THE ROAD TO
THE
DARK
TOWER

THE ROAD TO
THE
DARK
TOWER

EXPLORING
STEPHEN KING'S
MAGNUM OPUS

BEV VINCENT

NEW AMERICAN LIBRARY

New American Library
Published by New American Library, a division of
Penguin Group (USA) Inc., 375 Hudson Street,
New York, New York 10014, USA
Penguin Group (Canada), 10 Alcorn Avenue, Toronto,
Ontario M4V 3B2, Canada (a division of Pearson Penguin Canada Inc.)
Penguin Books Ltd., 80 Strand, London WC2R 0RL, England
Penguin Ireland, 25 St. Stephen's Green, Dublin 2,
Ireland (a division of Penguin Books Ltd.)
Penguin Group (Australia), 250 Camberwell Road, Camberwell, Victoria 3124,
Australia (a division of Pearson Australia Group Pty. Ltd.)
Penguin Books India Pvt. Ltd., 11 Community Centre, Panchsheel Park,
New Delhi - 110 017, India
Penguin Group (NZ), Cnr Airborne and Rosedale Roads, Albany,
Auckland 1310, New Zealand (a division of Pearson New Zealand Ltd.)
Penguin Books (South Africa) (Pty.) Ltd., 24 Sturdee Avenue,
Rosebank, Johannesburg 2196, South Africa

Penguin Books Ltd, Registered Offices:
80 Strand, London WC2R 0RL, England

First published by New American Library,
a division of Penguin Group (USA) Inc.

First New American Library Printing, October 2004

(NAL) REGISTERED TRADEMARK—MARCA REGISTRADA

LIBRARY OF CONGRESS CATALOGING-IN-PUBLICATION DATA:
Vincent, Bev.
The road to the dark tower : exploring Stephen King's magnum opus / Bev Vincent.
p.   cm.
ISBN 0-451-21304-1 (trade pbk.)
1. King, Stephen, 1947– Dark Tower.   2. Fantasy fiction, American—History and criticism.
3. Roland (Fictitious character) I. Title.
PS3561.I483D376 2004
813'.54—dc22   2004005816

Set in New Times Roman
Designed by Ginger Legato

PUBLISHER'S NOTE
While the author has made every effort to provide accurate telephone numbers and Internet addresses at the time of publication, neither the publisher nor the author assumes any responsibility for errors, or for changes that occur after publication.

I have not forgotten the face of my father,
Donald Vincent,
gone to the clearing at the end of the path
July 1, 1927–January 3, 2003

CONTENTS

KEY TO REFERENCED WORKS

DT1: *The Gunslinger*

DT2: *The Drawing of the Three*

DT3: *The Waste Lands*

DT4: *Wizard and Glass*

DT5: *Wolves of the Calla*

DT6: *Song of Susannah*

DT7: *The Dark Tower*

SL: *'Salem's Lot*

TS: *The Stand*

DS: *Different Seasons*

TT: *The Talisman*

ED: *The Eyes of the Dragon*

TK: *The Tommyknockers*

INS: *Insomnia*

RM: *Rose Madder*

LS: "The Little Sisters of Eluria"

HA: *Hearts in Atlantis*

OW: *On Writing*

BH: *Black House*

EE: *Everything's Eventual*

FB8: *From a Buick 8*

THE ROAD TO
THE
DARK
TOWER

MORE WORLDS THAN THESE

*There are quests and roads that lead ever onward, and all of them end in the
same place—upon the killing ground. Except, perhaps, the road to the Tower.*
[DT1]

*"Everything in the world is either coming to rest or falling to pieces," he said
flatly. "At the same time, the forces which interlock and give the world its
coherence—in time and size as well as in space—are weakening. . . .
The Beams are breaking down."*
[DT3]

"When one quests for the Dark Tower, time is a matter of no concern at all."
[DT1, foreword]

A gunslinger rides into town, sitting tall in his saddle. He wears two
sinister guns low on his hips. He grieves the memory of his one true
love, long dead. A honky-tonk piano plays inside the saloon near
where he puts up his horse. Someone approaches him stealthily from behind and he turns in a blur, guns drawn, ready for a fight, only to find either the town drunk or the village idiot.

Though this description resembles the scene in *The Gunslinger* where
Roland enters Tull and meets Nort the Weedeater, recently raised from the
dead, it actually comes from the opening page of "Slade," a Western po-
litical satire[1] that Stephen King serialized in *The Maine Campus* between
June and August 1970.

Elements from this story are mirrored in *Wizard and Glass*, written a
quarter of a century later. The love of Slade's life—Miss Polly Peachtree
of Paduka (sic), Illinois—is dead. Sam Columbine killed Sandra Dawson's rancher father and is trying to take over her land. It's a short hop
from Sandra Dawson to Susan Delgado, whose father was murdered and
whose land and possessions have fallen to Hart Thorin. Sandra Dawson's
top man is also named Hart.

Columbine hired a bunch of hardcases—Big Coffin Hunters, in other
words—and "Pinky" Lee rides about with Regulators. A sinister character with a deadly pet snake evolved into the witch Rhea. Slade utters Clint

Eastwood–like epithets.[2] A character loses the index and middle fingers from one hand, though it isn't Slade. The story even directly mentions its author, Steve King. Of course, Slade is slightly more cavalier about killing people than Roland is,[3] and the story ends with the gunslinger wrapping his arm altogether too fondly around his horse's neck as they wander off into a romantic sunset.

While Jack Slade and his "sinister .45s" stalked the streets of Dead Steer Springs, his creator, Stephen King, was beginning a more serious endeavor, one that would occupy him off and on for the next thirty-five years.

In his introduction to "The Little Sisters of Eluria," King writes, "If there's a magnum opus in my life, it's probably the yet unfinished seven-volume series about Roland Deschain[4] of Gilead and his search for the Dark Tower which serves as the hub of existence." [EE] Using "unfinished" and "magnum opus" in the same sentence may seem presumptuous, but by the time *Everything's Eventual* appeared in early 2002, King was well on his way to completing the series.

Shortly after King finished the last three books and publication dates were established, a joint press release from Viking, Scribner and Donald M. Grant quoted the author: "The Dark Tower has been a major part of my life and writing career. I wanted to finish it both for the readers, who have been so devoted, and for myself. . . . For me, it's like a finale and a re-union, all at once. I've put everything I've got into these three books."[5]

As you should already know, the *Dark Tower* series chronicles the adventures of the last gunslinger in a strange world that is somehow related to our own. (If you haven't read all seven books, stop now, for herein there are spoilers aplenty.) Roland's world has moved on. Time speeds up and slows down unpredictably. A night might last ten years, or nightfall might begin early in the afternoon. Compass directions shift.

Everything is slowly falling apart and at the center of the world's ills, literally and symbolically, is the Dark Tower, which "stands at the root of time."[6] It is the nexus of all possible universes, and was originally supported by Beams powered by an unending supply of magic. Lacking faith in the persistence of magic, men replaced it with rational—but mortal—technology.

When he is barely more than a boy—but already a gunslinger who has killed many times—Roland receives a vision of the Tower and realizes that it is failing. If it does, his world—and every other reality, including many only subtly different from our own—will be destroyed, leaving behind only chaos. In one version of America, there is a car model called the Takuro Spirit, and in another Lincoln's picture appears on the one-dollar bill. In some dimensions, Ronald Reagan was never president, and in others a superflu decimated the population. Between these infinite universes lie dark places containing unimaginable creatures.

The Crimson King, who intends to rule the chaos after the Tower's fall, has amassed hostage workers known as Breakers to speed up the destruction of the Beams supporting the Tower. Reaching the Tower and somehow fixing what has gone wrong is the quest Roland has chosen, or that fate chose for him.

Getting Roland and his followers, his ka-tet, to the Tower has been Stephen King's lifelong work.

This book is the first to examine the series in its entirety. Chapter 1 follows its long and harrowing road to publication, from the time King wrote its famous first line in 1970 until the publication of *The Dark Tower* in late 2004.

Each book—including both the original and the revised versions of *The Gunslinger*—is examined individually in the following seven chapters, and the nonseries novels and stories with strong ties to the *Dark Tower* mythos are discussed in chapter 9. Chapter 10 explores the series' major characters.

Chapter 11 considers the epic nature of the quest, identifies some of King's literary influences and explores ka, while chapter 12 reflects on art and creation from King's perspective as both the author of the seven *Dark Tower* books and as a character within them.

After some concluding remarks that consider the *Dark Tower* series as King's magnum opus, appendices chronicle the factual publication timeline for the series and the fictional timeline of events in Roland's world and in the various versions of Earth he and the members of his ka-tet travel. A glossary of Mid-World terms, a list of online resources and the text of Robert Browning's mysterious poem "Childe Roland to the Dark Tower Came" complete the appendices.

Come with me as we cross a blazing desert, traverse mountains and the beach that lies beyond, cross corrupt bridges, ride an insane train, shoot it out with deadly Wolves, skip between worlds, preserve a vacant lot in Manhattan, battle to free the Breakers and cross the desolate lands laid waste by the Crimson King until we join the last gunslinger at the top of a hill, when he sees the object of his lifelong quest for the first time.

I promise to treat you better than Roland treated many whose paths crossed his.

ENDNOTES

[1] "Slade was a peace-loving man at heart, and what was more peace-loving than a dead body?"

[2] "Friend, smile when you say that."

[3] "I guess you can't win them all," he says after accidentally shooting an innocent by-stander.

[4] King pronounces Roland's last name "dess chain." It's likely that the mysterious and solitary gunslinger Shane who befriended a young boy influenced King's choice of this name.

[5] www.simonsays.com, Scribner's Web presence, June 2003. Extracted from a press re-lease issued February 2003.

[6] "The Gunslinger," *The Magazine of Fantasy and Science Fiction,* October 1978. This is King's description of the Tower in the author's note at the end of the story in its first appearance.

CHAPTER 1

THE LONG JOURNEY TO THE TOWER

[T]ell me a story, one that has a beginning and a middle and an end where
everything is explained. Because I deserve that. . . . Jesus, you guys
can't stop there!

He was wrong, we could stop anyplace we chose to.

[FB8]

He who speaks without an attentive ear is mute.

[DT7, dedication]

The publication of *Pet Sematary* in 1983 was notable for several reasons. First, it was a book Stephen King had frequently told interviewers was too terrible to see in print. Second, the name on the spine was Doubleday, a publisher King had left several years earlier.

Of most significance to King's Constant Readers, though, were three words on the author's ad-card, opposite the title page. Near the bottom, squeezed between *Cujo* (1981) and *Christine* (1982), was this entry: *The Dark Tower* (1982).

What was this? A Stephen King novel no one had heard of? This innocuous listing initiated a twenty-year obsession by readers around the world who frequently clamored for the next installment in Roland Deschain's quest to reach the Dark Tower.

In 1983, bookstores had no record of *The Dark Tower*. No one—it seemed—knew how to acquire this mysterious volume. This was before the Internet era; information wasn't yet a mass-market commodity. Fan communities weren't interconnected. Today, a curious reader encountering such a puzzle could post a query to a newsgroup or scan fan pages and official Web sites via a judiciously phrased search engine request. Searchable inventories of independent and chain bookstores across the continent are available online. Internet-based auction sites routinely offer out-of-print and rare editions.

Back then, such resources didn't exist, so King and his publishers (past and current) were bombarded with letters, all asking the same thing: "How can I get *The Dark Tower*?" Doubleday reportedly received more than three thousand letters.[1]

The book that caused such a stir had a rather inauspicious genesis. King showed a couple of fantasy stories he had written to his agent, Kirby McCauley, who thought he might be able to sell them.[2] In October 1978, shortly after the hardcover release of *The Stand, The Magazine of Fantasy and Science Fiction* (F&SF) published "The Gunslinger," which opened with the line, "The man in black fled across the desert and the gunslinger followed." The forty-page novelette ended with a parenthetical doxology from King:

"Thus ends what is written in the first Book of Roland, and his Quest for the Tower which stands at the root of Time."[3]

The promise of more to come.

The second installment didn't appear until the April 1980 issue of F&SF. After another yearlong hiatus, the final three segments of the story that would become *The Dark Tower: The Gunslinger* appeared in rapid succession in February, July and November 1981.[4]

The fifth installment, described as the last story in the first cycle, contained the following harbinger above the title: "The series will be published in a limited hardcover edition by Donald M. Grant in the spring of 1982." This was the first announcement of the book that would, two years later, cause such a clamor.

King originally had no plans to republish these stories. Not only was the tale set in an unfamiliar world—a departure from his previously published books—it was incomplete. In "The Politics of Limited Editions," King says the stories were well received, but F&SF's audience was somewhat different than his normal readership.

Donald M. Grant, Publications Director at Providence College, owned a small press that issued lavishly illustrated fantasy novels, including the works of Robert E. Howard.[5] In 1981, while at Providence College on a speaking engagement, King praised the books Grant had produced over the years. At dinner, Grant asked King if he had anything that would lend itself to a Donald M. Grant edition. King suggested the *Dark Tower*, and the publisher immediately recognized the series as the kind of project he could do and sell.[6] King rescued the wet and barely readable manuscript from a mildewy cellar and tweaked the stories for publication.[7]

Getting Michael Whelan to illustrate the first book was a stroke of good fortune. Whelan was an award-winning illustrator who had previously created drawings for the limited edition of *Firestarter*.[8]

Ads announcing the Grant edition appeared in only a few places, including volume 5 of *Whispers* magazine in August 1982,[9] the Stephen King issue, which featured artwork inspired by *The Gunslinger*. The cover illustration was "Nort the Weedeater" by John Stewart, and six other *Gunslinger*-inspired Stewart works appeared in a folio section of the magazine.[10]

Whispers editor Stuart David Schiff's news section said, "[Grant] has just produced what might possibly be the most important book from a specialty press." He goes on for more than half a page praising the book's merits, its production quality and Michael Whelan's illustrations, finishing with the following advice: "Do not miss this book."

Alas, most people did.

The ten-thousand-copy first printing[11] of *The Gunslinger* was the largest small-press edition in history[12]—this from an author whose later first-edition printings would run to seven figures. Grant's previous press-runs had been 3,500 books or less. The ad in *Whispers* doesn't mention the signed edition, but Schiff's editorial states that this version, limited to five hundred copies, would be available for $60, compared to $20 for the trade edition.

THE STORY THAT WOULD BECOME CENTRAL to Stephen King's body of work and his career had its genesis almost a decade before the first story appeared in F&SF, when King and his wife-to-be, Tabitha Spruce, each inherited reams of brightly colored paper nearly as thick as cardboard and in an "eccentric size." [DT1, afterword]

To the endless possibilities of five hundred blank sheets of 7" x 10" bright green paper, King added "Childe Roland to the Dark Tower Came" by Robert Browning, a poem he'd studied two years previously in a course covering the earlier romantic poets. "I had played with the idea of trying a long romantic novel, embodying the feel, if not the exact sense, of the Browning poem." [DT1, afterword][13]

In an unpublished essay[14] called "The Dark Tower: A Cautionary Tale," King says, "I had recently seen a bigger-than-life Sergio Leone Western,[15] and it had me wondering what would happen if you brought two very distinct genres together: heroic fantasy and the Western."

After graduating from the University of Maine at Orono in 1970, King moved into a "skuzzy riverside cabin" and began what he then conceived of as a "very long fantasy novel," perhaps even the longest popular novel in history.[16] He wrote the first section of *The Gunslinger* in a ghostly, unbroken silence—he was living alone—that influenced the eerie isolation of Roland and his solitary quest.

The story did not come easily. Sections were written during a dry spell in the middle of *'Salem's Lot,* and another part was written after he finished *The Shining.* Even when he wasn't actively working on the *Dark Tower,* his mind often turned to the story—except, he says, when he was battling Randall Flagg in *The Stand,* which is ironic since both Flagg and a superflu-decimated world became part of the *Dark Tower* mythos many years later.

In *Song of Susannah,* the fictional Stephen King claims that by 1977 he had given up on the story, daunted by its magnitude. It had become "too big. Too complicated. Too . . . outré." Roland also concerned him. His hero seemed like he might be changing into an antihero.

DONALD M. GRANT released *The Gunslinger* in 1982. The first printing—then envisioned as the only printing—sold out based on word of mouth and their limited advertising in specialty magazines.

Then came *Pet Sematary* the following year[17] and the ensuing deluge of letters. The mail King received concerning *The Gunslinger* was occasionally rancorous, especially from readers who felt they had the right to read anything King published. "You must trust me about one thing: I did not include *The Dark Tower* on the 'other works' [page] in a mean spirit— picture if you will, a man teasing a hungry person with half a hamburger and then gobbling it himself. The inclusion was the result of complete *naivete.* It took the resulting flood of mail to make me uneasily aware that

I had either wider responsibilities in the matter of my completed work, or people *thought* that I did."[18]

This was probably King's first indication that he and his readers might not always see eye to eye on the relationship between a writer and his audience. As Paul Sheldon in *Misery* learned, readers could be demanding, fans—fanatics—single-minded in their pursuit of all things King. The fictionalized version of himself is less restrained on the subject. "On the other hand, God and the Man Jesus, people are so fucking *spoiled*! They just assume that if there's a book anywhere in the world they *want,* then they have a perfect *right* to that book. This would be news indeed to those folks in the Middle Ages who might have heard *rumors* of books but never actually saw one." [DT6][19]

Several times over the next two decades, King labored to clarify his position—that he's not Scheherazade, a captive storyteller, subject to the whims of his audience, spinning tales to save his life. Ultimately, he decides how and if he will present his creations. "To *write* and to *make* has always been an act of necessity to me; to **show** has always been an act of need, and may express some deep insecurity in myself."[20]

Recent reports of King's impending retirement underlined this schism by highlighting the difference between writing and publishing. When asked to confirm these rumors, King usually responds that he might retire from publishing, but couldn't imagine not writing.[21]

But in 1985, King still saw publication as a necessary part of the creative process. "A novel in manuscript is like a man with one leg and a novel which has been printed and bound is like a man with two. . . . To not publish is to see the book as a creation which has been willfully crippled."[22]

Even at this relatively early point in his career, King didn't need to publish for financial reasons. But he had dangled the hamburger in front of hungry readers and learned, to his chagrin, that some of them were angry. "I tried to find a middle ground between publishing in a trade edition where I would be unable to control the number of copies printed, and not publishing at all, which I find an offense to the work."[23]

King had less sympathy with booksellers who claimed that his decision to not publish *The Gunslinger* in a widely available trade edition deprived them of income. If the book had been released traditionally, it would have generated a "rolling gross" on the order of several million dollars.[24] This money would have profited King and his publisher but also printers, secretaries, salespeople, distributors and booksellers.

> If the idea of a writer having an economic responsibility to publish what he writes seems absurd to you, I can assure you it does not seem at all absurd to the booksellers of America, or to a writer himself after he has been told that his seemingly whimsical decision to publish a book in a small-distribution format had actually taken the bread out of children's mouths or might have been a contributing cause to the closure of an independent small-town bookstore that might otherwise have turned the corner . . . or at least staggered on a while longer before collapsing.[25]

After discussing the situation with Donald M. Grant, King authorized a second printing of *The Gunslinger* equal in size to the first. He sent out a form letter (see next page) to people who had mailed him seeking the novel.

The second printing shipped in January 1984 and was out of print by the end of the year. The book's text and layout remained unchanged from the original printing. Other than the copyright page information, the only difference was that a four-color process was used for the endpapers of the first printing, and for the second printing a single-color process was used.[26]

Starting in 1985, the *Castle Rock Newsletter,* published by King's assistant and sister-in-law, Stephanie Leonard, was readers' main forum for up-to-date information about King in the mid-to-late 1980s. It also served as a place for them to vent. In letters to the editor, they advocated for a mass-market edition of *The Gunslinger.* Some thought fans were paying too much for the limited edition on the secondary market, and many weren't able to read the book at all because they couldn't afford it or were unable to locate a copy.

Even the second printing was fetching as much as $100 by early 1986. It was the first King item to penetrate beyond the book market, showing up in comic book stores, displayed under glass. Some experts speculated that—with so many carefully preserved copies in print—*The Gunslinger* would eventually lose its "inflated" resale value.[27]

> I was a little bit horrified by what happened afterward when the book became a collector's item and the price jumped. It hadn't

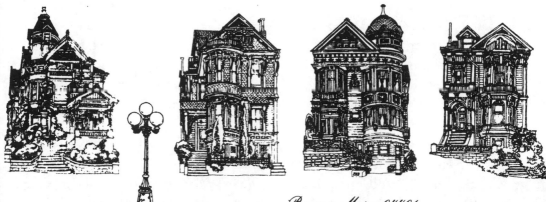

December 1, 1983

Bev Vincent

Halifax, Nova Scotia
Canada B3H 4J5

Dear Bev Vincent:

Thanks for your letter concerning THE DARK TOWER. Since PET SEMATARY was
published, I have been deluged with questions, comments, and also quite a
few brickbats about this little book.

Because of all the requests for, and questions about THE DARK TOWER, I have
given Don Grant the go ahead to print another 10,000 copies. If you still
want a copy, what I suggest you do is this: Write Donald M. Grant, Publisher
                          a letter requesting that he reserve a copy of this
second edition for you, and include a photocopy of this letter with your
request. I am going to ask Don to service the people who have specifically
requested THE DARK TOWER from me, Doubleday or Viking Press before anyone
else. I hope this will be of some help.

The original cover price of Grant's Trade Edition was $20. That seemed a
fair price at the time for a book bound in cloth, printed on good rag quality
paper, and profusely illustrated.

One last thing. THE DARK TOWER was done as a limited edition because it was
a story with limited appeal. It is a fantasy novel set in a fantasy world,
and it is really only the long opening section of a much larger work that is
still in progress. I am only telling you this because the story may not be
exactly what you have come to expect from me.

Thanks for your interest.

Best wishes,

Stephen King

SK/ss

been my intention to see these books climb from $20 to $50 to $70 to whatever. I wanted to do something about it, and Don Grant, who was upset, wanted to do something about it. We talked on the phone one night and I said, "What if you publish another five hundred or five thousand?" Don sighed. And I said, "That would be like pissing on a forest fire, wouldn't it?" Don agreed.[28]

KING HAD ALREADY WRITTEN SECTIONS of the next cycle of stories, originally titled *Roland Draws Three,* by the time *The Gunslinger* appeared in 1982. The first forty handwritten pages of the book vanished, and he still doesn't know what happened to them.[29]

He confessed in the afterword to *The Gunslinger* that his vision of the overall arc of the epic was unclear. He didn't yet understand exactly what had befallen Roland's world, the nature of Roland's confrontation with Marten, how Roland's friends Cuthbert and Jamie died or who Susan was. But he hadn't forgotten entirely what was on the missing pages or what he intended for the story.

King fictionalizes this stage in his development of the story in *Song of Susannah* when Eddie and Roland visit him in 1977. His character knows Roland, but he hasn't created Eddie yet. He doesn't know about Blaine or the implications of nineteen. "Except somewhere I do. Somewhere inside I know all of those things and there's no need of an argument, or a synopsis, or an outline. . . . When it's time, those things—and their significance to the gunslinger's quest—will roll out as naturally as tears or laughter." [DT1, afterword]

Once the world at large knew about the *Dark Tower* and a small percentage of King's readership sampled *The Gunslinger,* clamoring for the next installment began, a tune that would haunt the author for the rest of his career. "When are you going to write the next book?" became one of his Frequently Asked Questions,[30] posed at virtually every public appearance. The *Castle Rock Newsletter* reported that the top two questions in his fan mail were: 1) what is the *Dark Tower* and how do I find it? and 2) when will the next installment be published?[31]

Before his appearance at Cornell University in 1994, King told one of the organizers, "Every one of [the five thousand people present] is going to raise their hand during the question-and-answer period and say, 'When's the *Dark Tower* going to go on?'" When King established his official on-line presence in 1998, "When will the next *Dark Tower* book be re-leased?" was near the top of his FAQ.

King told an interviewer, "I have three women who work in this office that answer the fan mail, and a lot of times they don't tell me what's go-ing on with fan mail except for the stuff I pick up myself. But they put every Dark Tower letter on my desk. This is like a silent protest saying, 'get these people off our backs.'"[32] King calls these "pack your bags, we're going on a guilt trip" letters.[33]

Still, in the mid-1980s, many of King's readers were unaware of *The Gunslinger* and most of those who did know about it either couldn't find or afford a copy.

In late 1985, the *Castle Rock Newsletter* announced a tentative 1986 publication date for *The Drawing of the Three*. It's hard to imagine how King had the energy to delve back into Roland's world after finishing the behe-moth novel *It*, published in 1986, but he wrote the novel during the course of that year and had it in the hands of his publisher by early 1987, a pro-ductive year for him with the trade publication of *The Eyes of the Dragon*, *Misery* and *The Tommyknockers*, in addition to the *Dark Tower* book.

Michael Whelan wasn't available to illustrate *The Drawing of the Three*, so Phil Hale—who had previously contributed to Grant's limited edition of *The Talisman*—did the artwork, starting a tradition of having different artists for each novel except for *The Dark Tower*, which was also illustrated by Whelan.[34]

Donald M. Grant started taking orders for the book early in 1987, with ads in specialty publications such as the *Castle Rock Newsletter*. The book was delayed slightly when Hale asked the publisher to correct the color of the book's internal plates, which gave King time to do a last-minute rewrite of several sections.[35]

The book was printed on thick buff-colored paper made in a mill in Brewer, Maine, across the Penobscot River from Bangor.[36] Learning the lesson of supply and demand from *The Gunslinger*, the print runs of both editions were increased: eight hundred signed and thirty thousand trade. Unsurprisingly, the cost had increased as well ($100 and $35 postpaid, re-spectively), given five years' worth of inflation and the fact that, at four hundred pages, *The Drawing of the Three* was nearly twice the length of *The Gunslinger*.

Grant offered matching signed/numbered editions to anyone who had previously purchased copies of *The Gunslinger.* Unclaimed numbers—and numbers 501–800 that had no counterpart in the first volume—were sold on a lottery basis to people who sent in their names for consideration.[37]

The book's dedication reads, "To Don Grant, who's taken a chance on these *novels,* one by one," mirroring the dedication to *The Gunslinger,* where King paid tribute to F&SF editor Ed Ferman for taking a chance on the stories making up that novel one by one.

The *Castle Rock Newsletter* published the first chapter of *The Drawing of the Three* in April/May 1987, accompanied by some of Hale's artwork, and the book shipped shortly thereafter. By September the signed edition was out of print and being offered for resale at prices in excess of $500.

In early 1988, King recorded *The Gunslinger* for NAL Audio using the studio at his Bangor radio station, WZON.[38] The six-hour, four-cassette package was the first of King's novels to be released on unabridged audio, and the first to be recorded by the author. He repeated the process for the next two *Dark Tower* books before turning over the reins to professional audiobook narrator Frank Muller, who rerecorded the first three books as well as performing *Wizard and Glass.*[39]

In September 1988, *The Gunslinger* finally became available to the masses in trade paperback from Plume. The large format allowed the publisher to include Michael Whelan's illustrations without shrinking them to the size of a mass-market paperback. *The Drawing of the Three* followed in the same format in March 1989.

The five-year gap between publication of *The Gunslinger* and *The Drawing of the Three* set a precedent that would be followed for the next three volumes. In 1989, King announced that *The Waste Lands* was still two or three years away from release. "Of everything I've written, *The Drawing of the Three* is my kids' favorite book, and they're pestering me. . . . That's the best incentive I know. Tell somebody a story who really wants to hear it."[40]

In the Overlook Connection winter 1990 catalog, King contributed his New Year's resolution, which said, "I resolve to get down to business and write the third novel in THE DARK TOWER series, *The Waste Lands.* It will be the only fantasy novel of 1990 (I hope) to feature a talking train."

Before starting to write, King reread the first two installments, taking notes and marking pages with highlighters and Post-it notes.[41] He finished the final draft and revisions early in 1991.

> [F]inding the doors to Roland's world has never been easy for me, and it seems to take more and more whittling to make each successive key fit each successive lock. Nevertheless, if readers request a fourth volume, it will be provided, for I still am able to find Roland's world when I set my wits to it, and it still holds me in thrall . . . more, in many ways, than any of the other worlds I have wandered in my imagination. And, like those mysterious slo-trans engines, this story seems to be picking up its own accelerating pace and rhythm. [DT3, afterword]

With the demise of the *Castle Rock Newsletter* in 1989, King fans no longer had an inside source of information concerning upcoming publications. The first indication that King had returned to Mid-World came in the December 1990 issue of F&SF. Billed as the Stephen King Issue, it contained a new short story ("The Moving Finger"), an author appreciation by the magazine's book review editor, Algis Budrys, a bibliography organized by King's assistant, Marsha DeFilippo, and "The Bear," an excerpt from *The Waste Lands*.

It also featured an ad from Donald M. Grant stating that the book would be published in early 1991. King was less optimistic. In his introduction to "The Bear," he says *The Waste Lands* may appear in 1991 or 1992.

The limited editions from Grant came out in August 1991, with the trade paperback from Plume coming close on its heels the following January. Because of this narrow window of exclusivity, the Grant trade hardcover didn't sell out.[42]

In the afterword to *The Waste Lands,* King apologized for ending the book with a cliff-hanger and said the fourth volume would appear in the "not-too-distant future." Years passed with no sign that he had returned to the series. However, the *Dark Tower* began to insinuate itself more and more into his nonseries books. While on a promotional tour in 1994, King responded to the inevitable question "When is the next *Dark Tower* book coming out?" by calling *Insomnia* the next *Dark Tower* book. It was the first of three books published in consecutive years with conspicuous ties to the series.

In mid-1994, King said for the first time that once he got his next novel out of the way, he would write the remaining four books back-to-back to finish the series.[43] In a fanzine essay, Stephen Spignesi, author of the *Stephen King Encyclopedia* and *The Lost Works of Stephen King,* suggested that this strategy might encourage readers who hadn't yet tried the *Dark Tower* series to start because there would be no other new King material for a couple of years.[44]

Rose Madder appeared in 1995 with references to elements from *The Waste Lands,* but King's plan to tackle the rest of the series that year didn't materialize.

He had a highly publicized and successful six-month run with the serialized publication of *The Green Mile* in 1996. All six installments appeared simultaneously on the *New York Times* best-seller list in September. In the first book's introduction, he compared the serial release to his ongoing work with the *Dark Tower* and discussed some of the fan reaction the series had inspired:

> I liked the high-wire aspect of [the serial publication process], too: fall down on the job, fail to carry through, and all at once about a million readers are howling for your blood. No one knows this any better than me, unless it's my secretary, Juliann Eugley; we get dozens of angry letters each week, demanding the next book in the Dark Tower cycle (patience, followers of Roland; another year or so and your wait will end, I promise). One of these contained a Polaroid of a teddy-bear in chains, with a message cut out of newspaper headlines and magazine covers: RELEASE THE NEXT *DARK TOWER* BOOK AT ONCE OR THE BEAR DIES, it said. I put it up in my office to remind myself both of my responsibility and of how wonderful it is to have people actually care—a little— about the creatures of one's imagination.[45]

The author's alter ego writes, "I still get a ton of letters about the cliff-hanger ending. They fall into three major categories: People who are pissed off, people who want to know when the next book is coming out, and pissed-off people who want to know when the next book is coming out." [DT6]

In April 1996, King told participants in an AOL chat that he was going to try to write *Wizard and Glass* during the coming summer. "I know a lot of what happens. Mostly now it's a matter of gathering my courage and starting." To prepare, he returned to the first three books, armed once again with a highlighter and sticky notes. He started writing in motel rooms while driving from Colorado to Maine after finishing work on *The Shining* miniseries. Ads announcing the book's upcoming publication appeared in the back of the final four *Green Mile* installments.

Courage he must have found in abundance. In October, during a conference at the University of Maine in Orono,[46] King read an excerpt, announcing that the first draft was more than 1,400 pages long and dealt mostly with Roland's childhood.[47]

King's twin books *Desperation* and *The Regulators* were released simultaneously in September 1996. Initially, they were bundled together with a battery-powered night-light. However, once supplies of the night-light were depleted, King suggested to his publisher that they could replace them with a small booklet containing the first two chapters of *Wizard and Glass*. Fans squealed with delight and shrieked in consternation. The next *Dark Tower* book was on its way, but to get this freebie they had to buy two hardcover books many already owned.

By now, the Internet had numerous places where fans could express their opinions. One of the most active was a USENET newsgroup called alt.books.stephen-king, which was occasionally monitored by King's publisher, Viking. Through them, he learned of reaction to his gift. His publisher posted the following message to the newsgroup on King's behalf.

Gentle Readers:

   It's reached my attention that there's been a fair degree of pissing and moaning about the Wizard and Glass *booklet which comes with a dual purchase of* Desperation *and* The Regulators. *I swear to God, some of you guys could die and go to heaven and then complain that you had booked a double occupancy room, and where the hell is the sauna, anyway? The major complaints seem to be coming from people who have already bought both books. Those of you who bought the double-pack got the light, right? A freebie. So whatcha cryin' about?*

The booklet was my idea, not the publisher's—a little extra for people who wanted to buy both books after supplies of the famous "Keep You Up All Night" light ran out. If you expect to get the booklet IN ADDITION to the light, all I can say is sorry, Cholly, but there may not be enough booklets to go around. If you bought the two books separately, because there weren't any gift packs left (they sold faster than expected, which is how this booklet deal came up in the first place), go back to where you bought them, tell the dealer what happened, show him/her your proof of (separate) purchase, and they'll take care of you. If they get wise witcha, tell 'em Steve King said that was the deal.

If you're just jacked because you want to read the first two chapters of Wizard and Glass, *wait until the whole thing comes out. Or put it on your T.S. List and give it to the chaplain. In any case, those of you who are yelling and stamping your feet, please stop. If you're old enough to read, you're old enough to behave.*

STEVE KING[48]

King's frustration with reader demands rings out loud and clear—so much so that many people refused to believe it was genuine.[49] The hue and cry was all for nothing as it turned out—Penguin posted the excerpt on their Web site two months later.

In the introduction to the preview—which he calls "a signal of good faith" for readers who have waited five years since the previous installment—King quotes Susannah from *The Waste Lands.* "It is hard to begin," she thinks while preparing to challenge Blaine the Mono in a game of riddles. Returning to the *Dark Tower* series has often been hard for King. "And sometimes *scary,* too."[50]

Wizard and Glass proved to be the longest book of the series—so long that the 780-page signed/limited edition from Donald M. Grant was split into two volumes. The first copies shipped on August 9, 1997. Betts Bookstore, an independent seller in Bangor specializing in King editions, sent a truck to the publisher's warehouse to speed up their delivery process. A trucking company lost or damaged about a third of the dust jackets for the deluxe signed edition, delaying its release until the end of September.

For the first time, Grant made a significant number of the forty-thousand-copy limited trade edition available to nationwide chain bookstores. *Wizard and Glass* became the first book from a specialty (that is, small-press) publisher to appear—albeit briefly—on the *New York Times* hardcover bestseller list.[51] The trade paperback from Plume appeared in November with a first printing of 1.5 million copies.

The dedication begins: "This book is dedicated to Julie Eugley and Marsha DeFilippo. They answer the mail, and most of the mail for the last couple of years has been about Roland of Gilead—the gunslinger." Shortly after the book was released, King reiterated his plan to continue working "until the cycle is done and then, that way, I can walk away from it."

It's always been my intention to finish. There isn't a day that goes by that I don't think about Roland and Eddie and Detta and all the other people, even Oy, the little animal. I've been living with these guys longer than the readers have, ever since college, actually, and that's a long time ago for me.[52]

He intended to start work on the fifth installment in 1998 so that he could finish while he "still drew breath" and "before I can hide my own Easter eggs," King's expression for senility.

Wizard and Glass was the last *Dark Tower* book readers would see in the twentieth century, but it wasn't Roland's final appearance. Robert Silverberg proposed an anthology of novellas by famous fantasy writers, where the stories were to be set in the author's best-known fictional universe. They were to be stand-alone tales so people unfamiliar with the associated works could enjoy the collection. King accepted Silverberg's invitation to write about Roland "in a moment of weakness."[53] Though novellas allow a writer to be more expansive than short stories do, he had trouble keeping "The Little Sisters of Eluria" to a manageable length. "These days, everything about Roland and his friends wants to be not just long but sort of epic," he wrote in the story's introduction when it was reprinted in *Everything's Eventual.*

Another novella released in F&SF in early 1997, "Everything's

Eventual," would ultimately turn out to be a *Dark Tower* story, though no one realized it at the time. The venue should have been a clue. Almost every story King has published in that magazine has been related to the *Dark Tower.*

His plans to complete the *Dark Tower* series were thwarted by reality. In 1997, he left Viking, his publisher since 1979, for Scribner. A three-book contract left little room in his schedule for the *Dark Tower,* though the series' influence would continue to be felt in books like *Bag of Bones* and *Hearts in Atlantis.*

King continued to get letters asking for more *Dark Tower,* including one from an elderly woman with cancer begging him to tell her the ending before she died. Another letter came from a fan on death row who promised to take the secret to the grave. As much as King may have wanted to respond to either letter, he couldn't. He didn't know yet where the story would take him. "To know, I have to write."[54]

In 1997, one reviewer,[55] marveling at the scope of the series and the length of time it took to reach the midpoint, implored readers to pray for the author's continued good health. His advice was eerily prescient. King's accident in 1999 almost spelled the end of the *Dark Tower.* During his *From a Buick 8* book tour, one fan told King that news of the accident made him think, "There goes the Tower, it's tilting, it's falling, ahhh, shit, he'll *never* finish it now."[56]

Despite concerns that he might not write again, King penned *Dreamcatcher* longhand during his rehabilitation and completed *On Writing* shortly thereafter. When Peter Straub suggested incorporating portions of the *Dark Tower* mythos into *Black House,* their sequel to *The Talisman*, King told Straub, "I'm glad you said that, because I don't know if I can keep it out. At this point, everything I write is connected to it."[57]

In August 2001, a month before *Black House* appeared, King announced that he had returned to the land of the gunslinger and intended to publish the remaining three books all at the same time. While he didn't commit to a firm publication date—"Well, that's ka, isn't it?"—he estimated the books would appear in about two years, "depending on all the usual variables, like sickness, accidents, and—scariest of all—a failure of inspiration. The only thing I know for sure is that all these old friends of mine are as alive as they ever were. And as dangerous."[58] He told Amazon.com, "I felt like if I didn't finish this time I never would."

In preparation for his reentry to Mid-World, King purchased a new desk for the office in his winter home in Florida. The custom creation of Vancouver furniture designer Peter Pierobon, the desk had ALL THINGS SERVE THE BEAM written in raised Gregg shorthand script on its black leather surface.[59] Instead of rereading the first four books, he listened to Frank Muller's audio narrations and hired a research assistant to document everything important from the published books and related stories.

To repay readers for their patience, King posted the prologue to the as-yet-untitled fifth volume on his Web site. He originally planned to call the book *The Crawling Shadow,* but later decided it was "sort of corny."[60] "I was younger then," he joked. This time there would be no complaining that the preview cost anything or was unavailable to anyone—except those without Web access.

The six-year gap between the publication of the fourth and fifth installments of the series equaled the longest interval between books. "[I]n my own defense, all I can say is that it's never easy to find the doorway back into Roland's world," he wrote.[61]

In June 2002, King updated fans about the status of the series.

> It's easily the biggest project I've ever taken on, and I'm throwing in everything I have. Including a little craft, actually . . . You have to remember that this project spans over thirty years of my life, and a lot of other books I've written have this as their basis. I feel a little like Cal Ripken, making his farewell tour of all the stadiums in the American League. But in the quiet room where I work, no one's cheering. I just hope some of them will when they read the pages. You have to remember that, for most Steve King readers, Roland the gunslinger's never been a priority. The Dark Tower books are . . . well, they're different.[62]

By then he had finished the first drafts of *Wolves of the Calla* and *Song of Susannah,* as well as the first third of *The Dark Tower,* a total of 1,900 manuscript pages. Confessing to burnout, King said he would be taking at least a month off before completing the final book.

While writing, King listened to the most boring, repetitive music he could find. He told Mitch Albom, "I've been working on these *Dark Tower* books for about fifteen months now and all I've been listening to is

Lou Bega Mambo No. 5. I've got a vinyl recording that's got four versions of Mambo No. 5—there's the radio version, there's the dance mix, there's a coupla instrumental [versions]."[63]

By early July, he was back at work on the 1,100-page manuscript that would see readers—and the author—through to the end of the epic. At each stop while promoting *From a Buick 8* in September, he updated his progress. Fifty pages left to go, he told a group in New York. Thirty-five, he told fans in Michigan. And while being interviewed by Mitch Albom for his radio show, King said he was down to the final two or three pages. "I wanted to finish it at home—I didn't want to finish it in a hotel room in Dearborn," he said, so he held off completing the book until he got back to Maine a few days later.[64]

King told Albom his tour in support of the *Dark Tower* books would probably be his farewell tour. He planned to get out and spread the message to the people who had been holding back, telling them that the whole story was now available.

In early October, the three books were done in first draft, a stack of manuscript pages that took up more than five reams of paper. King had reached the end of his story. For fans, another year would pass before they could return to Mid-World and the surprises King had in store for them.

An excerpt from *Wolves of the Calla* appeared in the anthology *McSweeney's Mammoth Treasury of Thrilling Tales,* edited by Michael Chabon, in February 2003. Titled "The Tale of Gray Dick," this vignette gave readers insight into what was being depicted in Bernie Wrightson's cover art, which started making the rounds of the Internet in April.

In May 2003, King's official Web site got a face-lift, adding a section devoted to the *Dark Tower.* Flash animation, audio excerpts and artwork samples previewed the remaining books. Both Scribner and Viking followed suit with sections of their respective Web sites devoted to the *Dark Tower.* This spirit of cooperation continued between these two corporate rivals when they cosponsored a contest where the grand prize was a chance to meet King in New York.

Viking released new hardcover editions of the first four books on June 23, 2003, featuring a new introduction by King.[65] Trade paperback editions from Plume followed one day later, and the NAL mass-market paperbacks appeared throughout the fall. The paperback versions of *Wizard and Glass* contained the *Wolves of the Calla* prologue, a rare instance in which one publisher promoted a book to be released by a rival company.

The new edition of *The Gunslinger* was revised and expanded. King completely rewrote the first book to bring it in line with the remaining books, feeling that its language and tone were vastly different from the others. He told an interviewer at Amazon.com that the original version seemed like it was trying too hard to be "something really, really important."[66] A week after it was reissued, *The Gunslinger* made number 17 on the *New York Times* hardcover best-seller list, not bad for a twenty-year-old book, especially considering the trade paperback and mass-market paperback editions of the new edition were available within a week of the hardcover release.

In July 2003, Scribner published Volume I of *Stephen King's The Dark Tower: A Concordance* by Robin Furth, King's research assistant. The book arose from her work ensuring continuity between the early novels and the remainder of the series. Volume I detailed characters, places and events in the first four books. The Calvins (the fictional *Dark Tower* scholars who work for Tet Corporation) would probably have produced a similar work.

Donald M. Grant published the deluxe signed editions of the remaining three books, but their limited trade edition was reduced to 3,500 copies. These artist's edition—featuring different dust jackets from the trade hardcover and signed by the respective artist—were released early enough to be the official first editions. Scribner and Grant jointly and simultaneously issued unlimited trade hardcovers, the first time new *Dark Tower* books were widely available in hardcover.

In November 2003, *Wolves of the Calla* broke a twenty-year tradition: It was the first *Dark Tower* installment shorter than the one that preceded it—950 manuscript pages compared to 1,500.[67] After a first printing of six hundred thousand copies, the book went back for a sixty-thousand-copy second-printing prepublication and a third printing of seventy-five thousand books was ordered the day after the book was released. A week later, the publisher ordered a fourth printing.

Song of Susannah, one of the series' shortest installments, followed in June 2004, and the final book, *The Dark Tower*, was published on King's birthday in September of the same year, with the second volume of Robin Furth's concordance appearing simultaneously.

Trade paperbacks followed approximately six months after the individual hardcover releases and mass-market paperback publication is scheduled to begin in 2006.

The *Dark Tower*'s long and arduous road to publication has at last come to its end.

ENDNOTES

[1] According to the quasifictional journal at the end of *Song of Susannah.*

[2] *NewsNight with Aaron Brown* on CNN, June 24, 2003.

[3] *The Magazine of Fantasy and Science Fiction*, October 1978. Roland's name doesn't appear in the story, only in this endnote.

[4] An intriguing aside—the November issue contained a story by Larry Niven and Dian Girard called "Talisman."

[5] King mentions Grant's editions of Howard's novels in *Wolves of the Calla.* Grant was awarded a life achievement World Fantasy Award in November 2003, the weekend before *Wolves of the Calla* was published.

[6] Garrett Condon, "King's 'Other' Publisher Well-Kept Collectors' Secret," originally in the *Hartford Courant*, August 28, 1987. Reprinted in *Castle Rock Newsletter,* Volume 3–4, No. 11–1, December 1987/January 1988.

[7] Introduction, *Stephen King's The Dark Tower: A Concordance,* Volume I, Robin Furth, Scribner, 2003.

[8] When *The Gunslinger* was released, Whelan was already a three-time World Science Fiction (Hugo) Award winner for Best Professional Artist and two-time World Fantasy Award winner for Best Artist. By 2002, Whelan had won the Hugo Award an unprecedented fifteen times after thirty-two nominations.

[9] This issue of *Whispers* also contained the first appearance of *The Shining*'s excised prologue, a piece that remained a rarity for fifteen years, until an abridged version was published in *TV Guide* in 1997.

[10] In his editorial, Stuart David Schiff is unsure what art will illustrate the magazine's cover, as Stewart's illustration, sent out for four-color separation, was lost somewhere in transit. As a backup, Donald M. Grant and Michael Whelan gave Schiff permission to use one of the Grant edition illustrations, but the Stewart pictures must have materialized at the last minute.

[11] Approximately 1,500 were misbound, affecting the order of the pages. [*Fear Itself,* Tim Underwood and Chuck Miller, editors. Underwood-Miller press, 1982.]

[12] Darrell Schweitzer, "Collecting Stephen King, part I," *Castle Rock Newsletter,* vol. 1, no. 10, October 1985.

[13] In a *Today Show* interview with Matt Lauer [June 23, 2003], King said he didn't understand what the poem meant but he loved the "gorgeous mystery of it."

[14] Referenced in *The Art of Darkness,* Douglas E. Winter. The essay discusses King's experience with *The Dark Tower* backlash.

[15] *The Good, the Bad and the Ugly,* he told an audience at Yale in April 2003. He also told them he was flying high on mescaline at the time.

[16] "On Being Nineteen (and a Few Other Things)," Viking, 2003.

[17] *The Gunslinger* was not listed on the ad-card in *Christine,* King's other 1982 hardcover release.

[18] "The Politics of Limited Editions," part 1, *Castle Rock Newsletter,* vol. 1, no. 6, June 1985.

[19] Since this comes from a fictionalized journal, these comments do not necessarily reflect King's real views.

[20] "The Politics of Limited Editions," part 1, op. cit.

[21] In the coda at the end of *Song of Susannah,* the fictional King considers the possibility that he may retire, or at least ease up considerably, when he finishes the *Dark Tower* series.

[22] "The Politics of Limited Editions," part 1, op. cit.

[23] Ibid.

[24] King says in "The Politics of Limited Editions" that *Pet Sematary* had a rolling gross of about $7 million.

[25] "The Politics of Limited Editions," part 1, op. cit.

[26] Donald M. Grant in *Castle Rock Newsletter,* vol 1, no. 12, December 1985. A third printing was issued with new cover art in 1998 as part of a boxed set containing the first three volumes of the series, and a revised and expanded edition was published by Viking in 2003.

[27] First and second printings currently garner about $500 and $200, respectively. The signed/limited first edition typically sells for several thousand dollars.

[28] "The Politics of Limited Editions," part 1, op. cit.

[29] Introduction to Robin Furth, *Stephen King's The Dark Tower: A Concordance,* Volume I, Scribner, 2003. No sinister inferences should be made concerning the author's initials. In *The Unseen King* [Starmont Press, 1989], Tyson Blue says that a handwritten fragment of the book was part of a notebook auctioned at a World Science Fiction Convention in 1986. It sold for $5,200.

[30] This was long before the Internet era popularized the notion of a FAQ.

[31] *Castle Rock Newsletter,* vol. 1, no. 10, October 1985.

[32] *Walden Book Report,* December 1997.

[33] A line he borrowed from the Charlie Sheen movie *Terminal Velocity.*

[34] "He'd be the only one to do pictures for two of the books, but since he was there at the beginning, it'd be great if he was there at the end." (www.stephenking.com, June 2002)

[35] Tyson Blue, *The Unseen King,* Starmont Press, 1989.

[36] Ibid.

[37] Grant has continued this matching number/lottery system throughout the publication history of the *Dark Tower* books, extending it to other King limited editions they have published, like *Desperation* and *Black House.*

[38] The station's call letters are derived from King's *The Dead Zone.* Careful listeners can hear traffic sounds—transports, especially—in the background of this recording.

[39] Muller was involved in a career-ending motorcycle accident in 2001. George Guidall, host of the Wavedancer Foundation Benefit to raise money for Muller's medical bills, recorded the final three *Dark Tower* books and the revised *The Gunslinger.* King had already dedicated *Wolves of the Calla* to Muller before his accident, calling him the

man "who hears the voices in my head." Muller narrated numerous other King novels, including *The Green Mile* and *Black House,* as well as books by John Grisham, Peter Straub, Pat Conroy and many others.

[40] *Castle Rock Newsletter,* vol. 5, no. 3, March 1989.

[41] Introduction to Robin Furth's *Concordance,* Volume I. Op. cit.

[42] In 1998, Grant issued a slipcased edition of the first three books to help relieve inventory of excess copies of *The Waste Lands.* This set contained a third printing of *The Gunslinger* (with new cover art), a second edition of *The Drawing of the Three* (with new illustrations throughout) and a first edition of *The Waste Lands.*

[43] *Larry King Live,* CNN, August 29, 1994. The novel was either *Rose Madder* (1995) or *Desperation* (1996).

[44] Stephen Spignesi, "A Piece of SKIN," *SKIN* newsletter, issue 1.7, November 1994.

[45] *The Green Mile: The Two Dead Girls,* introduction, March 1996, NAL.

[46] The speech was part of a two-day symposium called "Reading Stephen King: Issues of Student Choice, Censorship, and the Place of Popular Literature in the Canon."

[47] It ended up being fifteen hundred pages in manuscript. *The Dark Tower* manuscript was "only" eleven hundred pages.

[48] alt.books.stephen-king, November 21, 1996.

[49] The language is classic King. "So solly, Cholly!" appears in *Wizard and Glass.* Two expressions, "pissing and moaning" and "put it on your T.S. List and give it to the chaplain," appear in *From a Buick 8,* and the first phrase also shows up in *Black House.*

[50] "An Excerpt from the Upcoming *Wizard and Glass,*" Penguin Books, 1996.

[51] It entered the *Wall Street Journal* list at number 3 on September 4, 1997, and debuted in a tie for the number 12 position of the *New York Times* list on September 21, King's fiftieth birthday. It dropped off the list the following week, but the Plume paperback debuted in first place two months later.

[52] *Walden Book Report,* December 1997.

[53] Interview with Joseph B. Mauceri, *The World of Fandom,* March 2001.

[54] "On Being Nineteen (and a Few Other Things)," Viking, 2003.

[55] Edward Bryant in *Locus* magazine, October 1997.

[56] *The Gunslinger,* introduction, Viking, 2003. King's response: "Thanks for the sympathy, guys." [Interview with Paula Zahn, CNN, October 31, 2003.]

[57] Peter Straub, interview with Jeff Zaleski, *Publishers Weekly,* August 20, 2001.

[58] www.stephenking.com, August 21, 2001.

[59] *Vancouver Sun,* January 11, 2002. The desk also has two secret drawers. Pierobon often uses language-based decoration in his work as a way to communicate with whoever uses the piece. Pierobon, obviously not a *Dark Tower* fan, said he didn't know the significance of the quote.

[60] AOL chat, September 19, 2000.

[61] www.stephenking.com, August 21, 2001.

[62] www.stephenking.com, June 2002. In *Song of Susannah*'s coda, fictional King expresses his disappointment with falling sales figures for the *Dark Tower* books and hopes that they improve once the series is done.

[63] *The Mitch Albom Show,* September 30, 2002.

[64] Ibid. The first draft of the manuscript has a completion date of October 3, 2002.

[65] The Phil Hale artwork in *The Drawing of the Three* came from the second Grant edition, previously only available as part of their gift set.

[66] Interview with Ben Reese, published on Amazon.com in May 2003.

[67] *Wolves of the Calla* clocked in at 736 pages, compared to 780 pages for *Wizard and Glass,* though the Viking hardcover reissue was only 672 pages long.

CHAPTER 2

THE GUNSLINGER (RESUMPTION)

The man in black fled across the desert, and the gunslinger followed.[1]

Welcome to the weird, weird west.[2]

The fictional Stephen King encountered by Roland and Eddie in *Song of Susannah* describes the first sentence of *The Gunslinger* as possibly "the best opening line I ever wrote." [DT6] It simultaneously introduces the protagonist, his adversary and the setting in a few well-chosen words.

King wrote this sentence and the rest of the story that would become "The Gunslinger" not long after he graduated from the University of Maine at Orono in 1970. At the time, he had written—but hadn't yet published—a few novels. His print appearances were limited to short stories in men's magazines and articles and columns in the campus newspaper. He decided "it was time to stop goofing around and get behind the controls of one big great God a'mighty steamshovel, a sense that it was time to try and dig something big out of the sand, even if the effort turned out to be an abysmal failure." [DT1, afterword]

The young author could never have envisioned that he was embarking on a journey that would bracket his long and prosperous publishing career or that the gunslinger's quest would consume nearly thirty-five years of his life.

At the time of its publication, *The Gunslinger* was significantly different than anything else he had written. Though his books often featured characters with otherworldly powers, the settings were familiar—a small town in Maine, a Colorado hotel, suburban Pittsburgh or, as in *The Stand,* the sprawling canvas of America. He believed that people responded to supernatural or fantasy elements when they're wedded closely to reality.[3]

In later years, King would dabble more in the fantastic with books like *The Talisman* and *The Eyes of the Dragon,*[4] but in *The Gunslinger* he ranged beyond modern America for the first time.[5] Within the first few pages it's clear that the gunslinger isn't traveling in familiar territory. A postapocalyptic version of Earth, perhaps. A land that has "moved on," though he doesn't explain what this implies. For all its strangeness, the setting contains familiar elements: humans, donkeys, tombstones, revolvers, Jesus and the omnipresent Beatles song "Hey Jude."

Before J.R.R. Tolkien started writing *The Lord of the Rings,* he spent much of his life creating the fictional universe populated by hobbits, elves and orcs. He knew the culture, languages and history of Middle Earth intimately. King, by his own admission, knew very little about Roland, his background or his destiny when he finished the stories that comprise *The Gunslinger.*[6] The Dark Tower itself isn't mentioned until almost the middle of the book.

King relies on his innate and subconscious understanding of the story to carry him through to the end of this epic quest, believing that the story will come to him when summoned. It is an act of faith both on his part and on that of the readers who join Roland on the journey from the Mohaine Desert to End-World and the field of roses surrounding the Dark Tower.

The Gunslinger is also quite different from the subsequent *Dark Tower* books. King metes out information about the gunslinger reluctantly, allowing the landscape to prevail instead of paying his usual attention to creating sympathetic characters. He doesn't even name his protagonist for nearly a hundred pages.[7] Artist Michael Whelan said that, though he found the book engaging, he sometimes had trouble working on the illustrations because the novel's mood was oppressive and unremittingly bleak.[8] Reviewer Edward Bryant said, "The *Dark Tower* series has a fundamental quality of strangeness which may account for why it is less popular than his other books."[9]

Some of King's faithful readers abandoned the book without finishing it. Others suggested that readers new to the series start with *The Drawing of the Three,* relying on that book's argument to fill in the background.

Those who followed this advice probably have a far different understanding of Roland from those who traveled with him across the desert and through the mountains in pursuit of the man in black.

Ultimately, even King recognized *The Gunslinger* as a stumbling block to some seeking entry into Roland's universe. "I had a lot of pretentious ideas about how stories were supposed to be told," he said.[10] In the new foreword, he confesses to "apologizing for it, telling people that if they persisted they would find the story really found its voice" in the next book. While editing the last three books in the series, he took a break and revised *The Gunslinger* completely. When asked if someone who had already read the original version would want to get the new edition, King said, "I guess if you were a completist you would, but otherwise maybe no."[11]

"The beginning was out of sync with the ending." He felt he owed it to the potential reader and to himself to go back and put things in order. "The idea was to bring *The Gunslinger* in line with the material in the new books as well as the material in the first four. The other thing I wanted to do was to rewrite to some degree for language because I always felt it had a different feel than the other books because I was so young when I wrote it. The material is about an additional 10% (about 35 manuscript pages) with changes on almost every page."[12] The increased length amounts to about nine thousand words,[13] but not all of the changes are additions. King deleted some passages nearly a half page in length.

Director Mick Garris compares the first night of his miniseries *The Shining* to winding up a clock. Not much of consequence happens, but the characters are developed and fleshed out and hints of what has been and what is to come are carefully established. *The Gunslinger* is similar— it sets the stage and the mood for what will follow. However, Roland's universe is winding down rather than up. "The dark days have come; the last of the lights are guttering, flickering out—in the minds of men as well as in their dwellings. The world has moved on. Something has, perhaps, happened to the continuum itself."[14]

Guided by ka, the mysterious force shepherding him toward success, the gunslinger uses people and discards them after they've served their purpose or if they stand in the way of his goal. In the abstract, his actions are understandable. Saving all of existence is surely worth sacrificing a few people.

The opening section, "The Gunslinger," covers a period of nearly two months, taking the as-yet-unnamed gunslinger[15] from Pricetown through Tull and southeast[16] into the desert, where he encounters Brown, a young hermit who owns a precocious talking raven named Zoltan.[17]

However, King begins the story five days after Roland departs from Brown's hut. He experiences a brief spell of dizziness because he has just been returned to the desert after reaching the Tower and found lacking, though his awareness of this fades from his mind quickly. Through a series of flashbacks, he reminisces about his recent history. Readers don't know his greater purpose or origin, only that he has been pursuing the man in black across the desert for some time. What the gunslinger wants and why the man in black is fleeing remain a mystery.

In *Song of Susannah,* King says he liked how the story seems to be going backward, starting with Roland, slipping back to Brown, then to Tull and finally to show Nort the Weedeater being resurrected by Walter. "The early part of it was all told in reverse gear." [DT6]

The gunslinger's sole companion is a moribund mule that he bought in Pricetown before reaching Tull. The arduous desert journey has drained the animal to the point where the gunslinger can no longer ride it. This isn't the first beast of burden he's ridden into the ground. In the opening paragraphs of "The Little Sisters of Eluria," which takes place many years earlier, Roland's horse, Topsy, is on its last legs as well.

The gunslinger estimates how far behind the man in black he is by the freshness of Walter's fires, analogous to Tuco from *The Good, the Bad and the Ugly,* who chased the man with no name across the desert. From Brown's vague estimate, the gunslinger believes he is gradually catching up but is still several weeks behind. Desperate for companionship, the gunslinger waits for Brown to question him; he has a need to confess. The events of Tull rest heavily on his heart and mind. Though he can be cold and calculating, ruthless in the pursuit of his goal, the gunslinger isn't heartless. Sometimes he shocks even himself.

"Do you believe in the afterlife?" he asks Brown. "I think this is it," the young man replies. It's a perceptive comment, because Roland has probably visited Brown countless times before, having returned to the desert after reaching the end of his life. There is no clearing at the end of the path for him, but he is reborn via the Dark Tower, the Hall of Resumption.

Tull is dead, he tells Brown, daring the young man to ask more. Like a vampire, he needs an invitation to cross the threshold and tell his tale. Brown finally asks.

A tiny blot on an ugly countryside, Tull is a few short side streets crossing the main road at the bottom of a shallow hollow. The stagecoaches Roland met heading away from town are occupied, but the ones that pass him on the way to Tull are mostly empty. No one but the gunslinger comes here anymore. It's a borderland with far less life than Calla Bryn Sturgis.

His greeting in Tull is "Hey Jude." The gunslinger knows the piano player, Sheb, from Mejis, but only in the expanded version do they acknowledge their common past.

At the saloon, the gunslinger meets a dead man, Nort the Weedeater, poisoned from chewing devil grass and reanimated by the man in black.[18]

I See You, Lad

One of the first indications that there is some relationship between Roland's world and our own comes when the gunslinger hears Sheb playing "Hey Jude" as he enters Tull. The song appears several more times over the course of the series. Eddie sings it on the beach at the Western Sea. Roland and Susan Delgado hear it the night they meet in Mejis. It plays from the speakers at Blue Heaven, and Stutterin' Bill the robot plays it on a CD when he transports Susannah, Roland, Patrick and Oy to the Federal Outpost.

In Mid-World, the song begins "Hey Jude, I see you, lad."

Nort is one of many traps left behind for the gunslinger by the man in black, whose name is revealed to be Walter o'Dim in the revised edition. Walter would likely be disappointed if his traps worked, but he sets them all the same. For the man in black, this pursuit is a game. He can run circles around the gunslinger, but Roland must chase, so the man in black must allow himself to be chased.

Nort speaks the High Speech, an ancient, dead language that the gunslinger hasn't heard in centuries, perhaps even millennia, since his days in Gilead. This is the first hint of the gunslinger's age and the malleability of time in his world. Whether Nort is as old as Roland—like Sheb—or if he learned the High Speech from Walter or while dead is unclear.

The gunslinger knows that stopping in Tull will make him lose ground on the man in black, but he seems unable to resist its allure, like Odysseus trapped on Calypso's island in *The Odyssey*. He befriends Allie, the bartender, and spends a week in her bed. He is a ship becalmed, wanting to continue his quest but unable to catch a wind in his sails.

Allie provides him with a clue that, had he understood it, might have pointed him in the direction of the Tower. The clouds near Tull all flow in the same direction, southeast across the desert.[19] Roland and Walter aren't on a Path of the Beam, but they aren't far away from one. The Beam is pulling them gently in the right direction, though Roland and, presumably, Walter aren't conscious of it.

After five days, he learns of Sylvia Pittston, a corpulent preacher who believes she is carrying the Crimson King's child.[20] She's yet another person who dates back to Roland's days in Mejis—she traveled through that distant barony a year before he and his friends arrived. She springs another trap, preaching words Walter supplied to her. Calling the gunslinger the Interloper, she raises the town against him. Roland has no choice but to shoot the entire population. He reloads on the fly, a skill it took him years[21] to learn, burning his fingers on the hot chambers. As he shoots, he screams.

Allie is the first to die, begging Roland to kill her because she fell for the man in black's trap and used the magic word he left her in a note that would get Nort to tell what he experienced in the afterlife. In the chronology of the *Dark Tower* novels—though not in the gunslinger's life—she is the first of those he cared for to die by his hands. The first sacrificial lamb.

By the end of his shooting spree, fifty-eight men, women and children lie dead in the dusty streets. The gunslinger's only act of mercy before leaving Tull is to cut Nort down from where Sylvia Pittston and her followers had crucified him, laying his body with those of his townspeople. This is reminiscent of Odysseus, who backtracks on his journey home to tend to the body of one of his fallen comrades on Circe's island. Respect for the bodies of the dead is an important part of classic and heroic fiction. Roland muses that, unlike Nort, the other townspeople will only have to die once.

The gunslinger finishes his story and spends the night at Brown's hut. After two more weeks of travel across the desert, delirious and dehydrated, he approaches a way station for the coach line. He sees someone sitting in the inn's shadow. Mistaking the figure for the man in black, and in spite of his weakened condition, he runs the last quarter mile, gun drawn, making no effort to hide. Not that there's anything to hide behind. When Roland finally nears the Tower, a similar urge to drop everything and run pell-mell for his goal sweeps over him, but then he will have Patrick Danville and the loaded cart to hold him back.

Once he realizes the figure is a young boy, he has only enough presence of mind left to reholster his gun before collapsing. Jake Chambers
has water and food ready for him when he awakens. Later, when Roland
rescues Jake from the Tick-Tock Man in Lud, the first thing he does is
provide water to slake Jake's thirst. He remembers this moment and mar-
vels at the role reversal. Sharing khef is an important ritual. Before the
battle of Devar-Toi, Roland performs this ceremony with his ka-tet for the
last time.

Jake says that the man in black—"the priest"—passed by sometime
within the past two weeks, though his concept of time is unreliable. Jake
hid, afraid the bypasser might be a ghost. Roland correctly assumes Walter knew Jake was there but left him as another trap. Roland can't linger
long at the way station. Neither can he leave the boy behind.

The boy doesn't remember how he got to the way station. "I knew
when I came here, but it's all fuzzy now, like a bad dream when you wake
up." He vaguely remembers his home city, the Statue of Liberty and his
school uniform.

The gunslinger hypnotizes Jake to learn more—a skill he acquired,
ironically, from Marten, who is another guise of the man in black. While
performing his dancing bullet trick, he muses about the nature of evil in
his world and, for the first time, mentions the Dark Tower. "The gunslinger's goal is not this half-human creature but the Dark Tower; the man
in black—and, more specifically, what the man in black knows—is his
first step on his road to that mysterious place." [DT2, argument]

Jake reveals enough about his upbringing for the gunslinger to see
similarities with his own. Through Jake, the gunslinger learns of New
York City, a place that will play a pivotal role in his quest. All his life he
accepted intellectually the idea of multiple worlds, but until now—and
perhaps even now—he doesn't believe such a place as New York could
exist. "If so, it had only existed in the myth of prehistory."[22]

Roland has been far beyond the world he knew for a long time and often encounters things he once thought were fictional. As a boy, he and his
friends believed the Dark Tower didn't exist except as a symbol. When he
encounters a guardian of the Beam, he is again surprised to find myth become reality. He even wonders if Mid-World—as opposed to In-World,
where Gilead was, and the desert borderland—is anything more than a
rumor.

Ultimately, Jake remembers his death. Someone who resembles the man in black pushed him in front of a car. Roland later learns the pusher was Jack Mort, but Walter was likely nearby, orchestrating. Before bringing him out of his trance, the gunslinger asks Jake if he wants to remember his final moments or not. Jake chooses to forget.

While in the inn's cellar looking for food, Roland hears a groaning sound and sees a hole forming in the foundation. From the other side, a Speaking Demon tells him, "While you travel with the boy, the man in black travels with your soul in his pocket." Digging to get at the source of the voice, Roland finds only a rotting jawbone so large that he believes it belonged to one of the Great Old Ones, one of the creators.[23] For no clear reason, he takes the bone with him when he clambers out of the cellar. "It occurred to him later that this was when he began to love the boy—which was, of course, what the man in black must have planned all along."

King makes no secret of the fact that Jake's future is grim. Before long, the gunslinger thinks of him as "the sacrifice."[24] Roland and the boy he will one day come to think of as his son, the makings of a ka-tet that won't be complete until the middle of *The Waste Lands,* set out toward the mountains. Unbeknownst to them—and to readers until *Wolves of the Calla*—as they leave the way station behind, a figure who will play a significant role in Roland's future—Father Callahan from *'Salem's Lot*—is drawn through from Earth in much the same manner as Jake was.

Before sending him through the UNFOUND door to Calla Bryn Sturgis as another trap for Roland, Walter points Jake and Roland out to Callahan, saying, "They're following me . . . but I needed to double back and talk to you. . . . Now I must get ahead of them again—how else will I draw them on?" [DT5] Roland already suspects that the man in black is letting him catch up. "'Ware the man who fakes a limp," he remembers his old instructor, Cort, saying.

After a few days, they are close enough to see the light of Walter's campfire. During one of their afternoon rest periods, Roland recounts an incident from when he was eleven, the same age as Jake. Cort sentenced Roland's friend and fellow gunslinger-in-training, Cuthbert, to an evening without supper as punishment for his behavior during lessons. Roland knows Hax, the west kitchen cook, will give them something to eat.

While they are eating dessert under the stairs near the kitchen, they overhear Hax, who has forgotten they are around, conspiring to send poisoned meat to Farson,[25] an insurrectionist plotting against the Affiliation, centered in Gilead.[26] The west is where failed gunslingers are sent in shame, so Hax's position in the west kitchen is symbolic.

Roland reports their news to his father, Stephen Deschain, senior gunslinger and leader of Gilead, the last lord of the light. Hax is sentenced to hang for his treachery; Roland and Cuthbert ask permission to witness the execution. It is an important coming-of-age event for Roland. For the first time he sees death as a permitted punishment for disloyalty. Cort gives the boys bread to feed the birds that flock around the gallows, a scene echoed in *Black House* when Ty Marshall sees crows gathered around a gantry in End-World.

Within five years[27] of that hanging, Roland's land fell and both his parents were dead, his mother killed by his own hand. Only dimly conceived at this point, King wove elements of Roland's history into subsequent books, culminating in *Wizard and Glass,* written twenty years after "The Way Station." He also added some of these later-conceived details to the revised edition of *The Gunslinger*.

After two days in the foothills, Roland and Jake see the man in black, a tiny dot moving up the slope ahead of them, for the first time. Throughout his quest, Roland knows things without understanding why, but he trusts these intuitions. They will catch up with the man in black on the other side of the mountain. "The knowledge was strong in him . . . but it was not a good knowledge." He knows that he will be tested when he catches Walter. He believes that the only way he can proceed to the next stage of his quest is through the man in black.

Roland's dreams reveal more of his past, but it is a vision cloaked in mystery. He sees Susan Delgado, his beloved, dying in a fire. Susan warns him to watch out for Jake, who appears in the dream as a statue with a spike driven through his forehead in the same place where Alice of Tull bore a scar.[28] Not an auspicious omen.

He awakens to find Jake standing in a speaking ring, entranced by a succubus. Roland uses the jawbone from the way station as a talisman—or sigul—to free the boy from her grasp.[29] The demon is a creature "with no shape, only a kind of unformed sexual glare with the eye of prophecy," an ancient being cast ashore on the beach when the waters of the Prim receded. Roland knows that the demon will act as an oracle—for a price.

To prepare for his encounter, he ingests mescaline, which he tells Jake "wakes you up all the way for a little while." Native Americans often used mescaline to enhance their receptivity to messages from their gods. Aldous Huxley advocated its use to open up the mind to new ideas in *Doors of Perception*. King said he was watching *The Good, the Bad and the Ugly* under the influence of the drug when he was inspired to start the *Dark Tower* series.[30] It is extremely dangerous because the lethal dose is quite small. Roland dislikes its effects because "his ego was too strong (or perhaps just too simple) to enjoy being eclipsed and peeled back, made a target for more sensitive emotions."

Like most prophecies, the oracle's message raises more questions than it answers. The succubus tells Roland that the number 3 is his fate:[31] a young man infested by a demon called heroin, a woman on wheels[32] and a third, "Death . . . but not for you," a nearly literal statement since the third is named Mort.

Jake is Roland's gateway to the man in black, the demon says. Walter will show him the way to the three he needs to reach the Dark Tower. To save Jake, he would have to cry off from his quest. This he cannot do.

The demon's nominal payment for her prophecy is sex, an encounter that nearly kills him. During his climax, Roland remembers the faces of women from his past. He thinks the vision of Susan Delgado is punishment meted out by the succubus for being forced to speak.[33] He has no idea how profoundly his thirst for knowledge will impact his life. By agreeing to the oracle's terms, Roland has set into motion the creation of his son, Mordred, whom he will share with Susannah Dean, the demon-turned-woman named Mia and his ultimate nemesis, the Crimson King. As in the legend of King Arthur, Mordred will hate his father from birth and pursue him with single-minded loathing. This is the real price Roland pays for the snippets of the future the oracle reveals.

The following evening, Roland tells Jake more about his homeland, New Canaan, the land of milk and honey, which no longer exists. He hasn't been there since he started casting about for the trail of the man in black.[34] There was a revolution, he says. "We won every battle, and lost the war." Only three remain from the old world: the gunslinger, the man in black and the Dark Tower.[35]

The desert that almost killed Roland is now a distant memory as he and Jake climb toward the pass through the mountains. Water and food—in the form of rabbits—are no longer a worry. A week after they see a single footprint in a patch of snow, they catch up with their prey for the first time.

Though he's only been in Roland's land for a few weeks, Jake has fallen under ka's influence. He now knows things without having to be told,[36] including a certainty that Roland is going to kill him. He pleads with the gunslinger to turn back.

Roland tells Jake he will take care of him. On the heels of that self-serving lie—which will ultimately become the truth when Roland gets a second chance with Jake in *The Waste Lands*—they come face-to-face with the man in black, the master of lies. Acting out of instinct, the gunslinger shoots at his adversary even though he seeks information from him. "It's not your bullets I fear, Roland. It's your idea of answers that scares me," he says. Walter promises to respond to Roland's questions when they reach the other side of the mountain, but only when they are alone, a clear sign that Jake's doom is at hand.

If Roland can't bring himself to sacrifice Jake, he thinks he will be proven unworthy of his quest, but to whom? Even the man in black doesn't know. If Roland plays his part, the man in black must play his. Roland genuinely believes Jake's death is unavoidable but never pursues the question "Who requires such a price?"

If Roland is to redeem himself in future incarnations, he may have to find a way to the Tower without sacrificing Jake, entrusting ka to guide him. Or will "greedy old ka" always demand a sacrifice? As it says in the Book of Mark, "What does it profit a man, if he shall gain the whole world but lose his own soul?" Or, in the words of Morgan Sloat, "What does it profit a man to gain the whole world, if he should lose his own son?" [TT][37]

Facing the possibility of success after countless years of pursuit and hardship, Roland detaches himself emotionally from Jake. By choosing to follow Walter into the mountains, he consciously sentences Jake to death. "That was the moment at which the small figure before him ceased to be Jake and became only the boy, an impersonality to be moved and used."[38] He is a pawn to be sacrificed in favor of a greater victory. After Jake rejoins the ka-tet, Roland occasionally refers to him as "the boy" and immediately reprimands himself for doing so.

The fourth section, "The Slow Mutants," puts Roland and Jake beneath the mountains. As it opens, Roland is telling Jake about how he and his friends Cuthbert and Alain[39] spied from a balcony on the annual court-ing ball in the Great Hall of Gilead. Below them, the younger gunslingers danced while the older ones sat—seemingly embarrassed—at a great stone table.

Marten the counselor and enchanter sat next to Roland's parents. Though still a boy, Roland recognized that his mother, the betrayer, formed a connection between Marten and his father. "What hand could have held the knife that did my father to his death?" he wonders, perhaps referring to his mother's involvement in a plot to kill her husband, though Roland may be speculating that someone else in the court was responsi-ble for his father's death. Exactly how Stephen Deschain ultimately dies is never revealed, except that Marten arranged it.

Roland is talking nervously and angrily, needing to explain himself. Jake knows what lies ahead for him and isn't very interested in Roland's tale. He is angered by the games adults play and is aware that he's a help-less participant in another one of those games right now.

Jake finds a railroad line and they decide to follow it. In the meager light, they see relics of the ancient world: lightbulbs, gasoline pumps, a sign labeled AMOCO. LEAD FREE. After several days walking blindly, they collide with an old handcar. Jake knows what it is, but the vehicle is un-familiar to Roland, who is pleased by its operation. It's the only functional old machine other than the pump at the way station he's seen in years.[40] It's also the first of many trains that will play an important part in their quest, including Blaine, Charlie the Choo-Choo and the train that runs from Fedic through Thunderclap to Calla Bryn Sturgis.

They're still traveling in darkness, but at a far greater pace. Roland, at-tuned to ka, senses that they are close to the end of the beginning.[41] Dur-ing one of their breaks, Jake asks Roland about his coming of age, which can also be considered the end of the beginning of Roland's life.

"Love and dying have been my life," Roland responds in the original version, as if this answers everything. He tells of the crucial day when Marten tricked him into taking his test against Cort before anyone thinks he's ready. The enchanter summons him to his mother's apartment. The scene speaks for itself—Marten's clothing and appearance are disheveled. His mother wears only a gown and is clearly embarrassed to have her son see her like this.

Marten taunts and insults Roland, provoking him to lash out in anger.

In a blind rage, Roland leaves the apartment, Marten's laughter echoing in his ears. The enchanter and counselor to the gunslingers believes he's accomplished his goal, the first of many occasions when he underestimates Roland.

Cort has trained three generations of boys to become gunslingers. Each, in his own time, has challenged him or, failing to find the requisite courage, dropped out to live a quiet life of self-imposed exile in a nearby barony. Those who defeated Cort became gunslingers. The others were immediately sent west, into exile, never to see their families or homes again.

No one as young as Roland has ever succeeded at the challenge. The average age is eighteen. Stephen Deschain, the youngest ever to become a gunslinger, was sixteen. Even Cort implores Roland to reconsider, saying he is two years too early.[42] Roland is fourteen, closer to being a man than a boy, but still young.

Roland picks his hawk, David, a faithful companion for many years, as his weapon. His future depends on what remaining fire the aging bird has left. David is the first of a long line of friends whom Roland betrays and uses in the furtherance of his objectives. His inspired choice of a weapon demonstrates his skill at improvisation, a talent that will follow him throughout his quest. Cort approves, though the salty tutor still thinks he will prevail.

When David claws his head, Cort bashes himself in the face to disable the bird, and it looks like Roland's career as a gunslinger has ended before it begins. Broken and dying, David fights on his friend's behalf, lashing and tearing at Cort's face. The tutor can't handle two assailants simultaneously. Roland breaks Cort's nose and gains his teacher's ironwood stick. Cort is still unwilling to cede the battle—he tries to counterattack, but Roland is ready and smashes Cort solidly on the side of the head.

Finally, Cort yields and surrenders the key to the chest containing Roland's reward: his weapons. His birthright. Not the heavy, weighted sandalwood guns of his father, but transitional revolvers used by his father during his apprenticeship.

Before collapsing into a coma from which he isn't sure he will ever recover, Cort offers Roland his last counsel as teacher: Let word of his accomplishments spread. The legend will grow in the retelling. Rather than immediately seeking his vengeance against Marten, Cort advises him to wait. Walter will later tell Roland this was bad advice, but the young gunslinger never gets the chance to decide whether to take it or not. After asking his friends to tend to their badly beaten teacher, Roland goes into town and spends his first night with a woman, a second rite of passage. The next morning, his father sends him to Mejis to keep him out of Marten's reach.

Like David, Jake is a weapon to be sacrificed in the name of the Tower. "Am I ready to throw this boy at the man in black?" he wonders. He dismisses the boy, hearing an echo in his words—Marten dismissing Roland from his mother's chamber.

Jake wonders if he underestimated the gunslinger when Roland saves him from the Slow Mutants who attack them the next day. Drawn by Roland's and Jake's life forces, these disfigured creatures—maimed by ill-advised wars and disastrous experiments by the Old Ones or from working too close to the King's Forge—swarm around the handcar. Roland shoots those he can, but there are too many. They grab Jake, threatening to pull him off the car. Roland isn't ready to give up the boy yet. He knows this isn't the right place for a sacrifice. He fights for the boy's life, finally pulling him to safety.

Roland surprises Jake a second time, sending him into the darkness to remove stones blocking the track. Again, Jake's suspicions that he is being offered in sacrifice are disproved. Roland keeps the mutants at bay long enough for Jake to clear the track and regain the handcar.

Several days later, Jake and Roland see light for the first time in over a week, and they enter a chamber containing a switching station for a series of train lines. The tunnel they enter has a sign saying TRACK 10 TO THE SURFACE AND POINTS WEST. Though he defeated Cort many years earlier, Roland is headed west after all.

The central terminal, which reminds Jake of a subway station, is another reminder that things in the world are winding down. The shops contain relics of a long-ago era. The recirculator makes a grating noise, and the air has a mechanized taste. After thousands of years of operation, it won't last much longer.

Jake's confidence fails him. He doesn't want to go any farther. "You won't get what you want until I'm dead," he says. To his surprise, the gunslinger agrees and pretends to leave. "How easily you bluff this young boy," Roland thinks, hating himself, knowing Jake has no one else in this world who will see to his survival, short as it may be.

For a moment, Roland is tempted to turn away from his quest and wait until Jake is older, the center of a new force. It's not his first such thought—while in Mejis, he considered running away with Susan Delgado. "The Tower did not have to be obtained in his humiliating nose-rubbing way, did it?" he wonders. But Roland knows that to turn back means death for both of them, and for all of creation.

Jake falls for the gunslinger's bluff and runs after Roland, who resists the brief urge to speed up and leave him behind. Holding Jake, who had to leap on board to catch up, Roland knows that the end—in whatever form it is to come—is very close.

Their last obstacle is a rickety trestle within sight of the tunnel's end. Jake distrusts the bridge and urges Roland to abandon the handcar. They can easily walk the rest of the way. After inspecting the decrepit bridge, Roland agrees. Rotten crossties break under their feet, and there are wide gaps in places.

The arduous crossing foreshadows the bridge Roland and his followers will cross outside Lud. As in that future crossing, the bridge fails Jake. With the end of the tunnel in their grasp, the man in black appears and, simultaneously, Jake falls. Roland is torn between two crises, a situation he will face often during his quest. Sometimes he and his ka-tet can find a way to handle multiple problems in turn, but this time Roland must choose one crisis or the other. Jake is dangling over the deep chasm, pleading for help, but the man in black says, "Come now . . . or catch me never."

The boy or the Tower? Roland can't resist the lure of his quest; he abandons Jake, who plummets to his second death. Though King later tries to accept the blame for having written Jake into this situation, ultimately the author says that Roland acted on his own. The boy's final words haunt the gunslinger: "Go then. There are other worlds than these."

Walter tells Roland, without explaining why, that this sacrifice was necessary to allow the creation of the doorways from which he will draw his ka-tet. Necessary or not, Roland considers himself damned by his betrayal, though he does achieve some measure of redemption later.

Enraged, Roland empties both guns at the man in black, but the enchanter merely laughs. "You kill me no more than you kill yourself." Roland's In-World weapons would have no effect on Walter anyway, as he discovers in the Emerald Palace many months in the future. In the revised edition, Walter tells him his guns don't open doors, "they only close them forever."

Clear of the mountains, the railway tracks are worn away as if they had never been. Their disappearance is symbolic, for soon Jake too will fade from the gunslinger's memory as if he had never crossed over at the way station. Walter calls Jake Roland's Isaac, but Roland doesn't recognize the reference to Abraham, who was ordered by God to sacrifice his son. "I was never a scholar of [the Bible]," Roland says.

Thus begins the story's denouement.[43] The man in black leads Roland to a Golgotha—a place of skulls and death—and commands him to gather wood for a fire, like Roland ordered Marten countless years earlier in his mother's chamber. Walter's ordinary appearance disappoints Roland. The enchanter bears "none of the marks and twists which indicate a person who has been through awesome times and who has been privy to great and unknown secrets." Roland refuses the rabbit the man in black cooks, instead eating the last of his jerky.

They begin their palaver[44] after the sun disappears from the sky. "You won't see another sunrise for what may seem a very long time," the man in black tells Roland. He produces a customized tarot deck to tell Roland's future. "I suspect I've never read one quite like yours," he says. "You are the world's last adventurer. Yet you have no idea how close you stand to the Tower now, how close in time."[45] Thousands of miles down the road, as Roland draws near to his goal, he thinks that Walter's deck was probably stacked.

The gunslinger's card is the Hanged Man, signifying strength. The second card, the Sailor, represents Jake. "He drowns, gunslinger, and no one throws out a line." The remaining cards lay out Roland's future, starting with those who will accompany him. The Prisoner card shows a baboon holding a whip, astride a young man's back. This is Eddie, the addict, a man with a monkey on his back. The Lady of Shadows card shows a woman smiling and sobbing at the same time. A Janus, indicating the dual personalities of Odetta and Detta, who will become Susannah Dean.

The fifth card is Death—"yet not for you." Indeed, many friends have died and will die during Roland's quest.[46] These four cards surround Roland's like satellites circling a star. The man in black places the sixth card, the Tower, directly over Roland's card and refuses to explain its meaning or why he is showing Roland these things. Questions appear to anger him.

The seventh and final card is Life—"but not for you." The man in black does not place this card in tableau but instead tosses it into the fire. Neither Roland nor the man in black are meant to know its meaning, which perhaps signifies the way the gunslinger will never live out his normal course of days unless he solves the great puzzle of his life. Like the missing horn of Eld, it may be an indication that Roland's personal quest will fail this time.

"Sleep now . . . Perchance to dream," the man in black tells Roland, echoing Hamlet's soliloquy. He narrates Roland's vision, a traditional creation drama, starting from a void, introducing light, stars, the Earth, water, land, plants and animals. Roland sees more of the solar system than he ever knew existed. The word "universe," which Walter calls the Great All, is unfamiliar to him.

At one point, the narration seems to expand beyond Walter to some greater being, never identified, perhaps the Voice of the Turtle. Later, in the presence of Black Thirteen, Roland will understand that he was sent todash by the residual effects of that Wizard's orb, which was recently in Walter's hands. During his todash journey, Walter hypnotizes Roland.

When the dream overwhelms him, he pleads for it to end. The man in black urges him to renege. "Cast away all thoughts of the Tower. Go your way, gunslinger, and begin the long job of saving your soul." Roland summons the strength to utter his "final, flashing imperative." In the closing moments of the vision, revealed by the man in black but unseen by him, Roland sees something of cosmic importance: a tiny purple blade of grass.

When he wakes up, the man in black congratulates him on his resilience. "I never could have sent that vision to your father.[47] He would have come back drooling." Even so, he says Roland will never complete his quest. "The Tower will kill you half a world away." He claims to be "the furthest minion of he who now rules the Dark Tower. Earth has been given into that king's red hand."[48] "I am not the great one you seek. I am only his emissary."

When Roland tells him about the blade of grass, the man in black seems confused. Walter's failure to see everything that was revealed in the vision shows Roland that he has weaknesses. He may have facilitated the dream, but he didn't cause it, in a manner akin to how fictional Stephen King facilitates the *Dark Tower* story without causing or creating it.

Walter tells Roland the history of his world, starting hundreds of generations in the past when Roland's world was much like Earth, with advanced technology, cures for cancer and space travel—a time that had a wealth of information but no insight. Though Roland knows that Walter is not to be trusted, at least some of what he learns about the Crimson King (originally called the Beast), the keeper of the Tower, is partly true.

His intention is to discourage Roland with the magnitude of his task, arguing that the universe they occupy may be merely an atom on a blade of grass that exists for only a day or two in another reality. "If a scythe cuts off the blade, would the rot of it dying seep into our own universe and our own lives? . . . We say the world has moved on; maybe we really mean that it has begun to dry up." Walter asks Roland if he would dare take on the enormity of the room at the top of the Tower where all universes meet, a room resting above the sum of all realities. "Someone has dared," the gunslinger responds. "God has dared . . . or is the room empty?"

Roland and Walter talk through the night, but the gunslinger remembers little of it later. "To his oddly practical mind, little of it seemed to matter." What he does recall pertains directly to his quest. He is to go to the sea, twenty easy miles to the west, where the heretofore unknown power of drawing that Roland possesses will be expressed. Walter says that he is compelled to provide Roland with this information partly because he sacrificed Jake but also because it is the "natural law of things." At the sea, Roland will draw three. "And then the fun begins," the man in black concludes.

Roland is right in thinking that little of what Walter tells him is important to his quest. The oracle had already told him about the three people he will draw. Knowing the number is vital to his future survival because he and Eddie will push Odetta farther north along the beach, reasonably confident that they will find another door. Beyond the metaphysics lesson, the sum total of Walter's useful information is this: Go west. For this he sacrificed Jake?

One of the most significant changes King makes in the revised version is to clarify the fact that Walter—the man in black—and Marten are the same person, or different facets of the same being. Walter admits to having been both Marten and a member of his entourage known to Roland. He claims that Roland will have to kill the Ageless Stranger before he can reach the Tower without revealing that this is Flagg, yet another of his own guises.

Roland awakens to find himself ten years older, or so he perceives. Exactly how much time has elapsed is impossible to ascertain. Walter tells Mordred, "We were in one of the fistulas of time which sometimes swirl out from the Tower, and the world moved on all around us as we had our palaver in that bony place."[DT7] Long enough for Roland's hair to thin and turn slightly gray, and for his campfire to seem to petrify, but not necessarily as long as Walter would have Roland believe. The bones that are supposed to be Walter's decomposed body were arranged by the sorcerer to mislead the gunslinger.

He later says to Mordred, "I could have killed him then, but what of the Tower if I had, eh?" [DT7] Though Walter claims he allowed himself to be caught, he will later imply that he was terrified of the gunslinger and afraid for his own life. Perhaps that's one of Walter's lies, or maybe ka is using Walter in ways that he isn't aware of.

Roland doubts the skeleton is really Walter.[49] He knows that the man in black has told him many lies. On impulse, he breaks off the jawbone and sticks it in his pocket, a replacement for the one he gave Jake in the oracle's speaking circle. Since it wasn't Walter's, the jawbone has no real power other than to prove later to Roland's confused mind that Jake did exist.

The first book ends when Roland reaches the Western Sea. Once this sea was only a thousand miles from Gilead, but the world is expanding and his journey has taken him many times farther than that. Neither time nor distance remains constant. He dreams that he would "some day come at dusk and approach, winding his horn, to do some unimaginable final battle" at the Dark Tower.

In "The Politics of Limited Editions," King writes, "Roland doesn't change substantially in *The Gunslinger*, but the potential for and the promise of change come through strongly." How much his capacity for change evolves on subsequent iterations of his journey will determine whether or not he ultimately succeeds in discovering what exists at the top of the Tower—or whether he decides that, having saved it, he needs to go to the Tower at all.

King's decision to revise a twenty-year-old book is certainly controversial[50] but not unprecedented in King's publication history. He frequently updated short stories when preparing them for collections. During the process of restoring excised material that had been removed from *The Stand* prior to its 1977 original publication, he moved the story ahead a decade and rewrote sections. Of *The Gunslinger*, King says, "It actually seemed not so much like a luxury . . . but like a real necessity, to say, 'Let's make this book more readable; let's make it more exciting; let's pick up the pace a little bit and really try to draw readers in.'"[51]

His revisions create a situation not unlike the one Roland finds himself in at the start of *The Waste Lands*. He has two slightly different versions of his past: the reality where he encountered Jake in the desert and the one where the way station was empty. With *The Gunslinger*, there is a reality where Walter may not be Marten, Roland doesn't learn about the Crimson King and his trek takes him south instead of southeast.

King's changes occur on almost every page. Some are simple reworkings of awkward, self-conscious writing—"hollow blather," as he calls it in the foreword. He removed most adverbs—following his own advice in *On Writing*—and clarified numerous cases of pronouns with uncertain antecedents. In the original version, Roland occasionally spoke in 1970s slang, saying things like, "Dig?"

King changes dialogue in numerous places to adopt the distinctive language used in later books, things like "if it do ya fine," "say thank ya," and "thankee-sai." He replaces the seasons with their Mid-World equivalents, Fresh Earth and Reaping, for example. Anonymous characters, like Cort's predecessor and the gunslinger who hangs Hax, are given names. Obscure references ("like a Kuvian night-soldier") are gone.

A second level of changes could be called "bug fixes," addressing continuity errors that crept into the story. Roland no longer reads magazines in Tull—unlikely since paper is such a scarce commodity. References to electric lights are replaced with "spark lights." Alain Johns is frequently called Allen in the original. King addresses the temporal confusion pertaining to the span of Roland's quest, which was alternately either measured in decades or millennia, by being less specific.

The third types of changes are those where King introduces elements that he hadn't yet conceived in the 1970s. Gilead is never mentioned in the original version, nor are Arthur Eld, the Crimson King, Sheemie, the Manni,[52] taheen, Algul Siento, bumblers or the commala dance. He foreshadows the loss of Roland's fingers and the ka-tet's discovery of the Beam (Allie notes that the clouds all flow in a particular direction). Sylvia Pittston's sermon presages both Roland's discovery of the jawbone at the way station and his meeting with Walter at the Golgotha.

King also strengthens Jake's character through the subtle use of dialogue. The boy was often passive and silent in the original, but he now speaks his mind more frequently. Jake understands what he is to Roland, and he spares no occasion to let the gunslinger know he's aware. King deletes narrative descriptions of the boy with negative connotation, things like "with dumbly submissive sheep's eyes" or a scene where he compares the boy's pounding chest to the beat of a chicken's heart.

Roland's relationship with Allie in Tull is subtly more intimate, too. When Allie warns Roland that the hostler is likely to make things up if he doesn't know them, Roland thanks her and she is touched beyond measure, unable to remember the last time someone who mattered thanked her. Roland also shows his concern for her when he counsels her to forget Walter's message, to banish the word "nineteen" from her mind rather than use it to access Nort's memories of what happened to him in death.

Finally, King injects a number of hints about the cyclical nature of Roland's existence, adding the sense of dizziness brought about by his shift backward in time. Walter frequently mentions how Roland never manages to get it right, though the gunslinger doesn't understand. "What do you mean, resume? I never left off." King also draws more attention to Roland's missing horn, a crucial factor in the series' final pages.

> He thought of that momentary dizziness earlier in the day, that sense of being almost untethered from the world, and wondered what it might have meant. Why should that dizziness make him think of his horn and the last of his old friends, both lost so long ago at Jericho Hill? He still had the guns—his father's guns—and surely they were more important than horns . . . or even friends.

Because of its dry, dark tone, the original version of *The Gunslinger*, like a threshold guardian, turned away many who wanted to join the quest.

King's revisions create a more internally consistent series of books for newcomers to the series. Whether it succeeds in its primary goal of being more accessible to readers who might have been turned away by the original remains to be seen.

ENDNOTES

[1] Unless otherwise specified, all quotes in this chapter are from *The Gunslinger*.

[2] Inscription King often uses when signing copies of *The Gunslinger*.

[3] *Walden Book Report,* July 2003.

[4] Peter Straub and King finished writing *The Talisman* around the time Grant published *The Gunslinger. The Eyes of the Dragon* was probably written around the same time, as it was first published in 1984.

[5] The science fiction Bachman books *The Running Man* and *The Long Walk* notwithstanding. In 1982, few people knew about these books or that they were by King.

[6] "But what of the gunslinger's murky past? God, I know so little. The revolution that topples the gunslinger's 'world of light'? I don't know. Roland's final confrontation with Marten, who seduces his mother and kills his father? Don't know. The deaths of Roland's compatriots, Cuthbert and Jamie, or his adventures during the years between his coming of age and his first appearance to us in the desert? I don't know that either. And there's this girl, Susan. Who is she? Don't know." [DT1, afterword]

[7] In the original version of the novel, Roland is first identified by name when he is in the cellar of the way station. King obviously knew his name before that because he mentions it in a teaser at the end of the "The Gunslinger" in F&SF magazine in 1978. In the revised and expanded edition, Roland's name first appears at the end of the first section, about a third of the way through the book.

[8] *The Art of Michael Whelan,* Bantam, 1993.

[9] Edward Bryant, *Locus* magazine, Vol. 27, No. 6, December 1991.

[10] *NewsNight with Aaron Brown,* CNN, June 24, 2003.

[11] Interview with Amazon.com, May 2003. In an interview published on the Walden Books Web site, King said that eventually he would rewrite the entire series.

[12] www.stephenking.com, February 25, 2003.

[13] Foreword to *The Gunslinger,* Viking, 2003.

[14] Synopsis at the start of "The Way Station," *The Magazine of Fantasy and Science Fiction,* April 1980. These synopses are interesting because they are King's commentaries on the story while he was in the process of writing it. See appendix V.

[15] King was inspired by the spaghetti westerns starring Clint Eastwood, who often went unnamed in those films. Jake Chambers makes the connection when he sees a movie poster featuring Eastwood on his way to Co-Op City.

[16] South in the original edition.

[17] The town is named after the rock group Jethro Tull, and the raven is named after a folksinger King knew at the University of Maine. Roland's vision in the Wizard's ball in Mejis included Brown and Zoltan, but he doesn't remember most of what he saw.

[18] During the scene where Walter raises Nort, he says, "Mistah Norton, he daid," in a sardonic tone, mimicking the manager boy's words in Joseph Conrad's *Heart of Darkness:*

"Mistah Kurtz—he dead." Susannah—as Detta—echoes these words later, speaking first of Joe Collins (Dandelo) and then Eddie.

[19] Roland's course is changed from south in the original edition to emphasize the Beam's proximity and influence.

[20] In the original edition, it is the man in black's child she thinks she carries.

[21] A thousand years according to the expanded version; twenty-five years in the original.

[22] The expanded version says, "unless it was the mythic city of Lud," which is New York's twin.

[23] In the original version, this is where Roland is named for the first time.

[24] King doesn't shy away from sacrificing children in his books, for example: Pie Carver *(Desperation),* Ralph Glick *('Salem's Lot),* Gage Creed *(Pet Sematary),* Cary Ripton *(The Regulators)* and Tad Trenton *(Cujo).*

[25] In the original version, Farson is the name of a place, but King mistakenly changes him to John Farson in subsequent books. In the revised edition, King corrects this error by changing the town of Farson to Taunton.

[26] Gilead is never mentioned in the original version of the book. When Roland and Eddie meet King in *Song of Susannah,* he says he hasn't thought of the Gilead part when Roland introduces himself. On Earth, Gilead is a region of Jordan located between the Sea of Galilee and the Dead Sea, best known for the "balm of Gilead," an aromatic gum used as a medicine, which is mentioned in Poe's "The Raven."

[27] Ten years in the original edition.

[28] The same place as Father Callahan's cross-shaped scar and where the Crimson King's minions bear open wounds that don't bleed.

[29] In the Bible (Judges 13–16), Samson killed a thousand Philistines armed only with the jawbone of an ass. Sylvia Pittston refers to Samson in her sermon, and Aaron Deepneau mentions Samson's riddle in *The Waste Lands.*

[30] Master's Tea, Yale University, April 21, 2003.

[31] In the revised edition, "another number comes later," referring to the importance of 19 in the final three books.

[32] The original edition continued, "her mind is iron but her heart and eyes are soft."

[33] Roland reflects on this when the subject of mescaline and hallucinogenic mushrooms comes up outside Calla Bryn Sturgis.

[34] In the original version he says he hasn't seen New Canaan for twelve years, but in the revised edition, King changes this to "unknown years." The confusion of time that makes up Roland's life is something that even the Calvin scholars could never resolve.

[35] There were others, including Sylvia Pittston and Sheb from Tull, but they are now dead, too. Sheemie Ruiz from Mejis, who was with Roland when he and his fellow gunslingers set out on their quest for the Tower, is still alive, though Roland doesn't know it. King mentions Sheemie in the revised edition, foreshadowing his importance not only in *Wizard and Glass* but also in *The Dark Tower.*

[36] Each of the New Yorkers who join Roland's quest develops special talents shortly after his or her arrival in Mid-World. Jake's is known as the "touch," a talent he shares with Alain Johns, a member of Roland's earliest ka-tet.

[37] Sloat, the villain, has enough moral awareness to raise the question, but he comes to the wrong conclusion.

[38] Revised edition. The original text is worded a little differently.

[39] Jamie in the original version.

[40] In the revised edition, the handcar—like many other machines in Mid-World—talks, but Roland soon silences it.

[41] Roland often identifies crucial transitions in his quest: the end of the beginning, the beginning of the end, etc.

[42] The original version says five years too early. This is unlikely since that would make him nineteen, older than the average, but Roland is the most promising student Cort has had in decades.

[43] The original title of this section, "The Gunslinger and the Dark Man," is changed to "The Gunslinger and the Man in Black" in the revised edition.

[44] In English, the word "palaver" usually refers to a discussion between people from different cultures or levels of sophistication, and can also mean misleading or idle talk. In Mid-World, though, it usually refers to a meeting where important information is to be exchanged.

[45] In the revised edition, the last clause is replaced with "as you resume your quest." King hints about the cyclical nature of Roland's existence—with the new subtitle, RE-SUMPTION, for example—without giving the ending away. Roland is very close to the Tower in time—but in the wrong direction. After reaching the Tower, he is sent back to a point little more than a month before where he is now.

[46] Near the Tower, Susannah Dean echoes this sentiment; death for everyone else who walks and rides with him, but never for him. Another hint at Roland's cyclical existence—he won't reach the clearing at the end of the path even after a thousand-year journey. The list of the dead includes Susan Delgado, Cuthbert, Alain, Jamie, Jake (three times), Oy, Callahan, Sheemie, Eddie, Mia, Mordred and Walter himself.

[47] In the original text, Walter says "to Marten" instead, implying that they are separate entities.

[48] In the original version, Walter claims to be a minion of the Tower, and he says that Earth has been given into his hand (that is, Walter's) rather than to the red king. The Crimson King was introduced in *Insomnia,* but before the revised edition appeared his first, brief mention in the series proper was in *Wizard and Glass.* Roland, though, doesn't understand who the Crimson King is until late in his journey.

[49] In 1985, Ben Indick expressed doubt over whether the bones belonged to the man in black. ["Stephen King as an Epic Writer," Ben Indick, in *Discovering Modern Horror I,* Darrell Schweitzer, ed., Starmont Press, 1985.]

[50] In the foreword to the new edition of *The Gunslinger,* King writes, "Dark Tower purists (of which there are a surprising number—just check the Web) will want to read the book again, of course, and most of them are apt to do so with a mixture of curiosity and irritation. . . . I'm less concerned with them than with readers who have never encountered Roland and his ka-tet."

[51] Interview with *Walden Book Report,* July 2003.

[52] Brown's deceased wife was of the Manni.

CHAPTER 3

THE DRAWING OF THE THREE
(RENEWAL)

Three. This is the number of your fate. . . .
The three are your way to the Dark Tower.

[DT1]

One reason King had trouble returning to the *Dark Tower* epic was his professed ambivalence toward his protagonist. Though Roland started out as a mysterious knight errant akin to Clint Eastwood's man with no name, he is driven by urges that make him seem like a borderline sociopath. He bedded Alice in Tull but had no troubled dreams after he killed her and everyone else in town. When he let Jake fall to his death so he could palaver with the man in black, Roland teetered on the edge of becoming either an antihero or "no hero at all." [DT6][1]

A substantial part of the second book takes place in familiar territory, New York, whereas *The Gunslinger* was set entirely in Roland's world. This—in addition to the increased number of major characters—may have made *The Drawing of the Three* more accessible to King's readership. Many readers were encouraged to start the series with this book, backtracking later to learn the details of Roland's trek across the desert beyond what's summarized in the argument. It's not an unreasonable approach. *The Gunslinger* can be treated as a flashback similar to the central story in *Wizard and Glass*.

Though Roland makes no geographic progress in his quest for the Dark Tower in *The Drawing of the Three*—his trek north along the beach is almost in the opposite direction to where he needs to go—he assembles the team who will accompany him across the thousands of miles he has ahead. He still doesn't know how to get to the Tower; he hasn't yet encountered one of the Paths of the Beam to point him in the right direction, and he overlooked the significance of what Allie noticed about the clouds all flowing southeast across the desert.

Until now, Roland Deschain has left behind everyone who started the quest for the Dark Tower with him or helped him along the way, most of them dead. Roland is capable of completing his quest alone and seems content to do so. He finds companionship and rejects it. Part of the difficulty some readers had with *The Gunslinger* may lie in the fact that the first book is locked inside the head of a man who doesn't yield up his secrets easily. In *The Drawing of the Three,* Roland is forced to embrace companionship; he has little other choice.

The book closely follows the structure of Walter's tarot reading. The people behind the cards enter the story. Vignettes between these major sections are called "Shuffle," playing off the multiple implications of the word "drawing" in the title—drawing cards from a deck, drawing people from another reality.

The book starts a few hours after Roland arrives at the Western Sea. He falls asleep on the beach, exhausted from his preternaturally long palaver with Walter and the relentless chase leading up to it. He isn't aware of the tide coming in around him until the freezing water reaches his guns and ammunition belt, nor does he notice the four-foot-long lobsterlike monstrosities that have come in with it.

In a few minutes, Roland's ability to fulfill his destiny is severely compromised. Some of his precious ammunition supply gets wet. Worse, in a stupor and preoccupied with preventing any more of his bullets from being ruined, he misjudges the threat posed by the lobstrosities. He loses the trigger and middle fingers from his dominant right hand, a chunk of his lower calf, a toe and a boot to one of the creatures. His responses are dulled by an overpowering exhaustion the likes of which he will not see until the night before he reaches the Tower. He feels only the numbing dread that occurs when something life altering happens but the mind hasn't fully processed the implications yet. "I see serious problems ahead," he thinks remotely.

For a man whose identity is completely defined by being a gunslinger, Roland's injuries—especially the loss of his fingers—are grievous. The first time he draws his gun he drops it in the sand. "What had once been a thing so easy it didn't even bear thinking about had suddenly become a trick akin to juggling." When he finally learns how to work his damaged hand, the hammer falls on dud ammunition. He can no longer rely on the iconic weapons passed down from the beginning of time, their barrels forged from Arthur Eld's sword. They may not fire when he needs them. Some bullets are obviously ruined; the rest are merely questionable.

And with thousands of miles to travel to the Dark Tower, he now has only one boot and no big toe on his right foot, though it isn't a serious enough injury to stop him from dancing before the Calla-folken several months down the road.

These injuries imperil his long-term chances of success. Of more immediate concern, though Roland doesn't realize it yet, is the infection at work in his wounds. He has no means of fending off a microscopic enemy. All he can do is sprinkle the stumps of his fingers and toe with tobacco to stop the bleeding, and bind his wounds with bandages torn from his shirt.

His training usually prevents Roland from losing control, but the direness of his situation pushes him briefly over the edge, as it did after Jake fell to his death. In a fit of rage, he squashes the lobstrosity with a rock and crushes its head with his remaining boot, stamping on it over and over again. "It was dead, but he meant to have his way with it all the same; he had never, in all his long strange time, been so fundamentally hurt, and it had all been so unexpected."

Without live ammo, his revolvers are "no more than clubs." He separates the twenty bullets that are probably okay from the batch of about forty that may or may not fire when called upon. While he cleans his revolvers, his missing digits haunt him. "Go away," he tells them when they throb. "You are ghosts now."

He struggles up the beach away from the water, away from where he was maimed, collapsing in the shade of a Joshua tree. When he awakens the next day, he sees the first signs of the fast-acting infection. Roland has faced many opponents in the centuries he has traveled thus far, but the poison in his system threatens to defeat him. In his inimitably dry manner, Roland sums up his situation:

> I am now a man with no food, with two less fingers and one less
> toe than I was born with; I am a gunslinger with shells which may

not fire; I am sickening from a monster's bite and have no medicine; I have a day's water if I'm lucky; I may be able to walk perhaps a dozen miles if I press myself to the last extremity. I am, in short, a man on the edge of everything.

Here is another way that *The Drawing of the Three* differs from its predecessor—tension. In *The Gunslinger,* Roland often told his story in flashback, which adds a layer of abstraction to the story. Since he's reminiscing over these events, it's clear he survived whatever dangers he faced. In the second volume, Roland is in crisis mode from the very beginning, and the tension and pace rarely let up. He goes from one problem to the next with barely a breath in between.

For no reason other than that his heart tells him it is right, Roland goes north.[2] The man in black, convinced he has tricked Roland into thinking he was dead, watches the gunslinger struggle along the beach. Satisfied that he is unlikely to complete his mission, Walter goes in the opposite direction and escapes through a doorway.

In three hours, Roland manages only four miles along the beach, falling twice. He sees something in the distance and crawls the last quarter mile on his elbows and knees. Without help—and soon—Roland may never leave the Western Sea.

Fortunately, Roland's creator has decided he needs new friends. Long ago he set out on this quest with a group of comrades who perished defending Gilead. The time has come for Roland to assemble a new ka-tet, akin to the gathering of the Fellowship that assists Frodo in taking the One Ring to Mordor in *The Lord of the Rings.*

The oracle foresaw three in his future who would be his way to the Tower, and Walter told him he had the power of drawing. Short- and long-term prophecies come to fruition through the gunslinger. Roland's Fellowship, though, will not be composed of kings-in-exile and wizards. It's a ka-tet of damaged souls. Eddie Dean summarizes the group this way: "First you got your basic white junkie, and then you got your basic black shoplif[ter]." The Fellowship is rounded out by a gunslinger missing his trigger finger, a young boy whose parents were oblivious to his existence and a billy-bumbler kicked out of its pack for being too uppity.

Also, his comrades don't join him voluntarily; Roland hijacks them from their own worlds without considering the ethics of taking them against their will. He needs them; therefore, they must come. This is the morality of ka.

The object he has struggled to reach with his last ounce of strength is a door, the first of many he will encounter during the months to come. The members of Roland's ka-tet will take interdimensional doorways for granted, but this is the first such door he has ever encountered during his millennium-long journey. Though he doesn't know it, another door recently played its part in shaping his destiny. Father Callahan was transported through one from the way station to Calla Bryn Sturgis shortly after Roland left with Jake.

These doors, whether of the magic kind or the more recent technological replacements, stand where no door should be. Their hinges aren't fastened to anything. The one on the beach appears to be made from solid ironwood, and the doorknob—filigreed with the grinning face of a baboon—looks to be of gold. Written on it in the High Speech are the words THE PRISONER. When Roland walks around the door to examine the other side, it disappears. Only its shadow in the sand is visible. He thinks he's hallucinating.

The baboon and the words on the door echo the tarot card Walter showed him, but the man in black did not explain the meaning of his fortune. Roland has no idea what is behind this door, but he doesn't have many options—if he leaves it closed, he'll die. He has no doubt that it will open to his hand since ka wants him to succeed, just like John Cullum will be there in Maine months later when needed.

Unlike the portals that Roland encounters later, the doors on the beach permit a special kind of access to what lies beyond. Once opened, he sees through the eyes of the person he is supposed to draw. When he crosses the threshold, he enters that person's body and mind. This may be ka's way of pointing him at the person of interest on America-side. He likely

---

The Power of Four

Including Roland, the ka-tet of the *Dark Tower* is composed of four people. King often assembles groups of four: Roland's youthful ka-tet consisted of himself, Alain, Cuthbert and Jamie. Gran-Pere Jaffords and three others, including Molly Doolin, stood against the Wolves the first time one was killed. Three others accompanied Arthur Eld when he slew Saita, the great snake. Stu, Larry, Ralph and Glen are sent to Las Vegas at the end of *The Stand*, four friends go hunting in *Dreamcatcher*, four boys wander abroad in *The Body* and the four-membered Sawyer Gang enters the Black House. In a vision caused by the rose, Eddie sees four men save a young boy from a monster with one eye, reminiscent of the Sawyer Gang saving Ty Marshall from Mr. Munshun.

wouldn't have given Eddie Dean or Detta Walker much thought as potential ka-mates otherwise, and if he hadn't entered Jack Mort through the third door he might have believed it was Jake he was after. Also, Roland is inept in New York and he needs the support of the person he enters to function.

As luck would have it, when Roland opens the door, Eddie Dean is looking out the window of an airplane flying from the Bahamas to New York. The view of the Earth far below is nothing Roland could have anticipated, even given his recent astronomy lesson. Overwhelmed, he slams the door shut without considering that it might never open again. He regains his composure and tries a second time.

Roland gets his first glimpse of a world he will visit several more times over the course of his quest. He will never be completely comfortable in this land—Eddie tells him he loses something in the translation when they cross over to New York. The letters in English words swim before his eyes, and he's never quite sure how things work. Even so, he suspects it's similar to the way his own world was before it moved on.

"With the simple resolve that had made him the last of them all," Roland steps through the doorway. When he looks back, he sees his body lying limp on the beach. Only his essence crossed the threshold. As long as he remains on the other side of the doorway, he's vulnerable to the lobstrosities and any other predators that might happen along.

Roland's presence is a benevolent possession. He can push himself forward to assert control when he needs to, or pull back to let his host operate normally at other times. Once Roland announces his presence, he and his host will be able to communicate. Mia's possession of Susannah's body is similar. She can move forward and back in Susannah's mind, exerting control when necessary but allowing Susannah to operate normally when Mia doesn't know what to do. Perhaps Mia entered Susannah through a doorway like this.

Roland understands immediately that the person he inhabits is an addict. He identifies the symptoms with those of Nort the Weedeater from Tull. The baboon on Walter's tarot card symbolizes—in part—the young man's affliction. Eddie is a heroin addict who is going "cool turkey" long enough to smuggle two pounds of cocaine from the Bahamas. In preparation for this trip, he stopped shooting up so his conspicuous needle tracks could heal.

The cocaine taped under his armpits will be exchanged for heroin for him and his older brother, Henry—mostly for Henry, who could never have stayed straight long enough to make the trip. Roland learns from Eddie's mind that his addiction was largely brought about by Henry's negative influence. Though Roland claims to be slow and unimaginative, he often exhibits flashes of insight that defy this characterization, which was pounded into him by his father and teachers in much the same way Eddie's self-esteem was damaged by his mother and brother.

Eddie isn't weak; he has a weakness—Henry. When his contact in Nassau—where Sombra Corporation is incorporated—tries several times to cheat him during the cash-for-drugs transaction, Eddie calls his bluff and bullies the man into completing the exchange as negotiated. Roland, who has access to Eddie's memories, recognizes his deep steel. Eddie reminds him "achingly" of his old friend Cuthbert Allgood.

Eddie notices his eyes changing color in the bathroom mirror when Roland asserts his influence, but he shrugs it off as a withdrawal-induced hallucination. The scenes where Roland coexists within Eddie's mind are among the cleverest in the book. Roland is addled and weakened from fever. Eddie's mind isn't terribly clear, either, but Roland finds it easier to think inside what he considers "a cleaner vessel than his own." At times, Eddie experiences things through ten senses and feels with two sets of nerves.

Roland doesn't know all the rules of doorway travel yet. While Eddie sleeps, he performs a few experiments. He learns that he can take things from Eddie's world to his and back again, but he can't bring things that originate in his world into Eddie's. Later, he will discover that if he travels through the doorway in person instead of hitchhiking via Eddie's mind, he can transport things—like his guns—from Mid-World to Earth.

Though Roland doesn't understand much of what is happening in Eddie's world, he knows that Eddie will be in big trouble if they don't do something about the drugs. One of the flight attendants has her eye on Eddie, and he doesn't stand a chance of getting past Customs. Eddie is Roland's only potential source for medicine to cure his infection. To get the medicine, he has to get Eddie through Customs, which means hiding the drugs on the beach. He can't do this without Eddie's cooperation, and he must establish contact without sending his host into a screaming fit of terror. Time is running out. The plane has landed and is taxiing toward the terminal.

Their first exchanges are awkward, partly because Roland speaks archaic English and has to search Eddie's mind for words to describe the situation, and partly because Eddie is paranoid enough to believe he's going mad. By the time the airplane reaches the gate, Roland has convinced Eddie that it's in his best interest to obey the voice in his head. He talks Eddie into the bathroom and instructs him to walk through the magic doorway into his world, where they race to rid Eddie of the drugs that have been so meticulously taped to his body.

The flight crew pounds on the door, threatening to break it in. Roland's recent injuries complicate their task, but he manages to get Eddie, sans cocaine, back through the door seconds before the lavatory door bursts open. Though Roland is frustrated with Eddie's clumsiness, Eddie thinks quickly enough to come up with a somewhat plausible explanation for the situation once he's back in the airplane lavatory.

Eddie also withstands a two-hour Customs interrogation. The agents know he was up to something, but they can neither prove it nor intimidate him into making a mistake. His innate strength is only partly responsible for the way he handles them. Roland's presence empowers him. Eddie isn't alone. He fears the stranger inhabiting him, but he likes him, too, and suspects that in time he could love him as he loved his brother.

Roland doesn't love Eddie, nor does he trust him very much. Though Eddie displays some inner strength, his addiction tells Roland he is a weak vessel. Everything he's accomplished so far was driven by self-preservation. Roland exhibits the same emotional detachment he had for Jake near the end. As he tells himself in the voice of Cort, "You did yourself ill to feel well of those to whom ill must eventually be done." He doesn't hide his own self-interest from Eddie very well, who knows he's ultimately expendable in Roland's eyes.

Roland tells himself that he will release the three destined to help him once he reaches the Tower. They might even be able to return to their original times and places, but he's honest enough with himself to admit that's unlikely. "Neither, however, could the thought of the treachery he contemplated turn him aside from his course." The morality of ka strikes again.

The man in black's voice chides him for his callousness. Roland has already sacrificed Jake in the name of the Tower, and now he's prepared to condemn those he draws "to something you would not have for yourself:

a lifetime in an alien world, where they may die as easily as animals in a zoo set free in a wild place."

It will be some time before Roland can see that there may be more important things than his quest, even though the future of all universes depends on his success. Eddie, weak and unworldly, identifies within Roland a common spirit. "You're a Tower junkie," he tells him.

Roland returns to his body long enough to move it away from the rising tide. As long as the doorway is open, it keeps pace with him regardless of which side he's on. However, when he intends to pass through it, some intuition tells it to stop moving. Though he's never seen a door like this before, Roland understands its truths. He could cross the threshold physically, but if he did so and the door closed, he would be trapped on the other side. Eddie will have to be on the beach the next time it closes, because it will never open again.

After the Customs agents release him, Eddie gets food and Anacin for Roland. The painkiller isn't enough to heal his infection, but it buys them a little extra time. Government agents are following Eddie, and drug lord Enrico Balazar's people are also watching him. One of Balazar's associates is Ginelli, presumably a member of the same family as Richard Ginelli, who appeared in the Bachman novel *Thinner* and died in 1983.

Balazar is curious to learn how Eddie made it through Customs and what became of the cocaine. He's not a man who likes mysteries, and is aware the cops may have turned Eddie. For leverage, he takes Henry Dean into "protective custody." Once he finds out what happened to his drugs, he'll have no more use for the Dean brothers.

King's reliance on coincidence becomes more obvious in this book. Things happen when they best suit Roland's quest. He found the first door on the beach when he needed it. If he had entered Eddie a couple of hours later, Eddie probably would have already been in custody or dead. His followers will eventually learn that coincidence is part of Roland's existence.

Balazar's headquarters is more Eddie's realm than Roland's, so the gunslinger steps back and lets Eddie operate, ready to take control if things go bad. Eddie knows about dishonor among thieves, so he pits members of Balazar's gang against each other by playing a game of interdimensional sleight of hand. He doesn't know that his brother is already dead from an accidental drug overdose administered by his minders.

Eddie's bravura performance makes his impromptu plan work. Exposure to Roland gives him newfound confidence; so much so that Balazar barely recognizes him as the drug addict they sent to the Bahamas. Eddie tells Balazar that the drugs have already been delivered and Jack Andolini, Balazar's lieutenant, is hiding them in the bathroom. He strips naked to prove he has nothing up his sleeves, and goes into the bathroom with Andolini to fetch the drugs.

Eddie's simple plan is almost foiled by Roland's wet ammunition. He pulls Andolini through the doorway and Roland draws his gun, but the hammer falls on a dud. Andolini, a professional killer, quickly recovers his wits. He has Roland dead to rights when Eddie—still naked—saves the gunslinger's life by whacking Andolini with a rock. Andolini's bullet goes wild, except "[w]hen you feel the wind of the slug on your cheek, you can't really call it wild."

Roland returns the favor by shooting the gun from Andolini's hand. His bullet strikes at the exact second Andolini pulls the trigger, causing it to explode in his face. Blinded, Andolini staggers into the claws of the waiting lobstrosities. This isn't the last they will see of Andolini, though. Roland and Eddie will face him again ten years in the past via another doorway.

Roland still needs medicine, so he and Eddie have to go back through the doorway. Eddie—who is *still* naked—has no chance of surviving alone against Balazar's men, so Roland returns with Eddie physically. Only one of Roland's hands is of any use to him, so he gives a gun to Eddie, something he couldn't bring himself to do with Jake when they battled the Slow Mutants beneath the mountain.[3]

If Eddie needed any motivation for the gun battle that ensues, he gets it when they return to the bathroom. While he's gathering packets of antibiotic from the medicine cabinet, he overhears one of the men report that Henry is dead. "I want to go to war," he tells Roland.

After a fierce gunfight, Balazar and all of his men are killed. In a final insult, one of Balazar's men throws Henry's severed head at Eddie. Roland hears the approaching police sirens and knows it's time to retreat through the doorway. He knows, too, that Eddie must come with him. Eddie asks what's on the other side of the door for him. "If you can tell me, maybe I'll come. But if you lie, I'll know."

Roland issues Eddie's call to adventure, the part of a quest when a character is challenged to leave his familiar surroundings for the unknown. He tells Eddie that death probably awaits him at the end of the journey. But it won't be boring, he promises. "If we win through, Eddie, you'll see something beyond all the beliefs of all your dreams."

Roland could drag Eddie through the doorway, but he leaves the decision up to the young man he still calls prisoner. "He had seen this hagridden man behave with all the dignity of a born gunslinger in spite of his addiction." In a wisecracking tone that Roland will grow to despise, Eddie says he "doesn't have anything else planned for tonight, anyway." Once through the doorway, he remembers the heroin that is likely in Balazar's desk and turns to go back for it.

"That part of your life is over, Eddie . . . your need will pass." With these words, Roland closes the door. Both of them forget about the cocaine that is still hidden on the beach, but it's unlikely this drug would have done much to satisfy Eddie's need for heroin, anyway.

Roland's life is in Eddie's hands in the following days. Time means little to either of them as Roland fights his infection and Eddie suffers intense heroin withdrawal. They can smell each other's illnesses. Both have the same choice, which echoes Red's sentiments in "Rita Hayworth and Shawshank Redemption": "Get busy living, or get busy dying." [DS]

Ironically, all Eddie can find for them to eat are the lobstrosities that poisoned and mutilated Roland. Eddie hates the gunslinger for kidnapping him to a place where he has no hope of finding drugs to cure his craving. Even so, he builds a travois and drags Roland north, the direction Roland intuitively knows they must go. Roland is tempted to ridicule the crude carrier, but he realizes Cort would probably have grudgingly approved of Eddie's resourcefulness.

Eddie contemplates suicide in the dreary nighttime hours. The only thing that keeps him going is the knowledge that without him, Roland will die, too. "After you're really on your feet again, I may, like, re-examine my options."

During their rest periods, Eddie talks about the life he left behind. Roland understands that his unbalanced relationship with his brother—eight years his senior—and their mother robbed him of his self-esteem. Eddie had been hooked on the drug of trust that Henry knew how to use and push so well. By the end Henry had been so badly hooked on drugs that their roles reversed. "Now Eddie held Henry's hand crossing streets."

Having told his story—to Roland, but also to himself for the first time—Eddie awaits Roland's response, but Roland has no use for philosophy. If the gunslinger were prone to introspection and questioning the cosmos, he would have asked himself why he had been blessed with a companion who "seems to promise weakness or strangeness or even outright doom." The question, however, never forms in Roland's mind. Eddie's past is irrelevant. All he knows—all he cares to know—is that Eddie is here with him now. "[W]hat's past is past, and what's ahead is ahead. The second is ka, and takes care of itself," a sentiment *Eddie* will grow to despise.

The antibiotics combat Roland's infection enough so that Eddie no longer has to drag him along the beach. Long before Eddie can see it, Roland detects the next doorway almost a full day's walk away.

For Roland, the portal labeled THE LADY OF SHADOWS represents his next companion. Eddie sees it as a way back to his own world and to the heroin he still craves. Roland knows what Eddie has in mind, and for the first time in his life Roland lets someone strip him of one of his weapons.[4] When it comes to his ka-tet, Roland always allows the other person to make his or her own decisions. He knew that Eddie might be weak, but he isn't stupid. Entrusting ka to set them on the right path, Roland places his life entirely in fate's hands.

Eddie knows what will happen to Roland's body when he goes through the doorway, and threatens to kill the gunslinger if he doesn't promise to take Eddie with him once his business with the Lady of Shadows is done. Like anyone in the grip of addiction, he knows how to dissemble. All he wants is something to eat other than lobstrosity, he claims. Fried chicken and doughnuts. That's all.

Roland knows better than to trust a junkie. "Until after the Tower, at least, that part of your life is done. After that I don't care. After that you're free to go to hell in your own way. Until then I need you." He tries to appeal to Eddie's good, strong side. The quest that lies ahead of them is a chance for Eddie to redeem his honor. "You could be a gunslinger. I needn't be the last after all. It's in you, Eddie. I see it. I feel it."

Eddie, who isn't so sure he's going to have a life after they reach the Tower, continues threatening to kill Roland as the gunslinger passes through the doorway. He can't follow without Roland's cooperation, but even with a gun and a knife to wield over the gunslinger's limp body, he doesn't have the power to coerce someone willing to yield his life to fate.

The second doorway reveals a world that Roland recognizes as Eddie's. Eddie—watching from the beach—knows that the setting is decades before his era. As they watch, the woman, who Eddie thinks is "one rude bitch," steals some cheap cosmetic jewelry from a store display.

"The Lady of Shadows" is Odetta Holmes, a young, affluent, disabled woman—she thinks of herself as Negro and is offended when Eddie refers to her as black—living in 1964. Her tarot card showed a woman who seemed to be "smiling craftily and sobbing at the same time." Walter called her a "veritable Janus," referring to the Roman god of gates and doorways, often depicted with two faces looking in opposite directions. It's an appropriate symbol for a woman who suffers from multiple personality disorder.[5]

Because she lost her legs from the knees down when she was pushed in front of a train, Odetta is wheelchair bound. This accounts for the strange, gliding view Eddie observes through the doorway, which reminds him of a Steadicam shot from Stanley Kubrick's *The Shining*. The accident also causes her second personality, Detta Walker, who first appeared after a head injury when Odetta was five, to manifest more strongly and frequently.

Odetta's history is revealed through a series of flashbacks, a different approach to how King disclosed Eddie's history. Roland learned about Eddie by sharing his memories and from Eddie himself as they walked along the beach. For Odetta, King switches perspective and tells who she is in narrative that Roland isn't privy to. The paragraph in which King describes Detta's existence runs three pages, most of it a single sentence, a rant that reveals something of her mental process.

Odetta is in one of her Detta phases, on a shoplifting spree at Macy's. Stealing is one way she expresses her rage. She never takes anything of value, and discards whatever she takes shortly after. The items are cheap, like she believes herself to be. The act of stealing is what is important to her.

Roland entered Eddie without being noticed, but Detta detects Roland's presence immediately and without apparent surprise. She's outraged because he's white, and tries to fight him off. Detta also briefly senses her other personality, "not the way one would look at her reflection in a mirror, but as separate people; the window became a windowpane and for a moment Odetta had seen Detta and Detta had seen Odetta and had been equally horror-struck." Eddie, looking through Detta's eyes, sees himself briefly in a disjointed, out-of-body manner.

Roland takes control and drives her into a changing room and through the doorway. By the time they reach the other side, Odetta has reasserted control.

Eddie is kneeling on the ground next to the gunslinger, knife in hand. The last thing Odetta remembers is being at home watching the news on television. A flood of questions flies from her. She asks, "Who am I?" before she even inquires who Roland and Eddie are. "Well, I'll tell you one thing, Dorothy," Eddie said. "You ain't in Kansas anymore," foreshadowing—or perhaps inspiring—events to come in *Wizard and Glass.*

Odetta reacts to her new situation with deliberate disbelief. She thinks she's either gone insane or suffered another head injury. Eddie tells her of his own experience, but she refuses to accept the reality of her situation and retreats into denial. She doesn't wear jewelry, she claims, and the fact that she has on cheap rings, and other contradictions, only makes her head hurt.

While Roland doesn't see how Odetta can possibly be of any use to him on his quest, he understands that she will be good for Eddie. She is vulnerable and afraid. Eddie has someone to look after, to replace his brother. Roland tries to warn Eddie about her other personality, as dangerous as the lobstrosities, but Eddie is smitten. He hears with his ears, but not with his heart. Roland, who has coexisted with Detta Walker, knows what she may be capable of. He also knows that Eddie will only truly believe how dangerous Detta can be by experience, so he loads his guns with spent casings and waits for Detta to prove herself.[6] "A child doesn't understand a hammer until he's mashed his finger at a nail," Cort once said.

After hearing Eddie's story about Detta's and Odetta's brief awareness of each other, Roland realizes that somehow he will have to make her two personalities face each other and unite. The person he needs at his side on the road to the Dark Tower must have Detta's "fight until you drop" stamina tempered by Odetta's calm humanity.

Odetta fills the gaps in her memory that are caused when Detta is in control with pleasant fabrications. Detta fills hers with false memories of being brutalized by white people. When she reemerges that night, she is convinced Eddie slapped her, fed her monster meat and taunted her with slowly roasted beef after tying her to her wheelchair. She steals Roland's specially prepared gun and pulls the trigger with the barrel pointed at Eddie's temple.

Roland's lessons are rarely gentle. He lets Detta pull the trigger several times to make sure Eddie knows what she tried to do. He doesn't intervene when she batters him with the gun butt. "If Eddie hadn't learned his lesson by now, he never would." Eddie doesn't argue when Roland suggests they tie up her hands and strap her into her wheelchair.

They continue north along the beach but, now that they have to push Detta's wheelchair, their progress slows to a crawl. Roland has another problem. The antibiotic regimen was insufficient to defeat the infection and it returns with a vengeance, meaning that Eddie has to do most of the work. After years as a junkie, he jokes that he has turned into a pusher. This pun anticipates Jack Mort, whose door will be labeled THE PUSHER, bringing to mind drug dealers rather than Mort's unique type of pushing.

Purely out of perversity, Detta does everything possible to thwart their progress. She uses her weight to make it harder to free the heavy wheelchair from the frequent sand traps they encounter. When Eddie finds a patch of solid ground and can move at a reasonable clip, she engages the chair's brake to topple herself over. At night, exhausted from their day's journey, Detta screams them awake. Roland appeals to the Odetta within to take control if possible.

Everything is working against them. Roland's illness is advancing rapidly. They are down to relying on the questionable ammunition. Even Eddie is getting sick from vitamin deficiency caused by a steady diet of lobstrosity. Detta's persistence is tiring him to the point of fatigue.

After several days of slow, plodding progress, Odetta reasserts control of her body. Roland has been holding himself together out of necessity, knowing he has to watch out for Eddie with Detta. Once Odetta is back, he collapses. Now he is the one holding up their progress. He sends Eddie and Odetta on alone, warning Eddie to be alert. If Detta returns, he tells Eddie to "brain" her. If he kills her, Roland's quest is probably doomed, but if she kills Eddie, Roland will die, either at her hands or from his illness.

Without Detta working against him, Eddie feels like they're flying up the beach. After their first day of travel without finding the third doorway, Eddie and Odetta make love on the beach under alien stars. The next afternoon, they reach the door.

Odetta knows the gunslinger doesn't want her to have his gun, but Eddie can't bring himself to leave her alone for two days with only a few stones to protect herself against the wildcats they hear screaming in the mountains. Roland knows that Detta armed would be a formidable creature, but the moment Eddie returns, Roland knows he has gone against orders.

When they reach the door, Odetta is gone, but Roland is sure she isn't dead, or the doorway would be gone, too. Roland's quest would die with her. Eddie won't abandon his search for her, and Roland is too weak to trick him through the doorway, where he would be safer. He leaves Eddie with his remaining gun and crosses the threshold to New York. Regardless of the doorway's label, Roland knows that it somehow means death.

The third mind Roland enters belongs to a sociopath. King is uncharacteristically unsubtle by naming this dealer of death Jack Mort. Mort has absolutely no awareness of Roland. He's too intent on his current task: preparing to push Jake Chambers in front of a car.

At first, Roland thinks he will be forced to witness Jake's fatal accident, a fitting punishment for sacrificing the boy beneath the mountains. His own hands, in a way, would be responsible. However, "the rejection of brutish destiny had been the gunslinger's work all his life," so Roland steps forward, distracting Mort long enough for him to miss his chance. Jake isn't crushed beneath the wheels of Balazar's 1976 Cadillac Sedan de Ville.[7]

It occurs to Roland that if Jack Mort had meant to kill the boy, he might have to stand aside and let it happen, but he can't allow himself to be responsible for Jake's death a second time. Through this instinctual act, Roland has performed selflessly for the first time. His extended contact with Eddie makes him consider the human implications of his decisions.

He doesn't stop to think about the paradox he has just created or whether he may have jeopardized his mission. Jake reached the way station not through a doorway but by being reborn into Roland's world after dying in his own. By apparently saving the boy's life, the gunslinger nullified Jake's part in Roland's past. Though he later realizes that this wasn't the day Jake died, because the boy told him Mort had been dressed like a priest, Roland's pending destruction of Mort makes the point moot.

Through the doorway, he sees that Detta has Eddie tied up at the mercy of the lobstrosities. He recognizes it as a trick to get him to come back to the beach. She could kill Roland by shooting his helpless body, but she wants more than that.

With intuition that defies logic, Roland knows what he needs to do. Jack Mort, who caused both of Odetta's life-altering injuries, isn't meant to join his ka-tet, much to Roland's relief. Mort represents death, not for Roland but for the individual entities that call themselves Odetta Holmes and Detta Walker. His plan is risky, and he needs Mort's cooperation to pull it off.

Once Mort realizes he has been possessed by another entity, his conscious mind faints, which is a great relief to Roland, who is repulsed by the man's worm pit of a mind.[8] Roland has complete control over Mort's body and memories, and uses him as a reference book for the information he needs to replenish his supply of ammunition and get his much-needed medication.

His first destination is a gun shop, where he finds more bullets than he could ever have imagined. Because he doesn't have a gun permit, Roland is forced to orchestrate an elegant scam involving a couple of police officers[9] and the shop owner. He can't imagine needing the two hundred bullets he can afford with Mort's money, but he can't deny the temptation to have them. He also takes the cops' guns, intending them for Eddie and Odetta, when and if she is ever ready to bear arms. He enjoys the sensation of being able to hold a weapon in a whole right hand again.

Next, Roland commits what the pharmacist believes to be the first penicillin robbery in history. Though he has to use his guns to control the situation, it's not really a robbery. After getting two hundred doses of Keflex, Roland leaves behind Mort's Rolex watch in payment. He even exhibits concern for the general safety of bystanders, something he didn't do in Tull.

His material tasks completed, Roland has one more job in Jack Mort's body. He hijacks a cop car and lets Mort drive to the Greenwich Village station where he pushed Odetta Holmes.[10] The police officers who follow Mort are more worthy of Roland's admiration than the ones at the gun shop. One cop almost takes down Mort, but the bullet is stopped by his cigarette lighter—perhaps placed there by ka—which he carried to curry favor with his superiors at work. Lighter fluid catches fire in Mort's pocket. Roland guides the burning man toward the coming subway train, not knowing for sure if it was the same train that struck Odetta, but knowing all the same because this is the way of ka.

Everything must come together in a split second. Roland projects a message to his Lady of Shadows, calling her by both her names. When she turns to look, Roland jumps Mort's body onto the tracks, where the train cuts him in half at the waist a split second after Roland crosses back to Mid-World with his boxes of bullets and antibiotics but without the cops' guns.

As Mort's body is divided, Odetta and Detta split into two physical entities and struggle with each other and the implications of what they witnessed through their own eyes and through Jack Mort's. Odetta embraces Detta and says, "I love you," at which the two become one again. This new person, whole for the first time since Jack Mort dropped a brick on her head, a woman of heart-stopping beauty, takes Roland's guns down to the beach to save Eddie from the lobstrosities.

The woman formed from Odetta and Detta adopts their middle name, Susannah, and will soon take Eddie's last name for her own. She's exactly what Roland hoped for: someone who possesses the strengths of her antecedents. At times she will revert to Detta, especially when she wants to distance herself emotionally from something or requires the heart and mind of a killer when in battle. Roland is never convinced that he has completely cured Susannah, and readily accepts the appearance of Mia as a new personality. Walter said she had "at least" two faces. "You can burn away warts by painting them with silver metal . . . but in a person prone to warts, they'll come back." [DT5]

Roland believes that Susannah is the third person he was meant to draw from New York. Her very nature is three: "I who was; I who had no right to be but was; I am the woman who you have saved." However, by killing Jack Mort, Roland has set up conditions for Jake, the real third person drawn to his ka-tet, to return to Mid-World.

After they reach the end of the beach, the trio travels through the hills, leaving the Western Sea behind. Roland dreams of the Tower again and hears its voices summoning him.

It stood on the horizon of a vast plain the color of blood in the violent setting of a dying sun. He couldn't see the stairs which spiraled up and up and up within its brick shell, but he could see the windows which spiraled up along that staircase's way, and saw the ghosts of all the people he had ever known pass through them. Up and up they marched, and an arid wind brought him the sound of voices calling his name.

Eddie knows that the gunslinger would sacrifice his new companions if his quest called for it, and tells Roland his brother taught him that if you kill what you love you're damned. Roland thinks he may already be damned for having sacrificed Jake but he sees the possibility of redemption. He isn't necessarily doomed by his inflexibility and narrow focus. He promises Eddie that he wouldn't consider sacrificing them—would not have sacrificed Jake—if there was only this world to win. His mission is to save everything there is. "We are going to go, Eddie. We are going to fight. We are going to be hurt. And in the end we will stand."

Roland and Eddie have a grudging respect for each other. They understand one another's strengths, but they also know each other's weaknesses. Though Eddie is destined to become a gunslinger as deadly as Roland—and he has already proven himself in battle—he hasn't yet lost his heart to the Tower. He has discovered love and despises Roland's callousness and single-mindedness.

In the weeks to come, Roland will instruct Eddie—and Susannah—in survival. Eddie will teach Roland about friendship and love. For his part, Roland has felt and seen the steel within Eddie, but his sarcastic humor and weak, insecure character annoy him. He's predisposed toward this irritation because he's been through it before with Cuthbert Allgood. Though they would be loath to admit it, the two men complete each other in much the same way Detta and Odetta complete Susannah. They counterbalance each other throughout the arduous journey ahead of them. Susannah is the wild card. Roland and Eddie know something of her constituent parts, but they still have to acquaint themselves with the composite person who has arisen from their ashes.

Critic Tony Magistrale says that Roland progresses toward a fuller realization of his heroic potential in this book. He's still violent, but the level of violence is more appropriate to the behavior of a hero.[11] The book is richer because it expands its scope beyond Roland by introducing two new major characters.

By the time he finished writing *The Drawing of the Three,* King had a rough idea of what would transpire in the next two volumes. "This work seems to be my own Tower, you know. These people haunt me, Roland most of all." For the first time, he raises the possibility that Roland won't reach the Tower, though someone from his group surely will.

In the afterword, King says that he still doesn't know what the Tower is or what awaits Roland when he reaches it. Roland himself wonders if it represents damnation or salvation. All King knows is that the Tower, whatever it is, is closer.

The haunting would continue for five more years, until King again heard the song of the Turtle and led his ka-tet to the Path of the Beam that leads to the Dark Tower.

ENDNOTES

[1] Unless otherwise specified, all quotes in this chapter come from *The Drawing of the Three*.

[2] Not only has time moved on in Roland's world, but geography is also unstable. Though he is heading north, the Western Sea is on his right-hand side.

[3] "*No one but the best ever held this baby in his hand,* Eddie thought. *Until now, at least.*" Eddie's low self-esteem rears its head.

[4] He lost his guns to the Little Sisters in Eluria, but here, on the beach, he actually permits it to happen.

[5] Eddie mistakenly calls her affliction schizophrenia, something he only knows about from movies like *The Three Faces of Eve*. Roland repeats this diagnosis to Father Callahan, and Callahan, who should know better, doesn't correct him.

[6] It won't be the last time Roland lies awake waiting for her to do something. When Mia appears, Roland spends nights tracking her on her quests for food.

[7] Jake and Eddie see this car parked outside Calvin Tower's bookstore in *Wolves of the Calla*.

[8] Not so long ago, Roland might have identified somewhat with the cold-blooded killer. Pop psychology says people hate in others things they resent about themselves.

[9] Though he identifies the cops as gunslingers, Roland isn't impressed with their performance. To one, he says, "You're a dangerous fool who should be sent west. . . . You have forgotten the face of your father."

[10] King says that this happened three years before, but this timeline is clearly 1977, since Mort was about to kill Jake. Odetta lost her legs in 1959. Also, King calls this Christopher Street station. In *Song of Susannah,* Odetta says that the A train never stopped at Christopher Street. "It was just another little continuity mistake, like putting Co-Op City in Brooklyn." King the author's mistakes become the realities of Eddie's and Odetta's worlds.

[11] Tony Magistrale, *Stephen King: The Second Decade,* Twayne Publishers, 1992.

CHAPTER 4

THE WASTE LANDS (REDEMPTION)

"The Drawers are places of desolation," he said.
"The Drawers are the waste lands."[1]

"Perhaps even the damned may be saved."

[DT2]

In his introduction to the excerpt of *The Waste Lands*[2] that appeared in *The Magazine of Fantasy and Science Fiction* in late 1990, King said that some five weeks have elapsed since the end of *The Drawing of the Three*. However, by the time the book was published the following year, he had revised that estimate to a lengthier and vaguer "some months." The newly formed trio has been at their present camp for two months, resting and recovering from their ordeals on the Western Sea, now about sixty miles behind them.

Eddie has rediscovered his childhood hobby of whittling, a pastime that reminds him of his late brother, Henry, who, as Roland points out, still visits him often. Henry shamed him into stopping whittling because he was good at it, and any sign of skill in Eddie made Henry nervous. Henry had no hidden talents or ambitions. Rather, he was content to rob Eddie of any aspirations he might have. Eddie has to remind himself that he's forever free of his older brother's passive-aggressive domination. If he wants to carve, he doesn't need to fear being ridiculed. "Beating heroin was child's play compared to beating your childhood."

Everything serves the Beam; Eddie's rediscovered hobby will soon become as important a skill as knowing how to shoot.

After working with them during the intervening months, Roland understands why he's been given two such unusual traveling companions.

Eddie and Susannah are born gunslingers. They learn their lessons quickly; not only how to handle weapons, but how to hunt and navigate by the unfamiliar constellations in his world—basic survival skills.

The most important lesson he must teach them, though, is how to kill. How to hit the target with every shot. Roland sees parallels between his new ka-tet and the one that died on Jericho Hill. Eddie reminds him of Cuthbert, and Susannah, in her way, is not so different from Alain Johns— though he will soon replace Susannah with Jake as a surrogate Alain.

Eddie asks Roland, "What if I told you I don't want to be a gunslinger?" Roland shrugs and says that what Eddie wants doesn't much matter in the face of ka.

Susannah Dean, now Eddie's wife, is Mid-World's first female gun-slinger. Though Roland never dreamt he would hear the gunslinger's catechism being said by a woman, the words sound natural coming from her. Natural, strange and dangerous. Though she is a newly created individual, her constituent personas occasionally emerge, especially trash-talking Detta.

Roland uses his knowledge of Odetta's past to drive her to anger during a training session, goading her to transcend rationality. He tongue-lashes her into shooting with her eye and mind and heart instead of with her hand. His strategy works, but his arrogance angers her. She calls him on it after the lesson, but Roland makes no apologies. They aren't playing games—he's training them to become gunslingers. "The end justifies the means" could be Roland's motto. Susannah tells Eddie later, "Roland's of the opinion that apprentice gunslingers who won't bite the hand that feeds them from time to time need a good kick in the slats."

During their debate over his teaching methods, Susannah and Roland hear the sounds of something enormous pushing over trees in the direction of their camp, where Eddie had stayed behind that morning. They run back to discover a seventy-foot-tall robotic bear running amok. Eddie is trapped up a tree.

The bear, known as Mir[3] to the old people who had feared it and Shardik[4] to the Great Old Ones who built it, is one of the twelve portal guardians.[5] Twelve doorways distributed in a circle around the Tower define the geography of Roland's world. Between each opposing pair of portals runs a Beam; together they somehow support the Tower and preserve its existence. The Beams are breaking down, but Roland doesn't know if that is the cause of his world's deterioration or an effect of it. He tells Eddie and Susannah:

> The Great Old Ones didn't make the world, but they did *re*-make it. Some tale-tellers say the Beams saved it; others say they are the seeds of the world's destruction. The Great Old Ones created the Beams. They are lines of some sort . . . lines which *bind* . . . and *hold* . . .

More than eighteen centuries in the past, the Great Old Ones panicked when the world's magic seemed to be receding. Enough magic remained from the Prim of creation to support the Tower forever, but this lack of faith made them replace the magic with finite technology, including guardians like the bear. Without the support of faith or magic, the machinery has progressively deteriorated over the centuries.

In Richard Adams's novel, the title character Shardik stands for all the promises religion ever made and then broke. The same could be said of him here—the religion of rational thought tried to improve on the Age of Magic but failed. Shardik has gone insane and is dying. North Central Positronics, Ltd., a shadowy organization that will make many appearances over the course of Roland's quest, manufactured him. The atomic pump at the way station was one of their creations.

Each of the three gunslingers does what is required of him or her to resolve the crisis. Eddie, knowing he can't shoot or outrun the monster, finds the only place where he is temporarily safe. Roland recognizes the threat for what it is and improvises a plan. Susannah, riding on his shoulders, wields Roland's gun and puts her training to the test.

Roland's harsh lesson serves her well, for it is the love of her life she is trying to save and she can't afford to let fear cause her hand to fail. Emotion falls away; all that remains is a deep coldness. Susannah realizes this is what Roland feels all the time and wonders how he can possibly stand it. Eddie feels a similar coldness when he shoots the other robots at Shardik's lair. After she dispatches Shardik, she says she hopes never to have to do anything like it again but, deep inside, part of her can't wait. Susannah has crossed the threshold into the realm of gunslingers. Ultimately, she will decide that she was made for a life like this.

Roland tells them what he knows of his world's creation story. Some of it is fairy tale, some of it rumor. He knows very little for sure, but he can guess at the parts he doesn't know. The portals that support the Beams are not like the doors through which Eddie and Susannah were drawn. They are more like the pivots of seesaws that balance the ka of the opposing forces in the universe. The ka of Roland versus the ka of Walter. The White versus the Red.

They follow the bear's trail back to the portal it once defended, which resembles the entrance to a subway station.[6] Here they discover one of the Beams. Everything in nature proves its existence. The needles of evergreen trees point the direction. Shadows and clouds form a herringbone path to the Tower. Flocks of birds crossing the Beam are momentarily deflected by it. Its energy ripples around the travelers like a fast-moving stream.

Allie had pointed out the clouds' motion to him in Tull, but Roland hadn't understood that a nearby Beam, a pull that was more than magnetism, was influencing him and Walter. After leaving Tull, he went southeast, twenty miles west to the sea, north along the beach where he drew Eddie and Susannah and then sixty miles east, inland, with his new followers. Since this Beam is running southeast, parallel to Roland's path across the desert, at times they will be almost retracing the gunslinger's course, which is about forty or fifty miles west of them.

If Roland had understood Allie's clue, he might have been tempted to give up his chase for the man in black and take this shortcut to the Tower, if ka had allowed him to do so. As the ka-tet will learn in Lud, ka has a way of shepherding them back on course should they take a route that would prevent them from accomplishing something vital.

Up till now, Roland has given no indication that he knows where the Dark Tower is or how to get to it. He didn't really believe in the guardians; they seemed too much like fantasy. If somehow convinced they were once real, he wouldn't have believed they still existed after two millennia. Now he thinks he's been searching for a guardian all his life.

They have found a path that will guide them directly to the Dark Tower, though Roland doesn't know how far away it is. Thousands of miles at least, and the distance grows longer every day. Half the size of his known world, for they are currently at its eternal edge. A long way to push a wheelchair. Roland seems to know something of their future, though, when he says to Susannah that the time may come when they travel faster than they'd like, surely alluding to their forthcoming roller-coaster ride on Blaine the Mono.

Though he shares what little he knows of their future with Eddie and Susannah, he is also hiding something from them. He's been traveling alone for so long with no one else to trust that he often keeps important information from others. What angered Cuthbert during their long summer in Mejis wasn't merely jealousy over Roland's reckless enchantment with Susan Delgado, but also that Roland had kept things from him and Alain, who relied on him for their survival as Eddie and Susannah do now.

He has smiled more in the past weeks than he has in years, but Roland believes he, like Shardik, is going insane. By preventing Jack Mort from pushing Jake in front of Balazar's car, Roland created a temporal paradox. Reality has split; so has Roland's mind.

Since Jake didn't die in 1977, he couldn't be reborn into Roland's world at the way station and Roland didn't sacrifice the boy in the name of his quest. Jake is no longer part of his past. This poses an interesting moral question. Does this mean Roland is no longer damned? Is this part of the redemption King alludes to in the book's new subtitle? Since Roland is allowed to make changes—course corrections—during subsequent iterations of his circular existence, perhaps a time will come when it isn't necessary for him to sacrifice Jake at all.

Roland still has memories of encountering Jake and picking up the Speaking Demon's jawbone in the way station's cellar. It's a history that isn't true, but should be. "He felt like two men existing inside one skull." The jawbone he has with him now reinforces his second memory. He took it from the pile of bones remaining after his long palaver with Walter to replace the one he gave Jake for protection from the oracle. It means something different to Eddie. "Remember this . . . the next time you get to thinking Roland's maybe just another one of the guys. He's been carrying [the jawbone] around with him all this time like some kind of a cannibal's trophy."

After their encounter with Shardik, Roland comes clean with his ka-tet, telling them both versions of his memory of the time between the way station and reaching the Western Sea. Eddie remembers Roland telling him on the beach that the way station was empty and that he traveled beneath the mountain alone. Eddie has a slight mental tickle associated with this memory, but nothing as profoundly dual natured as what Roland experiences.

While he speaks, the voices of the line of Eld tell Roland to throw the jawbone into the fire. "When one hears such a voice, not to obey—and at once—is unthinkable." Roland says something similar when he and Eddie are swept up by aven kal, the tsunami of the Beam. The Beam itself means to speak to them. "You would do well to listen if it does." [DT7]

Though the jawbone isn't Walter's, it is still a powerful sigul. As the fire consumes it, Eddie sees the shape of the key he is to carve and then glimpses "a triumphant rose that might have bloomed in the dawn of this world's first day, a thing of depthless, timeless beauty . . . as if all love and life had suddenly risen from Roland's dead artifact." Eddie doesn't know what the rose represents or what the key is for, but he is driven to have it ready for when its time comes. His childhood Henry-induced insecurities make him doubt his ability to get it right, though.

That night he has a dream that sums up their quest, much of which he doesn't understand. He dreams of a deli in New York located at the site of the future empty lot where the rose—the Tower's representation in New York—grows. He hears Jake's words ("there are more worlds than these") spoken by his old nemesis Jack Andolini, dreams of Blaine the Mono and sees the Tower itself, surrounded by a field of bloodred roses. Red eyes, the eyes of the Crimson King, stare at him from the Tower, though only Roland knows the name of their greatest adversary.

From the top of the Tower, he hears a horn, the one that Roland lent to Cuthbert during the battle of Jericho Hill and neglected to retrieve after his friend was killed. The instrument is an important sigul dating back to Arthur Eld. Roland's failure to pick it up is an indicator that this iteration of his quest is doomed to fail.

Eddie also dreams the first line of *The Gunslinger,* though in his vision it comes from *You Can't Go Home Again* by Thomas Wolfe. This is the first significant hint of the nature of the ka-tet's existence—that they are the fictional creations of an author from another plane of reality.

The book's cover is illustrated with three symbols—a key, a rose and a door—that bring to mind a line from the introduction to another Wolfe novel, *Look Homeward, Angel,* which is used as an epigraph in the revised edition of *The Gunslinger.* These icons also appear on the box containing

Black Thirteen, the dangerous Wizard's Glass that allows them to travel between worlds and save the vacant lot containing the rose.

After his dream, Eddie realizes that he and Susannah are no longer prisoners in Roland's world. His quest is their quest.[7] Roland is like Dorothy in *The Wizard of Oz,* picking up traveling companions along her trek to find the Wizard, each one developing his own reason for completing the journey.[8]

Eddie's dreams the following night take him to the streets of Manhattan, but Roland's sleep is troubled by his mental schism. He is so profoundly affected by his dual memories that he surrenders his guns—the very items that define him—to Eddie and Susannah. Eddie protests—though he and Susannah had already discussed the danger they might be in if Roland went insane—but Roland insists, saying, "Until the wound inside me closes—if it ever does—I am not fit to wear this [gun belt]." He even hands over his knife, which Eddie uses to start carving the key, keeping what he's doing a secret, in much the same way Roland often hides his plans.

In 1977 New York, Jake Chambers also thinks he's going insane. Just before he should have been killed, he develops an awareness of his impending death. After the moment passes, he has dim flashes of Roland and the events after he arrived at the way station, but the knowledge that he should be dead is what preys on his mind.

He develops a fascination with doors, convinced that one will open onto the desert, returning him to a world where he has never been. He's not the only one with this obsession. Susannah will later muse that doorways have dominated her life, starting with the one that slammed shut on the jail in Mississippi.

Jake fears his English end-of-term paper will reveal his growing insanity. He has no recollection of writing the surrealistic, rambling essay entitled "My Understanding of the Truth," which hints at what would have happened to him if Roland had not altered the timeline by killing Jack Mort, and his desire to return to the gunslinger. It also foreshadows events that lie ahead: Blaine the Mono and the contest of riddles. He decorated it with a picture of a door and one of a train. It has epigraphs from poets T. S. Eliot and Robert Browning, upon whom Jake has bestowed the nicknames "Butch" and "Sundance," calling to mind the classic Western.

Astonished by what he has written and terrified of how his teacher

will react to it, Jake goes truant from school for the first time in his
short academic career.[9] He wanders the streets, ending up at a used bookstore called The Manhattan Restaurant of the Mind, where he meets the
proprietor—auspiciously named Calvin Tower—and his friend Aaron
Deepneau,[10] both of whom will play important roles in Roland's quest in
days to come.

Two books capture Jake's attention: *Charlie the Choo-Choo* by Beryl
Evans and a collection of riddles with the answers torn out.[11] He leaves
the bookstore with his acquisitions—believing incorrectly that he will
never be back here again—and is drawn to an empty lot at the corner of
Second and Forty-sixth Street, the former site of Tom and Jerry's Artistic
Deli. If he had looked back over his shoulder, he would have seen Balazar
pull up in front of the bookstore in a car that should have killed him three
weeks earlier.

He feels like he is standing on the edge of a great mystery. On the
fence around the lot he sees graffiti mentioning Bango Skank, the Turtle
and the Beam, and senses the coming of the White. When he relates the
episode to the ka-tet later, Roland says, "What happened to you in that lot
was the most important thing ever to happen in your life, Jake. In all our
lives."

After he climbs over the fence, he finds a key that is the same shape as
the one Eddie is carving.[12] He also sees the dusty pink wild rose growing
among a mass of purple-paint-coated grass. In the vision Walter enabled,
Roland saw a blade of purple grass but never got far enough to see the
rose.

Jake understands that the rose is in danger and feels the overwhelming
need to protect it—the same force that drives Roland to the Dark Tower.
A voice tells him the rose doesn't need to be guarded against normal injury—it can protect itself from being plucked or crushed.[13] This rose will
draw the ka-tet back to New York again and again in the coming months.

Within the pages of *Charlie the Choo-Choo,* Jake discovers several
clues. First is the train itself, which is supposedly benign but appears evil
in the illustrations. The passengers on board look as if they're afraid
they'll never get off alive. The president of the Railway Company is Raymond Martin, a subtle reference to Marten, the wizard from Gilead. The
engineer's daughter is named Susannah. The other engineers mock Charlie's driver, saying, "He cannot understand that the world has moved on."

The Ubiquitous Bango Skank

Peter Straub originally created Bango Skank for *The Talisman* but never used him in that book. In a personal communication, King said that Bango keeps popping up in his work like "a kind of graffiti boogeyman." Jake notices his repeat appearances and muses, "Man, that guy Bango gets around." Susannah calls him the Great Lost Character and identifies him as one of the voices that speaks to her in her dreams of being reunited with Eddie and Jake in Central Park.

When he's not around, the ka-tet notices his absence. On the graffiti-free streets of Pleasantville in Algul Siento, they note, "If Bango Skank had been here, his mark had been erased."

Graffiti is a recurring element in the series, providing information and warnings. In King's short story "All That You Love Will Be Carried Away," the main character, a traveling salesman, obsessively collects snippets of graffiti from his travels. As early as *The Talisman*, characters receive graffiti warnings: GOOD BIRDS MAY FLY; BAD BOYS MUST DIE. THIS IS YOUR LAST CHANCE: GO HOME.

The ka-tet sees signs of Bango Skank in the following locations:

- On the fence around the vacant lot containing the rose defacing a drawing of the Turtle Bay Condominiums
- On the back of a road sign outside Topeka
- In the Topeka jail cell where Father Callahan spends time after hitting bottom
- In Co-Op City
- In the bathroom at the hotel where Mia and Susannah hide. His message there is BANGO SKANK AWAITS THE KING
- In the lavatory at the New York public library where Father Callahan travels in 1977
- In the tunnel to the Fedic doorway behind the Dixie Pig (BANGO SKANK '84)

Jake underlines all the passages that resonate with him.

The key Jake finds in the empty lot calms the feuding voices in his head and also gives him the power to persuade others in the same way the Turtle sigul Susannah finds in the bowling bag in 1999 does for her.[14] It also facilitates a telepathic link between Jake and Eddie. Jake transmits a message to Eddie— whom he has never met, it must be remembered—suggesting his carving will calm Roland's mind, too. Roland, tormented to the point of welcoming death to bring silence to his mind, weeps with relief when Eddie gives him the wooden key to hold.

Jake receives a dream message to go to Co-Op City, Eddie's old neighborhood.[15] In the dream, Eddie is about thirteen, the age he would have been in Jake's time. The young Eddie is to be Jake's guide to the doorway he has been seeking, the one that will return him to Mid-World. Before heading for Brooklyn the next day, Jake steals his father's Ruger and a half-full box of shells, as if he knows his destiny is to become a gunslinger.

Meanwhile Roland, Eddie and Susannah reach the boundary of Mid-World and see Lud's skyline in the distance.[16] Time is moving slower in Jake's world than in Mid-World. Later, the ka-tet will discover that in Keystone Earth—the primary American reality where time moves in only one direction and all deaths are final—time runs faster and faster than in Mid-World, putting additional pressure on them.[17]

Two doors are needed to birth Jake back into Roland's world, both located in "thin" and "attractive" places. One is in a dilapidated house in Dutch Hill, significant, perhaps, because Calvin Tower is of Dutch heritage. The other is in a speaking circle, where Eddie uses his hand-carved

"Roland" beats Bango to the punch, leaving his mark outside the "real" tower in NYC. (*Ron J. Martirano, 2004*)

key to try to open a portal he sketches in the ground. The term "drawing" has two meanings in this context: Jake is being drawn into Mid-World through a doorway that is itself a drawing. This duality appears again when Patrick Danville draws a doorway for Susannah.

The demon doorkeeper guarding the passage between worlds is the oracle that Roland and Jake encountered in the mountains, though it has pulled itself inside out to change from its female aspect to male. On Earth-side, the doorkeeper is the condemned house itself, which is reminiscent of the black hotel in Point Venuti, California, from *The Talisman*. As soon as Jake enters it, he realizes he's left his world.

Eddie is the midwife for Jake's rebirth. The magnitude of his responsibility overwhelms him, amplifying his insecurities. His key doesn't work, and Roland strikes him when he says he doesn't care about forgetting the face of his father. The gunslinger deals his harsh lessons, confronting Eddie with his fears of failure, forcing him to decide. "Come from the shadow of yourself, if you dare." Eddie comes very close to shooting Roland before he breaks down.

Susannah hates Roland for what he did to the man she loves. "Sometimes I hate myself," Roland says, but Susannah won't let him escape with that thin confession. "Don't ever stop you, though, do it?" The words come from deep within her. The voice is Detta's.

Roland returns the key to Eddie to complete. Eddie apologizes for being afraid, but Roland doesn't want an apology; he wants Eddie to remember his lessons. "[H]ere was the last of Eddie's childhood, expiring painfully among the three of them." The gunslinger adds this little death to the scorecard of things he's done in the name of the Tower. It's a bill he's not sure he will ever be able to pay, but he manages to reassure Eddie, and goes so far as to tell Eddie that he loves him.

The demon, drawn by their presence in the speaking circle, appears in male form, so it falls to Susannah to divert it. Sex is its weapon, but also its weakness. Eddie struggles to finish his key and keep the door open while his wife is being sexually assaulted by an invisible entity. Jake scrambles on the other side to find the key he dropped, as the doorkeeper approaches. Eddie and Jake project messages back and forth, encouraging each other, but it is the voice of the rose that calms Jake, a powerful force that wants him to succeed.

Roland plucks Jake from the jaws of death, lifting him up instead of letting him fall like he did before. Jake arrives without his pants and sneakers, but otherwise intact. The voices he and Roland have been hearing are silenced. What happens to Susannah during her long sexual struggle with the demon is left open, but it clearly will have serious implications in the future.

The ka-tet becomes complete four days after Jake's rebirth when the boy is adopted by a billy-bumbler, a creature resembling a badger crossed with a raccoon.[18] He can speak, but usually only repeats what he hears. Roland has been told that bumblers are good luck. Dubbed Oy by Jake, he gradually becomes an integral part of the group and his heroic actions will be crucial to the completion of their quest.

A few days from the decaying city of Lud, the ka-tet stops in River Crossing, where they spend a pleasant day in the company of a group of old people who remember the world before it moved on. The foursome won't see another meal like the one they are served here until they reach Calla Bryn Sturgis. After dinner, Susannah displays the first signs that her encounter with the demon may have yielded more than Roland antici-pated. She considers the possibility that she's pregnant, but dismisses it and doesn't mention it to anyone else. Though they are a closely knit group, each member of the ka-tet will keep at least one secret from his or her companions.

River Crossing's matriarch, Aunt Talitha Unwin,[19] tells them about con-ditions in Lud, a fortress-refuge where two factions continue a generations-old civil war that isolated the city from the world. The degenerate combatants use technological relics of the Great Old Ones against each other. She advises Roland to circle around the city, but he is loath to leave the path of the Beam. Also, if they bypass Lud, they will miss Blaine the Mono, whom Jake fears but knows intuitively is an important part of their quest without realizing that Blaine is the only way for them to cross the poisoned territory beyond Lud.

The old folk of River Crossing remember the sleek pink train that once traveled out from Lud faster than the speed of sound across the wastelands, reminiscent of the blasted lands near Conger Road in *Black House* and a similar region in *The Talisman*. These wastelands and the proliferation of mutant humans and animals seem to indicate that Roland's world had a nuclear war in its past. In some areas the mutations are lessening, as in Mejis. Roland says this Old War took place more than a thousand years ago, which puts it at about the same time as the fall of Gilead.

Their discussions at an end, Roland and his group take their leave. Even staying overnight would be a mistake, for the people of River Crossing, like the oracle in the mountain, could never be satisfied. The longer they stayed, the harder it would be to break away. Roland would find himself becalmed again, like he was in Tull.

As a parting gift, Aunt Talitha gives Roland a silver cross, asking him to wear it and lay it at the foot of the Dark Tower. The gunslinger accepts her gift, but makes no promise as to its ultimate destination. This sigul of an olden age will come in handy later on and will ultimately reach the Tower on America-side via a member of Tet Corporation.

On the way to Lud, the group encounters the wreck of a Nazi airplane. Eddie wonders if aircraft that disappear in the Bermuda Triangle end up in Mid-World. The pilot was the fabled outlaw prince David Quick, leader of the army that attacked Lud nearly a century before. Later, the Tick-Tock Man will ask Jake if he is a "Not-See"; his mispronunciation of "Nazi" is also a phrase that forms the opening question in stanza XXXII of Browning's poem: "Not see? because of night perhaps?"

During a break in their travels, the foursome takes turns retelling their stories up to that point. Jake shows the others *Charlie the Choo-Choo,* which they examine in detail. Eddie and Susannah recognize the book from their respective childhoods,[20] though both remember losing their copies, Susannah after being hit by Jack Mort's brick. Ka has been trying to place the book into their hands, but other forces may be working to keep it away from them. Roland dismisses the riddle book, perhaps because intuition tells him it isn't important.

Before they reach Lud and whatever challenges that city poses for them, they must first solve the riddle of the decrepit, rusting bridge that spans the Send River.[21] Eddie's recent retelling of *The Bridge of San Luis Rey,* about people who die together when the bridge they're crossing collapses, adds to their nervousness. This bridge is a three-quarter-mile-long shattered maze of steel and concrete, perhaps as old as Roland. The scene where the ka-tet crosses the bridge, evading holes and navigating tilted walkways is a cross between Larry Underhill's trek though the Lincoln Tunnel to escape New York in *The Stand,* and Roland and Jake's earlier experience on the trestle.

While King seems to foreshadow that Eddie's acrophobia will be the source of any trouble they have during the crossing, the wind is what brings about their crisis. A strong gust sweeps Oy over the edge while they are navigating the gap in the middle, and Jake leaps to his rescue. Eddie functions like a gunslinger, running to Jake's rescue mindless of his fear.

While all attention is focused on saving Jake and Oy, an intruder, Gasher by name, arrives wielding a hand grenade.[22] He threatens to kill everyone—himself included—unless they turn Jake over to him. It's another Mexican standoff. Jake demonstrates his faith in Roland by choosing to go with Gasher, trusting that Roland won't let him down this time.

Roland sends Eddie and Susannah to find Blaine, while he and Oy follow Jake's trail through the booby-trapped streets of Lud. The warlike drum track from a ZZ Top song emanates from speakers hanging around the city, once part of a public address system for emergency announcement during some ancient war. The city's residents hear within the drumbeats an invitation to commit ritual murder.[23] They sacrifice themselves by lottery to appease the ghosts they believe responsible for the noise, reminiscent of Shirley Jackson's famous short story "The Lottery."[24] From each speaker pole hangs a "grisly garland of corpses." Thousands of bodies line the streets, a scene familiar to Dorcas from *Rose Madder*.

In this section, King deftly juggles three parallel story lines, following Jake and Gasher, Roland and Oy, and Eddie and Susannah simultaneously. Each subplot is a crucial part of the gunslingers' mission in Lud, and each has its own thread and building tension. The Fellowship of the Ring was similarly split into fragments during Frodo's journey to the Tower. This is the first time the ka-tet is subdivided, but it won't be the last.

Eddie and Susannah encounter a simulacrum of Roland's universe—six streets radiating from a central square. They follow the street whose entrance is guarded by a giant turtle, a logical choice since they are on the path of the Bear heading in the direction of the Turtle. Susannah kills a human being for the first time, shooting a childlike dwarf—one of the Pubes—who approaches with a grenade hidden behind his back. She and Eddie kill several others before the mob dissipates.

They force two Pubes to lead them to the Cradle of Lud. Atop the station's roof they see the Guardians of the Beam and a statue of Arthur Eld, the father of all gunslingers, the King Arthur of Roland's land. The Pubes are afraid of Blaine, who they believe is the most dangerous of Lud's ghosts. Inside, Eddie and Susannah find the monorail, made by North Central Positronics, who was also responsible for Shardik. From the front, the train looks like it has a face, reminiscent of *Charlie the Choo-Choo*.

Blaine, who hasn't run in a decade, is more than the train; he's the voice of Lud, the one who brought the city's technology back to life, deliberately driving its residents to battle. His brain is a vast array of computers buried in the city's bowels. Like Susannah, he has two personalities: Big Blaine, a brash, confrontational lover of puzzles, and Little Blaine, a conscience who speaks only when Big Blaine isn't paying attention. Little Blaine begs Eddie and Susannah not to disturb the train, who apparently isn't aware of his alter ego.

When Blaine comes to life, Little Blaine disappears, afraid Big Blaine will kill him. Blaine is angry at being awakened and a little out of touch with reality. He thinks the doorways between worlds are closed and believes gunslingers haven't walked Mid-World or In-World in three centuries.

After Eddie convinces Blaine they really are from New York, the games begin. The monorail doesn't care where they came from; he just wants to hear some good riddles. The penalty for failure is death.

Meanwhile, Gasher takes Jake deeper into the bowels of Lud to the lair of the Tick-Tock Man, "a cross between a Viking warrior and a giant from a child's fairy tale," named, perhaps, after a Harlan Ellison story.[25] He was once Andrew Quick, the great-grandson of David Quick, and he rules with an iron fist. To Jake, he's the only person in Lud who "seemed wholly vital, wholly healthy, and wholly alive." Tick-Tock doesn't have a short fuse; he has no fuse at all. Jake easily angers him and is battered as a reward for his pertness.

Oy picks up Jake's scent and leads Roland through the decaying city. The ka-tet can communicate with each other telepathically, though their power most often manifests as a kind of knowing—the "touch," Roland calls it, likening it to sending out his ka. His old friend Alain was strong with it, and Jake's touch is growing, too. Roland tries to see through Jake's eyes, but he can't establish contact for fear that Jake will inadvertently reveal something to Tick-Tock.

Roland knows how intelligent some billy-bumblers can be. He sends Oy to scout the room where Jake is being held. Oy reports the number of people in the room by tapping on the floor. The gunslinger finally contacts Jake and tells him to create a diversion. Jake imitates Eddie in Balazar's lair, turning Tick-Tock's suspicions on his own men.

Oy breaks into the chamber through a ventilation grid and attacks Tick-Tock with the same determination and disregard for his own well-being that he will later use against Mordred. Tick-Tock bends Oy almost to the breaking point; Mordred will break Oy's spine in the bumbler's final battle. Though Oy survives, Roland knew it was possible that he was asking one member of his ka-tet to sacrifice himself for the sake of another, which indicates that, although he is evolving, Roland hasn't yet reached a point where he won't risk another being's life to further his goals.

Jake is distracted from opening the door to admit Roland, but it opens anyway, triggered remotely by Blaine. Jake joins the ranks of gunslingers when he shoots Tick-Tock Man with his father's gun. The wound only appears to be fatal, though.

If Roland hadn't already redeemed himself by preventing Jack Mort from killing Jake, he does so now, validating Jake's faith by rescuing him.

Blaine contacts Roland over the citywide PA system, demanding a riddle, having learned from Eddie and Susannah that he knows many good ones. Roland asks one and uses the promise of more as a bargaining tool to get the train to cooperate. Blaine sends a sphere to lead Roland and Jake to the Cradle, where the ka-tet is reunited. Before they can board the train, however, they have to solve a puzzle. Susannah, hypnotized by Roland, draws on Detta's memories to figure out the riddle of the prime numbers.

Blaine activates the city's warning sirens. Panicked, many of Lud's residents commit suicide. As they leave, Blaine detonates a stockpile of chemical and biological weapons. He clearly has no intention of returning. Blaine rationalizes his actions by saying that he's serving the residents by fulfilling their belief that he is a god who dispenses both favor and punishment on a whim.

The trip southeast to Topeka along the Path of the Beam will cover more than seven thousand miles in eight hours. The distance was once much less, Blaine tells them, "[b]efore all temporal synapses began to melt down." The chasm outside Lud is reminiscent of the abyss beyond the walls of Castle Discordia, where terrible creatures battle each other and fight to escape.

The ubiquitous Randall Flagg enters the *Dark Tower* mythos, materializing in the underground passages, where he forces the injured Tick-Tock Man to repeat words once said by another of Flagg's minions, Trashcan Man[26] from *The Stand*: "My life for you." Tick-Tock, the ruthless leader of the Grays and descendant of a great warrior, becomes completely subjugated to Flagg—who calls himself Richard Fannin—within moments of his appearance. When Flagg rips a giant flap of loose flesh from his head, the man regards him with "dumb gratitude."

Perhaps King's 1990 work on updating and revising *The Stand*—a book written during the period when the original stories that comprise *The Gunslinger* were composed—had him thinking about this villain and his part in the larger *Dark Tower* universe. Flagg is anti-ka, an agent of Discordia. His purpose is to ensure Roland and his ka-tet fail. "They're meddling with things they have no business meddling with. . . . They must not draw closer to the Tower than they are now."

Readers speculated for the next decade about who Flagg really was. With the reissue of *The Gunslinger* in 2003 and the appearance of the final three books, King confirmed that Flagg had been in the series from the very first page as Walter, the man in black.

While none of the volumes in the series have definitive conclusions, most wrap up at least some of the particular book's business. Roland catches the man in black in *The Gunslinger* and assembles his ka-tet in *The Drawing of the Three*. *The Waste Lands* doesn't have a goal, per se, other than to get the group to Lud, onto the train and across the blasted lands between there and Topeka. That goal accomplished, the book ends with a cliff-hanger. Reviewer Edward Bryant of *Locus* magazine said, "While clearly a symphony of traveling music, this novel is rather like an enormous chapter in some sort of cosmic radio serial."[27] A serial with five- to six-year gaps between installments

After accelerating to breakneck speeds, Blaine tells the group he will only deliver them safely to Topeka if they can stump him with a riddle. Otherwise, he will crash and kill them all. Blaine is aware of his own degeneration and also professes boredom. "I CAN ONLY CONCLUDE THAT THIS IS A SPIRITUAL MALAISE BEYOND MY ABILITY TO REPAIR," the suicidal train tells them. Like everything else manmade in

Mid-World, Blaine is coming apart at the seams. Still, he knows the answer to every riddle Roland can remember. If the group's riddle expert can't stump the insane train, what hope do they have for survival?

In the author's note, King writes:

I am well aware that some readers of *The Waste Lands* will be displeased that it has ended as it has, with so much unresolved. I am not terribly pleased to be leaving Roland and his companions in the not-so-tender care of Blaine the Mono myself, and although you are not obligated to believe me, I must nevertheless insist that I was as surprised by the conclusion to this third volume as some of my readers may be. Yet books which write themselves (as this one did, for the most part) must also be allowed to end themselves, and I can only assure you, Reader, that Roland and his band have come to one of the crucial border-crossings in their story, and we must leave them here for a while at the customs station, answering questions and filling out forms. All of which is simply a metaphorical way of saying that it was over again for a while and my heart was wise enough to stop me from trying to push ahead anyway.

The song of the Turtle had stopped for the time being.

ENDNOTES

[1] Unless otherwise specified, all quotes in this chapter are taken from *The Waste Lands*.

[2] The book's title is taken from T. S. Eliot, and quotes from that and other Eliot works appear in the text.

[3] "Mir" means both "world" and "peace" in Russian. Mir is running down; Roland's world is running down.

[4] The eponymous gigantic bear in the novel by Richard Adams. Eddie associates the name with rabbits: *Watership Down* is another Adams novel.

[5] On the other side of the Tower from the portal of the Bear is the portal of the Turtle, called Maturin. The other ten guardians are: Fish, Eagle (sometimes just Bird), Lion, Bat, Wolf, Hare, Rat, Horse, Dog and Elephant. The portal of the Bear is twinned with Brooklyn in Keystone Earth.

[6] In the Cradle of Lud, Eddie refers to this portal as the unfound door, foreshadowing the real UNFOUND door that lurks in their futures. The Cradle of Lud is a kind of portal, too, decorated as it is with the guardians of the Beam and a statue of Arthur Eld.

[7] Outside Lud, Eddie tells Roland, "We're with you because we have to be—that's your goddamned *ka*. But we're also with you because we *want* to be. . . . If you died in your

sleep tonight, we'd bury you and then go on. We probably wouldn't last long, but we'd die in the path of the Beam."

[8] Eddie and Susannah promise to tell Roland the story of Oz, but they don't get around to it until they are at the Emerald Palace, thousands of miles down the Path of the Beam, a Mid-World analog to the yellow brick road.

[9] Before he leaves, his teacher hands out the summer reading list, which includes *The Lord of the Flies*. Ted Brautigan gives this book to Bobby Garfield in *Hearts in Atlantis*. Brautigan will mistake Jake for Bobby when he first sees him at Thunderclap Station. Alas, Jake never gets to read this book. O, Discordia.

[10] Deepneau is distantly related to Ed Deepneau from *Insomnia,* the man who became the Crimson King's tool.

[11] The book discusses how riddles are perhaps the oldest of all the games people still play today, and tells the story of Samson's wedding-day riddle, but the account is inaccurate. It sets the story at Samson's wedding to Delilah, but according to the Bible, it took place when Samson was supposed to marry a Philistine woman. Samson's riddle of the lion and honey is a complex play on words that derives from the fact that "lion" and "honey" are outwardly identical in Hebrew.

[12] The key isn't the only thing Jake will find in this lot that proves crucial to their quest. The bowling bag that allows them to carry Black Thirteen in the Calla will also materialize in this lot for him to find on a future journey.

[13] The roses growing near the Tower are so firmly rooted that their thorns sever another of Roland's fingers when he tries to pick one.

[14] The ability Jake and Susannah get when they wield their siguls is a more powerful version of Andy McGee's "push" in *Firestarter,* which was created by science, not magic. Andy McGee's power also damages him physically when he uses it, in the same way that using mechanical doorways (like the one the Wolves use to get to the Calla) sickens people. As King says in *Wolves of the Calla,* "Gods leave siguls. Men leave machines."

[15] Co-Op City is really in the Bronx, not Brooklyn, so Jake's world isn't Keystone Earth, even though the rose exists here. Jake and Eddie may or may not come from the same reality.

[16] Though Lud is twinned with New York, its location in Mid-World is comparable to St. Louis. Eddie jokes, "Today we're studying Wacky Geography in Mid-World. You see, boys and girls, in Mid-World you start in New York, travel southeast to Kansas, and then continue along the Path of the Beam until you come to the Dark Tower . . . which happens to be smack in the middle of everything."

[17] When Jake arrives in Mid-World, his digital watch displays an impossible time and runs backward. Roland comments that "as a rule no timepiece did very good work these days." The Tet Corporation gives Roland one that works fairly well until he gets close to the Tower.

[18] Oy is based on King's Welsh corgi, Marlowe.

[19] At least 105 years old, she is reminiscent of Mother Abigail from *The Stand*. Unwin was the name of the original publisher of *The Lord of the Rings*.

[20] Jake's housekeeper, Greta Shaw, had a copy, too. In High Speech, "char" means "death," as in the charyou tree that was Susan Delgado's destiny, which may be an omen.

[21] Eddie and Jake see the resemblance to the George Washington Bridge in New York. Roland will see that bridge from the window of the boardroom at the Tet Corporation's office and agree.

[22] King credits having read *The Quincunx* by Charles Palliser as his inspiration for Gasher's dialect. [DT6]

[23] Eddie is apoplectic when he discovers what's going on, "You're killing each other over a piece of music that was never even released as a single!"

[24] In that story, people in a village take part in an annual lottery in which the person who draws a piece of paper with a black circle on it is stoned to death. King discusses "The Lottery" briefly in *Danse Macabre,* saying that it turns the concept of the outsider into something symbolic, created arbitrarily by the bad luck of the draw.

[25] "'Repent, Harlequin!' Said the Ticktockman."

[26] "He ended up betraying me, but he was a good friend for quite some time, anyway, and I still have a soft spot in my heart for him."

[27] Edward Bryant, *Locus* magazine, December 1991.

CHAPTER 5

WIZARD AND GLASS (REGARD)

*"You have the right to know all those things, I suppose, and I'll tell them to
you . . . but not now. It's a very long story. I never expected
to tell it to anyone, and I'll only tell it once."
"When?" Eddie persisted.
"When the time is right," Roland said, and with that they had to be content.*

[DT3]

*I asked one draught of earlier, happier sights . . .
One taste of the old time sets all to right!* [1]

For six long years, King left Roland, Jake, Eddie, Susannah and Oy
on board Blaine the Mono, hurtling toward seemingly certain death.
Part of his reticence about tackling the follow-up book came from
his knowledge that a large section of it would be about the heat and passion of teen love, and he wasn't sure he knew the truth of that anymore.
"Suspense is relatively easy," he writes. "Love is hard."

He told an audience at the University of Maine in Orono, "At first I
thought it would be extremely short: The train crashed and they all died."
Instead, he produced the longest book of the series in an amazingly short
amount of time—six months.

Wizard and Glass starts by repeating the section of *The Waste Lands*
explaining the rules of the riddle challenge. Blaine, the insane monorail,
loves to solve riddles. "What's happening to the rest of the world is happening to me, I reckon," he says. If the ka-tet can't stump him before they
reach Topeka, he will commit suicide by smashing into the terminus barrier, going faster than the speed of sound, taking them with him. [2]

To Eddie, everything in Roland's world is a riddle. You don't shoot
with your hand, but with your mind. Roland thinks they have a chance to
win. Why else would Jake have purchased a book of riddles from Calvin
Tower's bookstore just before he was drawn into Roland's world?

When the contest begins, the route map indicates they have nearly eight hours until the end of the line. Time moves differently in Mid-World and aboard Blaine, though. Roland tries to tempt the monorail into slowing down with the promise of harder, more interesting jokes, but Blaine knows the story of Scheherazade,[3] even if Roland doesn't.

Blaine's knowledge reaches beyond Mid-World; he knows about New York, Marilyn Monroe and Raquel Welch. He recognizes one of Roland's puzzles as having originated in England.[4] Roland learned most of his repertoire from Cort during the Fair-Days of his youth. He isn't surprised to discover that his old tutor may have known about other worlds, probably from the Manni who lived on the perimeter of Gilead.

The first sign that Blaine might have a weakness comes when he thinks Edith Bunker is a real person rather than a TV character.[5] Roland uses up most of their time before giving the others a chance. It only takes Jake a few minutes to go through the hardest entries his riddle book has to offer, with no success. The fact that the answers had been ripped from the back of this book is perhaps a subtle hint from ka that normal riddles with sensible answers weren't the way to defeat Blaine, a clue reinforced in *Charlie the Choo-Choo.*

Susannah passes her turn and Blaine skips over Eddie, asking instead if Roland remembers any more Fair-Day riddles. Blaine mocks Eddie repeatedly during the trip, perhaps sensing that his wisecracks pose the greatest challenge.

Blaine and Roland both take riddles seriously, and they have often been serious business in classic fiction all the way back to the Greeks and the story of Oedipus, who had to answer the Sphinx's riddle at the gate of Thebes to gain entry. The penalty for failure was to be eaten by the Sphinx. When Oedipus correctly answered the challenge—a riddle that Roland uses against Blaine—the beast committed suicide by throwing itself from the city walls, in contrast to Blaine's threat of suicide if no one can stump him.

Eddie often irritates Roland with his illogical jokes. He wonders if Blaine might react similarly. Then he realizes that the clue to winning against Blaine comes from *Charlie the Choo-Choo.* Charlie's song began, "Don't ask me silly questions, / I won't play silly games. / I'm just a simple choo-choo train / And I'll always be the same."

He launches into a string of school-yard jokes that annoy Blaine, who is irritated by having to lower himself to Eddie's level. He cannot refuse to answer, though, because the rules stipulate that no one can "cry off." The contest must be played to the end. The train lurches each time Eddie poses a joke. Little Blaine warns Eddie that he is killing Big Blaine, but that's exactly Eddie's intent.[6]

A dead-baby joke defeats Blaine. He can't answer, and Roland won't allow him to crash the train with a joke unanswered. Like a verbal gunslinger, Eddie shoots more inane jokes from the hip, answering himself while he prepares the next. He doesn't have to stop to reload—he is an endless font of tasteless humor. Blaine dies in a blaze of hateful words, and no one is seriously injured when the train coasts into the barricade at the end of the track and derails.

In eight hours, Roland has covered more territory than he has in a thousand years wandering in search of the Tower. The world they find when they climb out of the train is more familiar to Eddie, Susannah and Jake than to Roland, though.

They are in Topeka, but in this version of reality a superflu virus known as Captain Trips[7] emptied the world a year before Eddie was drawn from New York. As Jake once said to Roland, there are "more worlds than these," some mostly the same as Earth, others radically different. The three New Yorkers may have all come from different Earths, not just from different times in the same one. In this Topeka, they encounter subtle differences from the world they knew, things like baseball team names, car models and soft drinks.[8]

They see no indication of the Beam. Roland tells them that though the Tower exists in all worlds, it may not be accessible from them all. In fact, there are only two worlds of cosmic importance: Roland's place of In-World, Mid-World, End-World and the one real Earth, known as Keystone Earth, which is probably at the highest level—level 19—of the Tower of all Earths.

They hear a distant, mournful wail, which Roland recognizes as a "thinny," a place where "the fabric of existence is almost entirely worn away." These dangerous pockets have increased in number since the Dark Tower's force began to fail. "[T]hey are sores on the skin of existence, able to exist because things are going wrong. Things in all worlds." Blaine probably took them through a thinny to cross between worlds.

Eddie finds a modern, light wheelchair to replace the one Susannah left behind in their mad scramble to board Blaine. Before they set out,

Concerning Twins

King and coauthor Peter Straub introduced the concept of Twinners, people who have one-to-one counterparts in an alternate reality, in *The Talisman*. While the *Dark Tower* series doesn't make the same use of this notion, twins feature prominently in the two central realities, Keystone Earth and Mid-World, themselves twins of a sort.

Early on, Roland sees strong similarities between Eddie and his old ka-mate Cuthbert. While under the gunslinger's hypnotic spell, fictional King refers to them almost interchangeably when Roland and Eddie visit him in 1977. Jake resembles another of Roland's childhood friends, Alain Johns. Both were strong in the touch. Susannah is twinned with the demon Mia who inhabits her body and steals her child, but she was already dual-natured, consisting of Odetta Holmes and Detta Walker. "If we are not used to such twinnings yet, I reckon that we never will be." [DT7]

Mordred Deschain is referred to as a twin because of his dual paternity and nature. The Crimson King also exists in two forms, Ram Abbalah and his physical form trapped in the Tower.

Even lesser characters have doubles. Twins are the rule rather than the exception in Calla Bryn Sturgis, and it is their essence that feeds the Breakers. Henchick of the Manni in Mid-World becomes Harrigan of the Church of the Holy God-Bomb in New York. Though Father Callahan and Ted Brautigan are both from America-side, their itinerate lives are strikingly similar and both are characters in books in some realities. Simple-minded Sheemie Ruiz is twinned with Bryan Smith, the driver of the van that struck Stephen King.

Places are also twinned. The Mohaine Desert is geographically similar to the Mohave. Mejis is twinned with Mexico. Residents of Stoneham, Maine, have the same last names as many of those in Calla Bryn Sturgis, and some of the towns' buildings are alike. New York is twinned with Lud. The Dixie Pig's kitchen is identical to the one in Castle Discordia where Mia feeds.

And what of Roland Deschain? Who is his twin? The gunslinger is, perhaps, twinned with the wordslinger, the writer from Maine. Both are the sorts of men who would straighten pictures in strange hotel rooms. When Roland and Eddie visit King, Eddie observes that Roland could pass for King's father. Why else would the gunslinger share the pain of King's accident injuries if they weren't empathically linked?

Jake spies their old buddy Charlie the Choo-Choo in an amusement park across the street from the train station. Father Callahan is familiar with this park, too. Topeka is where he hit bottom during his drunken binge tour of America in the early 1980s.

At the entrance ramp to the interstate, they see graffiti that says WATCH FOR THE WALKIN' DUDE, a reference to Randall Flagg, who appeared to Tick-Tock Man in Lud under the name Richard Fannin. In another place they see ALL HAIL THE CRIMSON KING written in red letters over a single red eye, referring to a character introduced in *Insomnia* and later woven into the revised version of *The Gunslinger*. Roland shakes his head as if he doesn't recognize the name, but he's troubled by it all the same. When Susannah asks him directly who the Crimson King is, Roland replies, "I know not."

Eddie still dreams of the empty field containing the rose, but now he sees a bulldozer, which tells Roland that their quest has doubled. They have to protect the rose as well as save the Tower. Troubled by the dream, Eddie asks Roland if he would ever betray them. The gunslinger can't answer to anyone's satisfaction, even his own. Roland believes his next betrayal would be his last and would spell defeat for him and his quest. Even so, he warns Eddie, "I bear watching, as you well know."

The thinny's wailing vibrates their foreheads and makes their eyes water. Roland tells his companions to put bullets in their ears to block the sound. The only ones that work are the few remaining "wets" from Gilead. Roland can't explain why this is so; he just knows it.[9]

At several times during their quest, a member of the ka-tet will need to perform some act akin to repentance before they are able to continue, like an alcoholic who performs acts of contrition to those he or she may have injured in the past. The thinny reminds Roland of a painful part of his youth that he hasn't yet told his friends about. He needs to summon the courage to start, like King summoning the courage to write.

> I'm not sure you need to hear, but I think I need to tell. Our future is the Tower, and to go toward it with a whole heart, I must put my past to rest as best I may. There's no way I could tell you all of it—in my world even the past is in motion, rearranging itself in many vital ways—but this one story may stand for all the rest.[10]

Before they reach the strange building looming on the road ahead—which appears to be a crystal palace—Roland finds the strength to tell his story, starting with Marten's ruse to goad him into taking his manhood challenge early. For the rest of the night, Roland talks. It may not have been an ordinary night, but one more akin to the time when Roland and Walter held palaver. "[S]torytelling always changes time," Roland tells them. "At least it does in my world."

The morning after his victory over Cort, Roland's irate father finds him in a prostitute's bed and castigates him for allowing Marten to drive him "like a cow in a chute." Emboldened by his recent success, Roland speaks back to his father, telling him what he knows of his mother's treachery with Marten. He wants to take his new apprentice guns and kill the enchanter. Stephen Deschain has the cool head of a seasoned gunslinger. He's known of his wife's deceit and Marten's duplicity for two years.

Without mentioning the Tower explicitly, Stephen tries to make Roland understand that the pending civil war isn't important. The gunslingers of Gilead consider all other problems minor compared to protecting the Beams and the Tower. Their view—which Stephen passes on to his son like a defective gene—proves to be shortsighted; they fail to realize that Farson's insurrection will destroy the Affiliation and those who guard the Tower.

Though he's now officially a gunslinger, Roland isn't any match for Marten, who is far slyer than Roland will ever be, according to his father. Gilead is no longer safe; Marten has sworn to kill Roland before he can grow to be a problem. Though he won his challenge, he is still to be banished, sent east rather than west. "My real growing up didn't start until my Da' sent me away," Roland once told Jake.

Stephen sends Roland and two friends, future gunslingers Cuthbert Allgood and Alain Johns, to Mejis,[11] where they may be beyond the reach of the leaders of the insurrection in In-World. The boys, barely teenagers, pretend to have been sent to count things that might aid the Affiliation in time of war as punishment for some unspecified youthful sins.

They don't expect to uncover treason and conspiracy. Mejis is supposedly faithful to the Affiliation, but the barony is a remote colony and the locals have little interest in the goings-on of some far-off empire. Because of its isolation, John Farson, the leader of the revolution,[12] chose this place to amass supplies for the coming battle. Farson is either Walter or is controlled by him to the extent that it makes no difference.

To oversee his projects, Farson sent three regulators—one a failed gunslinger—who call themselves the Big Coffin Hunters[13] to Hambry, the barony seat, taking the powerful and legendary rose-colored Wizard's Glass with them. Farson has no use for it at present and sends it away because it consumes those who use it.

The pink "grapefruit" is part of Maerlyn's Rainbow. There are thirteen glass balls, one for each of the twelve guardians and one for the Dark Tower. Roland's father told him that his grandfather believed it wasn't wise to talk about Black Thirteen, "for it might hear its name called and roll your way." Stephen believes most of the balls are broken, but the Crimson King possessed six in his castle. The Talisman—also known as the Globe of Forever—emitted white light, the sum of all colors, and may have been an opposing or unifying power.

The Big Coffin Hunters entrust the grapefruit to Rhea Dubativo, called Rhea of Cöos, a witch who lives on the outskirts of town. The moment she removes the glass from its sealed box, she is addicted. She can't control what she sees within it, but it shows her the people of Hambry at their vilest. Using it sucks the life and vitality out of her like a vampire sucks blood. When she isn't looking into it, she's thinking about looking into it.[14]

The lives of those in Hambry who won't agree to support Farson are at risk. Pat Delgado, who for years was in charge of the barony's horses, was killed—though the murder was made to look like an accident—because he wouldn't cooperate with a plan to hide the increased number of horses in Mejis.

Mayor Hart Thorin of Hambry turns a blind eye to the goings-on in his town. As a payoff, Farson's local conspirators steal Pat Delgado's papers of ownership for his land and horses. This puts Delgado's daughter, Susan,[15] in a difficult financial situation. Thorin seems like the only solution to her problem. He offers money to Delgado's sister Cordelia,[16] effectively purchasing Susan as his gilly.[17] Susan's aunt claims the arrangement is necessary for them to survive.[18]

While Susan is at Rhea's house (sent by Thorin to have the witch vouch for her purity), she spies on Rhea basking in the aura of the Wizard's Glass. During the examination, Rhea takes liberties with Susan, and plants a posthypnotic suggestion designed to spoil Thorin's pleasure.

Rhea vouches for Susan's suitability as a bride, and then proclaims that Thorin isn't to touch her for another three months. This is a relief for Susan, but Aunt Cordelia doesn't consider it good news; Thorin is holding two-thirds of her payment until the deal is consummated. By setting this condition, Rhea unwittingly sets up the tragedy that follows, for otherwise Thorin would have bedded Susan immediately and she would have felt bound to him. During her reprieve she has time to fall in love with Roland.

What happens next is inspired not by spaghetti westerns but rather by

Romeo and Juliet.[19] Ka thrusts the two star-crossed[20] lovers together almost immediately. They meet while Susan is returning from Rhea's house mere hours after the three boys arrive in Mejis. Roland introduces himself by his cover name, Will Dearborn. His manners and diction betray him as coming from the Inner Baronies. He says he is from a small village in New Canaan, the center of the Affiliation—a place less grand than Gilead.[21]

Thus begin the first steps in their dance of courtship. Susan is evasive when Roland asks if she's promised to another and mentally curses her poor timing.[22] Concerned about appearances, she turns down Roland's repeated offer of a ride back to town on his horse. Roland tries to charm her with news of insurrection in the baronies thousands of miles west. He implies that he and his friends got in trouble back home and were sent on a make-work project that is a step short of exile.

The sixteen-year-old girl soon has Roland's measure. "[H]e's the sort to burn bridges and upset mail-carts, then go on his merry way without a single look back." Roland is "far from the relentless creature he would eventually become, but the seeds of that relentlessness were there."

The three boys are to present themselves in town the next day. Susan knows Mayor Thorin will invite them to his house for an official welcoming dinner. Without explaining why, she asks Roland to pretend they've never met. He assumes she is a servant. She also warns him about the Coffin Hunters, who work as private guards at Thorin's house.

When they part, she kisses him briefly, but not in a sisterly way. It's Roland's first kiss. The prostitute in Gilead took his virginity but wouldn't kiss him. He is so swept up with emotion that he rides in the dark for hours. What is promised can also be unpromised, he thinks. He's not so lovesick that he fails to notice signs that something may be amiss in Mejis. There are far too many horses in the fields.

Though Cuthbert suspects something is preoccupying Roland, the young gunslinger decides without thinking not to tell his friends about meeting Susan. "Most of his decisions, certainly the best of them, were made in this same way." It's unclear if this was ultimately a good decision, but it's typical of him. Even at fourteen, Roland hides things from the people who rely on him and might help him.

The Big Coffin Hunters—Eldred Jonas, Clay Reynolds and Roy Depape—have important business in Mejis that won't be done for months.

Having three Affiliation brats around counting things makes them nervous. They can't kill the boys—that might draw the wrong kind of attention—but they arrange quarters for them in an abandoned ranch, far enough out of town to keep them from being constantly underfoot. "If ye'd steal the silver from the dining room, first put the dog in the pantry," Jonas says. He doesn't know who Roland and his friends are, but he smells "quite a little wrong on them." The failed gunslinger is the most dangerous of the Big Coffin Hunters. He also knows about the Manni, and sometimes talks about the other worlds he has visited through special doors.

Roland meets no one at Mayor Thorin's formal dinner that he likes or trusts except Olive, the mayor's wife.[23] When he sees Susan, he struggles to maintain his composure and keep up the pretense that they haven't met previously. He mentally upgrades her from Thorin's servant to a relative before hearing Coral Thorin describing her as the mayor's "quiet little woman." Roland is incensed. He says hurtful things to Susan when they are forced to dance together. If he'd been wearing his guns, he might have been tempted to shoot her.

Later that night, the "brats" tip their hand to the Big Coffin Hunters during a showdown at Coral Thorin's saloon, where the music is courtesy of Sheb McCurdy, who will move on to Tull and have his wrists broken by the gunslinger before being shot, along with the rest of the town.

The boy who cleans the saloon, Sheemie Ruiz, gets in Depape's way. Cuthbert tries to talk him out of beating Sheemie but has to shoot the Big Coffin Hunter with his slingshot to get his full attention. A daisy chain Mexican standoff ensues, with Reynolds drawing on Cuthbert, only to find Alain's knife at his throat. Eldred Jonas pulls his gun on Alain and is surprised to feel Roland's knife between his shoulder blades. Sheriff Avery defuses the situation, threatening to run all six out of town if they don't shake hands and promise to forget their argument. The Big Coffin Hunters are beyond Avery's authority, but they comply because it is in their self-interest to do so.

Jonas needs to know more about these boys, who act like apprentice gunslingers. He sends Depape to follow their back trail and ask questions. Depape eventually finds a man who recognized one of the boys as the son of a gunslinger.

Roland regrets the way he treated Susan at the mayor's party. He sends her a note via Sheemie, apologizing and asking to see her on "a matter of importance." Susan rejects his request at first, but she can't get him out of her head. If she hadn't met him, she would have been resolved to her situation. After a fight with her aunt, she rides to where she first encountered him, only half hoping to see him.

Roland has two purposes for wanting to see her—he wants to profess his love for her, but he also needs her help. He suspects the level of cooperation they're receiving from the locals is meant to hide something. Even Susan only vaguely supports the distant Affiliation. Why is everyone else bending over backward to help them? He has to trust someone, but Susan isn't sure she wants his trust any more than she wants his love.

Together they uncover the lies being told to the Affiliation. Mejis has at least three times as many horses as reported and, contrary to what they've been told, very few of them are born mutant. Most of the locals—except those who have taken to calling them Little Coffin Hunters after their run-in with Jonas and his crew—regard the boys with genial contempt, planning to shift around their stock to confuse the boys when the time comes for them to count horses.

Roland suggests that Pat Delgado's death may not have been an accident, which Susan is reluctant to accept. He helps her confront her shame by telling the story of his mother's treachery. Susan asks if he will wait for her to complete her bargain with Thorin by bearing his child. Roland replies that he'd do anything for her except wait while she goes with another man.

Roland refuses to report the suspicious activity they've uncovered to his father via the carrier pigeons they use to communicate. First he wants to understand the complete plot. Alain and Cuthbert suspect that he's reluctant to send news because it might bring an end to his developing romance with Susan. They have to respect his authority, though, because he alone is a gunslinger and the son of their leader.

Mejis has a thinny in Eyebolt Canyon, like the one that triggered Roland's memory of this time. It appeared before Susan was born but during her father's lifetime. She tells him that an earthquake heralded its appearance but it may have been a Beamquake instead, corresponding to one of the Breakers' successes. The three boys explore the thinny, evaluating its possible use. As they near the edge of the canyon, familiar voices tell Roland to jump in. Each of them hears a different person, an effect similar to the Cave of Voices outside Calla Bryn Sturgis.

Roland, Cuthbert and Alain dawdle for months, counting only what's safe, avoiding the delicate subject of horses. They're playing a game of Castles, where players who emerge from cover become vulnerable.

When Roland asks to meet Susan again, she refuses at first, thinking her late father would have counseled her to honor her commitment to Thorin. She reconsiders, deciding to give in to her attraction for Roland.

He tells Susan their suspicions and his real name. They explore the nineteen abandoned oil wells outside Hambry, which Susan believes have been dry for years. Here Roland uncovers the real reason behind the local conspiracy: dozens of camouflaged oil tanks ready to be sent west to Farson, who plans to process the oil into fuel to power war machines that either came from the Old People or from another dimension. If Farson can get them working without the Affiliation finding out, he could wage surprise attacks that would win him the war.

Susan asks, "Is it me you're concerned about or yourself and yer plans?" He doesn't answer. "This'll have no good end," she predicts. She asks Roland to make her break her promise to Thorin, but Roland resists, partly because they sense that someone is watching them, not realizing that it is Rhea with the Wizard's Glass.

As the Reaping Day festival draws close—the day when her promise to Thorin is to be fulfilled—Susan argues with her aunt and rides to her secret thinking spot, where she finds Roland. He tells her to ask him again, for this time he will say yes.

King has already revealed that Susan will never see Gilead and that her destiny is a stake. She senses this deep down, but is unwilling to change what ka wants for her. After they make love, she suggests that she might already be pregnant. Her child would be the next generation of the Eld line. Roland replies, "If you carry my child, such is my good fortune."

Rhea's posthypnotic suggestion takes effect while Roland sleeps. Susan goes to the river and tries to shear off her long blond hair with a sharp rock. Rhea loses contact with them through the ball, so she doesn't see Roland break the enchantment before much damage is done. She is furious when she discovers that someone has foiled her, and decides Susan deserves to die for standing against her, but only after she's been humiliated.

With Susan's permission, Roland hypnotizes her but is unable to see everything that happened that night at Rhea's house. Part of it is hidden in a cloud of pink.

The lovers have numerous clandestine meetings in the ensuing weeks. Cuthbert is jealous of Roland for winning the most beautiful girl any of them has ever seen, but he also hates her for stealing his best friend and distracting him from their mission. Roland is the weapon they count on, but now he's like a revolver dropped into water. "God knows if it'll ever fire again, even if it's fished out and dried off," Cuthbert says, a simile an older Roland would appreciate after the Western Sea wets his ammunition. Roland refuses to even argue with them.

Cordelia Delgado tells Eldred Jonas her suspicion that something is going on between her niece and Will Dearborn. Jonas is surprised by the revelation. If Roland has been able to keep that big a secret, what others might he have?

He uncovers evidence that the boys have been to the oil fields. After searching the ranch where they are staying and finding their guns, he kills their messenger pigeons and covers his tracks by pretending it is an act of vandalism. He then meets with Walter, the man in black. A hundred of Farson's men are coming to town to escort the oil tankers west. They concoct a plan to frame the Affiliation brats as traitors to get them out of the way.

When he realizes that Roland sensed what was going to happen at the ranch, Cuthbert is ready to hit Roland. Alain holds him back, saying that they have to trust Roland or fail. Roland is a gunslinger; they're not. Alain can't intervene a second time, though, when Cuthbert encounters Sheemie on his way from Rhea's house. Sheemie has a note he's supposed to deliver to Cordelia, announcing Rhea's knowledge of Susan's relationship with Will Dearborn.

Cuthbert carries the message back to Roland, calls him outside and strikes him in the face, then thrusts out the note before Roland can react. "I've been a fool," Roland says, and cries. His mistake, he says, is not falling in love but "thinking that love could somehow be apart from everything else." He thought he could live two lives, one with his ka-tet and one with Susan. He thought love could lift him above ka. Love made him blind.

Roland and Cuthbert make peace and then ride out as gunslingers to deal with Rhea, who Roland calls "daughter of none."[24] Roland doesn't want to kill her unless he must, a decision he would come to regret. He was still a boy and the decision to kill "does not come easily or naturally to most boys." They warn her off, but she doesn't emerge from her house.

She wails in sorrow when Roland shoots her pet poison snake, a parallel to Arthur Eld's victory over the great snake Saita. In that legend, Arthur Eld wore the dead snake around his neck as a trophy. In Mejis, it is Rhea who wears her dead pet around her neck until it turns into a stinking carcass.

Roland knows their time is running out. They have to destroy the oil before it leaves Mejis. He, Cuthbert and Alain meet with Susan to sketch out a general plan. They trust ka to sweep them out of the situation it has swept them into. The thinny is an integral part of their plan—they think they can drive Farson's men into the canyon and destroy them.

Working near the thinny, with its haunting voices, puts their tempers on edge, though. Alain tells Cuthbert, "You'll die young," which is meant in jest but perhaps comes from Alain's touch, for it proves true. A few years later at Jericho Hill, the ka-tet will make its last stand against Farson's men. Alain dies under Roland's and Cuthbert's guns, an accidental nighttime shooting. A sniper kills Jamie DeCurrie. They are a dozen against thousands, but Roland and Cuthbert go out in a blaze of glory, fighting to the end. The arrow in the eye that fells Cuthbert comes from the bow of Randolph Filardo, aka Randall Flagg.

Roland hypnotizes Susan again when Alain questions how Rhea knew what was going on. He has grown to suspect that the witch possesses one of the Wizard's glasses. His father thought Farson owned one because of the way he seemed to know things he shouldn't have known. With Alain's help, he gets Susan to reveal where the "grapefruit" is hidden.

Bolstered by her knowledge of what is going on in Mejis, Susan searches her father's office and finds evidence to support Roland's suggestion that he had been killed. After another fight with Cordelia, she moves out of the house. She meets Roland in a hut, where he shows her his guns. If things go badly for him, she's to take them to Gilead and show them to his father.

After they make love for the last time, Susan expresses a sense of dread about their future, a feeling akin to ka-shume, the sense of an impending break in a ka-tet. Roland realizes later that some part of her knew what lay ahead. Like Eldred Jonas, Roland has a sudden urge to pack up and leave, but he knows that the faces of his friends and those who would die against Farson would haunt him if he doesn't complete this mission.

The next day, the Big Coffin Hunters make the first move by murdering Mayor Thorin and his chancellor and framing Roland and his friends. During their arrest, Roland exposes Jonas as a failed gunslinger. Jonas limps because Cort's father broke his leg with his ironwood club, then disarmed the boy and sent him into exile. Roland tells him, "The soul of a man such as you can never leave the west."

Jonas goes to retrieve the Wizard's Glass, only to discover that Rhea's become little more than a walking skeleton. She believes she's the ball's chosen one, its mistress, and tells Jonas it will do Farson no good without her. Jonas knows about the ball's seductive power, but rather than kill her to get it back, he agrees to take her along.

Susan decides to free Roland and his friends from jail, defying his orders to flee west and save herself. Sheemie is waiting for her in town to help her. His foreknowledge of what she would do is an indication that there's more to the boy than meets the eye, that he has powers that will lead him to become a Breaker a thousand years down history's long trail.

During the rescue, Susan is forced to kill both the sheriff and his deputy. For a brief time, she is a part of the ka-tet of gunslingers. Roland hides her in one of their secret meeting places with Sheemie to watch over her, and makes her promise again to go to Gilead with warnings of Farson's plans if he doesn't return. It's the last time he sees her in person.

Before tackling Farson's men, Roland, Cuthbert and Alain set the oil fields ablaze, destroying Farson's fuel source. They know that Jonas has the Wizard's Glass and are worried it will reveal their plans. Instead, it shows Rhea where Susan and Sheemie are hiding.

Jonas captures Susan and sends her to Coral Thorin with Reynolds. Then he takes the Wizard's Glass and evicts Rhea from the camp. "May it damn you the way it's damned me," she tells him. She finds her way to Cordelia Delgado's house, where the two bitter women plot their final revenge on Susan, whom they both blame for their downfall. Rhea replenishes her energy with Cordelia's blood.[25]

Sheemie follows Susan's trail and seeks Olive Thorin's help in freeing Susan. Olive and Susan escape north but Clay Reynolds, told where to wait by Rhea, recaptures them.

Roland and his friends prepare to ambush Jonas and Farson's cowboys. "Today it was Cuthbert and Alain's turn to be tested—not in Gilead, in the traditional place of proving behind the Great Hall, but here in Mejis, on the edge of the Bad Grass, in the desert and in the canyon." They lie in hiding, wait for the posse to pass, then attack from behind, killing a quarter of the contingent before the group realizes it's under assault. What they lack in training they make up for with the keen eyes and reflexes of the young. Within minutes, those not dead flee in panic. Roland takes the Wizard's Glass from Jonas before killing him.

The ball sweeps Roland away in a vision of the future, showing him disjointed images of his undeclared quest, all the way to the edge of End-World and beyond, where he sees Oy impaled on a tree branch. He sees his destiny: the Dark Tower. "[He] senses both the strength of the place and the wrongness of it; he can feel how it is spooling error across everything, softening the divisions between the worlds, how its potential for mischief is growing stronger even as disease weakens its truth and coherence, like a body afflicted with cancer; this jutting arm of dark gray stone is the world's great mystery and last awful riddle."

The vision is his call to adventure, a call that he never questions or refuses. Now Roland understands why his father felt that the pending civil war was comparatively unimportant. He swears to reach the Tower and conquer the wrongness within. A voice tells him he will kill everyone he loves and "still the Tower will be pent shut against you." Roland defies the voice, drawing on the strength of every generation before him. Then he passes out.

When he comes to, he doesn't remember much of his vision, but he knows his destiny is forever altered. He and his friends may be going back to Gilead, but not for long. If they survive the day, they will search for the Dark Tower. They will still fight Farson's men, but only because they're in their way and gunslinger ethics demands they forbid these thieves their prize.

Cuthbert argues that the Tower is a myth, no more real than the Holy Grail. Roland replies, "Its existence is the great secret our fathers keep;

it's what has held them together as ka-tet across all the years of our world's decline."

Roland's choice between the Tower and a full life with Susan is both difficult and easy. He knows she's pregnant with his child and he would choose her in an instant, except the Tower is crumbling. "If it falls, everything we know will be swept away. There will be chaos beyond our imagining. . . . I choose the Tower. I must. Let her live a good life and long with someone else. . . . As for me, I choose the Tower."

Their attack on Farson's men goes exactly as planned. Alain blows up several of the tankers with a machine gun taken from the Big Coffin Hunters' posse, and the rest explode on their own. The defenders get off only a single shot in return before the three boys lure them into Eyebolt Canyon, where Roland sets a fire that drives the men closer to the thinny. Those who don't ride into it by accident are drawn by the voices emerging from it.

After their victory, the bloodred moon rises and Roland realizes how the Wizard's Glass misdirected him into believing Susan was safe. "Sometimes it sees a future that's already happening." He watches in the glass as Susan is taken into town, tied on the back of a cart. The people of Hambry are in a frenzy, believing Susan was a traitor and that her death will bring life for their crops. Cordelia throws the first torch onto the cornshucks surrounding her. Rhea is only a second behind her. With her final breaths, Susan screams her love for Roland.

Roland remains in a trance while Cuthbert and Alain take him back to Gilead. Along the way, he eats and drinks but does not speak or sleep and cannot be separated from the Wizard's Glass. He wasn't traveling inside the glass, he says later, but rather inside his head, where everyone has a Wizard's Glass.

When they reach the outskirts of Gilead, the ball comes to life and shows him everything that happened in Mejis. "It showed me these things not to teach or enlighten, but to hurt and wound. The remaining pieces of the Wizard's Rainbow are all evil things. Hurt enlivens them, somehow."

At home, he keeps the glass from his father. It continues to show him the Dark Tower, but he also sees the fall of Gilead to Farson. Their triumph in Mejis only bought the Affiliation another couple of years.

• • •

EDDIE, SUSANNAH AND JAKE are amazed by Roland's story. "To have gone through all that . . . and *at fourteen,*" Susannah says. They see the gunslinger in a new light, understanding better how and why his emotions have been stripped away.

Roland feels better for having told the story. Jake hugs him, and Eddie thinks it's probably the first hug the gunslinger has received in a long time.[26] Eddie had been afraid Roland was going to tell him that he had killed Susan himself, for his "damned Tower." Susannah realizes that Roland believes that's exactly what he did.

They continue along the interstate, asking questions. Jake asks what became of Sheemie. Roland says he followed them, though he doesn't know how. When they left in search of the Dark Tower, Sheemie started out with them as a sort-of squire. He understands how the boy managed to keep up with them when he later learns of Sheemie's teleportation skills.

Jake spots a note left under a vehicle's windshield wiper. "The old woman from the dreams is in Nebraska. Her name is Abigail.[27] The dark man is in the west. Maybe Vegas."[28]

They encounter four pairs of shoes[29] and a set of four booties lined up on the road before them. The footwear is tailored for the gunslingers' individual personalities. Susannah's are designed to fit over her stumps. The three erstwhile New Yorkers immediately make the connection to *The Wizard of Oz*.[30] Jake clicks the heels of his red leather oxfords together, to no effect. They tell Roland the story—which Eddie and Susannah had mentioned to him near Shardik's portal—and he identifies with Dorothy's desire to get back home again. The ka-tet wants that, too, but for them home is the Path of the Beam. They carry their new footwear toward the Emerald Palace. Ka will tell them when to use the shoes.

A flag bearing the Crimson King's eye flies over the palace. A gate of neonlike tubes blocks their way. Each bar is a different color, representing the thirteen Wizard's balls. Living creatures—fish, birds, horses—swim within the colored lights, some disquietingly human, perhaps symbolic of the twelve guardians.

The interstate expires beyond this barrier. Jake senses they can get through the gate using their shoes. Once they successfully train Oy to click his heels together, the black bar explodes. On the other side, omens and warnings attempt to discourage them from their path.

They enter the palace and find a chamber that is a cross between the Wizard of Oz's domain and Blaine's Barony Coach. The putative Wizard greets them in Blaine's voice over a PA system. As in *The Wizard of Oz,* doglike Oy pulls away the curtain to reveal the Tick-Tock Man. Eddie and Susannah kill him before he can do anything, never stopping to consider that the only way he could have gotten here ahead of them is by magic, perhaps through a door.

The real wizard sits behind them: Randall Flagg, whom Roland knew as Marten, the betrayer in his father's court. Marten reminds Roland that they met during the last days of Gilead, when his first ka-tet was preparing to go west in search of the Tower. "I know you saw me, but I doubt you knew until now that I saw you, as well."

Like Lucifer tempting Christ, Flagg promises Roland and the others an easier life if they would just "give over this stupid and hopeless quest for the Tower." To a man, woman, child and billy-bumbler, the members of the ka-tet all answer "No."

Roland's Mid-World gun is useless against Flagg, so he draws Jake's father's gun. His maimed hand fails him briefly and the gun sight gets caught in his belt buckle long enough for Flagg to disappear, leaving the pink Wizard's Glass behind. Flagg was genuinely taken by surprise and if Roland hadn't faltered, the wizard might have been killed—or so he later claimed.

Winning the Emerald Palace returns them to the Path of the Beam. The voice of ka tells Roland he can't continue until he tells the last scene of his story. The only way to show his friends the truth is to take them inside the Wizard's Glass. Everything around them is tinged pink. When they travel via Black Thirteen, a black pall clouds their vision. As in her later todash trips, Susannah's legs are restored to her.

"I lost my one true love at the beginning of my quest for the Dark Tower. Now look into this wretched thing, if you would, and see what I lost not long after."

After he got back from Mejis, the ball showed Roland an assassination plot against his father. Farson's agents passed a poisoned knife to the castle's chief of domestic staff, who was to pass it on to the actual assassin, Roland's mother. The toxin came from Garlan, the same place Flagg got the poison he used against King Roland of Delain. Roland reported the intermediary to his father, but decided to give his mother a chance to stop her foolishness, recover her sanity and return to her husband's side. "He has saved her from herself once, he will tell her, but he cannot do it again."

Filled with dread, Eddie, Jake, Susannah and Oy follow the young Roland and see with their own eyes what Roland can't bear to tell them.

Roland's mother stole the grapefruit to give to Marten as a consolation prize for failing to murder her husband. Inside Gabrielle Deschain's chamber, the ka-tet sees what Roland does not—a pair of shoes beneath the drapes near the window. A shadowy figure appears with a snakelike object in its hands. The ka-tet believes it is Rhea of Cöos, still bearing the decaying body of her dead snake, Ermot, come to retrieve the Wizard's Glass and punish the boy who caused her so much trouble.

Roland sees her reflection in the ball. He turns and fires at the figure, which transforms back into his mother. In her hands she carries a belt she had made for him.[31] It's a scenario befitting any Greek tragedy: Roland used his father's guns to kill his mother.

Rhea appears to the ka-tet in the pink ball, first as the Wicked Witch of the East, again beseeching them to cry off their quest. Like any good deceiver, she tempts them with the truth, telling them to ask Roland what happened to Cuthbert, Alain or Jamie. "He never had a friend he didn't kill, never had a lover who's not dust in the wind!"

The pink ball—the only real thing in this group vision—self-destructs, returning them to Mid-World. Roland tells them he saw Rhea once more and, without elaborating, implies that he killed her.

Time has slipped again and they have no way to tell how much. They've apparently been walking during the vision: The Emerald Palace is at least thirty miles behind them. The cloud pattern tells them that they are back on the path to the Tower.

In their packs they find food and drink, provided by ka or Flagg (or, according to Eddie, the Keebler Elves). They find a message from Flagg: "Next time I won't leave. Renounce the Tower." Beneath it, a sketch of a cloud emitting a bolt of lightning, the symbol for Thunderclap.

Roland suggests that the others should consider Flagg's advice, since he has a reputation for getting his friends killed. "I'm aware this is probably my last chance to love. . . . For the first time since I turned around in a dark room and killed my mother, I may have found something more important than the Tower."

However, ka has changed the New Yorkers. They don't want to go back to the worlds they came from—and how would they get there if they did? In Stephen Donaldson's *Chronicles of Thomas Covenant, the Unbeliever,* the protagonist is drawn from the normal world into a fantasy land and refuses to believe or participate in what happens to him there. Eddie, Susannah and Jake not only believe in their situation, but they also make the quest their own. Hand in hand, the four travelers, with Oy two paces ahead, return to the Path of the Beam, leaving their red shoes behind in a pile as they continue on the road to the Dark Tower.

While the contemporary action in *Wizard and Glass* takes Roland and his ka-tet much closer to their destination—they start at the beginning of Mid-World and arrive close to where End-World begins, traveling farther in a few hours than Roland has covered in a millennium—that part of the journey does not demand much growth from its participants, which is the normal result of a quest. Travelers must usually scratch and claw for every inch of progress, but King put his cast on an express train and rocketed them halfway across the continent.[32]

Through his story, Roland lays himself bare as he explains how he came to be the hardened loner the members of his ka-tet met when they arrived through their respective doors. His development since leaving Mejis isn't growth; it's attrition. It will take this ragtag group of erstwhile New Yorkers—and one billy-bumbler—to help him recover his soul.

Cleansing the soul to attain the purity required to achieve a goal is another element of questing. Roland willingly accepts responsibility for his crimes—killing his mother and causing Susan Delgado's death—though the members of his ka-tet do not blame him for his actions. His decision to forsake the woman he loved to undertake a seemingly impossible quest to save all existence impresses on his followers the seriousness of their task.

The story of *Wizard and Glass* is tragedy upon tragedy. The star-crossed lovers are straight out of Shakespeare, and Roland's matricide owes a debt to the ancient Greeks. That Gabrielle Deschain—who betrayed her husband and planned to execute him with her own hands—perhaps earned her death does not mitigate the tragedy. Just as no parent should live to see a child die, no child should have to live knowing he was the instrument of a parent's demise. "A man doesn't get past such a thing," Roland says. "Not ever."

In an online interview at the *Dark Tower* Web site in 1997, Peter Straub said the flashback "offers a nice counter-rhythmic backwash to the surging forward progress of the saga as a whole." Fans and reviewers expressed admiration for King's literary style in this flashback section while simultaneously admitting to impatience at wanting him to get on with the contemporary story. "I think this is a very interesting way to tell a story, that is, by literalizing the story-telling," Straub said, comparing the technique to one Joseph Conrad used in *Heart of Darkness*.[33]

In 1994, King said he knew the remainder of the series, and in the afterword to *Wizard and Glass,* he outlines the general shape of the final three books. He could never have foreseen how his own personal version of ka would intervene. In July 1999, King's world was turned upsidedown when he was struck by a Dodge minivan. The incident changed his life, but it also provided inspiration for his writing and became an important plot element in the finale of the *Dark Tower* series.

ENDNOTES

[1] Robert Browning, "Childe Roland to the Dark Tower Came." Unless otherwise specified, the quotes in this chapter are from *Wizard and Glass*.

[2] This is reminiscent of the game of riddles Bilbo Baggins and Gollum play beneath the mountain in *The Hobbit*.

[3] One of the inspirations King used in *Misery*—as long as Paul Sheldon continued to work on his next *Misery* novel, Annie had reason to keep him alive.

[4] In the original version of *The Gunslinger,* Walter claims to have come from England.

[5] Archie Bunker's wife from *All in the Family* in the 1970s.

[6] Susannah tells Little Blaine that the world would be a better place with his "big brother" gone. These words must resonate with Eddie, whose world was likely better off without Henry, his big brother.

[7] The same flu that ravaged the world in *The Stand,* a book that introduced an evil man named Randall Flagg. Roland is familiar with Flagg—more familiar than he realizes—from the final days of Gilead. He believes Flagg is a demon. "Hot on his heels had come two young men who looked desperate and yet grim, men named Dennis and Thomas"—two characters from *The Eyes of the Dragon,* which also featured a demonic wizard called Flagg.

[8] Kansas City Monarchs, Takuro Spirit and Nozz-A-La, respectively. Some of these brands will appear in future *Dark Tower* books, usually as an indication that a world is not Keystone Earth. Nozz-A-La is also featured prominently in *Kingdom Hospital,* a TV miniseries written by King that aired on ABC in 2004.

[9] The bullets work in much the same way that Eddie's hand-carved key blocked the ricocheting dual memories Roland had been suffering from before Jake was drawn into Mid-World. Roland and Eddie use bullets as earplugs in the Doorway Cave near Calla Bryn Sturgis to block the voices.

[10] This is a hint of Roland's repeat journeys through his past, doing things a little differently each time. After he passes through the Tower, the past rearranges itself to put Arthur Eld's horn among his gunna.

[11] Mejis is a twin to Mexico. Many of the barony's cultural traditions, including garb and vocabulary, are Mexican.

[12] His sigul is the red eye of the Crimson King. He started as a stage-robber in Garlan and has grown to a general. His "persuasive" style of politics is rather like Greg Stillson's from *The Dead Zone*. Like Randall Flagg, whom he may well be, he brooks no intolerance and has been known to leave cities after "state visits" with the local politicians' heads on spikes at the town's entrance. "Death is what John Farson is all about," Roland tells Susan Delgado, warning her that his influence may one day extend to Mejis.

[13] The blue coffin-shaped tattoos the Big Coffin Hunters sport on the webbing between thumb and forefinger of their right hands is also used by the low men/Regulators in *Wolves of the Calla*.

[14] Addictions plague the cast of the *Dark Tower*. Eddie has drugs, Callahan has alcohol, Calvin Tower has acquisitiveness, Patrick—who lies much farther down the road—has drawing and Roland has the Tower. Rhea has the pink Wizard's Glass.

[15] Named after a victim of Ted Bundy who survived.

[16] Cordelia was King Lear's disinherited daughter in the Shakespeare play that was the source of the line "Childe Roland to the Dark Tower Came."

[17] Thorin has a wife, but she can't bear him children. As a "gilly," it will be Susan's obligation to bear Thorin's child or children until he has an heir.

[18] Cordelia is reminiscent of Bobby Garfield's mother from "Low Men in Yellow Coats" in the way she uses her parental authority to mislead her ward into believing their financial situation is poor to justify her actions. Cordelia sold Susan to the mayor for twenty-four pieces of silver and twelve pieces of gold.

[19] In Mid-World, every town has its version of a story about star-crossed lovers, a tale that often ends in a murder-suicide. The Hambry version featured lovers named Robert and Francesca.

[20] Literally—a meteor passes over their heads on the night they meet.

[21] Cuthbert's alter ego, Arthur Heath, is from Gilead, which, to the people of Mejis, is as if he were from heaven.

[22] Her father would have told her it was ka, which will "come like a wind, and your plans will stand before it no more than my da's barn stood before the cyclone when it came."

[23] Olive Thorin can't bear children, which was "what opened the door to this horrible situation in the first place."

[24] Mia, who will bear Roland's child, also calls herself daughter of none.

[25] Though Rhea isn't a vampire per se, she shares some characteristics with those creatures and is, perhaps, an augury of the real vampires that will enter the series in the next book.

[26] Mercy, the blind woman in River Crossing, hugged Roland.

[27] "I think she's part of another story," Roland says. "But a story close to this one. . . . Next door maybe," Eddie replies.

[28] The west—the direction where failed gunslingers were sent when banished—is where Flagg set up his encampment in *The Stand*.

[29] Roland saw shoes tumbling through the air during his trip inside the Wizard's Glass in Gilead. The title of this section, "All God's Chillun Got Shoes," derives from a spiritual. In the slavery era, sons wore shoes and servants went barefoot. "When I get to heaven I'm goin' to put on my shoes/I'm goin to walk all over God's Heaven."

[30] It's not Roland's first exposure to Oz. During his vision in Mejis, Roland saw Rhea saying, "I'll get you, my pretty," like the Wicked Witch of the West.

[31] Roland promises to tell the others the tale of how he ultimately lost the belt, covered with his mother's blood, that he wore for many years. It bears on his quest, but is a tale for another day, one that hasn't yet been told.

[32] When Jack Sawyer finished his quest in *The Talisman,* rather than have him plod all the way back across America to his mother, he is conveniently driven back home in a chauffeured limousine.

[33] Peter Straub, in "The Dark Tower's Architecture," posted to the Penguin Web site in 1997. King pays homage to Conrad by naming a character in *Dreamcatcher* after Kurtz.

CHAPTER 6

WOLVES OF THE CALLA (RESISTANCE)

When gunslingers come to town, things get broken. It's a simple fact of life.[1]

The six-year gap between the publication of *Wizard and Glass* and *Wolves of the Calla* equals the longest pause in the story. Earlier, King had indicated that he wouldn't write an argument summarizing the events in the previous books, saying that Book V wasn't the place where readers should start the series. He must have had a change of heart, as "The Final Argument," a six-page synopsis, appears at the beginning of the book.

Unlike previous *Dark Tower* books, the opening of *Wolves of the Calla* doesn't feature Roland or any of his ka-tet. Instead, it starts in Calla[2] Bryn Sturgis, a rustic community on the banks of the River Whye—a long and busy commercial river similar to the Mississippi—at the edge of End-World. Farmer Tian Jaffords is plowing a rocky, cratered field he calls Son of a Bitch, "a thankless tract which mostly grew rocks and blisters and busted hopes." Mules are too valuable to risk on such a hellish field, so Tian's twin sister, Tia, drags the plow. Tia is "roont"—mentally handicapped and grown overlarge—and not good for much else.

Andy, a seven-foot messenger robot known to the Calla-folken for many generations and manufactured by North Central Positronics, arrives with grim news: The Wolves will come again in thirty days. Andy—who reminds Eddie of C3PO from *Star Wars*—doesn't always bear bad news; he's usually cheerful, bringing gossip, telling horoscopes or singing songs. No one knows where he gets his information, but he's never been wrong about the Wolves.

His announcement isn't a complete surprise. Once during each of the past five or six generations,[3] several dozen Wolves from Thunderclap—rumored to be warriors of the Crimson King—have descended upon Calla Bryn Sturgis.

The town's name acknowledges the classic Western *The Magnificent Seven*[4] as part of King's inspiration. In the movie, the people of a small Mexican village hire gunslingers to protect them from bandits who raid their village for food. They leave only enough so the people can struggle to survive and produce more food for the next raid.

The Wolves don't steal food; they steal children, one of every set of twins in a village where single births are the exception. Ka determines which twin is taken. Tian's great uncle was chosen because he was closer to the road than his grandfather. Tian and his wife, Zalia, have five children—the rare singleton will always be safe from the Wolves.

No one knows where the children are taken or why. After several weeks, most return on a train from the east, sunburned, covered in food and feces, and roont like Tia and Zalman, Zalia's brother. The older children come back with some vague understanding of what was stolen from them. Some commit suicide. Childlike until puberty, they suddenly grow into giants. Family members describe hearing bones grow inside the ruined bodies, calling to mind Brown's description of how his corn sighed and moaned after one of the desert's rare rains. The roont children all die long before their natural span of days.

Tian is a good man to receive this news. Smarter than the average farmer and semiliterate, he knows there was a time when the Wolves didn't raid his village. While others in the Calla accept the Wolves like drought or nightfall, Tian thinks it's time to fight back. He sends out the opopanax feather (the word "opopanax" was used frequently throughout *Black House*) to call a meeting of the menfolk, including a delegation of the Manni, a reclusive Amish-like religious sect who live on the edge of town.[5] Like Stu Redman in *The Stand,* Tian is an uncomfortable leader, but his anger drives him.

The town hall meeting is reminiscent of the scene in *Storm of the Century* where the townspeople debated over the future of a single child. The Calla faces the loss of half of its children. Several ideas are proposed, ranging from the cautious to the absurd. Leaving isn't an option. The Wolves would destroy the Calla in their absence and might even follow their trail and take the children, anyway. The men are farmers and know no other way of life. They are ill equipped to fight. A few rusty old rifles, spears, rocks and bows are poor weapons against guns, light sabers and flying metal drones called sneetches.[6]

Tian speaks passionately: "Each time they come and take our children, they take a little more of our hearts and our souls." Once the richer, more influential farmers speak, though, the meeting's momentum starts to shift. No one believes they can defeat the Wolves. They're farmers, not fighters.

An unlikely savior comes to his rescue: the man known as the Old Fella or Pere Callahan. Father Donald Callahan, late of 'Salem's Lot, Maine.[7] Tian feels like "a character in a silly festival play, saved at the last moment by some improbable supernatural intervention." Saved by ka, in other words.

Callahan has been in the Calla for about ten years, long enough to build a church and convert half the village to his religion, but he's still an outsider. He's never been there when the Wolves come. He's like the wise old man who lives on the edge of town in *The Magnificent Seven* who is consulted by the villagers, except Callahan doesn't wait to be asked, and ignores the ritual of passing the feather. His solution is similar to that suggested by the old Mexican—go north and hire men who deal in lead[8] to fight the battle for them; this refers to the gunslingers Andy told him are following the Path of the Beam four days northeast of town. Andy told Tian this news, too, but the farmer had been too overwrought to absorb it.

The Mexicans offered their hired guns a pittance: $20 each for several weeks of dangerous work. The people of the Calla get a better deal. Gunslingers are forbidden to take payment. Callahan has an ace in the hole, an object buried beneath the floor of his church that a gunslinger won't easily resist. Something that will kill Callahan if he doesn't get rid of it soon.

DURING THE APPROXIMATELY SEVEN WEEKS[9] since the ka-tet's run-in with Flagg, the clock has given them a slight reprieve, a little time-out, but it has started running against them again. Eddie's sensitivity to the passage of time might be attributed to his latent awareness of their somewhat unreal circumstances. When time slips back into gear, King may be answering the song of the Turtle.

Summer has come to an end, and fall, the time of harvest and festivals, is upon them. The weather reminds Eddie of the first week of November, which corresponds—coincidentally?—to the week *Wolves of the Calla* was published. But the Wolves' pending harvest is not a time of celebration for the people of Calla Bryn Sturgis.

The mystery number 19 has started appearing to the ka-tet everywhere they look. Eddie carves it on the side of a slingshot. They carry firewood in armloads of nineteen logs. Tree branches form the number's shape against the sky. Nineteen is the sum of the number of portals, Beams and the Tower that stands at their intersection, and was the magic word Walter provided Allie to access Nort's memories in Tull. It's also the number of oil derricks Roland encountered long ago in the fields of Mejis.[10]

Though he normally believes in omens and portents, Roland dismisses his ka-tet's infatuation with the number. He has other things on his mind. Susannah has manifested a new personality calling herself Mia, daughter of none. Roland recognizes her name as a word that was almost holy in Gilead, where it meant "mother" in High Speech.

Susannah has been experiencing some of the signs of pregnancy, but her periods have been regular except for one occasion before the ka-tet passed through Lud. She thinks it's a false pregnancy brought about by her strong desire to have Eddie's baby. Roland knows she's pregnant by the demon in the speaking circle.

Mia, fiercely protective of the "new chap" she carries, forages in the swamp for food at night, thinking that she's feasting in a castle banquet hall. Though she isn't an aspect of Susannah, Mia isn't yet fully formed, and some of Susannah's old memories merge with Mia's. The blue plates in the banquet hall remind the Detta within her of the "forspecial" one that belonged to her aunt. She smashes each one she encounters without understanding why.

Roland, who has been following her on her nightly expeditions, watches her strip to keep her clothes clean before she wades into a bog, devouring hand-crushed frogs and water rats, bringing to mind the lines from Stanza XXI of Browning's poem: "It may have been a water-rat I speared, / But, ugh! it sounded like a baby's shriek." She picks leeches from her legs and swallows them like candy. After her repast, she cleans herself and covers her tracks. Roland decides to keep this to himself for the time being, another of his many secrets.

Fueled by dream-inducing muffin balls[11]—berries the size of tennis balls—and their proximity to Black Thirteen, the Wizard's Glass Callahan possesses, Eddie, Jake and Oy travel to New York on the day in 1977 when Jake saw the rose in the vacant lot. Roland knows what's happening because he learned about todash from Vannay, the court tutor who taught his students from books. He sees them fade away, their bodies replaced by a dull gray glow that approximates the shapes and positions of their bodies, "as if something was holding their places in reality." In New York, they are invisible to others, though passersby sense their presence. As they cross over, they detect things—looming shapes behind weird phosphorescent eyes[12]—in the darkness between universes.

Jake notices subtle differences between this version of the day and what he remembers living through. Stephen King's name appears in place of John D. MacDonald's on the deli board at Calvin Tower's bookstore, for example. *Charlie the Choo-Choo* is now written by Claudia y Inez Bachman, the fictional widow of Richard Bachman, the pseudonym under which King wrote several novels. The extra *y* pads her name out to nineteen characters. The copyright date, 1936, adds up to 19. McCauley House published the book; Kirby McCauley was King's agent at the time. These are the first hints that King will become pivotal to the survival of the Dark Tower. Roland believes *Charlie the Choo-Choo* is important enough to ka that, in different worlds, different women wrote the same story.

Jake and Eddie learn that Calvin Tower has problems with Enrico Balazar, the crime lord Eddie would smuggle drugs for ten years later. That Balazar is involved personally impresses Eddie. Balazar and his thugs have Tower cornered in his storage-room office[13] leaving Aaron Deepneau to run the store.

Todash chimes announce that their time in New York is running out, but Eddie resists long enough to get the gist of the agreement between Balazar and Tower. He is drawn to see the paper Balazar is waving around, in the same way the Beam draws the ka-tet to the Tower. Balazar, acting on behalf of Sombra[14] Corporation, paid Tower $100,000 to not sell the vacant lot for a one-year period that expires in six weeks. Sombra is interested only in the rose, but they can't get at it until they own the ground it grows on. On the contract, Eddie sees Richard Patrick Sayre's name (which has nineteen characters), which Father Callahan will recognize when the group exchanges stories.

The next morning, Susannah suggests that they buy the land with her inheritance, which was worth millions in 1964. Roland believes that Tower has been holding the property for them. Subconsciously, he's the rose's guardian and has resisted selling the last piece of property he owns, in spite of its enormous value. Still, Balazar and his thugs could terrify him into selling it, even though everything else in the universe compels him not to.

They need two doors to accomplish their plan: one opening on 1964 to safeguard Susannah's fortune and the other to physically take them to 1977 to negotiate with Tower. Roland reminds his friends that the first time he ever encountered a door like the ones they need was on the beach a few months earlier. "You speak as though my world was . . . filled with magical doorways."

Father Callahan, part of the contingent from the Calla that has been clumsily shadowing the gunslingers for days, interrupts their palaver and introduces himself. He traces his history from Detroit in 1983, to Topeka, to New York, back to 'Salem's Lot, Maine. His first question of the ka-tet is not *where* they are from, but *when*.[15]

As a gunslinger, Roland must accept any formal plea for help even if it takes his ka-tet far afield from their quest. Even if it means they might die. "The way of ka is always the way of duty." He won't try to convince the people of the Calla to hire him, though. They must make that choice for themselves by answering affirmatively to three formal questions.

Callahan hints that he possesses something of value to offer if they agree to help. Though the suggestion angers Roland, he senses that Callahan wants to get rid of this object regardless of whether they help or not. Callahan is afraid of it, believing it has come alive. Roland guesses correctly that the object is Black Thirteen, the most powerful of the Wizard's glasses, "very likely the most terrible object from the days of Eld still remaining on the face of the earth." Dangerous as it is, it might provide the solution to their time-travel quandary.

The other members of the contingent join the group, including Wayne Overholser,[16] Ben Slightman and his son, Benny. Benny had a twin sister who died, apparently of pneumonia. No one is sure if he is still vulnerable to the Wolves or if he is now considered a singleton.

Andy predicts another trip todash for the ka-tet that night. Eddie quizzes him about the Wolves, their origin and how he knows they are coming. The robot requests a password to access this information, citing Directive Nineteen, the first hint that there might be more to him than meets the eye. The people who created Andy more than two thousand years ago couldn't have prevented him from speaking about something that has been going on for roughly two hundred years.

Overholser, the village's richest farmer, is also the strongest holdout to asking the gunslingers for help. Eddie is amazed by the way Roland handles the man, surprised primarily that Roland didn't simply kill him. Roland convinces Overholser to at least listen to their proposal. The farmer is frightened and wants to say yes, but he needs a reason to change his mind. If the Calla-folken choose badly, it could mean death for everyone. Part of his reluctance comes from not believing that Roland is really a gunslinger. Gilead has been dust in the wind for a thousand years. Roland stages an impromptu but convincing demonstration of their skills.

Roland proposes spending time surveying the land and talking to the folk. Later, they will request a meeting where he will tell the people if their town can be defended and how many men they'd want to help them. Though he now has a female gunslinger among his tet, he doesn't antici-pate that it will be primarily the women of the Calla who help during the battle.

That night, everyone goes todash to New York, including Susannah, who is delighted to find that she has legs again, not realizing they belong to Mia. Her new legs are either black—indicating that Mia hasn't sub-stantially taken over her body yet—or the darkness hides their color from the others. This New York is as novel to Susannah as it is to Roland; much has changed in thirteen years. Clouded by a pall cast by Black Thirteen, Roland senses despair and loss.

An extra day has passed in New York compared to in the Calla. If they spend a week in the Calla, two weeks might elapse here, perhaps more. Parallel sets of deadlines like this will haunt the ka-tet during the remain-der of their quest. While they attend to business in the Calla they will need to keep a watchful eye on what is happening in New York.

At the vacant lot, Jake notices that the graffiti about the turtle of enor-mous girth[17] has been replaced with "Oh **SUSANNAH-MIO,** divided girl of mine, Done parked her **RIG** in the **DIXIE PIG,** in the year of '99."

The message was probably written by the low men to tell Mia where to go to have her baby, but it will also help the ka-tet figure out where to look for Mia when she escapes after the battle with the Wolves.

Susannah stays behind while the others climb the fence to see the rose. She uses the excuse of having no shoes, but Roland suspects that Mia fears something dreadful might happen to her and her baby if they get too close to the rose. While she waits, seven minutes slip by during which Mia takes control of Susannah's body. When Mia recedes, Susannah's legs vanish, as does her fear of the rose.

Eddie and Roland see the rose for the first time. It opens at Roland's approach, as if in greeting. Its nineteen petals surround a scarlet furnace and a yellow sun burning at the center, but also a flickering purple glare that doesn't belong there, an indication of its illness. In the rose's glow, Eddie sees how ka intervened to enable many great events—or to prevent many horrible disasters—throughout history, and also how it influenced numerous small incidents to make people's lives better. The Big Combination powered the multiverse's evils, big and small; the rose is the advocate for multiuniversal good. The song it sings is "All might be well, that all manner of things might be well."[18]

Before they leave the vacant lot, Jake finds a pink bowling bag near where he found the key that got him back to Mid-World. Roland knows that ka has provided the bag made of metallic fiber to contain Black Thirteen and perhaps shield some of its terrible power, like the hat Burnside used to block Ty Marshall's strong powers in *Black House*. When Eddie later questions how they were able to bring the bag back with them when they found it while todash, Roland says that perhaps the bag is todash, too.

Susannah's scream at the sight of one of the vagrant dead brings the ka-tet rushing out of the vacant lot. The vags are people who either don't know they've died or refuse to accept it. Why King introduced vags into the story is unclear, as no further use is made of them. Susannah tells about her missing seven minutes, but Roland doesn't voice his concerns about what the lapse—coupled with the disappearance of her legs—might signify.

The next day, while riding back to the Calla, Benny Slightman invites Jake to stay at his ranch. Though they are similar in age, Jake's display of gunmanship permanently changed the dynamics of their relationship.

Jake gives Roland adult reasons for accepting Benny's invitation. Roland regrets that Jake is ashamed to just accept a friend's invitation to sleep over like the young boy he is. The gunslinger presided over the end of Eddie's childhood in the speaking circle outside Lud, and he knows that Jake's childhood is nearing its end, too.

Nearly a thousand people welcome the travelers, and the evening turns into a festival. After introductions—including of Oy, who wins the townspeople's hearts with a bow and a verbal greeting—Roland surprises and angers Eddie by turning the gathering over to him. He later realizes that Roland was getting him warmed up to talk to people during the ensuing banquet.

As they socialize, the gunslingers learn things that may prove important. Susannah hears that Tian's grandfather has evidence the Wolves can be killed. When Eddie later follows up with Gran-Pere Jaffords, he learns about the Wolves' vulnerable spots. The old man also tells them something crucial that King hides from readers.[19] He probably intends to build tension, but it seems like cheating to arbitrarily suppress one detail from a conversation when all else is revealed. Like Roland, King doesn't tell his followers everything and risks breaking his ka-tet by doing so. It reminds readers that they are at the whim of the author. The relationship between reader and storyteller can't be taken at face value.

Later, they dance and sing. Roland mounts the stage and, in the full emotion of the moment, asks the crowd two of the three questions necessary for the ka-tet to become involved in their affairs. The crowd answers as one: yes.[20] Roland reserves the final question for another time—he will only ask it once he knows what the answer will be. Then he surprises and charms everyone by performing the Rice Song, a chant combined with a jiglike tap dance familiar both to the people of the Calla and those of Gilead. At the height of the song's passion, Roland tumbles off the stage into the crowd and is swept away like a body surfer in a mosh pit.[21] Nothing could possibly top this performance—the party ends.

Roland is keeping two secrets from his ka-tet: Susannah's pregnancy and his suspicion that he's suffering from the dry twist, a fast-spreading arthritis that will eventually claim his most valuable tools—his hands.[22] Father Callahan's housekeeper, Rosalita Muñoz, treats his pain and welcomes Roland to her bed, his first lover since Alice in Tull.

He finally tells Eddie about Susannah's pregnancy and new personality, saying that the baby she carries isn't human. He knows this because Susannah is still having her periods. "The thing she's carrying scorns her woman's blood." Roland worries she may "foal" on the day the Wolves arrive. After all, coincidence has been canceled. They decide to keep the secret from Susannah. Eddie knows Roland is only interested in making sure she isn't distracted during their upcoming business, but he goes along to protect the rose. "That's the only thing worth risking her for." With this decision, Eddie becomes more like Roland than he'd ever admit—willing to keep secrets from his wife and entertain the possibility of sacrificing her for the quest.

Father Callahan tells his life story, starting with his part in the battle against 'Salem's Lot's vampires. He is sharing khef, which means he is part of their ka-tet. Roland believes Callahan will leave the Calla with them when their job is done.

When Callahan mentions author Ben Mears, Eddie recognizes the name. However, Eddie doesn't seem aware of Stephen King although he knows about Kubrick's movie version of *The Shining*. Perhaps in Eddie's world *The Shining* had a different author, as did

---

Concerning Vampires

Father Callahan, the resident expert on vampires, created a taxonomy of the creatures. He identified three types:

Type Ones, the grandfathers like Barlow, are few in number, live a long time, and may spend centuries hibernating. They're capable of making a large number of Type Two vampires in a short period of time. The scuttling black bugs known as grandfather fleas may herald their presence.

Type Twos, the undead, like those created in Salem's Lot, can make new vampires, but they're barely smarter than zombies. They can't go out in daylight without being blinded, badly burned or killed. Their ravenous hunger undoes them, so they normally don't survive very long. Type Two vampires generally create other Type Twos in a relatively small area, usually after the Type One vampire has moved on. Sometimes they create Type Threes.

Type Threes, which Callahan also calls pilot sharks, are like mosquitoes. They can't create other vampires, but they feed constantly and are AIDS carriers. Their victims are marked, drawing other vampires to feed on them. Type Threes are somewhat smarter than Type Twos. They can go out in daylight and take their principal sustenance from food. When killed, they leave behind only clothing, hair and teeth in a manner reminiscent of the creatures in "The Ten O'Clock People" from *Nightmares and Dreamscapes*.

The *Dark Tower* series features other kinds of vampires, too. The witch Rhea draws energy by drinking blood, as she does from Cordelia Delgado. The Little Sisters of Eluria are vampire nurses who once served the White but were later corrupted by the Great Poisoning, and Joe Collins, aka Dandelo, is an emotional vampire. Young Steve King feared that the red spiders in the barn would bite him and turn him into a vampire.

Charlie the Choo-Choo. Eddie later believes that King either exists only in Keystone Earth or what he does in other worlds doesn't matter.

Callahan tells about meeting and falling in love with Lupe Delgado in New York. Roland, of course, recognizes this surname. "Another coincidence that cannot possibly be a coincidence. Another click in a great turning cog." He leaves the city after the low men become aware that he's killing vampires. In Sacramento, Callahan works with a group of illegal aliens whose last names he will later encounter in the Calla.

He journeys across different versions of America on what Eddie dubs todash turnpikes. Callahan says they are as addictive as booze. Roland says, "Wandering's the most addictive drug there is, I think, and every hidden road leads on to a dozen more."

He dies on December 19, 1983, at 4:20 P.M. (the digits in 12/19 and 4:20 add up to nineteen) in a Detroit office tower when he falls for a trap set by Richard P. Sayre, the man whose name Eddie saw on the document in Tower's office. Under the threat of being infected with AIDS by vampires, Callahan commits suicide by throwing himself through a plate glass window.

After he dies, he finds himself in the presence of Walter o'Dim, who circled back to the way station to meet him shortly after Roland and Jake left. Callahan sees the gunslinger and the boy on the horizon. This is the only time Walter appears bearing the open red wound on his forehead identifying him as an agent of the Crimson King, which is usually an indicator of lesser minions like Sayre or the low men.

When Callahan demands to know where he is, Walter provides a literary answer: "So much backstory, so little time." He takes Callahan into the stable and shoves him through the freestanding doorway labeled UN-FOUND, sending Black Thirteen—the Eye of the Crimson King looking down from the Dark Tower—with him. Callahan is Walter's backup plan, another trap for the gunslinger. If Roland dies before reaching Calla Bryn Sturgis, Callahan will live a quiet, pastoral second life. If he somehow survives, Black Thirteen will surely kill Roland.

In the Calla, Callahan begins to preach again. The residents who already know about Jesus build him a church, and he hides Black Thirteen beneath its floor. The ball is another of the great EVILS Callahan once sought as a young priest. It seduces people to do terrible things by making them think they are doing something good. It encourages a kind of optimistic grandiosity. Black Thirteen sent him todash twice, once to Los Zapatos,[23] Mexico, in the mid-1990s for Ben Mears's funeral and once to the Castle of the Crimson King.

Callahan takes Roland into the church to see Black Thirteen. The ball is in a box made of black ironwood—called ghostwood in the *Tales of Arthur*—with three objects carved on top. Callahan says they are symbols from *Look Homeward, Angel*.[24] "A leaf, a stone, an unfound door." Perhaps the leaf of a rose plant. Roland feels the object's evil power and thinks that only the faith of the people in the church has kept it in check.

In the coming days, Roland surveys the community for people and weapons. Vaughn Eisenhart,[25] who opposes fighting the Wolves, owns a couple of dubious firearms.[26] His wife, Margaret, has a surprise for Roland. She relates the legend of Lady Oriza, who killed Gray Dick by decapitating him using a weighted dinner plate with a sharp rim after he murdered her father.

Margaret is Henchick of the Manni's granddaughter, but she abandoned the tribe because they are a peaceful people and below the surface she is not. The Manni call her one of "the forgetful." They believe she is damned for leaving them, which may be true given her fate during the battle with the Wolves.

She and her friends, the Sisters of Oriza—a women's social club with a deadly pastime that includes Zalia Jaffords and Rosalita Muñoz, Roland's new lover—have kept Lady Oriza's legacy alive, using modern plates made of titanium instead of glass. Though flustered with excitement, Margaret impresses Roland with her skill. He asks her to gather the four best throwers for a contest, and has Zalia instruct Susannah in the way of the Oriza. Susannah masters the skill quickly but she deliberately loses the contest so that a local woman can win. The victor is Roland's new companion, Rosalita. The gunslingers have their local help.

Things were easier for Roland when he traveled alone. He didn't have to decide with whom he could share information. He can't trust Susannah because of Mia, nor Eddie because he loves Susannah. Jake might let something slip to Benny Slightman, and Roland is suspicious of Benny's father, the only person in the Calla who wears glasses. Slightman says he got them by trading a colt to one of the merchants on the riverboat shops that occasionally passed the Calla. Jake's "touch" tells him Slightman is lying, but doesn't reveal that the glasses were actually part of his payment for betraying his neighbors and friends to the agents of Thunderclap.

Jake learns about Mia on his own through a dream about one of her foraging excursions where Mia thinks she's eating a roasted pig that resembles a baby but is really devouring one of Tian's pigs raw. In his dream, Jake hears her muttering about the Dixie Pig in New York, which will help him track her down when Mia takes her through the doorway later.

Roland's disease of secrecy infects other members of the ka-tet. Jake, alerted by Oy, sees Andy and Benny's father meeting clandestinely one night. Afterward, Slightman wades across the river in the direction of Thunderclap. Jake keeps this suspicious activity to himself, but he knows that if he takes matters too much into his own hands he'll have to face Roland in a test of manhood that he would surely lose. He would be sent east into Thunderclap in exile and shame.

He does confront Roland with his concerns about Susannah as they ride along the East Road, where the final battle against the Wolves will take place, a symbolic location for this tense confrontation between leader and follower, father and surrogate son. When Jake mistakes Roland's shame for anger, Roland realizes how badly their ka-tet is broken. They agree to tell Susannah before the Wolves come, but as late as possible. Jake reluctantly agrees to monitor Susannah with his touch to see if Mia is exerting more control.

Henchick, the Manni leader, takes Roland to the cave where they found Callahan. Someone local knew he was coming and left a message on a tape recorder[27] revealing where to find him. Both the door and the box containing Black Thirteen were open slightly. Henchick had been terrified by the glow coming from the door, which made him feel *dim,* perhaps Walter's lingering influence. In the box's blackness, Henchick saw the red eye of the Crimson King, someone Roland has heard of before but doesn't know much about. He knows only that he's either in Thunderclap or farther east. "I believe he may be a guardian of the Dark Tower. He may even think he owns it."

When Henchick shut the box, the door slammed closed, too, and hasn't opened since.

People who enter what was once known as the Cave of Voices hear condemning voices drawn from their memories, in a manner similar to the visions seen by the Sawyer Gang when they entered the Black House in Wisconsin.[28] Roland hears his mother and father, Walter, Cuthbert and Rhea.

The door is exactly like those Roland encountered on the beach. Etched upon it are a rose and the word UNFOUND in hieroglyphics. Roland knows Black Thirteen will open the door, and could take them to any place or any time.

While Roland and Henchick explore the cave, the members of his ka-tet go shopping using gold and silver coins and gems from a magic grow-bag, the last thing of magic Roland owns. Took,[29] the shopkeeper, opposes the gunslingers' mission because the Wolves once burned down the store when the townspeople tried to hide children there. However, he cannot turn down hard currency, though he drives hard bargains. Susannah enjoys bartering with him and putting him in his place when he gets too flippant.

Afterward, they sit on the porch in front of the store and greet the townspeople for five hours, answering a thousand difficult questions.

Callahan's Catholicism comes into play in three different ways during the buildup to the battle with the Wolves. First, he hears Roland's confession, which consists of his story from the time he draws Odetta from New York through his awareness of her pregnancy. Roland isn't looking for absolution, and gets none. Callahan tells Roland he has been a fool, "ka-mai."

Roland is afraid that Mia will take control of Susannah and go off somewhere to have the child. "I have every reason to believe it would begin its work by slaughtering the mother," he says, calling the child "poison with a heartbeat." Callahan chastises Roland for being more concerned about the breaking of the tet than the death of a friend. "I wonder if your friends know what sort of man you are," Callahan says. "They know," he responds.

Callahan's religious training also permits him to see another possibility for Susannah's predicament beyond Roland's assumption that Mia is a new personality, a notion that depresses Susannah once they as a group finally talk about her pregnancy. Callahan suggests that Mia might be possessing Susannah, though he doesn't go so far as to propose an exorcism.

Finally, when Roland proposes aborting the demon child, Callahan stands firm. Not only won't he let Roland suggest it, but Roland also must dissuade Susannah if she comes up with the idea herself. Callahan promises to raise the townspeople against the gunslingers if Roland won't agree.[30]

Callahan's strong beliefs concerning venal sins are hard to rationalize with his own suicide in Detroit. Roland doesn't know enough about Catholicism to raise this issue, though, and arguments about saving Susannah's life or all of creation won't sway Callahan. Roland regrets raising the subject, for in doing so he's eliminated a possible solution to their problem. Callahan tells him, "It won't be first time you mistook your will for ka, would it?"

Eddie is nervous about the passage of time in New York. He believes that the world containing the rose is a special reality where they can't double back. Each time they cross over, it will be later. They can't afford to miss the July 15 deadline.

He has a simpler plan than the one they discussed outside the Calla. He believes Tower will sell them the vacant lot for a token amount—a dollar—because he's been waiting for them to come along. Even though Tower thinks he'd be better off without the lot, he's kept it all these years, in much the same way that Father Callahan has guarded the black Wizard's Glass.

Eddie and Roland take Black Thirteen to the Doorway Cave in Jake's bowling bag. Roland waits in the cave with bullets in his ears to block out the cave's voices.

Three weeks have passed since their last trip to New York. Eddie finds two of Balazar's thugs, George Biondi and Jack Andolini, threatening to burn Tower's valuable books unless he will make a verbal commitment to sell the lot to them after their option expires. Eddie surprises the men, whom he knows from his own time, though they won't know him for another decade. He uses his knowledge of Andolini's family to intimidate the thug before sending him back to Balazar. He's sufficiently brutal to make Balazar's chief lieutenant believe the message he is to deliver: Calvin Tower is off-limits. Eddie invents a new company and tells Andolini that Tower will be selling the lot to Tet Corporation, not Sombra.

After Andolini is sent on his way, Tower comments that some of Eddie's diction reminds him of language from a book by Benjamin Slightman Jr.[31] The cover shows a building that resembles a wooden Quonset hut. On the title page, the book is called *The Hogan,* but the cover says

The Dogan, a word that doesn't exist. Tower tells Eddie that this and other printing mistakes make the book valuable.[32]

Tower begrudgingly agrees to sell the vacant lot for a dollar, with the promise of fair market value later. Aaron Deepneau is a lawyer, as ka would have it, and Eddie tells Tower to get him to draw up the contract. Once he recovers from his scare, though, Tower has second thoughts, displaying the stubbornness that kept him from selling to Sombra long ago.

He finally agrees that if Eddie can tell him the name on a piece of paper in an old envelope with Tower's great-great-great-grandfather's name and the UNFOUND hieroglyphics on it, he'll do as Eddie asks. Another riddle for Eddie to solve, this one affecting the fate of all of creation. He guesses true: The paper says "Roland Deschain, of Gilead, The line of ELD, GUNSLINGER."

Eddie knows how Balazar will react to Andolini's report and warns Tower to get out of New York until July 15. Tower resists until Eddie finally convinces him of the danger he's in. Eddie instructs him to have Deepneau write the zip code of where they're going on the vacant lot's fence. Before Eddie leaves, Tower convinces him to transfer a shelf of his most valuable books through the UNFOUND door. He correctly assumes that Balazar will burn down the store when he discovers Tower has left town.

Jake takes it upon himself to figure out why Benny Slightman's father and Andy are sneaking around at night. Oy leads him along the path Slightman took toward Thunderclap, where they find a Quonset hut resembling the Dogan from Benjamin Slightman's novel.

Inside the North Central Positronics outpost—which he accesses by guessing the entry code—Jake finds a bank of monitors. Of those that still work, some show different parts of the Calla, explaining how the Wolves know where the townspeople hide their children or if they plan to resist. Fortunately, the ka-tet held most of its palavers out of sight of these cameras.

On another monitor Jake sees Andy and Slightman approaching. From his closet hiding place, he learns that Slightman is cooperating with Andy to guarantee Benny's safety. His son's twin sister is dead, making Benny especially vulnerable to the Wolves.

Andy relays an intelligence report to Finli O'Tego at Algul Siento[33]— where the Breakers are being held—and reveals the real reason he warns the townspeople about the Wolves: He enjoys the grief it brings them. "Each tear's a drop of gold." Shortly after meeting the robot, Eddie had suspected Andy's pleasure at the discomfort of humans, but he didn't follow up on it.

Jake understands the conflict of duty. In spite of their friendship, he must report Benny's father as a traitor, thinking it might be a worse betrayal than when Roland let him fall to his death. His dilemma is complicated by the fact that he's never been good at making friends his own age and now he has a good one he will have to let down.

After he reports what he learned, he begs Roland to spare Slightman. Roland says he'll do what he can, but he's not sure it's a mercy because Slightman will be through in the Calla if they win.

As the day of the battle draws near, Roland sends Callahan to New York to retrieve the zip code of Tower's destination. Only one day has elapsed, but The Manhattan Restaurant of the Mind has been torched. Callahan hears the voice of the rose for the first time and understands the nature of Roland's quest. He feels part of their ka-tet.

While Callahan is in New York, Roland finds *'Salem's Lot* on Tower's bookshelf in the cave. He keeps his discovery secret—even from readers—not wanting to distract the ka-tet from the upcoming battle.

Eddie accompanies Callahan to the Doorway Cave the next time. While Callahan delivers a note to Tower and Deepneau in Stoneham, Maine, Eddie notices something sewn into the lining of the bowling bag Jake found in the vacant lot, but the voices in the cave distract him from exploring further.[34] Callahan realizes that he can no longer see Eddie through the open doorway. He returns just in time to save Eddie from jumping off the edge of the cliff, having been convinced by the voices that he could fly to the Tower.

The time comes to learn how the Calla-folken want to proceed. Roland gathers them at the pavilion where he danced the commala. Tian, plagued by worries about what he's set into motion, fears Roland will perform the death dance this time.

After asking the first two questions again, Roland poses the third, crucial question: Do you seek aid and succor from us? The townspeople respond with a resounding yes, except for a few dissenting voices and abstentions. Much of the plan Roland lays out is a lie, since he knows that Slightman will report what he says to whoever is in charge of the Wolves.

With Tian's help, the night before the battle Eddie sets a trap for Andy and shoots out the robot's eyes. He guesses the robot's access code based on Jake's experience at the Dogan and shuts him down permanently. Rosa suggests they bury him beneath the floor of Father Callahan's privy. Roland believes Andy killed Benny's sister to make someone in the village vulnerable to being coerced into spying on his own people, and suspects that the robot has been doing something similar for generations.

Slightman realizes he's been uncovered, partly because of what they've done to Andy and partly because he's sensed a change in the way Jake relates to him. The morning of the battle, he asks Roland what will become of him. Roland tells him that if he fights hard to save the children, and the ka-tet defeats the Wolves, Roland won't expose him as a traitor. However, he says the best thing that could happen is for Slightman to die a hero. That way there's no chance Benny will ever find out that his father sold out for a pair of glasses and some other trinkets.

Slightman tells Roland about the Breakers,[35] humans with extrasensory powers who eat normal food but also need something extra to nourish their mental talents. The only source of this brain food is twins, who possess a chemical that links them mind to mind. Slightman doesn't realize that the Breakers are working to destroy the Tower.

Finally, Roland reveals what he and the ka-tet have known since Eddie's talk with Gran-Pere: The Wolves and their horses are robots. Their hoods cover tiny rotating dishes like the one atop Shardik and his robotic menagerie.

The moment a cloud of dust in the distance heralds the Wolves' arrival, things start to go wrong. Jake, Benny and two other children are trapped in the open while leaving a false trail. Roland knows what's happening but leaves Jake to handle the situation. He can't justify risking the hundred children hiding in the rice fields for four, even if one of them is his surrogate son.

Roland's fears about Susannah bear out. Her water breaks before the battle begins. Mia tries to take control, but Susannah fights her. She promises to help Mia with the baby if Mia will allow Susannah to finish her part. Rather than struggle in the middle of a war, Mia agrees.

The Wolves enter Roland's trap. The gunslingers and the Sisters of Oriza, a total of seven defenders, arise from the blind and attack their sixty-one opponents (19 upside-down), dispatching many of the Wolves before they realize they've been misled.

Margaret Eisenhart is the first defender killed, beheaded by one of the Wolves' glow sticks, reminiscent of a *Star Wars* light saber.[36] Her head lands next to Benny Slightman, surprising him into leaping from cover only to be destroyed by a sneetch.[37] Later, Roland asks Father Callahan for a blessing against the curse Vaughn Eisenhart promised to bring upon him if Margaret died during the battle.

Eddie, Jake and Roland, assisted by Rosa, destroy most of the remaining Wolves. Jake, enraged by Benny's death, turns into a killing machine, much like Roland was in Tull. Eddie and Roland leave the last two Wolves for him. He in turn leaves the last one for Susannah, who couldn't follow them up the path.

As Roland predicted, "you'll wonder what all the planning and palaver was for, when in the end it always comes down to the same five minutes' worth of blood and stupidity." He tells the people of the Calla that they now know the secret of how to defeat the Wolves, though they'll probably never see them again.

> ### Lucky Seven
>
> Seven is a mystical number in many cultures, but the seven defenders of the Calla refer directly to *The Magnificent Seven*. Susannah lost seven minutes as Mia in New York. Andy the robot is seven feet tall. Seven weeks have elapsed at the beginning of the book since the ending of *Wizard and Glass*. Mia was promised seven years with her chap. Young Stephen King was seven when he was sent to the barn as punishment. Walter's tarot reading consisted of seven cards, and seven Losers stood against the creature in *It*, who commented on the number's talismanic quality. And, of course, there are seven volumes in the *Dark Tower* series.

In the confusion following the battle, Mia takes charge of Susannah's body. After she wrecks Susannah's wheelchair, she transfers to an ATV that someone—probably Andy before he was decommissioned—left for her, so she can make it up the hill to the Doorway Cave. When she passes through, she takes Black Thirteen with her, sealing the door.

Rosa notices Susannah is missing, and the ka-tet follows her trail. Along the way, Eddie finds the hand-carved wooden ring that Susannah wore around her neck because it was too big for her hand. Mia had no use for it and cast it aside, but told Susannah that the Crimson King is on her trail and she doesn't want Eddie's scent associated with her. "Later, if ka wills, you may wear it again." [DT6]

When the ka-tet reaches the cave and realizes the door is locked against them, Roland shows them *'Salem's Lot,* saying it represents the heart of perhaps the greatest mystery. Jake recognizes the author's name from the deli board outside Tower's bookstore. The church on the dust jacket resembles both the Calla Gathering Hall and the Stoneham Methodist Meeting Hall, which Father Callahan saw earlier.

Like Sancho Panza from *Don Quixote,* who also discovers he's a character in a book, Father Callahan doesn't understand how someone could have written a story that contains details only he knew, things that happened when he was alone. Unlike Don Quixote, Callahan isn't concerned over whether he has been portrayed accurately or adequately in the novel. Don Quixote knows he's real; Father Callahan is no longer sure.

Apart from being Father Callahan's creator, Stephen King will become an increasingly important presence in the series. His fate and ka are inextricably commingled.

The ka-tet still has a dual imperative. Where once they had to save the Calla from the Wolves and protect the rose, now they have to find Susannah and protect the rose. The rose, which represents the Tower, is ultimately the more important task, but Roland has softened enough to accept that he cannot ignore one of his ka-tet as he once abandoned Jake in the name of his quest. The linear nature of time in Keystone Earth means they have to carefully plan their strategy. They can't go back to fix any mistakes they make, a catchall of time-travel stories.

Wolves of the Calla's ending is not as much of a cliff-hanger as the ending of *The Waste Lands,* but it leaves some pressing business—the question of Susannah's pregnancy—unfinished. King says the fifth and sixth books of the series "both end on notes that [make] you really want to know what happens next."[38]

For the first time, though, readers knew exactly how long they had to wait for the next installment—seven months—because the follow-up was already written and its publication date set well before *Wolves of the Calla* was released.

ENDNOTES

[1] Unless otherwise indicated, all quotes in this chapter come from *Wolves of the Calla*.
[2] "Calla" isn't pronounced like the first part of "Callahan," but more like the beginning of "cauliflower"—Kaw-la.
[3] Pennywise from *It* also returned once per generation to prey on the children of Derry.
[4] Which is in turn based on the Japanese movie *The Seven Samurai,* directed by Akira Kurosawa.

[5] They also lived on the perimeter of Gilead in Roland's time. Brown the farmer's wife was of the Manni. They are also known as sailors on ka's wind.

[6] George Telford says, "They can strip a man from top to toe in five seconds, leaving nothing around him but a circle of blood and hair."

[7] While King once considered doing a sequel to 'Salem's Lot, he later declared that the time for such a story had passed, but he was still interested to see what happened to the failed priest who snuck out of town on a Greyhound bus. He hinted in the afterword to Wizard and Glass that Callahan would have a part to play in the story.

[8] This famous phrase was uttered by Steve McQueen's character in The Magnificent Seven. King—as Richard Bachman—also used it as an epigraph in The Regulators.

[9] This is Eddie's rough estimate, corroborated by the fact that Susannah has had two menstrual periods since they left the Emerald Palace.

[10] Once readers start combing King's other works, they will undoubtedly turn up 19 everywhere. When Roland robs Katz's Drugs, the police dispatcher calls Code 19. Many characters have things happen to them at that age, but it's also the page of the manuscript in Bag of Bones where Mike Noonan finds his subconscious message, and the last number Johnny Smith played at the Wheel of Fortune just before his accident in The Dead Zone. The digits in Donald M. Grant's zip code add up to 19.

[11] Eddie is reluctant to try them at first because they remind him of the poisoned mushrooms served in the Shirley Jackson novel We Have Always Lived in the Castle. This is Jackson's first direct mention in the series, though her spirit was invoked by the deadly lottery Eddie and Susannah witnessed in Lud.

[12] In Black House, Jack Sawyer goes todash during his first dream of Speedy. "[I]t is the mad sound of that laughter which follows Jack Sawyer down into the darkness between worlds" [BH], which seems to describe todash spaces. Later, when Jack remembers how to flip, he dissolves into a shimmering gray glow like those Roland saw, but he goes farther and the glowing placeholder vanishes as he goes fully to the other side.

[13] The wall calendar behind Tower's desk features a picture of Robert Browning, author of the poem "Childe Roland to the Dark Tower Came." The shop cat's name is Sergio, a nod to Sergio Leone, director of spaghetti westerns often featuring Clint Eastwood.

[14] "Sombra" means "shadow" in Spanish.

[15] He asks Eddie, who is the only one from a when later than his own, whether the Red Sox, King's favorite baseball team, had won the World Series yet. As of 2003, this team still has not found favor with ka. In fact, mere days before Wolves of the Calla went on sale, the Red Sox once again played the role of ka-mai, losing to their longtime rivals, the Yankees, a mere five outs away from making it to the World Series.

[16] Overholser is named for a real Western writer who started publishing in the 1930s. Calvin Tower told Jake his name "sounds like the footloose hero in a Western novel— the guy who blows into Black Fork, Arizona, cleans up the town, and then travels on. Something by Wayne D. Overholser, maybe." Fictional King made this connection after Roland and Eddie leave him, also mentioning the auspiciously named real-life Western author Ray Hogan.

[17] "On his shell he holds the earth / If you want to run and play, / Come along the BEAM today."

[18] The origin of the quotation is a fifteenth-century English mystic named Julian or Juliana of Norwich. In her book Revelations of Divine Love, she wrote, "All shall be well, all

shall be well, and all manner of things shall be well." Peter Straub encountered this quote in a novel by Muriel Spark and used it first in *The Talisman*. [Personal communication.]

[19] In *From a Buick 8,* Sandy Dearborn (Will's distant relative?) picks up something from the shed, but King hides what it is until it comes into play during a climactic scene.

[20] Will you open to us if we open to you? Do you see us for what we are, and accept what we do? Roland later asks these questions of individual people. Even those against confronting the Wolves can agree to these two questions.

[21] "Roland stage-dives like Joey Ramone," Eddie says. The Ramones are one of King's favorite rock bands. He wrote the liner notes for the 2003 tribute album *We're a Happy Family.*

[22] Roland realizes later that his ailments reflect the injuries Stephen King will suffer on June 19, 1999.

[23] "All God's Chillun Got Shoes."

[24] By Thomas Wolfe. In his vision of a rose, a key and a door in *The Waste Lands,* Eddie saw a copy of Wolfe's *You Can't Go Home Again.*

[25] Perhaps named for actor Robert Vaughn of *The Magnificent Seven.*

[26] In a rare display of droll humor, Roland tells Eisenhart he might as well stick one of his rifles in the ground. "Maybe it'll grow something better."

[27] The cassette player also played a song, "Someone Saved My Life Tonight," that made Callahan weep.

[28] Thinnies produce a similar effect. In the vacant lot, the phenomenon is extended to the visualization of the phantoms of people's lives.

[29] Another nod to *The Lord of the Rings*. The Tooks were a well-respected hobbit family. In the Calla, the greedy store owner's name is almost literal.

[30] Roland has already had at least one town rise up against him. However, he's here to save the people of the Calla. He wasn't similarly invested in the folks of Tull.

[31] Slightman's full name consists of nineteen characters. While Wayne D. Overholser is named after a real writer, Slightman isn't, probably because Slightman the Elder is traitorous. The fictional Slightman also wrote science fiction novels about multiple universes under the name Daniel Holmes, which is Odetta's father's name.

[32] An error on the dust jacket and its small first printing is why *'Salem's Lot* appears among Tower's collection of rare books, though King isn't particularly famous in 1977.

[33] First mentioned in the revised edition of *The Gunslinger*. Roland met a taheen looking for a place by that name.

[34] "[It] was Susannah who eventually found it, and when she did, she was no longer herself."

[35] Breakers were introduced in "Low Men in Yellow Coats" *(Hearts in Atlantis)*, and play an important part in *Black House*. Ted Brautigan, who will return in *The Dark Tower,* is a Breaker.

[36] They don't just seem to be light sabers—they really are *Star Wars* light sabers. The Wolves' masks are all Dr. Doom from Marvel Comics. Eddie remembers him as being from *Spider-Man* but Dr. Doom was primarily a *Fantastic Four* villain.

[37] They are the Harry Potter model. None of the ka-tet recognizes the reference, since the first Harry Potter novel was published after Eddie's time.

[38] Interview with Ben Reese, published on Amazon.com, May 2003.

CHAPTER 7

SONG OF SUSANNAH (REPRODUCTION)

Terrible surgeons waited to deliver her of her equally terrible chap.[1]

Except for a short preamble in Calla Bryn Sturgis, *Song of Susannah* takes place during a twenty-four-hour period, though the action occurs in two different decades: July 9, 1977, and June 1, 1999. Instead of chapters, the book is divided into stanzas, each ending with a "stave" and a "response," like the Rice Song Roland performed for the people of the Calla.

Only a few hours have elapsed since the ka-tet learned that Susannah and Mia passed through the UNFOUND door, taking the key—Black Thirteen—with them. The group descends from the Doorway Cave to Callahan's rectory to plan their next steps.

Their main problem is figuring out how to open the door again. Roland has two destinations in mind: Maine in 1977 to complete their property deal with Calvin Tower, and wherever and whenever Susannah went. The Manni—who know the secrets of traveling to other worlds—might be able to use their magic to reopen it on the last two places it accessed.

Concerned that Susannah may deliver her cannibalistic baby at any time, Eddie is eager to get started, but the Manni won't go to the cave at night. The ka-tet has several clocks running against them—Susannah's pregnancy, the deadline to close the deal with Calvin Tower and the omnipresent decline of the Beams supporting the Tower.[2] The latter concern is always with them, but its immediacy is brought home when a

Beamquake rocks the Calla. The Breakers' work is progressing, and they have successfully disrupted another Beam.[3] It's not the Beam they are following, or else the damage would have been much worse. "The very birds would have fallen flaming from the sky," Roland says. This brings to mind the earthquake that occurred when Jack Sawyer finally took possession of the Talisman.

Two Beams remain, but time is running out. They have to handle each crisis in its turn. "We can't win through to the Tower without [Susannah]. For all I know, we can't win through without Mia's chap." Mia will need Susannah's cooperation to survive in Keystone Earth. "If they can't find a way to work together now that they're there, they may die together."

On the way to the Doorway Cave in the morning, the ka-tet and the Manni pass the battle site, where the Calla-folken have built a funeral pyre of dead Wolves and their mechanical horses. Susannah's beaten-up chair is nearby, positioned as a tribute to her. The Manni form a ring around the site and pray for success to their god, the Over,[4] which Henchick sometimes calls The Force.

In the cave, the Manni use plumb bobs and magnets to gather their force. Their equipment is in boxes covered with stars, moons and odd geometric shapes, reminiscent of the japps, mirks, bews, smims and founders Dinky Earnshaw used in "Everything's Eventual." Jake's powerful touch focuses their power. He grabs an imaginary hook—like Bill Denborough performing the Ritual of Chüd—and the Manni pull the door open through him.

Roland intended to send Jake and Callahan to 1977 while he and Eddie followed Susannah's trail. Ka has a different plan. Roland and Eddie are sucked through the door to 1977, where they are caught in an ambush. Jake and Callahan are sent after Susannah, accompanied by Oy, who was supposed to stay behind with the Manni.[5] Oy is part of the ka-tet and ka needs him for this part of the mission.

Mia arrives in New York on June 1, 1999, near the once-vacant lot where a skyscraper now stands at 2 Dag Hammarskjold Plaza, which the people who work there jokingly call the Black Tower.[6] Susannah and Mia struggle for control. That they're experiencing strong labor pains doesn't help.

With Mia in charge, their body has white legs, and the longer she's in control, the more the white coloration spreads up Susannah's body. If

The tower that currently stands on the corner of Forty-sixth and Second in Manhattan.
(Ron J. Martirano, 2004)

Susannah controls the body too long, though, her legs tend to vanish, as they did during her todash trip to New York.

Mia materializes in front of an accountant named Trudy Damascus.[7] Since she has no shoes, she accosts Trudy, threatening her with an Oriza and demanding footwear.

Trudy is only a minor character whose part is over as soon as she gives her shoes to Mia. However, in the minute between 1:18 P.M. and 1:19 P.M. her entire worldview was pushed off balance. A former doubter of all things supernatural and extraterrestrial, her experience puts her in a league with Donnie Russert, John Cullum's friend from Vanderbilt who explored the walk-in phenomenon, and Ted Brautigan, who tried to convince people to make use of his psychic skills. They all discover that there are some things that people—especially those like Irene Tassenbaum's husband, David—just won't believe even when you can prove it. Trudy eventually learns to stop fighting this entrenched disbelief or trying to counter the mundane explanations others have for Mia's appearance. She also comes to recognize the sympathetic nods her story receives as being similar to those afforded madwomen to keep from upsetting them.

Outside the Black Tower, she encounters the former acne sufferer whom Father Callahan met twenty years earlier. He tells her that visiting this place cleared up his acne when he was a young man, expecting that she will think he's crazy. Her strange confrontation with a materializing shoe thief gives them a common bond. Singing still attracts people to the corner, but Trudy senses that something is very wrong. The world is tipping and in danger of toppling completely.

Susannah and Mia figure out what Roland already knew: If they are to survive in New York, they have to cooperate. Mia has full access to Susannah's memories, but she has no experience living in a place like this, which is almost as foreign to Susannah as it is to Mia.

Susannah creates a mental control room reminiscent of Jonesy's storage room in *Dreamcatcher*. Here she can control Emotional Temperature, Labor Force and whether her fetus—the "chap"—is awake or asleep. She reduces her Emotional Temperature to a comfortable level, sets the Chap switch to SLEEP, then wrests the Labor Force setting from nine out of ten all the way down to two. Unbearable pain prevents her from reducing it to one. The control room trembles and quakes under the strain, like Poe's House of Usher.

Susannah visualizes her baby for the first time and is confused to see that it has Roland's eyes, not Eddie's. Before leaving, she adds a microphone that she tries to use to talk to Eddie, but she gets no response.

Her mental Dogan is more than mere visualization. All three ex–New Yorkers have been changed by their experience. Jake has the touch, Eddie can make powerful talismanic objects like the key, and Susannah can see things hard enough to make them real. However, she isn't in complete control. Her microphone was supposed to be a Zenith, but it bears the markings of North Central Positronics.

In the now-crimson bag containing Black Thirteen, Susannah finds the object Eddie had noticed while in the Doorway Cave: a scrimshaw turtle—Maturin, a Guardian of the Beam, with a question mark scratched on his shell.[8] Like the singing rose, people are drawn to it. Like the key Jake found in the vacant lot, the turtle makes people susceptible to suggestion. It is can-tah, one of the little gods, a term first seen in *Desperation*. Susannah believes the scrimshaw turtle belongs to the Dark Tower. In a pocket park (Katharine Hepburn Park) next to 2 Dag Hammarskjold Plaza, Susannah discovers a statue that also depicts the turtle.

We're All Going Crazy

Insanity—or concerns about going insane—is a common theme in the *Dark Tower* series. The first truly insane creature the ka-tet meets is Shardik the bear, once great Guardian of the Beam. Soon they will learn that most of the ancient sentient machinery has gone mad, including suicidally depressed Blaine the Mono.

Eddie thinks he may be going crazy when Roland enters his mind aboard the flight from the Bahamas. Both Roland and Jake fear for their sanity after Roland inadvertently causes a doubling of time by killing Jack Mort, a sociopath who is clinically insane. Greta Shaw helped Jake "hold up the Tower" of his sanity.

Living in the shadow of the Dark Tower for millennia and coveting its power drives the Crimson King insane. Father Callahan thinks the Crimson King's eye, trapped in Black Thirteen, is mad. The Doorway Cave goes insane after the Beamquake.

Susannah frequently worries about her sanity, especially when Mia possesses her. Mia, mother of Mordred and daughter of none, goes insane giving birth, even before she realizes the true nature of her son.

And even author-character Stephen King doubts his sanity when the fruits of his imagination appear to him one sunny day in 1977.

She uses the totem to convince a Swedish businessman[9] to rent her a room at the Plaza-Park Hyatt and divests him of nearly $200. Under the sigul's influence, the hotel receptionist says, "Soon comes the King, he of the Eye. . . . When the King comes and the Tower falls, sai, all such pretty things as yours will be broken. There will be a darkness and nothing but the howl of the discordia and the cries of the can toi."[10]

In room 1919, Mia stores the Orizas and Black Thirteen in a safe. She's expecting a call, though Susannah wonders how Mia knows anything about telephones. While they wait, Mia goes todash with Susannah so they can talk face-to-face. They meet on the parapet wall—the allure—of the Castle on the Abyss. Once known as Castle Discordia, it is deep in End-World, "near the place where your quest ends, for good or for ill." Susannah feels very close to the Tower. Mia tells Susannah that Roland has finally come to the Crimson King's attention and will surely be destroyed before his quest is over: "I carry his doom in my own belly, and I care not."

Past the castle's inner keep is the town of Fedic. The abyss beyond the outer wall is filled with monsters trying to escape its confines, much like those in the chasm outside Lud.

Mia's baby will be called Mordred, a name she drew from Susannah's mind. Part demon, the child will grow quickly[11] and, like his namesake in Arthurian legend, will strive to slay his father. Mia believes Mordred will be the avatar (ideal) of every gunslinger that ever was. Susannah is stunned when Mia confirms that Roland, not Eddie, is the baby's father.

Mia tells Susannah the Mid-World creation story. Discordia, called the Over by the Manni, is the soup of creation, also known as the Prim. From it arose the Beams, supported by a supply of magic that would have lasted forever. However, when the magic left everything else in the world except the Tower, men despaired and replaced the magic sustaining the Beams with mortal machines supported by rational thought. Now these machines are failing and the world is running down. "Maerlyn retired to his cave in one world, the sword of Eld gave way to the pistols of the gunslingers in another, and the magic went away," Mia says. Like Shardik and Blaine the Mono, the machines are slowly going mad. The Crimson King's Breakers are only hurrying along their decay.

The Crimson King has been promised—or perhaps he only promised himself—he will survive when the Tower falls and will rule the resulting chaos forever. Mia tells Susannah that Roland's real quest is not to save the Tower. If he managed to free the Breakers and kill the Crimson King, he would only be slowing down its eventual collapse. She wants Susannah to believe that Roland's goals are less noble than saving creation.

What he wants of the Tower is only to see it. Or, perhaps to enter it, and climb to the room at the top, his ambition may strike so far. He may dream of standing on its allure . . . and chant the names of his fallen comrades, and of his line all the way back to Arthur Eld. But save it? . . . Only a return of the magic could possibly save it, and . . . your dinh deals only in lead.[12]

Mia recounts the demon hierarchy: six demon elementals, one for each Beam, who rule above the other creatures left behind on the beach of existence when the Prim receded; Speaking Demons; ghosts; and demons called disease. Each demon elemental is both male and female, so there are twelve demon aspects to counter the twelve Guardians of the Beams. They have no need of names. They are what they are.

Mia tries to tell Susannah that she is one of the demon elementals, but Susannah forces her to admit she doesn't really know what she is or where she came from. Roland had intercourse with a female demon in the place of the oracle. His seed was preserved and given to Susannah by the demon's male aspect in the speaking ring when Jake came through from New York.

Mia has been told she'll get to raise Mordred, but Susannah thinks Mia's overwhelming need to be a mother made her susceptible to believing lies. Detta raises a crucial question: If Roland's semen entered Susannah, why is it Mia who is pregnant now that they are separate?

The ringing telephone takes them back to New York. Richard Sayre, the man who lured Father Callahan to his death, summons Mia to the Dixie Pig. Susannah and Mia's palaver has raised doubts in Mia's mind. She asks Sayre if he will keep his promises. Sayre placates Mia, saying her son is the most important child to ever be born and, though Mordred's childhood will be short, she will have him for several years.

Sayre taunts Susannah, saying Eddie and Roland will be killed in an ambush. Susannah is livid that Mia—who had access to Susannah's memories and the zip code where Tower was hiding—bartered Eddie for her monster. "No wonder you wanted to take his ring off! How could you bear to have it lie against your skin, knowing what you'd done?" Mia seals Susannah in a triply locked prison in her mind, making her flash back to Odetta's experiences in jail in Oxford.

• • •

A SMALL ARMY led by Jack Andolini is waiting for Roland and Eddie when they arrive in Maine. Sayre underestimates Roland's "divine combination of training, observation and hair-trigger intuition"—he drags Eddie inside the nearby general store in a hail of machine gun fire, leaving all their belongings behind except for their guns.[13] The ambush reminds Roland of Jericho Hill.

Some of the men taking part in the ambush are people Eddie and Roland killed previously—ten years in the future. This is the Keystone World, though, and anyone they kill here will stay dead. This interference with the timeline might have created dual memories similar to the ones Roland and Jake experienced after Roland killed Jack Mort, but it doesn't. Perhaps this is because nothing they do affects the mortality of a member of the ka-tet.

Roland and Eddie take the shopkeeper and John Cullum, the only surviving customer, with them as they retreat out the back of the store. Cullum, the first of two useful people ka delivers to Roland in the general store, is an army veteran who follows Roland's instructions without question. He sets fire to the storeroom, preventing the attackers from coming through the building. If they circle around the building, Roland and Eddie will pick them off.

Approaching sirens give Roland, Eddie and Cullum the distraction they need to retreat farther. Cullum takes them across the lake on his motorboat. During the crossing, King implies for the first time within the text[14] that one of the ka-tet will die, and it will be either Eddie or Roland. Eddie reminds himself to ask Roland something later but he "never got the chance; before the question occurred to him again, death had slipped between them."

Cullum, a cottage caretaker, asks Roland and Eddie if they are "walk-ins," which is what locals call the strangers who have appeared over the past two or three years. They wear old clothing or are naked, and some speak unknown languages. From Cullum's description, Roland recognizes some as Slow Mutants. Not all of the walk-ins are friendly.

Like any good caretaker, Cullum is familiar with visitors and locals alike. He shows Roland and Eddie where Tower and Deepneau are staying and agrees with Eddie's suggestion that the first walk-ins appeared at about the same time Stephen King moved to nearby Bridgton. As they part, Roland tells Cullum he'd be wise to take a short vacation to keep Andolini off his trail.

For someone supposedly in fear of his life, Tower hasn't been keeping a very low profile—he's been out in the community buying books. Eddie is mad enough to kill him. Roland tells Eddie that if Roland could manage not to kill the whining and self-involved young drug addict he met many months ago, then Eddie should be able to resist killing Tower.

Time on this side is speeding up. Tower's contract with Balazar expires in less than a week. When they arrive at cabin number 19, Deepneau is alone. Roland asks the retired lawyer to draw up a contract of sale, but Tower has changed his mind again and Deepneau thinks it will probably take torture tactics to make him reconsider. "We will convince him," Roland states.

Eddie launches into Tower when he returns from his latest book expedition. Roland doesn't interfere—Eddie understands Tower. They share addictions. The combination of Eddie's rage and Deepneau's calm counsel brings Tower around. He interrogates Roland in High Speech.

Deepneau and Eddie exchange pleasantries while Roland and Tower go outside to talk. When Eddie mentions that he's from Co-Op City in Brooklyn, Deepneau says that Co-Op City is in the Bronx.[15] Eddie feels overwhelmed by all the worlds and the column of truth with a hole in it.[16] As the endgame draws near, this hole becomes more and more obvious to him.

Roland closes the deal with Tower. "It isn't every day I get called the scum of the earth by a man who promises to make me a millionaire and also to relieve me of my heart's heaviest burden," Tower says before signing the paper that gives ownership of the vacant lot to the ka-tet.

Roland operates on Eddie to remove a bullet in his lower leg from the shoot-out. Roland tells Eddie pain rises from the heart to the head and puts a belt in his mouth to catch the pain.[17] Eddie turns down the painkillers Deepneau offers; they're too close to heroin for comfort.

While Eddie reminisces about scenes like this from countless Westerns,[18] he makes the connection between their battle in Calla Bryn Sturgis and *The Magnificent Seven,* and even thinks of actors who would play him and Roland in the movie version of their quest, an exercise often undertaken at online *Dark Tower* fan sites.

After the procedure, Tower explains to Eddie why he priced his copy of *'Salem's Lot* so high. The book had a low first printing, and the dust jacket refers to Father Callahan as Cody. The book's original price was raised and then lowered again, so most first editions have a price-clipped dust jacket. "Suppose this man King becomes famous or critically acclaimed? I admit the chances are small, but suppose that did happen. Available first editions of his second book are so rare that, instead of being worth seven hundred and fifty dollars, my copy might be worth ten times that."[19]

Eddie convinces Roland to go to Bridgton to visit King. He trusts that by the time they get there, ka will tell them why they need to go. This is the last time Eddie or Roland see Tower or Deepneau. The partings have begun. "It's the end-game now. . . . All I've worked for and waited for all the long years. The end is coming. I feel it. Don't you?" Roland asks. However, the gunslinger's feelings are ambivalent. He says, "It's as if, after all these years, the quest itself has become the point for me, and the end is frightening."

IN A DREAM, Susannah hears several obituaries on the news. One of them is the future death of Stephen King, but since she wasn't in the cave when Roland showed *'Salem's Lot* to the others, the name means nothing to her. She won't remember hearing this or realize its significance until they reach Blue Heaven.

She receives a mental message from Eddie telling her to burn up as much of the day as she can while he and Roland complete their business in Maine. When Mia has a panic attack in the now-crowded hotel lobby on the way to her birthing rendezvous at the Dixie Pig, Susannah sees her opportunity to barter information for cooperation.

They retreat to a bathroom stall. Mia's confidence in Sayre is shaken when Detta tells her that Roland and Eddie survived the ambush in Maine. They take another todash voyage, this time to Fedic, the ghost town between the inner and outer keeps of the Castle on the Abyss. Susannah finds one of the Wolves' masks near Patricia the Mono's station. This is where they brought the twins stolen from the Callas. A one-way doorway underneath the castle led them to the Calla side of Thunderclap.

Magic doors worked in both directions, but North Central Positronics has never been able to master that feat with technology; their doors can only go one way. Some technological doorways lead to endless todash spaces between universes that contain monsters—such as Tak and It, perhaps—like the rats between the walls of a house. People who end up in these places may wander in darkness for years, but ultimately something always finds and devours them. The Crimson King reserved one for his worst enemies.

Keeping Eddie's request in mind, Susannah entices Mia, who hasn't had anyone to talk to for centuries, to tell the rest of her story, a kind of Scheherazade in reverse. When Mia came to Fedic two thousand years earlier, around the time Andy the robot was built, the city was alive, but most people were either sterile or gave birth to mutants. She saw one perfect baby and knew that her destiny was to bear and raise such a child. Then came the Red Death,[20] and the few people who were untouched by the plaguelike disease left Fedic on Patricia the Mono.

Trapped in Fedic, Mia spent centuries alone until the Crimson King's men came, with the endlessly bleeding hole in their foreheads, followed by Walter, Sayre's boss, who told her the Crimson King would give her a child. In the Dogan of all Dogans, the headquarters of North Central Positronics, Walter made Mia mortal. She doesn't remember how her transition from demon to the world of flesh was accomplished. It was a Faustian bargain—give up near immortality to become a woman who can carry a baby, but is unable to conceive one.

Mia believes she's part of ancient prophecy: "He who ends the line of Eld shall conceive a child of incest with his daughter, and the child will be marked, by his red heel shall you know him." Susannah reminds Mia that she isn't Roland's daughter, but Mia asks if she understands all the implications of the word "dinh."

Mia admits that she was the oracle and that she had met Jake and Roland before. She never mentions being involved in impregnating Susannah. Possibly she has no memory of it, but it's just as likely that the male demon was a different creature and by then she had become what Susannah accuses her of being: a receptacle or an incubator. The baby is to be transmitted to Mia cell by cell like a blood transfusion. Susannah enrages Mia with her persistent and demanding questions, so she returns them to the hotel bathroom. Susannah hasn't burned up the entire day, but she's dragged it out until dusk.

ON THE WAY to Stephen King's house, Eddie suggests that if they could convince Susannah's godfather, Moses Carver, to merge Tet Corporation and Holmes Dental, he could turn the new company into one of the richest corporations in the history of the world with their knowledge of the future. One of its missions would be to keep Sombra and North Central Positronics from becoming strong and perhaps save all the Beams that haven't yet been broken. The company could also set up a mechanism to take care of the immortal rose forever.

Nearing Bridgton, Eddie and Roland feel like they are approaching an awesome source of power. King represents one of the two surviving Beams supporting the Tower. The rose represents the other. The gunslingers realize the full implication of finding *'Salem's Lot;* they are literally going to meet their maker.

Both creator and creation react strongly upon meeting. Roland becomes physically ill. King thinks he's having a breakdown and tries to run away from them. He recognizes Roland,[21] but he hasn't yet imagined Eddie. "You'd be gunslingers, if you were real," he says. "Gunslingers seeking the Dark Tower." Then he faints. King, their god and creator, isn't immortal. Eddie sees a faint black nimbus around him, like the colored halos Ralph sees in *Insomnia*. Roland calls it todana, the deathbag. Ka has marked King. Some of his stories might be immortal, though.

The three men size each other up. Eddie thinks King is likable enough for a god, but he is responsible for the deaths of people like his sister and brother. For his part, King is afraid that Roland has come to kill him.[22] "Believe me when I tell you this," Roland says. "Killing you is the very last thing we'd ever want to do, sai King." He asks King the three questions that he asked of the people of Calla Bryn Sturgis, changing the last one to reflect the fact that he and Eddie are now seeking succor instead of offering it.

King confides to Eddie that he gave up on the *Dark Tower* series because he doesn't much care for Roland. The story was going to be his *Lord of the Rings,* his *Gormenghast.* "One thing about being twenty-two is that you're never short of ambition. It didn't take me long to see that it was just too big for my little brain. . . . Also, I lost the outline."[23] He relegated the manuscript to a box of busted stories in the basement.

King says the book has "maybe the best opening line I ever wrote." He knows the story only as far as Roland's palaver with the man in black.[24] The gunslinger reacts when King mentions his betrayal of Jake beneath the mountains. "No need to look so ashamed, Mr. Deschain. It was me after all. I was the one who made you do it." A few minutes later, he recants. He says Roland, who started out as a version of Sergio Leone's Man with No Name, became a problem. "When you let the kid drop, that was the capper."

Roland says, "You said you made me do that." King responds, "I lied, brother." Roland thinks there is another reason why King stopped writing. Something doesn't want him to work on this particular story. Perhaps the low men stole his outline.

Seeking clues to help them on their quest, Roland interrogates King about things from their recent past. King recognizes the name Claudia y Inez Bachman, but not as the author of *Charlie the Choo-Choo*. She's his pseudonym Richard Bachman's wife. The *y* doesn't mean anything to him, but Eddie knows it is there to make her part of the ka-tet of nineteen. All King knows about 19 is that prime numbers have always fascinated him.[25]

King knows Roland's hypnotizing trick with the bouncing bullet but still succumbs to it. He says the story of the Dark Tower "just comes. It blows into me—that's the good part—and then it comes out when I move my fingers. Never from the head. Comes out the navel." King isn't ka—he's just an intermediary—and he hates some of the things ka makes him do, like writing Susan Delgado's death.

The Crimson King first tried to terrorize King when he was seven during a panic attack he had when he and his brother were banished to the barn as punishment for trying to run away, but Cuthbert—or Eddie, his twin—freed him. From that time on, he had a fear of spiders and associated them with the Crimson King, whom he calls the Lord of the Spiders. Over the years, the Lord of Discordia tried many times to kill King or convince him to stop writing. Sometimes others stepped in to save him; sometimes he stepped aside.

Roland asks him why he stopped writing his story. King responds, "I don't want to be Gan.[26] I turned aside from Dis, I should be able to turn aside from Gan, as well. . . . When I open my eyes to your world, he sees me."

Roland tells the hypnotized author to listen for the song of the Turtle, the cry of the Bear. Then he must begin writing again, starting with Roland losing his fingers. He is to write until he's tired, and then rest until he hears the Turtle's song again. The ka-tet will try to protect him when he's working. Eddie suggests Roland hypnotize King into stopping smoking and drinking, but Roland thinks he's meddled with his mind—and ka itself—as much as he dares.[27]

King tells Roland and Eddie that Susannah's baby will kill her if they don't reach her in time and that Black Thirteen must be destroyed. If it wakes, it will become the most dangerous thing in the universe. "Take the ball to the double Tower," he says.[28] Since King hasn't written this part of the story yet, this advice must come from deep within him, via ka.

He tells Roland he is allowed to send a letter to himself, perhaps even a small package, but only once. The message he chooses to convey is another key, which he sends to Jake. Roland wakes King from his hypnotic trance with an order to forget everything except in the depths of his mind.

CALLAHAN, JAKE AND OY pursue Mia's trail. In New York, they encounter Reverend Earl Harrigan, Henchick's twin and pastor of the Church of the Holy God-Bomb. He tells them that Susannah, who communicated with him via her Dogan microphone, got into a taxi less than half an hour ago. They visit the skyscraper on the site of the former vacant lot and discover the wild rose is still there in a flower garden in the lobby, behind velvet ropes where it receives sun through the building's tall windows. Many of those who pass it on their way to work weep. A sign says GIVEN BY THE TET CORPORATION, IN HONOR OF THE BEAM FAMILY, AND IN MEMORY OF GILEAD.

Jake checks for messages at the hotel where Susannah stayed and is given the note King sent upon emerging from Roland's hypnotic trance. The writing on the envelope is in half-script and half-printing.[29] Inside the envelope is a hotel card key and a message that begins, "This is the truth," echoing Jake's essay.

Jake and Callahan realize Black Thirteen is still in Susannah's room, and the Crimson King's men will come back for it when Mia shows up without it. "I thought I was rid of it," Callahan says. "Some bad pennies just keep turning up." The card key gets them into Mia's room—they don't have any doubt which room is hers—and Jake guesses the safe combination. He arms himself with Orizas, which he learned to use in the Calla. The Wizard's Glass tries to get Callahan to kill Jake. Jake, Callahan, Oy and a passing maid all invoke the name of God to quiet it. Their victory here renews Callahan's faith and emboldens him for their coming mission.

Callahan steals the maid's tip money and they take a taxi to a building with the safest storage in New York—the "double Tower." They purchase enough tokens to store Black Thirteen indefinitely in a basement locker of the World Trade Center.[30] Jake jokes that the locker is safe unless "the building falls down on top of it." Without realizing it, Jake and Callahan have solved the problem of Black Thirteen. "Even a ball filled with deep magic wouldn't be much good underneath a hundred and ten stories of concrete and steel."

Callahan worries that their enemies at the Dixie Pig might pick the location of the locker from their minds. "It might be a bad idea for us to be taken alive." Both Jake and Callahan believe this is their night to die. Callahan hears Jake's last rites before they enter the restaurant.

Jake lays out a general plan of attack for their assault. Like the man who trained him, he knows to allow room for improvisation. He gives Callahan his father's Ruger and arms himself with Orizas, but Oy finds another weapon that will help them immeasurably in the Dixie Pig: the scrimshaw turtle talisman that Susannah left behind in the gutter while Mia was distracted.

A FORTUITOUS TRAFFIC JAM caused by a bus—in other words, an event orchestrated by ka—prompts Mia's taxi driver to drop her off a block short of the Dixie Pig. On the street, she encounters a singer performing "Man of Constant Sorrow," a song Susannah associates with her days of social activism and that she sang for the people of the Calla. After all she's been through with Roland, Susannah knows that hearing that song can't be a coincidence. Mia, without Susannah's influence, offers the man $50 to play it again. The song transports Susannah back to Odetta's experiences in Oxford, Mississippi, and Mia feels their glorious hope and love, exalted by the simplicity of what they believe.

Mia sees how deeply she's been misled when she asks Susannah what her mother was like. Susannah shows her a simple scene of coming home from school to find her mother waiting with warm gingerbread in the oven. From that moment, Mia understands what motherhood could be if allowed to run its course uninterrupted. "I agreed to mortality but I missed most of what makes the short-time life worthwhile, haven't I?" ("Short-Timers" is how immortals describe mortals, a term used by the bald docs in *Insomnia* and by the ghosts in *Kingdom Hospital*. The creature in *It* also comments on the short lives mortals lived.)

During Mia's momentary distraction, Susannah throws the scrimshaw turtle into the gutter, entrusting ka to get it to the ka-tet. Detta—Susannah's other demon—emerges to suggest that they might use Mia's mothering instinct to turn her into an ally.

Susannah's attempts to keep her labor under control reach their limits. The system overloads. She flips the Chap switch from ASLEEP to AWAKE, but it's not enough. The only solution is to increase the Labor Force, going all the way to ten, sending Mia into full labor.

Inside the Dixie Pig, the smell of roasting meat greets them. The restaurant is full of low men and women, and vampires. Sayre is there, too, with a hole in his forehead, looking like he had been shot at close range. Blood swims there but never overflows the "wound." He claps for Mia and the others join in, crying, "Hile, Mia!" and "Hile, Mother." Strange bugs scamper beneath the table, echoing the cheer in bug language that Mia hears in her head.

Detta takes momentary control and pulls the masks from a low woman. Beneath, she has the face of a red rat with yellow teeth growing up the outside of her cheeks. Detta tries to stay in charge, but Mia is stronger and takes over again.

Sayre humiliates Mia in front of his minions, forcing her to lick his boots.[31] "You have been an excellent custodian . . . but we must also remember that it was Roland of Gilead's gilly [that is, Susannah] who actually bred the child."

Behind a tapestry, she sees a dozen of the man/woman-beast hybrids called taheen dining on the roasting corpse of a human baby. The restaurant's specialty is "long pork," a euphemism for roasted human flesh. The kitchen is a twin of the one from Castle Discordia where Mia fed in her dreams.

Mia and Susannah rendezvous briefly on the castle ramparts.[32] Mia finally accepts that she's been misled. Her epiphany is reminiscent of Harold Lauder's eleventh-hour realization that Flagg had misled him in *The Stand*. She begs Susannah to help her get away with her chap, even if it means escaping into the todash darkness. Wandering forever in darkness with her son by her side is better than the alternative. "And if there's no way for us to be free," Mia says, "kill us."

As they pass through a doorway between New York and Fedic, Susannah overhears the password. Though it is in a strange language, she knows she could repeat it. She is taken to a room in the Fedic Dogan filled with hospital beds, one of which is occupied by Mia in her corporeal form and is covered with the bugs Susannah saw in the Dixie Pig. These are the same parasitic little doctors used by the Little Sisters of Eluria to heal their patients.

Susannah and Mia are connected by something straight out of *Star Trek*. The link is required to transfer the fetus to Mia, so she can accomplish the final labor and push the baby out. After Mia delivers, neither Susannah nor Mia will be needed. Susannah is slated to appear on the menu at the Dixie Pig. She screams in pain as the baby is transmitted to Mia to be born. "And on the wings of that song, Mordred Deschain, son of Roland (and one other, o can you say Discordia), came into the world."

THE STORY ENDS here. The book, though, contains a coda: Stephen King's journal from three days after he meets Roland and Eddie through the date of his accident, less than three weeks after Mia gives birth to Mordred.

He records the process of returning to work on the *Dark Tower* series and the journey to publication of the constituent stories followed by *The Gunslinger*. Nine years after Roland and Eddie's visit, he decides to give Roland some friends and starts *The Drawing of the Three*. "It seems to me that a lot of the other things I've written (especially *It*) are like 'practice shots' for this story." He decides it's a good book, but "in many ways it seems like I didn't write the damn thing at all, that it just flowed out of me . . . the wind blows, the cradle rocks, and sometimes it seems to me that none of this stuff is mine, that I'm nothing but Roland of Gilead's fucking secretary."

Two years later, he quits drinking, and a couple of years after that he gets a dozen roses for his birthday and hears the call to start *The Waste Lands*. There are hardly any strikeouts or retakes. Other than a few continuity glitches, the huge manuscript is clean. He expresses concern over Susannah's pregnancy, but reassures himself that he won't have to deal with that for another book or two. He knows the fans are going to howl at the cliff-hanger ending. The book feels like the high point of his make-believe life, perhaps even better than *The Stand*.

He gets fan mail from a seventy-six-year-old cancer victim who asks how the series will end. He feels bad because he can't answer her. "I have no more idea what's inside that damned Tower than . . . well, than *Oy* does! . . . The wind blows and the story comes. Then it stops blowing, and all I can do is wait, the same as you. . . . They think I'm in charge, every one of them from the smartest of the critics to the most mentally challenged reader. And that's a real hoot. Because I'm not."

The coda takes readers through his work on *Wizard and Glass* and discusses arguments he has with his wife about the dangers of his long walks along the narrow country roads near their lake house. He's pleased to see Flagg show up again and muses that he may turn out to be Walter, Roland's old nemesis. "I can see now how to a greater or lesser degree, every story I've ever written is about this story. . . . Writing this story is the one that always feels like coming home."

But it also feels dangerous. He is aware of some anticreative force to which he's more vulnerable when he's working on this series. He's worried he might die of a heart attack while writing, and he doesn't want to leave behind an unfinished work.[33] "*The Dark Tower* is my *uber*story, no question about that."

He sees the series' influence in other books. In mid-1999, though he is between *Dark Tower* books, he dreams more and more about baby Mordred, Discordia and June 19, 1999. He and Tabby continue to argue again about his walking route. The coda ends with a clipping from the *Portland*

Telegram announcing King's accident on June 19, 1999. In this timeline, King succumbs to his injuries.[34]

While characters may have encountered their own creator in fiction before, the *Dark Tower* series may be the first to explore the implications of what happens to characters if their creator dies before they reach the end of their story.

King remarked in 1994 that he knew the general layout of the rest of the series; he said in a personal communication that he had an accident in mind for his fictional counterpart, but nothing as dramatic as what would befall him five years later.[35] Reality, which is often stranger than fiction, stepped in and provided King with unexpected material that would dramatically influence his magnum opus.

Everyone faces mortality. Everyone has work they want to accomplish before they reach the clearing at the end of the path. By inserting himself and his accident into the series, King acknowledges how important finishing Roland's quest is to him.

ENDNOTES

[1] Unless otherwise specified, all quotes in this chapter come from *Song of Susannah*.

[2] They will discover before long that they have another deadline in 1999, but the only vague notion Roland has of that situation is his worsening arthritis.

[3] The Beam of the Wolf and Elephant, according to Pimli Prentiss in *The Dark Tower*. Roland believes it might be the Fish-Rat Beam.

[4] Part of their prayer includes "Over-can-tah," bringing to mind the language of the unformed and Tak.

[5] Oy dutifully accepted this plan but cried tears of sorrow at the thought of being separated from Jake.

[6] This building really exists and is somewhat as King describes it, though it is only sixteen stories tall instead of the seventy to eighty stories in *The Dark Tower*. The nearby pocket park with the turtle statue also exists in this region of New York, known as Turtle Bay.

[7] Perhaps a symbolic name. Saul had a strange encounter on the road to Damascus that changed his life. Trudy works for Guttenberg, Furth, and Patel. Robin Furth is King's research assistant. Surendra and Geeta Patel are friends to whom *From a Buick 8* was dedicated.

[8] Named for Stephen Maturin, a character in seafaring novels by Patrick O'Brian. Maturin describes a fictitious species of turtle that he discovers in the South Pacific. Jack Aubrey, for whom *Testudo* ("tortoise" in Latin) *aubreii* was named, is Maturin's friend. According to an e-mail message from King's office posted at Anthony Schwethelm's Dark Tower Compendium Web site, King has a pet turtle named Maturin that he had recently discovered is actually female.

[9] He calls the talisman skölpadda, the Swedish word for turtle.

[10] Susannah uses the turtle to convince the receptionist that an Oriza is actually her driver's license, reminiscent of Andy McGee "pushing" a cabbie to believe a one-dollar bill is $500 in *Firestarter*. Jack Sawyer makes similar use of a posy of white blossoms Speedy gave him in *Black House*. The can toi, a term also applied to the low men, are Tak's children of the desert in *Desperation*.

[11] This demon-spawned child is reminiscent of "Little Brother" from *Kingdom II* by Lars von Trier, the Danish miniseries that King adapted as *Kingdom Hospital* in 2004. His father was a demon, and he grew abnormally fast both in utero and after. "Little Brother" refused to accept his demonic nature, unlike Mordred, who will embrace it. King, however, said that he had only seen the first part of von Trier's series, which ends with the demonic baby's birth. Nevertheless, the name Mordred Wilder is seen on the cover of a book, Mia Dean is paged to the maternity ward and numbers 19 and 99 appear regularly on the show. In a private communication, King referred to Antubis, the program's anteater guardian, as Roland's old trailmate. Antubis's name is a pun on the Egyptian god of the dead, Anubis.

[12] Echoing a line by Steve McQueen's character, Vin, in *The Magnificent Seven*. Roland does want to save the Tower, but having done so, he carries on beyond what is required of him by ka. Not everything Mia says can be believed. When the Breakers are freed, the Beams start to heal themselves and regenerate those that were broken.

[13] Eddie laments losing a lock of Susannah's hair. Roland says their guns are all they need.

[14] In the afterword to *Wizard and Glass,* he wrote, "All may not live to reach the Tower."

[15] When Eddie meets King, he asks his future creator where Co-Op City is. King erroneously says Brooklyn. Eddie says, "I refuse to believe that I was raised in Brooklyn simply because of some writer's mistake, something that will eventually be fixed in the second draft."

[16] King's *Danse Macabre* closes with this passage:

> We fall from womb to tomb, from one blackness and toward another, remembering little of the one and knowing nothing of the other . . . except through faith. That we retain our sanity in the face of these simple yet blinding mysteries is nearly divine. That we may turn the powerful intuition of our maginations upon them and regard them in this glass of dreams—that we may, however timidly, place our hands within the hole which opens at the center of the column of truth—that is . . . well, it's magic, isn't it?

[17] A similar scene appears in "Low Men in Yellow Coats" when Ted Brautigan helps replace Carol's dislocated shoulder. "Pain rises from its source to the brain . . . but you'll catch most of it in your mouth as it rises." [HA]

[18] Eddie calls the scene "Pulling the Bullet," a play on "Riding the Bullet," perhaps.

[19] Tower was optimistic. First editions of *'Salem's Lot* typically sell for $750 to $1,500, depending on condition.

[20] After Poe's "The Masque of the Red Death." This plague was probably caused by the Crimson King, hence its name. "Some folks said something had been opened in the castle, some jar of demonstuff that should have been left shut forever," Mia says.

[21] King isn't sure he's thought of the "Gilead" part yet, but acknowledges that it is good. "There is no balm in Gilead" (a misquote).

[22] Though he hasn't written *The Dark Half* yet, this echoes Thad Beaumont's fear of one of his own creations, a pseudonym.

[23] King says in the introduction to *The Gunslinger* that he did indeed lose an early outline, but it "probably wasn't worth a tin shit anyway."

[24] King takes some liberties with history. The final sections of *The Gunslinger* weren't written until 1979 or 1980.

[25] They also turn up in *Dreamcatcher,* when the aliens recite streams of prime numbers.

[26] King claims Gan is the creative force in Hindu mythology. Gan made the world and tipped it with his finger, setting it rolling, thereby creating time. Note the syllable's presence in Dogan and Harrigan.

[27] Roland thinks tobacco prolongs life. It keeps away ill-sick vapors and dangerous insects. Since they are going ahead to 1999, they can't come back to check on him after today. In *The Dark Tower,* Roland and Eddie find a solution to this dilemma.

[28] That is, the World Trade Center. Jake and Callahan will do this without benefit of King's advice.

[29] This is King's normal writing hand, as seen in the reproduction ledgers Scribner used to promote *Dreamcatcher.*

[30] In the afterword, King writes, "[T]o the best of my knowledge, there were never coin-op storage lockers in the World Trade Center."

[31] In Mejis, Big Coffin Hunter Roy Depape made Sheemie Ruiz do the same thing.

[32] The castle allure is Mia's safe place, a retreat reminiscent of the Mohonk hotel used by Audrey in *The Regulators*.

[33] He mentions Chaucer's *Canterbury Tales* and Dickens's *Mystery of Edwin Drood* as examples of unfinished works.

[34] The article's byline is that of Ray Routhier, a real-life journalist for the *Portland Press Herald,* who gave King permission to use his name in the book.

[35] Personal communication, August 2003.

CHAPTER 8

THE DARK TOWER (RESUMPTION)

*My quest—the quest of my ka-tet—is the Dark Tower. It's not saving this world
we're about, or even this universe, but all universes. All of existence.*

[DT5][1]

What we're playing for, Roland, is the ages.

[DT6]

The Dark Tower begins immediately after the end of *Song of Susannah*. Father Callahan, Jake and Oy are on the street outside the Dixie
Pig, ready to begin what could be their final battle. For weapons they
have Jake's father's gun, Susannah's Orizas, and the scrimshaw turtle Susannah left for them in the gutter. Callahan knows that Jake must survive,
but his own part in the story is almost done.

Inside the restaurant, they both sense that something exciting has just
happened. They are vastly outnumbered, but the turtle sigul levels the playing field, entrancing most of the entities in the room except for the black
bugs scuttling under the table, the little doctors—also known as Grandfather fleas—that Roland encountered in Eluria. Their presence in such
numbers indicates that the Grandfathers—Type One vampires—aren't far
behind. Oy kills a few, and the others retreat quickly. Callahan muses that
Oy seems to have been bred to destroy these parasites.

Eddie and Roland, swept from Maine on a Beam hurricane, witness
the onset of the confrontation from a vantage point high up in the room.
They both know how this battle is going to turn out. Roland confirms
Callahan's belief that he is to sacrifice himself so Jake can continue. The
gunslinger inhabits Callahan's body to speak to Jake, telling him to leave
the priest behind and go after Susannah. Noticing his reluctance, Roland
thinks, "I should have schooled him better in betrayal." Eddie's sugges-

tion that the vampires will kill and eat Oy spurs Jake into action better than Roland's orders do.

The sigul has no effect on the Type One vampires who emerge from the kitchen, but Callahan's faith works through his cross. He doesn't waver in the face of EVIL when the vampires—echoing Barlow—dare him to throw his cross aside. "I needn't stake my faith on the challenge of such a thing as you. . . . I'd never throw away such an old friend in any case." He lets the cross fall inside his shirt, but the power of God and the White radiate through his very being. He gets a second chance to correct an error he made in a previous life, in much the same way that Roland has been given multiple attempts to get his quest right.

Fear of Sayre, who answers to Walter, who in turn answers only to the Crimson King, spurs three taheen to take action. They knock the turtle from Callahan's hand to the floor. It bounces under one of the tables and "there passes out of this tale forever,"[2] releasing the taheen from its glammer. Callahan invokes God's name, but the Crimson King's minions exist outside His power. They fall on him and bite into his neck. The smell of blood outweighs the power of the cross, drawing the vampires to him.

God—or ka—answers Callahan's call for strength. He shoots the taheen who attacked him and wonders if that makes him a gunslinger. Before the vampires sink their teeth into his neck, Callahan turns the Ruger on himself. He salutes Roland, who returns the salute, saying, "Hile, gunslinger!" Callahan pulls the trigger and dies, satisfied that he has fulfilled his duty, committing suicide without apparent moral conflict for the second time in his existence.

THE BEAM HURRICANE, called aven kal, strikes Eddie and Roland in Cullum's car on the way to Turtleback Lane in Lovell, a looping road along the shore of Kezar Lake[3] and the center of walk-in activity. The Beam means to speak to them. Roland's tutor used to say, "You would do well to listen if it does."

Their bodies float inside the car briefly, then the hurricane carries their essences to Fedic, where they hover over Susannah and Mia. Susannah sees them—naked and surrounded by a cloud of detritus from inside Cullum's car—and says, "Chassit," a word Roland knows from a song his mother used to sing. It means "nineteen," the mystical word they have been encountering since leaving the Emerald Palace. The hurricane then takes them to the Dixie Pig before returning them to Cullum's car. In its wake, they sense Callahan's death.

Roland expects to find a magic doorway at Turtleback Lane. Before they leave in pursuit of Susannah, Eddie wants to arrange to have the title to the vacant lot—a document that may not withstand close scrutiny—delivered to Odetta's godfather, Moses Carver. Time is running out for Susannah, but the Tower takes precedence. He gets perverse pleasure from knowing that the agreement, perhaps the most important piece of paper in the world, has a silly pun ("Dam important things to do") at the top.

They need someone besides Aaron Deepneau as a go-between because Deepneau doesn't know enough of the ka-tet's story to resist Tower's nagging. The only other person they know is John Cullum, whom they earlier ordered to leave town until the heat died down. Roland believes that since they need him, ka dictates that Cullum will still be at home. Eddie argues that, in a story, a minor character like John Cullum would never come in off the bench to save the day. It wouldn't be considered realistic. Roland says, "In life, I'm sure it happens all the time."

Roland's faith is validated. Cullum answers his phone when he hears Eddie's voice on the answering machine, and agrees to meet them on Turtleback Lane. On the way, they pass a being Roland calls a Child of Roderick.[4] They are wandering folk, Bedouins from beyond any land Roland ever knew, although before the world moved on they honored Arthur Eld. Now they act as trustees at Devar-Toi, where the Breakers are held. Their mutation is caused, according to Pimli Prentiss, from working near the red glow of the King's Forge, aka the Big Combination.

Roland shows it Aunt Talitha's cross to prove his identity. In exchange for the name of the town standing near Castle Discordia where Susannah has been taken, Roland puts the mutant out of his misery. In the wake of this incident, Eddie contemplates the gunslinger and, for the first time, thinks of him as his father.

Roland is elated. Once their business in Fedic is done, they will turn east and head straight for the Dark Tower. "I have never been so close. I hear all my lost friends and lost fathers whispering to me. They whisper on the Tower's very breath."

• • •

FROM HER HOSPITAL BED, Susannah assesses her situation. She has eleven adversaries, including Sayre and the human doctor, whose gun she thinks she can steal. Her link with Mia is fading and her labor pains are over, but she continues to scream to keep the enemy disoriented. When the connection is severed, she feels like she has lost a sister. One look at Mia tells her that finally achieving the imperative of her existence—giving birth—has driven her insane.

Baby Mordred seems normal at first, other than being born with a full set of teeth and an erection. On his left heel he bears the bloodlike mark of the Eld, which becomes a crimson brand on the back of the spider-monster he turns into while suckling at Mia's breast. A white growth rises from its back containing the baby's tiny, deformed face and blue eyes. According to legend, the Guardians of the Beam each carried an extra brain on the outside of its head. The satellite dishes that controlled them inspired this myth, but Mordred's form seems analogous.

Susannah is so stunned by the transformation that she misses a chance to shoot both Mia and Mordred. Even Sayre is surprised. Mia dies praising her beautiful son as the monster drains her lifeblood. Susannah snaps out of her trance, seizes the doctor's gun and shoots everyone in the room, mentally thanking Roland for showing her how to become a killing machine. When Sayre tries to surrender, Susannah shoots him twice, once each for Callahan and Mia.

She stumbles over a body and only wounds Mordred with her last bullet, shooting off one of his legs, an injury that translates when Mordred is in human form to an arm wound that will never heal. As the spider escapes, Susannah hears his outrage projected into her mind. "You cannot! You must not! For I am the King's only son!"

The only being left in the Dogan is Nigel, the robotic butler. Memories of Andy and the Calla fresh in her mind, Susannah shoots out his eyes and then gets him to carry her to the door from New York, where she waits for Jake.

A washer boy—originally from the outskirts of Lud—warns Jake on his way through the Dixie Pig's kitchen to beware the "mind trap." Oy follows Susannah's scent down a long corridor decorated with travel posters. People from Mid-World used these rational doors to access Earth like time-traveling tourists.[5]

When Jake tries to use his touch, he realizes that he is open to mental infiltration, which he mistakenly thinks is the mind trap. To empty his head, he sings "The Lion Sleeps Tonight." The real mind trap captures these images and creates a jungle populated with cartoonish dinosaurs from *The Lost Continent,* a movie Jake saw when very young. Though they are only mental projections, the dinosaurs are real enough to kill him.

To get around the trap, Jake exchanges minds with Oy,[6] who doesn't see the dinosaurs. Oy awkwardly operates Jake's body and carries the billy-bumbler containing Jake's mind past the holographic projector. They switch minds again just as their pursuers from the Dixie Pig catch up. It's an amusing scene but ultimately irrelevant, as there are no lingering effects from their exchange and Jake and Oy's relationship does not gain any permanent new insight from it.

Exhausted, Jake reaches the door and readies himself for a battle, but Susannah hears him and gives him the password. Sayre hadn't entrusted his minions with this information, so they are thwarted. Roland's ka-tet is beginning to reassemble itself.

ROLAND AND EDDIE meet Cullum at Turtleback Lane, where King owns the house at number 19, named Cara Laughs.[7] They tell Cullum as much of their story as they think he can take, starting with Roland entering Eddie during his flight from Nassau. Cullum believes in the importance of their mission because they seem to want all the right things.

Cullum and Deepneau are to persuade Moses Carver, using a secret Susannah shared with Eddie that Carver would know, that his goddaughter is still alive. Roland turns Aunt Talitha's cross into a magic recording device to deliver this message in Susannah's voice. They want Carver to form a corporate giant that will use Susannah's fortune to protect the rose, watch over Stephen King and thwart Sombra and North Central Positronics at every possible juncture.

Eddie appoints Cullum vice president of Tet Corporation, though the caretaker isn't impressed by the title. He jokingly calls his new group the Three Elderly Stooges, the Three Toothless Musketeers, and the Old Farts of the Apocalypse. "[It] appears to me you're offering the keys to one humongous great engine. Who wouldn't want to turn it on, and see what it does?"

Before they part, Cullum presents the gunslingers with their gunna, which he retrieved from the general store. Eddie and Roland drive to the lake, where the building storm hints that the doorway will close soon. Walk-ins, many of them mutants, wander through the woods by the hundreds. This part of Maine is thin and close to many worlds. The doorway, one of the original magic portals from the Prim, can take them wherever they want to go.

Navigating by Jake's touch, Roland and Eddie arrive on the New York side of the Fedic door and make short work of Jake's pursuers. They open the door, and the ka-tet is reunited for the first time since the battle against the Wolves. Eddie and Susannah fall into each other's arms. So, too, do Jake and Roland, who for the first time treat each other like proud father and son.

The ka-tet believes the items they've been finding—like the scrimshaw turtle—indicate King is working on the *Dark Tower* series again. Susannah is about to mention dreaming about King's death, but Nigel, who has been reading *The Dead Zone,* distracts her. His impressive book collection includes classics, Westerns, and a complete set of Stephen King through 1999's *Hearts in Atlantis,* except for the *Dark Tower* books, which he claims to know nothing about. From his stuttering pattern, Susannah is sure he's lying. Eddie suggests taking the King books with them, but Roland worries their content might mislead them.[8]

Mordred monitors the ka-tet from a subterranean control room. Part of him wants to be invited to join them, but he could never acknowledge Roland as dinh, so he will always be on the outside.

Randall Flagg, aka Walter o'Dim, arrives after Nigel—who has been bringing Mordred food—dies from instabilities caused by Susannah's bullets. Like the low men who watch over the Breakers, to ward off mental attack Walter sports a metallic screen inside his hood that he "borrowed from a certain deserted house in the town of French Landing, Wisconsin." It's one of the metal-lined hoods that Charles Burnside put on potential Breakers to disrupt their mental powers when he abducted them. Walter may have made a serious error in wearing it. Mordred's appearance—he is barely a toddler—causes Walter to underestimate him.[9]

Walter's goal is now the same as Roland's—to get to the Dark Tower and see if anything occupies the room at the top. With the Crimson King imprisoned there, only two people can enter: Roland and Mordred. Walter intends to use Mordred to gain access to the Tower and take over as God of Everything, if he can get there in time. King's fatal accident is less than five days away in End-World time. When King dies, his Beam will break and the Tower will fall.

Mordred penetrates Walter's feeble defenses and extracts the information he needs from his mind. He paralyzes the old wizard and switches to spider form to feed. He makes Walter pluck out his eyes and tongue before devouring him.[10] "Walter had been quasi-immortal and made a legendary meal."

Readers may be disappointed at the unspectacular demise of this legendary villain who outwitted great minds for centuries without ever truly achieving any of his goals. He failed in Delain, in Las Vegas and in Mid-World. Roland isn't present when this ancient deceiver who bedeviled him all his life finally pays for his prodigious list of sins. Still, perhaps it is fitting that Walter, like Dr. Frankenstein, dies at the hands of a creature he was instrumental in creating: Roland's ill-begotten offspring. Walter's death also disproves his own prophecy that Roland would have to slay the Ageless Stranger to gain the Tower. Perhaps this is a harbinger that Roland's quest to defeat the endless loop of his existence won't succeed this time.

Mordred follows Walter's back trail and picks up the scent of the ka-tet. He's eager to attack, but knows his limitations. He's vulnerable to their bullets in either form, so he bides his time and follows. The ka-tet's next destination is Thunderclap, to stop the Breakers, either by killing them or freeing them. Roland believes Mordred intends to free the Crimson King, imprisoned in the Dark Tower, to slay what lives at the top.

Oy tracks the Wolves' scent to the Thunderclap portal, a technological door that will probably not work much longer. The overwhelming nausea they experience when they pass through explains why robots were sent to the Callas. No living being would eagerly pass through a second time.

Three temporarily AWOL Breakers greet them at the Thunderclap train station. The elderly man who mistakes Jake for Bobby Garfield is Ted Brautigan from *Hearts in Atlantis,* a book the ka-tet saw on Nigel's shelf a little earlier. His two younger companions are Dinky Earnshaw, the e-mail assassin from "Everything's Eventual," and a boy named Stanley whom Roland recognizes as Sheemie[11] from Mejis, which means he is as ancient as the gunslinger.

Sheemie blames himself for Susan Delgado's death, but Roland absolves him, laying the blame on Rhea and himself. "If anyone was blameless in the business . . . it was you." Roland tells Sheemie that he and his friends always knew he was special.

Thunderclap is in a perpetual eclipse, the lingering result of the Crimson King's madness. Stanley, assisted by the combined powers of the others, teleports the group to a mountain eight miles away. From their vantage point, the ka-tet sees artificial sunlight illuminating a prison that resembles a college campus. It has dorms near a village that looks like Main Street, America—Brautigan calls it Pleasantville—except the streets end in desert, reminiscent of the transformed community in *The Regulators*. Six high towers and three fences guard the area. Its real name is Devar-Toi, known by the taheen as Algul Siento, or Blue Heaven.

More than three hundred Breakers live here, mostly misfits who don't require much to make them happier than they were in their former lives: great food, movies and simulated sex with any person imaginable. United, they could easily overpower their captors, but they have no reason to escape. Most of them don't know what they're doing, but Ted does. He asks Roland if they've been eating "the children the Greencloaks bring from the Borderlands." Roland won't confirm Ted's suspicions. "So you can eat yourself alive? Eat yourself instead of them?"

Pimli (nee Paul) Prentiss and a taheen named Finli—whom Andy reported to from the Dogan outside the Calla—run Devar-Toi. Prentiss, a former Attica prison guard, is a compassionate warden who treats his wards well and calls them by name. He's an unlikely person to be leading the end of creation: a religious man who believes their work at Devar-Toi is God's work, as well as the Crimson King's. He and Finli are Mid-World civil servants. They drink together after work and try hard not to think about what they're doing.

Their future is uncertain because the Breakers are close to completing their work. The Bear-Turtle Beam is beginning to bend. Once it goes, the last Beam, Eagle-Lion, might hold for another few weeks. Since the last Beam snapped, Devar-Toi has been cut off from the outside world. Prentiss and Finli don't know why the Wolves didn't return. With the Breaker's work so near completion, Finli worries—with good cause—that Brautigan is planning something.[12]

Ted and his friends knew who was coming and prepared accordingly:

Four sleeping bags, and a towel-covered mattress for an animal, are set up in the cave. They have an ATV ready for Susannah. When Roland sees the tarot card—the Lady of Shadows—propped on its dashboard, he senses that Walter is dead.

A feeling of foreboding encompasses the ka-tet. Jake is reminded of how he felt before Roland let him fall under the mountain. Roland recognizes the sensation as ka-shume, the awareness of an approaching break in a ka-tet. Someone will die soon. "It never once crossed Roland's mind that the one to die might be him." He performs a communionlike sharing-of-water ritual and tries to reassure his friends, reminding Jake that he had felt the sense of impending death for both himself and Callahan when they entered the Dixie Pig.

Mordred, lurking outside the cave, shares their ka-shume, even though he is an outsider. He could report their presence to Prentiss and Finli and be on his way, but he wants the pleasure of killing Roland himself.

The ka-tet listens to the audiotapes Ted left for them, telling his history. He has a safe place where he can go, a Gingerbread House created by Sheemie outside of time and reality. Ted uses it as his command center for his munitions-gathering excursions. It's the only place he can be where he doesn't have to constantly guard his thoughts.

Ted tells of how he came to Blue Heaven and how he once escaped through a hole Sheemie made for him. From reading the thoughts of one of Blue Heaven's guards[13] Ted knows that King, the incarnation of Gan in Keystone Earth, isn't writing anymore, leaving him vulnerable. The ka of 19 and the ka of 99 will get together (1999) to bring about his end.

Susannah finally remembers to tell the others about her dream. All the 19s they've been seeing point to a date, probably June 19. They know King is still alive because they wouldn't still exist if he died. Roland's aches mirror the injuries King will suffer, and only living things feel pain, which tells him King won't be killed instantly. Roland is angry because one of the two simultaneous crises confronting them is due to the writer's laziness. Saving him by changing ka will cost them dearly. He looks forward to kicking "the lazy tale-spinner's yellow ass."

They have to decide which emergency to handle first. Sheemie tells them of a dream he had the previous night about a small boy who asks why they are hurting him when he loves them so. The members of the ka-tet realize that each one of them had this dream. The boy represents the

Beam, which is analogous to love. "When love leaves the world, all hearts are still." The answer is clear: They must first free the Breakers.

Roland sends a Roderick with a few sneetches to start fires that will create confusion and panic. Fire is the most feared thing in Blue Heaven, much of which is constructed of wood. Susannah sets up her ATV on the north side of town with enough firepower to make it seem like she's a small army. They plan the attack for shift change, when the prison is most vulnerable.

When the fire alarms go off, Dinky mentally guides the Breakers out of the building and tells them to put their hands up so the gunslingers can distinguish prisoners from guards. Roland waits for Prentiss and Finli to appear before opening fire; cut off the head of the snake and it dies. He shoots Prentiss, then gives the order to the others to fire. What follows is the pandemonium of a vast and multifronted battle. King describes the confusion in discrete vignettes. "The historians can later assemble it into a comprehensive narrative," he writes. Susannah drives the battle from the north with her guns and laser beams. By the time she reaches Main Street, the shooting is over and Pleasantville's gutters run with the blood of Blue Heaven's personnel.

From the moment the ka-tet reached Thunderclap, King started establishing the vector leading to the first major death in the series, Father Callahan notwithstanding. When Ted tells the history of Algul Siento, King draws attention to the gun used by Prentiss's predecessor to execute a low man who raped a Breaker, warning that it will play a grim part in future events. This is the gun passed to Prentiss when he took charge of the prison camp. On the morning of the battle, he tucks the weapon into his belt without giving it much thought. He didn't normally arm himself, but he was nervous—perhaps influenced by the same sense of déjà vu known to the ka-tet.

The ka-tet gathers for their last group hug. Prentiss isn't dead, only mortally wounded. He can't change the outcome of the battle, but its one-sided nature angers him. Eddie's reflexes aren't quick enough to avoid Prentiss's bullet, which enters above his right eye and exits from the back of his head. Gran-Pere Jaffords would have said it was the only end that a gunslinger such as him could expect. Prentiss is struggling to get off a second shot when Roland kills him.

Roland and Jake take care of the remaining guards while Ted and

Dinky help Susannah comfort Eddie. Roland kills only those who shoot at them. The others he disarms and frees, giving them until sundown to get out of Dodge. "You've done bad work here, hell's work, but hell's shut, and I mean to see it will never open these doors again." This is a far different gunslinger from the one who obliterated every living soul in Tull and offered no quarter to those who chased Jake from the Dixie Pig.

To Jake, Eddie's lingering death is pointless and endless. He didn't want to remember his wisecracking friend looking frail, old and stupid. He's afraid that even kissing Eddie might be enough to kill him. Roland tells him they attend Eddie for Susannah's sake because "later on she'll remember who was there, and be grateful." Jake wonders how grateful she'll be to Roland, without whom Eddie wouldn't be dying. On the other hand, Susannah would never have met Eddie without him. No one says "better to have loved and lost," but this is what Jake thinks.

Though they've saved the Beams and prevented the fall of the Tower, Roland and Jake can take no pleasure in their victory. Their fourteen-hour bedside vigil puts the pressure on. King will meet his own destiny in less than a day, but Roland won't leave until Eddie dies. On his deathbed, Eddie promises Susannah he will await her in the clearing at the end of the path. His message to Jake is more cryptic, telling him his job (and Oy's) is to protect his dinh from Mordred and Dandelo. He calls Roland Father and, with his final words, thanks Roland for the better life he has had since the gunslinger drew him from New York.

"The rest of the tale will be short compared to all that's gone before. Because when ka-tet breaks, the end comes quickly."

Roland had planned to destroy Devar-Toi, but he leaves it for the Breakers who wish to stay. There's enough food to last them a lifetime. He tells them how to get to the Callas, where the people will likely forgive them. He urges them to go that way if only to find absolution for what they've done. "If you prefer purgatory to redemption, then stay here."

Susannah stays with Ted to bury Eddie, while Sheemie sends Jake, Oy and Roland to Maine to save King. Teleporting is dangerous business for Sheemie. Ted estimates he can only do it one or two more times before it kills him. They don't know that he's already dying from an infected foot wound he suffered during the battle.

Roland arranges to meet Susannah in Fedic in two days. She agrees to rejoin them because Eddie wanted her to, but Jake thinks she still wants to see the Tower as much as he and Roland do. The ka-tet might be broken, but ka remains.

Roland and Jake arrive outside the general store twenty-two years after Andolini's ambush. Roland has no time for pleasantries. He pulls his gun and demands the store owner's truck keys, but they also need a driver; Jake can't drive, and Roland's hip aches too much. For the second time, Roland finds a useful person in the general store. Irene Tassenbaum agrees to take them where they need to go. She's afraid, but she also enjoys being at the center of something important.

King is on one of the country-road walks his wife nags him about. He reaches a crucial point, a crossroads. If he takes the shorter route back home, he will start working on the next *Dark Tower* book. By choosing the longer road, he announces his intention to procrastinate. Ka decides he's outlived his usefulness.

His fate lies in the hands of Bryan Smith, a local in a blue minivan who is on his way into town to satisfy his drug-induced munchies. Jake can sense Smith and tries to use his touch to slow him down. The minivan driver is distracted from the road by his rottweillers, Bullet and Pistol, who are digging in a cooler of meat behind his seat. He doesn't see King on the roadside ahead, or the truck approaching from the opposite direction.

To save one life, the ka-tet will have to exchange another. Roland has already sacrificed Jake—the boy he now thinks of as his son—once on his quest for the Tower; he will not do so again. If anyone dies this day, Roland is determined it will be him.

When it comes to ka, Roland doesn't always get his way. Ironically, pain from the very injury he intends to prevent causes his bad leg to betray him when he leaps from the truck. Without a second's hesitation, Jake steps on and over Roland and seizes King, shielding him.

King doesn't escape completely. The impact throws him off the road, and the van hits him again and stops on top of him, breaking his hip. Roland rushes to Jake, but the boy pushes him away. Roland needs to make sure King will live. He tries to convince himself that Jake's injuries are slight, but Jake knows otherwise. He has died twice already.

The van did Roland's job of kicking the lazy tale-spinner's yellow ass. King looks worse than Jake, but Roland is sure he'll survive. King

The Accident

Most readers will be aware that the incident depicted here bears some resemblance to the accident King suffered in the summer of 1999. In the endnotes, the author calls it a "funhouse mirror" version of the real event. How close are truth and fiction?

Though it isn't stated in the text, King's fictional accident takes place around 4:20 P.M. on Saturday, June 19, 1999, the same time as Father Callahan's fatal appointment with Sombra Corporation fifteen and a half years earlier. The real accident happened at 4:30 P.M.[14]

In *The Dark Tower*, Jake attempted to slow down Smith by having him stop to urinate. In reality, it was King who stepped into the woods. He later said, "It was two months before I was able to take another leak standing up." Two women observed Smith's minivan weaving on the road, and one said that she hoped the van didn't hit King, whom they had just passed. King has the women picking berries, but in reality they were driving.

King was struck as he walked along the shoulder of the road. He had earlier been reading a Bentley Little novel, but he stopped reading when he reached a stretch of road with poor sight lines due to blind curves and hills. He was thrown about fifteen feet off the road by the impact, landing in a grassy patch near a wall of rocks.

As in the fictionalized account, Bryan Smith—who was driving from his campsite into town for groceries (Mars bars)—was distracted from the road by his dog Bullet,[15] who was rummaging around in a cooler of meat behind him. Smith's other rottweiler, Pistol, didn't accompany him in the van in the real version of the accident.

Police reports indicated that King probably heard the van at the last minute because he turned slightly, which may have saved his life. He later said that he thinks he tried to leap out of the way. In the fictional version, of course, it was Jake Chambers who was responsible for deflecting the potentially fatal impact. King admits to a break in his memory here—the time during which a gunslinger from Mid-World hypnotized him?

In *The Dark Tower*, King is alone when struck, but in reality a pedestrian witnessed the accident and another driver arrived on the scene shortly after it happened. Smith, who never saw King and thought he'd struck a deer until he noticed the author's bloody glasses inside the van beside him, was sent off to call the police while the resident stayed with King. As in the book, Smith reportedly told King he'd never even had a parking ticket before, which later proved to be patently untrue. King responded that he'd never been struck by a van before and, as in the book, asked for a cigarette.

King said, "It occurs to me that I have nearly been killed by a character out of one of my own novels." [OW] How far apart are truth and fiction?

recognizes Roland, greeting him by saying, "You again," before asking where Eddie is. He hasn't written about Eddie's death yet and tries to tell Roland he lost the Beam, but Roland forces him to sit up in spite of his injuries, and points to the sky, where it is perfectly clear. "You didn't lose it, you turned your coward's eye away."

King promises to continue the story, no matter how it comes out, but he chastises Roland for his anger. "Save your hate for those who deserve it. I didn't make your ka any more than I made Gan or the world and we both know it."

Roland is devastated that he has to leave Jake's dying to Oy and Irene, a woman they met less than an hour earlier, to deal with two men he doesn't like. While he's making sure King won't surrender if Death calls on the way to the hospital, Jake, whom he loved even more than Susan Delgado, answers that same call. In one of the series' greatest ironies, Jake sacrificed his life to save Stephen King in 1999, thereby allowing King to finish writing the series in 2003, including the section depicting Jake's death in 1999, which will happen again and again as Roland repeats the quest cycle until he gets it right. In the words of Andre Linoge from *Storm of the Century,* "Hell is repetition."[16]

Roland sends Irene away until the accident scene is cleared, trusting her to return because she is a companion of the Beam. In the woods, he digs a shallow grave for Jake and says a Manni prayer over him. He thinks Oy might decide to perish at Jake's grave, but the bumbler rejoins Roland at the roadside before Irene returns in her own car.[17] Oy's decision strengthens Roland's resolve.

Jake asked Irene to drive Roland to New York, and she agrees to do so. On the first night, she watches the TV news long enough to learn that King survived his accident.[18] Later, she finds Roland sitting on the stoop in the dark. "I'm afraid to go to sleep," he tells her. "I'm afraid my dead friends will come to me, and that seeing them will kill me." This is a very different Roland from the man who was able to push thoughts of his upcoming sacrifice of Jake from his mind and sleep dreamlessly in the desert.

The second night, they make love in a motel in Harwich, Connecticut—the former home of Bobby Garfield and Ted Brautigan. King does not say whether Roland straightens any of the room's pictures. Afterward, she dreams of the field of roses and the Tower and hears the voices of Roland's lost friends. Roland has transferred some of his touch to her temporarily, like Ted Brautigan did with Bobby Garfield. Her part in the adventure is almost over, though, and soon she will return to her husband and her former life.

Roland's pain is with King now, so they walk from Irene's New York apartment to the high-rise at 2 Dag Hammarskjold Plaza housing the Tet Corporation. The building stuns him. It's not his Dark Tower, but it's the

Tower's representation in this Keystone World, just as the rose represented a field filled with them.

Irene draws his attention to the pocket park outside the building that contains a fountain and a turtle sculpture, the place where Susannah and Mia rested after stealing Trudy Damascus's shoes. Roland leaves Irene in the park, a perfectly serene place for her to bide while he attends to business inside.

The rose is exactly where Roland last saw it. The garden lobby and the building are shrines built around it. He's so fascinated by the rose that he doesn't hear Nancy Deepneau—Aaron's brother's granddaughter—approach him from behind, a serious lapse for a gunslinger. Roland, who normally has trouble with written English, can read the sign in the garden because the inscription devoted to Eddie and Jake changes into the Great Letters of Gilead. Before June 19, the plaque had been more generic, honoring the "Beam family" and Gilead.

Nancy takes him to the nineteenth floor, where he learns about the deaths of John Cullum (in 1989 at the hands of low men[19]) and Aaron Deepneau (in 1992 of cancer). Moses Carver, the last of the Ka-Tet of the Rose, is still alive at the age of a hundred. He retired as president of Tet Corporation two years earlier in favor of his thirty-year-old daughter, Marian Odetta Carver. The business is now worth $10 billion.

To confirm his identification, Marian asks to see Roland's gun. Carver is awestruck. "Might as well tell your gran-babbies you saw Excalibur, the Sword of Arthur, for't comes to the same!"

Carver understands what the young women do not: that saving the Beams wasn't Roland's quest but a means to an end. "Had they broken, the Tower would have fallen. Had the Tower fallen, I should never have gained it, and climbed to the top." Nancy is incredulous. "You're saying you cared more for the Dark Tower than for the continued existence of the universe?" Roland tells her he sacrificed his friends, a boy who called him father and his own soul pursuing the Tower.

Carver tells Roland that a team of telepaths and precogs believe that Eddie told Jake something important before he died. Jake may have passed the message on, either to Irene or to Oy. They present Roland with a copy of one of King's novels, *Insomnia,* telling him that even his earliest books touch on the *Dark Tower* in one way or another. A group of Tet scholars—the Calvins—spend their days reading his works, cross-referencing them

See the TURTLE of enormous girth, on his shell he holds the Earth—from a pocket park near the Tower in NYC. (*Ron J. Martirano, 2004*)

by setting, character and theme, looking for references to the Tower and to real people.

Insomnia is the keystone nonseries book. Its red-and-white dust jacket signifies evil and good.[20] The Calvins believe King named the villain Deepneau as a subconscious way of getting Roland's attention. They tell him to be on the lookout for Patrick Danville, whom they believe will be important to his quest. The Calvins—and King—implicitly support Roland's second quest. Patrick Danville isn't important to saving the Tower, only to assisting him on his journey there.

Tet Corporation's final gift is a watch. Engraved upon its gold cover are three objects: a key, a rose and a tower with tiny windows marching in an ascending spiral around its circumference. According to one of Tet's precogs, when Roland nears the Tower, the watch may stop or begin to run backward. Moses tells Roland that in his world, giving a man a gold watch signifies he's ready for retirement, but he knows Roland doesn't plan to retire.

Outside the Manhattan Tower, Roland asks the bumbler what message Jake left for him. Oy tries to speak, but words fail him. Roland presses his forehead against Oy's, closes his eyes and hears Jake's voice one last time: "Tell him Eddie says, 'Watch for Dandelo.' Don't forget!" Oy had not forgotten.

Roland says good-bye to Irene at the Dixie Pig. She fared better than most of the people he used and left behind on his way to the Dark Tower and can return to her former life, though she is much changed by her adventure.

Susannah greets Roland in Fedic. She knew someone had died but hadn't been able to tell whom. Part of her wants to let Roland go on alone for what he has given her and then taken away. Instead, she kisses him, not on the cheek but on the lips. "Let him understand it's no halfway thing— if I'm in it, I'm in to the end." She tells him that Sheemie died on the train ride to Fedic.

Before going through the doorway toward Calla Bryn Sturgis, the Breakers used their powers to map out the labyrinth beneath the castle and find the passage Roland and Susannah need to get past the chasm beyond the outer walls.[21] The Breakers warn of creatures in the fissure that have been tunneling the catacombs for a long time and are close to breaking through. These beasts are neither for the Crimson King nor against him; they're only for themselves.

In Sayre's office, Susannah and Roland find surveillance files containing photographs of Jake and Eddie that are too painful to look at. They also see a painting signed by Patrick Danville depicting Mordred beside Llamrie, Arthur Eld's horse, which is dead. Though Roland doesn't know it yet, this painting—and another featuring the Dark Tower that can have been done only by someone who has seen it—comes from the future and is inspired by Patrick's experiences after he joins Roland and Susannah. The portrait of Llamrie symbolizes how Mordred, the last of the line of Eld, died partly because he ate Dandelo's dead horse.

> Narrow windows rise in an ascending spiral around it. At the top of the 600-foot tower is an oriel window of many colors, each corresponding to one of the Wizard's Glasses. The innermost circle but one was the pink of Rhea's ball. The center was the dead ebony of Black Thirteen. Outside the barrel of the tower were balconies encircled with waist-high wrought-iron railings. On the second of these was a blob of red and three tiny blobs of white: A face that was too small to see, and a pair of upraised hands. The Crimson King, locked out of the only thing he ever wanted.

"The room behind that window is where I would go," Roland says, indicating the multicolored oriel window at the top, similar to the window in his nursery in Gilead. "That is where my quest ends." He reassures Susannah that he won't be alone, that she and Oy will help him deal with the Crimson King and climb the stairs with him to the room at the top. The words feel like a lie to both of them.

They stock up on provisions, including Sterno for fires, and Roland rigs a set of straps so he can carry Susannah. Oy leads them to the passage the Breakers found. Something big—either from the fissure or to-dash space—follows them. When the lights fail, it closes the gap in a scene reminiscent of Jake's passage through the tunnel near the Oatley Tap in *The Talisman*. Susannah uses Sterno torches to hold the beast at bay while Roland runs in the darkness with her strapped to his shoulders, Oy keeping pace at their side. Eventually, they emerge into the cold land east of

Fedic, where they find a sign saying THIS CHECKPOINT IS CLOSED. FOR-EVER.

Though they have food for about a month and water, they don't have heavy clothing. Past this barren land there will be animals to kill for their hides, but that is weeks away and they are in for a very hard stretch of energy-draining cold. It would have taken very little—a sweater and gloves—to make them comfortable, but even the blankets in Fedic had rotted to almost nothing.

They set out along the Path of the Beam again, mother and father, but never husband and wife, with their ill-begotten son trailing behind.

The village in the shadow of the Crimson King's castle is deserted, the houses haunted. No wood will burn for them because this is "his place, still his even though he's moved on. Everything here hates us." The castle is off the Path of the Beam, but Roland wants to make sure the Crimson King is really gone and he thinks that they may also find a way to trap Mordred. They haven't seen the red pulsing that Susannah observed from the ramparts of Castle Discordia. Roland says it probably died when they put an end to the Breakers' work. The Forge of the King has gone out. This may also be the Big Combination, the Crimson King's child-powered energy plant, extinguished by Ty Marshall at the end of *Black House*.

Roland prepares for whatever traps the Crimson King may have left for them at his castle. Before victory comes temptation, and the greater the victory to win, the greater the temptation to withstand. He instructs Susannah to let him do the talking.

A banner welcomes them by name. In the castle's forecourt, two men who look like 1977 versions of Stephen King greet them. A third hangs back, staying on the far side of a dead-line set by the Crimson King.[22] The polite one calls himself *Fee*malo, the ego. The rude one is *Fum*alo, the id, and the one behind is the superego, *Fi*malo. Their names bring to mind "Jack and the Beanstalk" and also *King Lear,* where "Fie, foh, and fom, I smell the blood of a British man" is the line after "Childe Roland to the Dark Tower Came." Wayne Overholser also says, "Fee fi fo fum" in the Calla when talking about how the roont children grew into giants.

The scene is also reminiscent of Tweedledum and Tweedledee from *Through the Looking-Glass,* which Susannah underscores by reciting the line "Jam yesterday, jam tomorrow but no jam today." The odd twins in that book warn Alice against awakening the Red King, who is dreaming about her. If the king should awake, they say, Alice would cease to exist, putting the girl in similar company to Roland and Susannah, who are the living dreams of Stephen King, a representation of whom stands before them.

Fumalo and Feemalo tell Roland that after the Crimson King witnessed the ka-tet's victory against the Wolves, he forced everyone in the castle to take poison—recalling the Jonestown massacre, which is mentioned earlier—and then killed himself with a spoon, fulfilling an ancient prophecy familiar to Roland, and putting himself beyond death. He's now trapped on one of the Tower's balconies. In a fit of rage, he scorched the red mark from his heel and without a sigul of Eld he can't get back in. However, he could take Roland's guns from him and use them to reenter the Tower. From there he could rule, but he'd prefer to bring the Tower down, which he can possibly do, Beams or no Beams. Fimalo and Feemalo remind Roland that no prophecy demands he go beyond this point. He completed his task by saving the Beams and Stephen King, thereby preserving the Tower. If he continues, he goes outside ka and risks endangering the Tower again by providing the Crimson King what he needs to breach it.

When Roland makes it clear that he plans to go on, they offer food and clothing. The journey will take months through the deadly cold of Empathica. Though sorely tempted, Susannah resists their offer, remembering Roland's warning. "She never would have suspected that her life's greatest temptation would be nothing more than a cable-knit fisherman's sweater."

The provisions in the baskets are an illusion. Feemalo and Fumalo reach inside for guns, but Roland and Susannah shoot them before they raise their weapons. Fimalo transforms into a dying old man who served as the Crimson King's Minister of State under the name Rando Thoughtful.[23] Roland tells Thoughtful to give Mordred a message. "If he stays back he may live awhile yet with his dreams of revenge . . . although what I've done to him requiring his vengeance, I know not. And tell him that if he comes forward, I'll kill him as I intend to kill his red father."

Roland's watch is losing a few minutes each day. Susannah hopes that his eagerness to complete his quest won't make him careless. If he makes the right mistake at the wrong moment, neither of them will see the Dark Tower. Back on the Path of the Beam, they find wood that will burn, and are warm for the first time since Fedic. Keeping pace behind them, Mordred is so cold that he lines his mouth with straw to keep them from hearing his teeth chatter. Only hatred stops him from turning back to his red father's castle.

The poisoned lands cause serious health problems for those who linger or pass through. The Breakers and minders in Devar-Toi had severe acne problems. Roland develops a dry, harsh cough. A cancerous tumor grows beside Susannah's mouth. As Detta, she asks Roland to remove it, but he advises her to wait. Ironically, this cancer will provide her with the clue she needs to solve the riddle of how to get back to Eddie.

After several nights without fire, Roland and Oy corral a herd of deer out of the woods. Roland and Susannah kill ten, from which they make food, clothing and medicine that cures Roland's cough. Roland isn't much of a tailor,[24] so Susannah resews his stitches. Each of them now has a leather vest, a pair of leggings, a coat and a pair of mittens.

Susannah cuts weeks from their uphill struggle through the snowfields by making Roland a pair of snowshoes. She's pleased by her contribution, and can let Roland pull her along on a travois—like he had once been pulled along the beach—without feeling too much guilt. Still, it takes them three weeks to crest the hill and start downward again. She dreams nightly about Eddie and Jake. Eddie tells her she must let Roland go on alone. Jake reminds her to beware of Dandelo.

Mordred falls farther and farther behind, struggling to eat, to catch up and to stay warm.

They reach two recently plowed roads, the intersection of Odd Lane and Tower Road. One of the cottages clustered nearby looks lived-in. Susannah wants to keep going, but Roland feels obligated to warn whomever lives there about Mordred, who will not pass by.

An old man, introducing himself as Joe Collins, comes out to greet them. If Collins looks decrepit, his horse, Lippy,[25] blind in both eyes and malnourished, is the ugliest quadruped Susannah has ever seen. Some of her good cheer melts away at the sight of it.

Collins has an ice machine, a hot-air furnace and electricity thanks to a generator. A robot changes the propane tanks periodically. He's the first person they've met since Ben Slightman who possesses modern conveniences, a potential warning sign Roland and Susannah overlook. As long ago as the days of Mejis, Roland found out that people with access to luxuries like ice should not be trusted because they have likely traded their souls for them.

Collins invites them to take cover in his house from the approaching blizzard. He has lived at Odd Lane for nearly seventeen years. The Polaroid photograph of the Dark Tower tacked haphazardly to the wall seems to Susannah almost sacrilegious. Roland is paralyzed with awe. Collins saw the Tower as recently as two years ago. Even walking, Roland can reach it in a few weeks.

Susannah is suspicious of inconsistencies in the story Collins tells them during dinner. He denies that the white lands are known as Empathica. She doubts much of his tale about how he came to live in this cottage, and she thinks she hears something crying. The only part she believes is when he tells about hiding in the cellar when the Crimson King blazed past in his own portable storm on his final pilgrimage to the Dark Tower six months earlier. He says he felt like "potential snack food." Time is beyond relative in Mid-World, so it's not clear what this six-month time span corresponds to for Roland. It hasn't been six months since the liberation of Algul Siento.

Roland seems unaware anything is wrong. He encourages Collins to tell them jokes from his old stand-up routine and doesn't seem to mind Collins's lowbrow sense of humor, which is barely better than Eddie's. Soon Roland and Susannah are laughing uncontrollably. The sore beside Susannah's mouth starts bleeding, so she retreats to the bathroom to get a styptic pencil and Band-Aids. Here, she finds a note that says, RELAX! HERE COMES THE DEUS EX MACHINA! The message urges her to think about Odd Lane and then look for something the note's author left her in the medicine cabinet.

She rearranges the letters in "Odd Lane" to get "Dandelo," which Eddie and Jake had warned them about. In the living room, Roland is almost choking with laughter. Collins, feeding off their emotions, has grown almost twenty years younger in the few minutes she's been out of the room.

Before she shoots Dandelo, the emotional vampire's face changes into that of a psychotic clown. King seems to be leaving hints that connect the *Dark Tower* series and *It*. Pennywise often presented himself as a clown, and a member of the ka-tet that fought It was called Stutterin' Bill, the same name as the robot who fills Collins's propane tanks. The encounter with Dandelo is reminiscent of Beverly Marsh's experience with Pennywise.

Mrs. Kersh—Pennywise in disguise—claimed that her father, Bob Gray, one of It's aliases, loved his jokes. It came from a place outside the Earth, perhaps in one of the todash spaces between universes. (Henry Bowers thinks that It "came from the spaces between the stars.")

Pennywise and Dandelo both feed on emotions—fear and imagination. Dandelo, however, doesn't *seem* to have an existence that extends into the multiverse, like Pennywise did. To that extent, It is more akin to Tak and, possibly, the Crimson King, who disappeared into the deadlights after being bested by Ralph Roberts in *Insomnia*. In 1977, King told Roland and Eddie, "When I open my eyes to your world, he [the Crimson King] sees me. . . . *It*."

Roland falls to his knees and won't get up until Susannah forgives him for being taken in. Inside the medicine cabinet, they find an envelope addressed to them. The note calls the gunslinger Childe Roland, an ancient, formal term Roland says describes a knight—or a gunslinger—on a quest. "We never used it among ourselves, for it means holy, chosen by ka. We never liked to think of ourselves in such terms." The message says, "You saved my life. I've saved yours. All debts are paid."

They also find a photocopy of Browning's poem "Childe Roland to the Dark Tower Came," with several stanzas circled[26] depicting the liar, set with his staff to waylay travelers. Susannah realizes that this poem was King's inspiration. Stanza XVI tells of how Cuthbert and Roland fell out over Susan Delgado. They wonder if Browning is also in some way responsible for their existence since the poet wrote about the gunslinger a century before King wrote the *Dark Tower* series. Was Browning an earlier channel for Gan?

Dandelo's main supply of emotional energy was Patrick Danville, whom Roland and Susannah find in the cellar. The boy's mind is terribly damaged. Dandelo fed him barely enough to stay alive, while consuming his laughter, tears and fears several times a week.

Unwilling to stay in the house—which degrades after Dandelo dies—they hole up in the barn for three days until the blizzard passes. Stutterin' Bill clears the road after the storm and gives them a ride to Federal Outpost 19, which is as far as his programming will let him go. Some of the monitors in the outpost still work, but the one that used to show the Tower has gone out. "I don't think the Red King liked being on television," Bill says.

Dandelo had forbidden Bill from repairing the computer glitch that caused him to stutter; Roland gives him permission to fix it. Behind the outpost, Bill shows them vehicles that could carry them the last hundred miles of their journey, but Roland wants to walk. "I'm not ready to be there yet. . . . I need a little more time to prepare my mind and my heart. Mayhap even my soul." Now that the Tower is within his grasp, he's lost a little of the imperative that has driven him for a thousand years. When he thought Walter was within his grasp at the way station, he ran to confront him. Now he needs more time. The temptation to run will come upon him again soon, though.

They take a pull-cart for their provisions and a battery-powered vehicle for Susannah. Five days at a comfortable pace will get them to the Tower. He'd like to arrive around sunset if possible, for that's when he's always seen it in his dreams.

Susannah suffers frequent bouts of weeping. Only Roland is meant to reach the Tower, and she doesn't know what is to become of her, Patrick and Oy. She dreams about Eddie and Jake waiting for her in New York, trying to tell her something. She sees product brands that tell her they aren't in Keystone Earth, and she begins to realize that this is where she needs to go.[27] Given her power to imagine things and have them manifest, it is possible that her repeated dreams of Christmas in Central Park turn this fantasy into her future reality.

Her dream also features a door decorated with two crossed pencils with the erasers cut off and the words THE ARTIST, a clue that Patrick is involved. In Dandelo's pantry, Roland found pencils like these. Dandelo removed the erasers because Patrick's drawings make things real and unreal, although he doesn't know it.

She needs to find this door before she sees any part of the Tower, or her choice between it and the door will be harder. She's worried that Eddie won't know her, or that he'll turn out to be a junkie. Even worse, she worries that Eddie will recognize her but deny it because that would be easier than trying to deal with how they could possibly know each other.

Her way to the door is through Patrick. Susannah tests her theory by having him erase the cancerous sore beside her mouth in his portrait of her. Roland had drawn her, Eddie and Jake. Now Patrick has drawn her, too.

Patrick draws a doorway to her specifications and copies onto it the symbols she dreamt. If he doesn't get these siguls exactly right, the door will either not open or open some place she doesn't want to go. When Roland shows Patrick how to put the doorway into the context of their surroundings, it materializes before them. Susannah invites Patrick to come with her but he, like the Breakers, is a misfit, afraid of going some-place new.

Susannah tries to distance herself from Roland by bringing Detta forward when it's time to leave. Roland reminds her that she hasn't asked Oy if he will go with her. If she asks as Detta, he'll surely stay. Susannah puts Detta away, but Oy decides to stay with "Ollan." He still has a job to do, one assigned to him by Eddie: protect Roland from Mordred.

Roland wants her to stay even though he knows he is to complete his journey alone. He's only had companions for a brief time during his epic quest, but now he seems afraid to go on without her. He warns that her dreams may be tricks and she might pass through the doorway into todash space, but Susannah has made her decision. If she is lost, then "I'll light the darkness with thoughts of those I love," she responds. Roland starts to beg her to stay, but she doesn't want to remember him this way. She can't bear to see him on his knees.

She has no second thoughts, believing that Oy and Patrick will soon meet the same fate as Jake and Eddie. She kisses Roland good-bye and tastes death in the breath of a thousand years and ten thousand miles. "But not for you gunslinger. For others, but never for you. May I escape your glammer and may I do fine."

She rides through the doorway into Central Park in a world that is close enough to the real one that in time she won't know the difference. The first person she sees is Eddie. Before she approaches him, she discards Roland's gun, which looks like it hasn't been used in decades. She is still enough of a gunslinger to regret throwing away such a weapon, but she's doesn't pause or look back once she does.

Eddie Toren from White Plains, a city about thirty miles from New York, doesn't know her, but he knows her name. He's been dreaming of her for months. He loves her already, though he doesn't understand how that can be. Eddie's younger brother, Jake, has been dreaming of her, too. It's the only reason Eddie knows he isn't going crazy. Susannah knows the enormous force of ka is working in her favor this time.

She tells Eddie that they may end up working for Tet Corporation, which still had about thirty years of work ahead of it in 1999. Susannah takes Eddie's familiar, well-loved hand. She thinks she will die of joy.

"Did they live happily ever after? There was happiness and they did live."

ROLAND HAS ONE MORE OBSTACLE before reaching the Tower: Mordred. His monster son is still following but he is dying, poisoned from eating Dandelo's horse. His time to act is running out. He must kill Roland before he reaches the Tower the following day.

The Tower calls out to Roland, but he's so disheartened, lonely and tired that even its lovely song can't lift him. He says cruel words to Oy, and when he later apologizes, Oy ignores him. King knows Oy is supposed to die, but the fictional writer thinks Oy seems fine, good to go all the way to the Dark Tower.

Shortly after noon, Roland sees the first wild rose growing by the side of the road. Light pink on the outside, it darkens to a fierce red on the inside—the exact color of heart's desire. He falls on his knees before it, tipping his ear to listen to the rose's singing. In its heart he sees a yellow center so bright he can't look directly at it: Gan's gateway. Unlike the rose in the vacant lot, this one is healthy and full of light and love. The field of roses is a living force field feeding the Beams with their songs and their perfume. In turn, the Beams feed the roses.

The night before he reaches the Tower is the longest of Roland's life, except for the one he spent in palaver with Walter and, perhaps, the night he told the story of Mejis. He knows Mordred is probably waiting for him to fall asleep, but he can't stay awake and has no choice but to ask Patrick to keep watch. Roland gives him something to draw, hoping it will keep the boy attentive for an hour or two. He knows Patrick is addicted to "the narrow line of graphite running down the center of his pencils."

Mordred is struggling to stay alive long enough to fulfill his destiny. He considers attacking while Patrick is still awake, but the Crimson King speaks to him from the Tower, telling him to wait, then sends out a soothing pulse that lulls Patrick to sleep. Mordred sweeps down on the camp, a black nightmare on seven legs, but in his zeal he overlooks the third member of Roland's group. Oy throws himself at the spider with the same reckless disregard for his own safety he displayed when he attacked Tick-

Tock in the bunker beneath Lud. His barking wakes Roland. If Oy hadn't rushed out of the tall grass to intercept Mordred, it would have been Roland in the spider's grip. Oy has a chance to escape Mordred's grasp, but he chooses to fight instead.

Roland commands Mordred to release Oy, promising to let him live another day, but Mordred can't overcome his hatred. He's going to die soon, one way or the other. He flings Oy into the branches of a tree, where he is impaled, fulfilling Roland's vision inside the pink Wizard's Glass in Mejis.

> Ahead is a tree like a crooked, clutching hand; on its topmost branch a billy-bumbler has been impaled. It should be dead, but as the pink storm carries Roland past, it raises its head and looks at him with inexpressible pain and weariness. "Oy!" it cries, and then it, too, is gone and not to be remembered for many years. [DT4]

Mordred turns to attack Roland, but he is too slow and the gunslinger's eye has never been clearer. He shoots Mordred several times, until he hears a howl of outraged fury in his head. The Crimson King is livid at the death of his only son, but Roland reminds the madman that it was his fault for sending Mordred after him. The outcome of Roland's quest might have been much different if Mordred had been able to resist his need to kill his White father and reached the Dark Tower ahead of him.

Oy is the last of Roland's ka-tet to die from the terrible germ of death the gunslinger carries. Patrick is immune because he was never part of the ka-tet. Roland thanks Oy for his sacrifice and extends his hand, aware that Oy might bite him and perhaps hoping that he will. Oy has only enough strength left to lick Roland's hand once before he dies. Roland regrets being short with Oy the previous day, and realizes now that the bumbler probably knew he was going to die and that the dying would be hard.

After Patrick and Roland bury Oy, they set out to cover the last few miles to the Tower. Roland is careful to make sure that the wheels of his cart don't crush any of the roses that grow in increasing numbers along the road, which is lined with the remnants of rock walls. Some look like the ruins of castles; others look like Egyptian obelisks. A few are speaking rings, and one ruin resembles Stonehenge.

At last, Roland sees for the first time something that has occupied his dreams for a thousand years—the top of the Dark Tower. He's surprised that the world doesn't come trembling to a halt, but he is the same person a minute after he sees the Tower as he was a minute before. Neither, though, does he feel a sense of disappointment that his quest is nearly at an end.

Through binoculars scavenged from Mordred's camp he sees the oriel window at the top, its many colors blazing in the spring sunshine. The black center peers back at him like an eye. A double antenna juts from the top. The two surviving Paths of the Beam cross in the sky above it. X marks the spot.

The voices grow louder, singing the names of all worlds. He feels so light that he asks Patrick to climb into the cart he's pulling. "I need an anchor. . . . Without one I'm apt to start running toward yonder Tower, even though part of me knows better. And if plain old exhaustion doesn't burst my heart, the Red King's apt to take my head off with one of his toys."

A few miles from the Tower, Roland sets down the cart handles and he and Patrick crest the last hill hand in hand. Below them, a great blanket of red stretches to the horizon in every direction. At the far end stands the sooty gray Tower, its windows gleaming in the sun.

The Crimson King—who looks exactly like Patrick's childhood depiction of him—greets Roland with a scream: "GUNSLINGER! NOW YOU DIE!" They duck behind a steel-lined stone pyramid[28] as a sneetch strikes their cart, blowing their belongings in every direction.

Roland taunts his nemesis, hoping to goad him into depleting his ammunition. The Crimson King rages, then falls silent and lets Roland hear the Tower, which is summoning the entire line of Eld, calling to him like the Talisman called Jack Sawyer. Its call is like a fishhook in his mind, drawing him out into the open where the Crimson King can kill him. Roland's watch runs backward, faster all the time.

Roland wanted to kill the Crimson King himself, but he comes up with another solution. He gives Patrick the binoculars and tells him to draw the Red King. Patrick's voice echoes in his head. "He's not entirely there. He darkles. He tincts," he says, echoing how Walter described the Ageless Stranger and how the Tower will describe Roland himself.[29]

Patrick's pencil drawing is perhaps his greatest work, but something is missing. The eyes need to be red. Roland springs from cover to pick the nearest rose. Its thorns slash through his leather glove, severing one of the remaining fingers on his right hand. He had been unable to convince Patrick to go for the rose, and he realizes now that had he been successful, the boy might have been injured badly enough to prevent him from finishing his drawing.

Once the rose is out of the ground, its thorns lose their bite. Patrick creates pigment the color of the Crimson King's lunatic eyes from saliva, attar of rose and Roland's blood of Eld, for the Crimson King is descended from Arthur, too. Roland believes it may be the first time Patrick worked in color, but Patrick often used crayons as a child.

Roland hands Patrick an eraser. "Make yonder foul dybbuk[30] gone from this world and every world." The Crimson King screams in pain, horror and understanding, throwing sneetches until he has no hands with which to throw. Patrick's eraser removes everything but his eyes.

Roland must go the rest of the way alone, but he won't abandon Patrick completely. The boy stands for all the murders and betrayals that brought Roland to the Tower. Roland's family is dead; Mordred was the last. He gives Patrick his remaining gun and shells, tells him to gather what he can of their provisions, and points him back in the direction of the outpost. Stutterin' Bill may be able to take him to a door to America. If ka leads him to Susannah, Roland asks Patrick to give her his love and a kiss. Patrick's fate is unknown, except that he would live long enough to create the paintings Roland and Susannah found in Fedic. Like Irene, he fared better than many who abetted Roland in his quest.

Roland approaches the Tower, naming all who have been part of his journey. Finally, he says, "I am Roland of Gilead, and I come as myself; you will open to me." The door opens and slams shut behind him.

Browning doesn't say what happens to the narrator of "Childe Roland" after he blows his horn and announces his presence to the Tower. King tells readers they should be content to have the story end here, too. What's behind this UNFOUND door may leave readers disappointed, even heartbroken. Straub and King do something similar in the closing pages of *Black House,* telling readers that the story could end with the Sawyer Gang rescuing Ty Marshall and the other children. "If you do choose to go on, never say you weren't warned: you're not going to like what happens next." [BH]

With an almost audible sigh, King accedes to the imagined pleas for more and draws aside the curtain to show the bumhug.

Here is the Dark Tower.

Giving in to the call of the Tower is the greatest relief of Roland's life, but only slightly greater than feeling nothing at either hip except for the loops of his jeans. He hadn't realized how heavy his guns had become.

The Crimson King's red eyes stare down from the balcony, burning with eternal hatred. The destruction of eyes is a recurring theme in the series. Another manifestation of the Crimson King lost one of his eyes to Ralph Roberts in *Insomnia,* and another of his eyes, Black Thirteen, is doomed to destruction beneath the World Trade Center. It's ironic that eyes are all that remain of his greatest enemy, but Roland has no weapons with which to extinguish them.

The horn that greets him is the voice of the roses, welcoming him with a kingly blast. In his dreams, the horn was his own, but he left his with Cuthbert at Jericho Hill. It would have taken only a few seconds to pick it up, and he will pay dearly for this oversight. Could Roland have avoided what comes next if he stopped here and retraced his thousand-year journey to see if he could recover this sigul?

The Tower isn't stone. It is a living thing, Gan himself. Its pulse is Gan's beating life force. The door swings open on its own, revealing the bottom steps of a spiral stairway. When Roland steps inside, the Song of the Tower, which he has always heard, even in Gilead, where it hid in his mother's voice, finally ceases. He smells alkali bitterness without realizing it is the Mohaine Desert that awaits him at the far end of his climb. Is this another omen from the Tower that he should turn away, warning him before he commits himself to the stairs that he's failed again?

The door swings shut behind him with a sigh.

At each level of Roland's climb he encounters a signature aroma and an icon from his life—his baby clothing, feathers from his hawk. After the floor where he sees the charred stake symbolizing Susan Delgado, he has no desire to see more. The Tower is a place of death, but only because his life has made it so.

The sense of déjà vu he experienced outside the door stays with him as he climbs, but he thinks this is because the Tower is relating his life. He passes Zoltan, the way station, the lobstrosities, climbing over a mile through history in nineteen-step increments to the present, a room containing a drawing pad bearing two red, glaring eyes. Is he wrong to bypass these rooms without giving each one due consideration? Many rooms represent decisions that, if he had chosen differently, might have resulted in a vastly different result for his quest.

By the time he reaches the top, the stairs have narrowed to a passage no wider than the inside of a coffin. Death for others, but not for him. These narrow steps at the top of the Tower may be as close to a coffin as he ever comes.

Unlike the other doors he passed on his ascent, the ghostwood door to the final room at the top of the Tower is closed. It has a single word carved upon it: ROLAND. The knob is engraved with a revolver, the iconic representation of his life, but Roland gave his remaining gun to Patrick. "Yet it will be yours again," whispers one of the Tower's voices.

As soon as the door opens and he sees what lies beyond its threshold, Roland realizes that his existence has been an uncounted series of loops. He isn't sent back to the beginning "when things might have been changed and time's curse lifted," but to a time in the desert when he has at last found the man in black's trail and "finally understood that his thoughtless, questionless quest would ultimately succeed." The same point where Walter o'Dim started to believe the prophecy that Roland would "begin the end of matters and ultimately cause the tumble of that which he wished to save."

Roland tries to pull back, but the hands of Gan pull him through the last door, "the one he always sought, the one he always found." Does this wording imply that not seeking the door is the change he needs to make?

King often called his series a cycle, hinting at Roland's fate. The ka-tet had a sense of this all along, saying at one point that King's work "has cast the circle." The day before he drops Jake, he thinks, "How we make large circles in earth for ourselves. . . . Around we go, back to the start and the start is there again: resumption, which was ever the curse of daylight." [DT1] Even Susan Delgado experienced what she called "the dim—that feeling of having lived a thing before." [DT4]

The book's subtitle becomes clear: "Resumption," the same as for *The Gunslinger*. Once back in the desert, Roland has a momentary sense of dislocation, the memory of having been in the Tower stolen by time. A voice whispers, "Perhaps this time when you get there it will be different." The voice seems to be encouraging him to return to the Tower.

King believes the ending will surprise people, but he hopes they will say, "Yes, it just has to be this way."[31] Roland's moment of desolation is tempered with hope. He may get it right someday.

During his previous iteration—perhaps during countless previous iterations—Roland learned that though his quest's objective was honorable, even pure goals must be tempered by consideration for those he meets along the way. He had once known love, which he called "the Bright Tower of every human's life and soul," [DT4] but he also saw the ruin love could bring, first to his parents, then to Susan Delgado and ultimately to himself. He was frequently reminded that he killed anyone he loved, so for many long years he withdrew emotionally, focusing on the Tower with single-minded determination.

By the end of his quest, he knows how to love again.

Though the members of his ka-tet have little doubt that he would sacrifice any of them if he deemed it necessary, letting Jake fall beneath the mountains is the last conscious sacrifice Roland makes. Others in the ka-tet die during the quest, but it is now *their* quest, too, and the decision to risk their lives is their own, not Roland's.

He has also learned the blessing of mercy. He released people who did him or others wrong—Slightman in the Calla and the minders in Devar-Toi, for example, people he would once have gunned down without a second thought. He even promises to let Mordred go free in exchange for Oy's life.

"You're the one who never changes," Cort told him once. "It'll be your damnation, boy. You'll wear out a hundred pairs of boots on your walk to hell." As the philosopher George Santayana is often quoted, those who cannot learn from history are doomed to repeat it—a saying Roland knew from his teacher Vannay.

This time, perhaps it will be different. His bag now contains the ancient brass horn that legend claimed had once been blown by Arthur Eld, lost at Jericho Hill in his previous life. Roland has a strange awareness of the horn, as if he'd never touched it before. The voice of the Tower tells him it is a sigul of hope, that some day he may find rest, perhaps even salvation.

The book ends as the series began more than thirty years earlier. "The man in black fled across the desert, and the gunslinger followed."

Though each member of his ka-tet discovers a new—and arguably better—life with the gunslinger, they, like Roland, are condemned to relive Roland's closed-loop existence. Each time he returns to the desert,

his trajectory will take him to the doorways that bring Jake, Eddie and Susannah from their former existences. Even if he takes a different course—
if he refuses to sacrifice Jake, for example, or finds a way to the Tower
without catching the man in black—there seems little chance that he
could succeed in attaining the Tower without help.

It's a double-edged sword, though. If Roland were able to achieve his
life's goal—or somehow modify it—without needing to draw the three,
he would be damning them to their former existences and depriving them
of the life-altering opportunities they experienced with him. Their sole
consolation would be that they only have to live their lives once.

Ka is the wheel that turns the world. Sometimes it's a big stone rolling
down the hillside.

The version of Roland's personal quest—reaching and claiming the
Tower—told in these seven books was doomed to failure before the opening pages. The missing horn of Eld, an item he needed to have in his possession when he reached the Tower, symbolizes a character flaw that he
has not yet overcome—focusing on his purpose without considering the
short-term consequences of his actions on himself and others. What does
it profit a man, if he shall gain the whole world but lose his own soul?

Interestingly, the herald of change comes from outside his closed
loop. That he now has Eld's horn means that his personal evolution somehow extended its tentacles back into time and made him a slightly different person. Is this a gift from ka, a deus ex machina reward for the lessons
he learned with his ka-tet? Perhaps Roland hasn't truly looped back to a
place in his past but has been elevated to a different level of the Tower, a
version of reality where he made different—hopefully better—decisions
along the way, improving his chances at success.

The total elapsed time in Mid-World during the seven books of the series is about one year,[32] not counting the indeterminate period of Walter
and Roland's palaver and other such time slips. Roland pursued Walter in
the heat of summer. The ka-tet reached the Calla in fall, and Roland and
Susannah crossed Empathica in winter. Roland sees the Tower for the first
time on a spring morning. Time, of course, is not an easily measurable
quantity in Mid-World, nor is it in our own, where faithful readers have
traveled with Roland for more than two decades.

How different the following year of Roland's existence will be is left to
readers' imaginations. Maybe the next time he will take note of the flow-

ing clouds Allie points out to him in Tull and realize that the Path of the Beam is close at hand. Will ka let him escape his humiliation on the Western Sea and still provide him with the ka-tet that will teach him about love and friendship, and whom he in turn will show the true value of their lives?

Roland isn't optimistic. In the Calla, while they prepare for the Wolves, he has the sense that he would fight battles similar to this one over and over for eternity. Sometimes, instead of losing fingers to a lobstrosity he might lose an eye to a witch, and after each battle he would sense the Dark Tower a little farther away instead of a little closer.

Which begs the question: Where does perfection lie in Roland's existence? Since the Tower still stands, even at his worst Roland has never made a serious enough mistake that he failed his primary quest and existence came to an end. Of course, he has ka on his side, pointing the way when he is at risk of going astray. Ka and Stephen King's little gifts.

What will he have to learn to break the cycle of repetition? To find a different path to the Tower that doesn't involve sacrificing others? To abandon the quest after saving the Tower? That it is the height of hubris for a mortal to presume to understand God and the nature of existence? Maybe he will come to realize that the only way he will ever be free is to let the Tower fall, and then he will have to decide between the good of the one—himself—and the good of the many.

Or perhaps the final door at the top of the Tower will lead him to a different fate should he ever reach nirvana. Perhaps he will someday find his way to the clearing at the end of the path, along with all those others who have gone on before, and learn whatever there is to be known of existence by those who reach this state.

It's a question with no easy answers that will surely engender discussion among readers for years to come.

It may take him several more tries,[33] but King leaves hope that eventually Roland will find what he seeks—his own humanity and the meaning of his existence—at the end of the road to the Dark Tower.

ENDNOTES

[1] Unless otherwise specified, all quotes in this chapter are from *The Dark Tower*.
[2] Like the paper boat does in *It*, the grains of poison that fall to the floor in *The Eyes of the Dragon* and the blue cell phone in *Black House*. In a few moments, Jake observes that Callahan, too, is gone from the story.

3 King has changed enough of the local geography to maintain his family's privacy.

4 Perhaps named in tribute to Poe's Roderick Usher from "The Fall of the House of Usher."

5 One poster reads VISIT SEPTEMBER 11, 2001.

6 The ability to switch minds was one of Dr. Doom's infrequently used powers. The Wolves who raided Calla disguised themselves with Dr. Doom masks.

7 Sara Laughs was the name of Mike Noonan's house in *Bag of Bones*. Mike goes on dream trips to the Fryeburg Fair that are reminiscent of todash trips.

8 How Eddie planned to tote the collected works of Stephen King across Mid-World defies understanding.

9 This section is called "The Shining Wire," a reference to *Watership Down* by *Shardik* author Richard Adams. The Warren of the Shining Wire is a place where rabbits gave up their freedom for security and a sense of complacency. In the control room, Walter is overly complacent and will pay for his carelessness. "Every sunlit field of scampering rabbits conceals its shining wire of death," King wrote in a review of a Harry Potter novel in the *New York Times,* July 23, 2000.

10 Perhaps another allusion to *King Lear,* where Cornwall plucked out Gloucester's eyeballs. Later, Mordred will feed Rando Thoughtful's eyes to the castle rooks. Dandelo plucked out Patrick Danville's tongue.

11 Stanley, believed to be Sheemie's father, was the bartender at Coral Thorin's saloon. His mother was Dolores Sheemer, hence his nickname.

12 Finli is reading *The Collector* by John Fowles, which reminds him of their situation, except he thinks their goals are nobler and their motivations higher than sexual attraction. King wrote a lengthy introduction for a Book of the Month Club reissue of this novel in 1989.

13 The low man is named Trampas, the name of a character from *The Virginian* by Owen Wister, one of the books on the shelf Calvin Tower and Eddie carry into the Doorway Cave.

14 Accounts of King's accident were published by the global media. The specific details mentioned here come primarily from the *Bangor Daily News* and from King's own account in *On Writing.*

15 The first thing King wrote after his accident was a novella called "Riding the Bullet."

16 King reiterates this philosophy in his endnote to the short story "That Feeling, You Can Only Say What It Is in French." He says, "There's an idea that Hell is other people. My idea is that it might be repetition." [EE]

17 A Mercedes-Benz. She and her husband also have a BMW, which Roland hears her describe as a "Beamer."

18 Roland can't see the TV picture, just a bunch of lines that make his eyes water. Later, Irene watches *Westworld,* a movie starring *The Magnificent Seven*'s Yul Brynner about a robot cowboy that runs amok.

19 Eddie told Cullum to stick around until at least 1986 for a doozy of a World Series.

20 In the Mid-World game of Castles, the opposing sides are red and white.

21 The labyrinth brings to mind the maze in *Rose Madder*.

22 The Pubes in Lud thought there was a dead-line around the Cradle of Lud where Blaine slept.

[23] Before that he was Austin Cornwell, from Niagara, but not in the Keystone World. He worked on advertising accounts for Nozz-A-La and the Takuro Spirit.

[24] He did mend Jake's torn shirt while waiting for the mescaline to kick in near the oracle's speaking ring, but leatherwork is more demanding.

[25] Named after the Robert Browning poem "Fra Lippo Lippi."

[26] Stanzas I, II, XIII, XIV and XVI. See appendix VI.

[27] People from the Keystone World or Mid-World who are killed die in all worlds. However, Eddie and Jake aren't from Keystone Earth, so their deaths (in Mid-World and Keystone Earth, respectively) aren't existence-wide.

[28] Arthur Eld's sword Excalibur was entombed in a pyramid like this before he extricated it.

[29] "Darkles" means "to become clouded or dark" or, perhaps, dim. The line "It darkles, (tinct, tint) all this our funnaminal world" appears in *Finnegan's Wake* by James Joyce.

[30] In Jewish folklore, the wandering soul of a dead person that enters the body of a living person and controls his or her behavior.

[31] Interview with Ben Reese, published on Amazon.com, May 2003.

[32] See appendix II.

[33] In *Kingdom Hospital*, a baseball player named Earl Candleton (Candleton is one of the stops on Blaine's route) gets to go back to redo an important event in his life. In a personal communication, King said, "With us wretched humans, I think the wheel of Ka has to turn many times, with only small changes accreting, before changes for the better finally occur."

CHAPTER 9

RELATED WORKS

I've known for some time now . . . that many of my fictions refer back to Roland's world and Roland's story.

[DT7]

I am coming to understand that Roland's world (or worlds) actually contains all the others of my making.

[DT4]

This business concerns the Dark Tower.

[BH]

Interconnections within Stephen King's books are not a recent phenomenon. As early as *The Dead Zone,* characters in his novels referred to other King novels ("He set it on fire by his mind, just like in that book *Carrie,*" a character in *The Dead Zone* says). Characters and events from previous books recur, as in the Castle Rock novels.

Many readers enjoy finding these cross-references. The authors of *The Stephen King Universe*[1] catalog many such links and define two realities: the "real" world of Derry and Castle Rock, and the world of the *Dark Tower.* Some of the connections they make are clear and unequivocal; others are more tenuous.[2]

The titles of King's novels and story collections related to the *Dark Tower* series were bolded on the author ad-cards in the last three books of the series. Some of these books came as a surprise. Previously, no definitive link had ever been made between *From a Buick 8* and the series. However, the Buick's mysterious driver was strongly reminiscent of a low man, and the car itself appeared to be a portal to another world.

Skeleton Crew was also a surprise member of this list, which comprised nineteen titles when it first appeared in *Wolves of the Calla.* Arguments could be made for several stories in this collection. Mrs. Todd's shortcuts, for example, possibly took her by way of a thinny. Technological doorways to facilitate travel across vast distances were the subject of "The Jaunt."

However, according to King's research assistant, Robin Furth, "The Mist" is the *Dark Tower* story in *Skeleton Crew*. In a personal communication, she theorized that the Arrowhead Project either created the first thinny, or else it ripped a hole into todash space. While the characters in "The Mist" believed Arrowhead caused some sort of genetic mutation, such things do not happen at the speed they occurred in the story. It is far more likely that the oversized creatures entered Maine through a tear between dimensions.

Furth also commented that Mrs. Carmody seemed to be a twinner of Sylvia Pittston from *The Gunslinger*. Their sermons about the last times bear remarkable similarities.

One book that occupies a borderland is *It*. There is clearly some relationship between Pennywise and the Crimson King, both of whom have business in Derry, Maine, and share the concept of deadlights. The Crimson King tells Ralph Roberts, "You may not know it, but shape-changing is a time-honored custom in Derry." [INS] The appearance of the song of the Turtle in *It* represents at least the germ of an idea that King developed more fully in the *Dark Tower*, but beyond these elements and a few passing references like Stutterin' Bill and an insane clown who feeds on emotions, the book does not contribute much to an understanding of the series.

One other passage strengthens the link between *It* and the *Dark Tower*. The house on Niebold Street has wallpaper decorated with runners of roses and capering elves wearing green caps. At the house on Dutch Hill, "elves with strange, sly smiles on their faces capered on the wallpaper, peering at Jake from beneath peaked green caps." [DT3]

The books discussed in this chapter directly illuminate the series, either through the introduction of a major character or of crucial concepts. Starting in the early 1990s, King found it increasingly difficult to keep the *Dark Tower* out of everything else he wrote. The Crimson King, low men and Breakers all appeared first in nonseries novels. People reading the series for the first time might consider pausing after *The Waste Lands* to read these related works to experience the evolution of King's mythos in the same way as people who read the books when they were published.

In *Song of Susannah,* he calls the *Dark Tower* his übernovel. The Dark

Tower is the nexus of all universes, an axle around which infinite realities rotate. In the Stephen King universe, the *Dark Tower* series is the axle around which his myriad fictional realities rotate.

The Stand

The Stand and *The Eyes of the Dragon* could be described as the two "Books of Flagg," for they relate two exploits of Roland's enemy. In the former, he tries to take over a devastated Earth similar to the one known to Jake, Eddie and Odetta. In the latter, he tries to overthrow the Kingdom of Delain, one of the baronies of In-World, the land of Roland Deschain. In both cases he ultimately fails, though he manages to wreak considerable havoc and destroy many lives.

When Roland and his ka-tet arrive in Topeka at the end of their journey aboard Blaine the Mono, they find a world ravaged by a superflu very much like the one depicted in *The Stand,* a cataclysm Walter o'Dim takes credit for.

The Stand is King's first full-length exploration of a character who reappears in many names and forms in his work. Flagg is a shadowy character known as the Dark Man in a poem of the same name that King published in college. Some people think of him as the hardcase, which also derives from one of King's college poems.[3]

Randall Flagg doesn't appear until well into *The Stand,* striding along US 51 from Idaho into Nevada. Drivers who pass him feel a slight chill. Sleeping passengers are touched with bad dreams. He is a tall man of no age wearing faded jeans and a denim jacket over well-worn, sharp-toed cowboy boots. His gunna is kept in an old, battered Boy Scout knapsack. His pockets are stuffed with pamphlets of conflicting opinions. "When this man handed you a tract you took it no matter what the subject."[4]

> There was a dark hilarity in his face, and perhaps in his heart, too, you would think—and you would be right. It was the face of a hatefully happy man, a face that radiated a horrible handsome warmth, a face to make water glasses shatter in the hands of tired truck-stop waitresses, to make small children crash their trikes into board fences and then run wailing to their mommies with

stake-shaped splinters sticking out of their knees. It was a face guaranteed to make barroom arguments over batting averages turn bloody.

His hands are smooth and blank, with no life line or other lines.

He's well known among the lunatic fringe and "even the maddest of them could only gaze upon his dark and grinning face at an oblique angle." For decades, he has been fomenting dissent across America, using names like Richard Fry, Robert Franq, Ramsey Forrest, Robert Freemont and Richard Freemantle. He can't speak at rallies because when he tries, microphones scream with feedback and circuits blow, but he writes speeches for those who speak and occasionally those speeches end in riots.

He met Lee Harvey Oswald and was behind the Patty Hearst kidnapping, but he always escaped before the police arrived. "[A]ll they knew was there had been someone else associated with the group, maybe someone important, maybe a hanger-on."

Many are afraid to say his name because "they believed that to call him by name was to summon him like a djinn from a bottle." They called him the Dark Man, the Boogeyman, the Walkin' Dude, or even "Old Creeping Judas." Glen Bateman says, "Call him Beelzebub, because that's his name, too. Call him Nyarlahotep[5] and Ahaz and Astaroth. Call him R'yelah and Seti and Anubis. His name is legion and he's an apostate of hell and you men kiss his ass."

Mother Abigail believes she is part of a chess game between God and Satan. Flagg, or "the Adversary," is Satan's chief agent in this game. "He's the purest evil left in the world." The other little evils in the world are drawn to him, as are the weak and the lonely. "He ain't Satan," according to Mother Abigail, "but he and Satan know of each other and have kept their councils together of old . . . this man Flagg . . . is not a man at all but a supernatural being."

"All things serve the Lord. Don't you think this black man serves Him, too?" Mother Abigail thinks God intends for them to confront Flagg. "It don't do no good to run from the will of the Lord God of Hosts. A man or woman who tries that only ends up in the belly of the beast."

Sounds like ka and "all things serve the Beam."

Glen thinks Flagg is the last magician of rational thought, gathering the tools of technology against the forces of good. The Earth has been given to him to master, Flagg believes, though he doesn't know by whom. He has a sense that some huge opportunity is presenting itself to him, that he is being reborn to his new destiny. "Why else could he suddenly do magic?"

He doesn't understand his powers; he merely accepts them. His magic allows him to shape-shift, broadcast dark dreams across the continent and send out an Eye of vision to spy on his enemies. He has dominion over the predators of the animal kingdom. He can levitate and kill people with a thought. He materializes anywhere he wants to go like a ghost—or does he travel through doors? Like Walter, he can project flames and light fires from the tip of his finger. Also like Walter, he tends to titter when he laughs. "When Flagg laughs, you get scared."

He can look normal, attractive even, but often his face is that of a devil and his eyes glow in the dark like a lynx's. Stu Redman says, "[H]e had the eyes of a man who has been trying to look into the dark for a long time and has maybe begun to see what is there." Dayna Jurgens said, "Looking into [his eyes] was like looking into wells which were very old and very deep."

The women he takes to bed feel "so cold, it seemed impossible they could ever be warm again." Nadine Cross thinks he's "[o]lder than mankind, older than the earth." He chooses her to mother his child, telling her she had been promised to him. When she asks him who promised her, he doesn't remember. Maybe, like the Crimson King, he has only promised himself.

All he asks is that his minions fall down on their knees and worship him. Those in the west who oppose him are either crucified or driven mad and set free to wander in the desert. He uses people like Harold Lauder and Trashcan Man to do his dirty work. Some of his followers are so loyal they grow to love him, but even those closest to him fear him.

He begins to lose confidence in his mission toward the end, when things seem to be unraveling. Memories of his life before the superflu and his rebirth slip away. "He was like an onion, slowly peeling away one layer at a time, only it was the trappings of humanity that seemed to be peeling away: organized reflection, memory, possibly even free will." Ordinarily when things go bad—as they have so often for him in the past— he would do a quick fade, but this was his place and time and he intended to take his stand. Threatened with death, though, he disappears like Flagg the magician in *The Eyes of the Dragon.* As he vanishes, he seems to change into something monstrous. "Something slumped and hunched and almost without shape—something with enormous yellow eyes slit by dark cat's pupils."

In the unexpurgated version of *The Stand,* Flagg survives and is transported to a tropical jungle paradise. At first he doesn't know who he is and remembers only echoes of his past, but slowly his memory returns. Birds, beasts and bugs drop dead at the sight of him. Though the people that gather around him bear spears, his terrible smile disarms them.

He doesn't know where he is, but "[t]he place where you made your stand never mattered. Only that you were there . . . and still on your feet." He introduces himself to the primitive people as Russell Farraday, a man whose mission is to teach them how to be civilized.

"Life was such a wheel that no man could stand upon it for long. And it always, at the end, came round to the same place again."

The Eyes of the Dragon

The Eyes of the Dragon tells the legend of how a demon named Flagg frames Peter, the rightful heir to the throne of Delain, for the murder of his father, King Roland, so that Peter's weaker younger brother, Thomas, will rule in name and Flagg can control the kingdom. Flagg fears Peter's strength of character. He knows he can control Thomas, but Peter would likely banish him from the kingdom, where he had been stirring up trouble for more than five hundred years.

Flagg returned to Delain from Garlan nearly eighty years before King Roland's reign began, but he appears to have aged a mere ten years in that time. The people convince themselves that having a real magician in the court is good, but in their hearts they know there's nothing good about Flagg.

Each time he comes to Delain, he uses a different name, but "always with the same load of woe and misery and death." Once he was Bill Hinch, the Lord High Executioner under three savage kings. Once he came as Browson, a singer who advised the king and successfully instigated a war between Delain and nearby Andua. "He always came hooded, a man who seemed almost to have no face, and he never came as a King himself, but always as the whisperer in the shadows, the man who poured poison into the porches of Kings' ears."

> He wanted what evil men always want: to have power and use that power to make mischief. Being a King did not interest him because the heads of Kings all too often found their way to spikes on castle walls when things went wrong. But the advisors to Kings . . . the spinners in the shadows . . . such people usually melted away like evening shadows at dawning as soon as the headsman's axe started to fall. Flagg was a sickness, a fever looking for a cool brow to heat up. He hooded his actions just as he hooded his face. And when the great trouble came—as it always did after a span of years—Flagg always disappeared like shadows at dawn. Later, when the carnage was over and the fever had passed, when the rebuilding was complete and there was again something worth destroying, Flagg would appear once more.

A great magician, he knows all about the worst poisons in existence. He owns a huge book of spells bound in human skin. After a thousand years, he has gotten through only a quarter of it. "To read too long of this book, written on the high, distant Plains of Leng by a madman named Alhazred, was to risk madness."[6] He possesses a magic crystal that allows him to see things, a device akin to one of the Wizard's glasses. "His mind was very complex, like a hall of mirrors with everything reflected twice at different sizes."

Flagg isn't a shape-shifter and has never seen that trick done. He can't make himself invisible, but he can go dim. He, too, can start fires from the tip of his finger. Though his powers are real, he also knows "it was not always necessary to make claims and tell people how wonderful you were to achieve greatness. Sometimes all you had to do was look wise and keep your mouth shut." This is reminiscent of Cort's advice to Roland to bide his time and let the legend go before him.

Like Randall Flagg and John Farson, he thinks deserters set a bad example. "If one or two were allowed to get away without paying the full penalty, others might try it. The only way to discourage them . . . was to show them the heads of those who had already tried it."

Flagg suspects something is amiss when Peter is planning his escape, but he can't grasp what. Fifty miles from the castle, he cries out in his sleep.

The soldier sleeping nearest Flagg on the left died instantly of a heart attack, dreaming that a great lion had come to gobble him up. The soldier sleeping on Flagg's right woke up in the morning to discover he was blind. Worlds sometimes shudder and turn inside their axes, and this was such a time. Flagg felt it, but did not grasp it. The salvation of all that is good is only this—at times of great import, evil beings sometimes fall strangely blind.

"[M]en like Flagg are full of pride and confidence in themselves, and although they may see much, they are sometimes strangely blind." Peter uncovers of one of Flagg's exploits, more than four centuries earlier, and realizes the King's magician's true nature. "I think that, sooner or later, things like you always begin to repeat themselves, because things like you know only a very few simple tricks. After a while, someone always sees through them. I think that is all that saves us, ever."

In the end, Thomas admits seeing Flagg deliver the poisoned wine to his father. He shoots Flagg through the eye[7] with an arrow, but the demon-wizard vanishes. Thomas decides to atone for his complicity in Peter's imprisonment by going south on a quest after Flagg, who he knows is out there somewhere, "[i]n this world or in some other . . . He got away from us at the last second." Peter's friend Dennis joins him, and they catch up with Flagg at some point, but the nature of their encounter is never revealed and Flagg apparently survived to make more trouble for the world. Roland met the two young men during the last days of Gilead.

Insomnia[8]

In 1994, King admitted to an audience at Cornell University that the *Dark Tower* elements in *Insomnia* came to him as a surprise, but he didn't think it was a coincidence. "It delighted me because it cast a light on what I have to do with the *Dark Tower,*" he said. The book was written during a period when King intended to complete the final books in the series back-to-back. It raises more questions than it answers, but all that keeps it from being a true *Dark Tower* novel is the absence of Roland and his ka-tet.

Published between *The Waste Lands* and *Wizard and Glass, Insomnia* introduces two important characters: Patrick Danville, the boy who accompanies Roland down the last stretch of road to the Tower, and the Crimson King, who awaits him there. Ed Deepneau is a herald of Aaron Deepneau, Calvin Tower's friend and future board member of Tet Corporation. Aaron had a distant cousin named Ed who died in 1947, the year King was born. He was a bookkeeper, "as inoffensive as milk and cookies."

In *The Dark Tower,* Roland learns that Tet Corporation created a group of Stephen King scholars, the Calvins, who study the author's non-Tower novels. The Calvins conclude that *Insomnia* is the keystone book relating to the *Dark Tower* series. The hardcover edition's dust jacket symbolizes the fight of good versus evil: White over Red. The Calvins believe that most of what (fictional) King has written contains veiled clues meant to help Roland attain his goal. Messages in bottles, Moses Carver calls them, cast upon the Prim. Messages from King's subconscious.

Ralph Roberts, *Insomnia*'s main character, suffers from a rare sleep disorder after his wife dies. Instead of having difficulty getting to sleep, Ralph wakes up earlier and earlier each morning. The resultant sleep deprivation puts him in altered mental status and opens his mind to different levels of reality going on around him in Derry, Maine, one of King's thin places where, until recently, a murderous creature from "outer space" came once every generation to steal the town's children, reminiscent of the periodic sweeps through the Callas by the Wolves. Ralph says, "It was as if a door in the wall of reality had come ajar . . . and now all sorts of unwelcome things were flying through," like the magic portal on Turtleback Lane.

Ralph is one of the few people aware that events of cosmic importance are happening in Derry. A neighbor and family friend, Ed Deepneau, begins acting strangely, having fallen under the power of the Crimson King, an evil force from another level of reality. Ed's goal is cloaked as anti-abortion activism, but the Crimson King really wants him to kill Patrick Danville, a talented four-year-old learning how to create art with crayons.[9]

Forces beyond his understanding are manipulating Ralph. He is terrified by the notion that some creature capable of foretelling the future has taken an interest in him. Events are orchestrated to facilitate his success; he describes it as "the sense of being pushed by invisible hands," as if he were "being *carried,* the way a river carries a man in a small boat." Roland knows that feeling well: ka, the great wheel of being. Like Roland, Ralph reaches a point in his newfound intuition where feeling and knowing something become nearly the same thing.

Ralph argues with Clotho and Lachesis—the two benign bald doc Long-Timers,[10] who represent Purpose[11]—that ka repudiates freedom of choice. Lachesis responds that freedom of choice is part of ka. Life is both random and on purpose, but not in equal measure.

Clotho and Lachesis can't lie, but they're very good at avoiding telling the truth. Though they induced the insomnia that opens Ralph's mind to heightened reality, thereby altering his ka, they serve creatures from higher reality.[12] These All-Timers are either eternal or so close to it as to make no difference. Something from one of these higher levels has taken an interest in Ed, and something else has made a countermove.

Atropos, an agent of Random, is terrified of his master. He tells Ralph, "If you succeed in stopping what's been started . . . I will be punished by the creature you call the Crimson King!" All three bald docs are responsible for severing the cord of life for people in this reality, sending their victims to "other worlds than these."

Dorrance Marstellar wanders through the story like deus ex machina personified, putting the can of pepper spray in Ralph's pocket so it will be available when fanatic Charles Pickering attacks him. "It isn't just like he knew I'd need the stuff; he knew where to find it, and *he knew where to put it,*" Ralph thinks. Old Dor would be at home in a certain vacant lot in New York, dropping a key or a red bowling bag for Jake to find. He knows much more than he is willing to reveal, but occasionally conveys important instructions—telling Ralph to cancel his acupuncture appointment, for example—in the same way Stephen King sends messages to Jake at the hotel in New York or to Susannah in Dandelo's bathroom. Dorrance tells Ralph and Lois that they are ka-tet, one made of many, bound together by the Purpose.[13]

Ed is a blank card, up for grabs by either Random or Purpose. Only Short-Timers like Ralph and Lois can oppose Atropos. Dorrance tells them that the work of the higher universe has "almost completely come to a stop as those of both the Random and the Purpose turn to mark your progress." It's possible that Ralph's interference with the Crimson King is one of the events that drive him insane.

In Atropos's lair, near a sneaker once worn by Gage Creed, who was run down by a tanker truck in Ludlow, Maine,[14] Ralph and Lois find a saxophone with JAKE printed on the side. King doesn't specifically link this to Jake Chambers, but it's an old saxophone, and Jake left New York for Mid-World nearly twenty years before the events in *Insomnia*.

Ralph first encounters Patrick Danville with his mother in a park. Ralph "touches" the boy—an ability similar to the one Jake acquires in Mid-World—and sees that his mother is a victim of domestic violence. He doesn't realize the significance of the boy's rose-pink aura and isn't aware that Patrick is at the center of everything going on in Derry. Ralph and Lois save his life twice, during Charles Pickering's attack on a women's shelter and later when Ed tries to crash his plane into the Derry Civic Center.[15]

Patrick is at the Civic Center because his babysitter cut her hand and canceled at the last minute. His mother planned for weeks to see feminist Susan Day speak, so she's forced to bring him with her. Ralph believes that the babysitter's injury wasn't an accident. Something is willing to move heaven and earth to make sure Patrick is there that day.

While they wait for the lecture to start, Patrick draws a picture of the Dark Tower in the middle of a field of roses. At the top of the Tower he colors a man in a red robe, whom he calls the Red King, looking down at a gunslinger named Roland with an expression of mingled hate and fear. Patrick dreams about Roland sometimes. "He's a King, too."[16]

Patrick is one of the Great Ones whose lives always serve the Purpose. His life affects not only all Short-Timers, but also those on many levels above and below the Short-Time world. Because Ed is without designation, only he can harm Patrick. If Patrick dies before his time, the Tower of all existence will fall. Lachesis tells Ralph that the consequences of this are "beyond your comprehension. And beyond ours as well."

When Patrick escapes from the Civic Center unharmed, "matters both Random and Purposeful resumed their ordained courses. Worlds which had trembled for a moment in their orbits now steadied, and in one of those worlds, in a desert that was the apotheosis of all deserts, a man named Roland turned over in his bedroll and slept easily once again beneath the alien constellations."

King gives no definite indication of the role Patrick will play in Roland's quest except to say that he would save two people. It would be another decade before he entered the *Dark Tower* series, by which time he is at least a teenager, perhaps older. How he became a prisoner in the basement of Dandelo's cabin on Odd Lane within the Dark Tower's shadow is never explained.

In *Insomnia,* King lays out the structure of his multiverse, symbolized by the levels of the Tower. The nature of the Tower is dual, both personal and universal. It represents individual lives but also all the different planes of existence.

Short-Time creatures like Ralph and Lois occupy the first two floors of the Tower. Clotho tells them there are elevators that Short-Timers are not ordinarily allowed to use. Ralph tells him that he has seen a vision of the Tower, and it doesn't have an elevator but rather "a narrow staircase festooned with cobwebs and doorways leading to God knows what." He wonders if God is in the penthouse and the devil is stoking coal in the boiler room, reminiscent of the Crimson King's Big Combination. Clotho and Lachesis don't confirm or deny this.

One mystery introduced in *Insomnia* that the *Dark Tower* doesn't clearly resolve is the nature of the green man who talks to Lois.[17] She feels he is a force of good, perhaps the counterpart to the Crimson King at the level of Higher Purpose—an agent of the White,[18] perhaps analogous to the Turtle in *It,* which might account for its green color.

Rose Madder

Rose Madder has only passing relevance to the *Dark Tower* series. According to the coda of *Song of Susannah,* though, King's fictional version of himself was under the *Dark Tower*'s influence when he wrote the book. "I have an idea for a novel about a lady who buys a picture in a pawnshop and then kind of falls into it. Hey, maybe it'll be Mid-World she falls into, and she'll meet Roland." [DT6]

Rose Madder was written immediately after *Insomnia,* so it's not surprising that Mid-World crept into the story. The woman named Rose Madder, whom Rosie meets in the painting, could be her twin. Wendy Yarrow, a victim of Rosie's husband's abuse, is twinned with Dorcas,[19] Rose Madder's intermediary. Wendy and Dorcas are black women whose diction is reminiscent of Detta Walker's.

Dorcas is conversant with Mid-World geography and history. She tells Rosie, "I've seen bodies on fire and heads by the hundreds poked onto poles along the streets of the City of Lud." Rose Madder knows about Mid-World philosophy, telling Rosie that repaying each other for their actions is their balance, their ka. "Should we rage against ka? No, for ka is the wheel that moves the world, and the man or woman who rages against it will be crushed under its rim."

When Rosie's husband, Norman, finally confronts Rose Madder, he thinks hers "was the face of a supernally beautiful goddess seen in an illustration hidden within some old and dusty book like a rare flower in a weedy vacant lot." Readers of the *Dark Tower* series already know that Jake found a wild rose in a weedy vacant lot, and Roland believes it is the Tower's representation in Jake, Eddie and Odetta's world.

Rosie saves a baby as part of her service to Rose Madder. Readers speculated that this infant might be important to the *Dark Tower* series, perhaps even be Susannah's child, but neither the child nor Rose Madder ever appear again. The infant does bear something in common with Mordred, son of Mia: Though Rose Madder gave birth to the girl child, she won't get to raise it and is to turn it over to someone, but who that is, King never specifies.

The book's other minor ties to the *Dark Tower* include a framed photograph of Susan Day, the activist decapitated in *Insomnia*, and Cynthia Smith—one of Rosie's friends from the Daughters and Sisters shelter for battered women—who goes on to encounter Tak in *Desperation*. Roland and Susannah traverse a maze beneath the Castle on the Abyss that brings to mind the one Rosie maneuvers to rescue the baby from the Minotaur.

In the fictional journal at the end of *Song of Susannah,* King calls the book "a real tank-job, at least in the sales sense." He says he doesn't like it "because I lost the song." In *On Writing,* he described it—and *Insomnia*—as a "stiff, trying-too-hard" novel.

Desperation *and* The Regulators

Unlike most of the other nonseries books, it's only in retrospect that these two novels' place in the mosaic of the *Dark Tower* universe becomes clear. *Desperation* and *The Regulators*[20] share a unique twinning relationship and take place in different realties—different levels of the Tower, as it were.

Desperation, Nevada, is situated among the Desatoya Mountains, the location of Eluria in the novella "The Little Sisters of Eluria." While Tak can be traced back to the China Pit mines in *The Regulators,* his appearance is described firsthand in *Desperation.* He was unleashed upon the world when the miners broke through a wall between dimensions.

From Mia's description of the creatures in the infinite todash spaces between universes, it seems that Tak is probably such an entity, akin to the beings that occupy the fissures outside Lud and Fedic. That Tak speaks the same language of the unformed used by the Little Sisters and the Manni supports this notion. He may also be related to the monster in *It.*

The authors of *The Stephen King Universe* speculate that the Outsider in *Bag of Bones,* the evil force that enhances Sara Tidwell's vengeful power, is another of these creatures. Jo Noonan says, "She's let one of the Outsiders in, and they're very dangerous." Since *Bag of Bones* is set in Derry and in western Maine, both thin places, and Mike Noonan's summer house, Sara Laughs, reappears in *The Dark Tower* as Cara Laughs, this may be a valid assumption, although Mike Noonan believes the Outsider is Death.

Some of Tak's power is invested in small icons called can-tah, the little gods like the turtle sigul hidden in the bowling bag Jake picked up in the vacant lot. Tak is also known as Can Tak, or "big god." He mentions the can toi, another name for the low men, creatures from between the Prim and the natural world.

In *The Regulators* Audrey Wyler escapes Tak by taking Seth to her imaginary safe place in Mohonk in 1982. This kind of todash trip in time and space is reminiscent of Mia's journeys to the allure of the Castle on the Abyss, where she and Susannah find respite from New York.

"The Little Sisters of Eluria"

After accepting an invitation to write a stand-alone *Dark Tower* novella, King had difficulty coming up with a story, but once he got going he had a hard time keeping it from turning into a novel. In its introduction in *Everything's Eventual,* he writes:

> I was about to give up when I woke one morning thinking about *The Talisman,* and the great pavilion where Jack Sawyer first glimpses the Queen of the Territories. . . . I started to visualize that tent in ruins . . . but still filled with whispering women. Ghosts. Maybe vampires. Little Sisters. Nurses of death instead of life. Composing a story from that central image was amazingly difficult. I had lots of space to move around in—Silverberg wanted short novels, not short stories—but it was still hard. [EE]

The Little Sisters, whose tent is currently set up near the Desatoya Mountains where the China Pit mine is located in *Desperation,* are vampires, Old Ones. They can go about in the daylight, but they cast no shadows.[21] Their vocabulary incorporates the language of the unformed used by Tak and by characters in the *Dark Tower* series. At this early point in his quest, Roland doesn't recognize the words they speak.

The story also introduces the little doctors, parasitic bugs that facilitate healing. Their presence indicates that the old vampires aren't far away, hence their nickname "Grandfather fleas." Mia hears them scuttling beneath the table in the dream banquet hall where she feeds, and Oy kills a few of them at the Dixie Pig in 1999. (Eluria's saloon is the Bustling Pig.) In *Insomnia,* Ralph has a vision of similar creatures pouring from his late wife's head. He decides that they are part of the black aura, the deathbag known as todana that surrounds dying people.

It's impossible to identify exactly when in Roland's quest this story occurs. The only indication of a date comes from Eluria's law office register, where the most recent entry is marked 12/FE/99, a designation Roland doesn't recognize. All that can be said is that it takes place after the final battle at Jericho Hill and before Roland picks up the man in black's trail. He has been traveling alone for at least ten months, but probably far longer. He looks at least twenty years older than John Norman, who is a teenager.

Shortly after he enters the abandoned town of Eluria, he is confronted by a threatening group of Slow Mutants. Roland attributes their mutations to their having worked in the radium mines beneath the mountains, but similar creatures worked as overseers near the Crimson King's Big Combination, and their proximity to this Rube Goldberg–like power-generating station may have caused their transformation. Roland hasn't grown callous enough to shoot them in cold blood, but he also hasn't fully developed the gunslinger skills he displays by the time he reaches Tull. He allows a mutant to sneak up behind him and knock him out, a mistake he would never make in later years.[22] He thinks ka must be a cruel mistress if his quest to find the Dark Tower is to end at the hands of one such as these.

When Roland wakes up, suspended in a harness inside a vast silk tent, he thinks he's dead. He hears bugs singing; when they stop, his pain returns. A female voice speaks to him, and the first person he thinks of is Susan Delgado. The Little Sisters, who remind him of Rhea of Cöos, are dressed like nuns and wear the sigul of the Dark Tower, a bloodred rose, on their uniforms. From the outside, their pavilion looks like an aging MASH tent but, like the Black House, it is vast on the inside.

The Sisters are ka-tet. They serve the doctors who in turn serve them by healing patients for the vampires to feed on. All that protects Roland is a religious medallion he picked up from a dead boy in the village square. Either its gold or its reference to God keeps the Sisters at bay. It identifies him as brother to John Norman, the boy in the hospital bed next to him, who is from Delain, sometimes known jestingly as Dragon's Lair or Liar's Heaven. All tall tales, including one about the last dragon killed by King Roland, perhaps, were said to originate there.

To keep him from escaping, the Sisters drug Roland's food and force-feed it to him. The youngest of the six Sisters, Jenna, who is special owing to her bloodline, befriends Roland. Sister Mary, the group's nominal leader, resents Jenna's position. Jenna supplies Roland with an herbal remedy to counter the drug's effects.

After the Sisters get a Slow Mutant to remove John's protective medallion, Roland is the only human left for them to feed on. Jenna returns Roland's guns on the night he must escape and brings with her an army of little doctors, held in command by the Dark Bells of her headdress. Roland is glad to see that Jenna can touch John's medallion, but it burns her hands and she can only tolerate it briefly. Roland kisses her injured hands, making her cry. Roland hasn't yet buried his sensitive side.

Jenna decides to leave the other Sisters and go with Roland. She confesses that she has supped of blood but plans to give it up. The other

Sisters tell her she's damned. She says, "If there's to be damnation, let it be of my choosing, not theirs." Roland knows a little about damnation himself, and his lessons on that topic are just beginning.

Sister Mary intercepts them outside Eluria. Neither Roland's weapons nor his hands are any use against her, but ka intervenes on his behalf. A dog with a cross-shaped patch of fur attacks the vampire leader, destroying her.

Roland and Jenna don't get very far that night because Roland is still weak from his injuries. Jenna tells him the remaining three Sisters will move on; their canniness in this respect accounts for how they have survived for so long. He kisses Jenna, who has never been kissed as a woman before. In his dreams, the cross-marked dog leads him to the Dark Tower.

Jenna underestimates her power to exist free from her group. "Ka was a wheel; it was also a net from which none ever escaped." Overnight she reverts to primal form: a swarm of little doctors who come together one last time to greet Roland before scattering.

Roland moves on westward, alone, leaving Eluria behind like countless other towns on his path.

The story doesn't greatly impact the *Dark Tower* series. Rather, it is a snippet that reveals Roland at a transitional, vulnerable phase. He's alone, but he doesn't shun companionship. His skills are still developing, and he's prone to making potentially lethal mistakes, but he is growing to understand that ka may want him to succeed.

"Low Men in Yellow Coats" (Hearts in Atlantis)

In "Low Men in Yellow Coats," the opening section of *Hearts in Atlantis,* King starts tying together the clues he's been leaving in previous books. The story introduces Breakers—people sought by the Crimson King for some unknown but undoubtedly sinister purpose—into the *Dark Tower* mythos.[23] Ted Brautigan, an escaped super-Breaker, spends most of the novel evading the low men, who want to return him to his task.

When Ted shows up at the boardinghouse where Bobby Garfield and his mother live, he has just escaped from Devar-Toi, the Breakers' prison. Roland's old friend Sheemie from Mejis made a hole that Ted passed through, sending him to Connecticut in 1960. Most of Ted's history isn't told in this short novel, but he fills in the backstory in *The Dark Tower*.

Ted was born with extrasensory powers, but for most of his young life he couldn't find any use for them. He volunteered to help Army Intelligence during World War II, but his talents threatened the hawks that wanted to fight, and he was turned away. Not only is Ted psychic, but he can also enhance the powers of others and can briefly pass on some of his own talent to those he comes in contact with.

He becomes aware that he is being watched by a certain kind of person. Men, mostly, who like loud clothes, rare steak and fast cars painted in colors as garish as their outfits. They wear special hats to block the psychic powers of those they pursue. Their symbols—astrological icons and the occasional red eye—are marked on fences, sidewalks, sometimes near hopscotch grids.[24] They think upside-down pictures—especially pet posters—are the height of humor. Some people say their shoes don't touch the ground.

Their cars look like normal vehicles, but they aren't—they are as alien as the low men. Bobby believes the cars are alive. "If you tried to steal one, the steering wheel might turn into a snake and strangle you; the seat might turn into a quicksand pool and drown you."[25]

Their long coats are reminiscent of the ones men sometimes wear in movies like *Gunfight at the O.K. Corral* or *The Magnificent Seven*. They're regulators, like in the movie with John Payne and Karen Steele—or the novel by Richard Bachman.[26]

These are the low men who work for the Crimson King. They wear his red eye on their lapels like a badge. They are loyal servants, not very bright, but effective. Their outlandish clothing and vehicles are disguises that cause most people to willfully ignore them. "A little of what's under the camouflage seeps through, and what's underneath is ugly." They are can toi, a cross between the beastlike taheen and humans. They worship humanity, take human names, disguise themselves to look human, and believe they will replace humans after the Tower falls.

Ted becomes a Breaker when he answers a job ad after wandering aimlessly for most of his life. By the time he's hustled through a doorway to Thunderclap, he realizes the offer of vast amounts of money is a trick. He accepts his new life without much protest. Finally being able to use his powers is like scratching an impossible-to-reach itch. He knows he's part of the process of breaking something, but at first he doesn't care to know what.

From a low man he befriends, he discovers what he's doing and how his very presence is facilitating the universe's destruction, so he escapes. He shows up at the boardinghouse in Connecticut carrying his worldly possessions in a few mismatched suitcases and brown paper shopping bags with handles.

He befriends Bobby Garfield and hires him to watch for signs of the low men, who he knows will come after him. Bobby turns a blind eye when the signs start appearing because he's afraid Ted will leave, but Ted already knows that the low men are getting close. He goes into fugues when they approach. His pupils dilate and constrict rapidly. He utters strange sayings, like, "One feels them first at the back of one's eyes," and, more tellingly, "All things serve the Beam." When Bobby touches him, he hears a bell tolling in his head, like todash chimes.

Ted's talents encompass what Roland calls the touch. Like Jake, Ted is mostly scrupulous about how he uses this power. He tells Bobby, "[F]riends don't spy; true friendship is about privacy, too." His insight isn't infallible, though. He never realizes that Bobby doesn't like root beer.

Ted introduces Bobby to the world of grown-up books, including *The Lord of the Flies,* which Jake was assigned to read, and *Ring Around the Sun* by Clifford D. Simak, a book that King acknowledges in the afterword to *The Gunslinger* as probably the inspiration for his concept of multiple universes.

When the low men finally catch up to Ted, he willingly goes with them to save Bobby's life. The low men are tempted to bring Bobby along as a gift for the Crimson King, but Ted is smarter than any low man and convinces them that he will cooperate if they don't harm Bobby. "If I give you what you want instead of forcing you to take it, I may be able to speed things up by fifty years or more. As you say, I'm a Breaker, made for it and born to it. There aren't many of us. You need every one, and most of all you need me. Because I'm the best." He also mentions the gunslinger who has reached the borderlands of End-World. The low men are unimpressed.

In the summer of 1965, Bobby gets a message from Ted, an envelope that emits a sweet smell and contains rose petals of the deepest, darkest red he has ever seen. He has one of those moments of understanding, perhaps transmitted to him by Ted. "There are other worlds than this, millions of worlds, all turning on the spindle of the Tower. And then he thought: He got away from them again. He's free again. The petals left no room for doubt."

Ted probably sent this letter after he escorted Susannah to Fedic. Bobby senses that Ted is not in this world or time, that he ran in another direction. When last seen in *The Dark Tower,* Ted and those Breakers willing to follow him were headed toward Calla Bryn Sturgis, where they planned to seek forgiveness for their part in the loss of the village's children, work as an act of contrition and perhaps someday find a doorway back to their own world.

Bobby is reunited with his childhood girlfriend, Carol Gerber, who was supposedly killed years earlier. She lives under an assumed name and tells Bobby that she's good at not being seen, a trick she learned from Raymond Fiegler, another incarnation of Randall Flagg, a creature familiar with fringe groups like the one Carol belonged to. Of Ted, Carol says, "For an old guy, he sure knows how to push the right buttons, doesn't he?" Bobby responds, "Maybe that's what a Breaker does."

"Everything's Eventual"

When it was first published a few months after *Wizard and Glass,* few people suspected that "Everything's Eventual" was somehow related to the *Dark Tower,* but by the time King and Peter Straub started work on *Black House* in 2000, King had decided that Dinky Earnshaw, the story's e-mail assassin protagonist, was a Breaker.[27]

Dinky is a high school dropout with a new job that seems like a step up from gathering shopping carts at the grocery store or delivering pizza. He has a house stocked with anything he asks for, and he gets an allowance. His situation sounds similar to the way the Breakers are treated in Devar-Toi. The only condition is that he must throw away any money he has left over at the end of each week.

Dinky was watching a Clint Eastwood movie[28] when he received a call from the mysterious Mr. Sharpton offering him this rather unique position. Sharpton describes himself as "two parts headhunter, two parts talent scout, and four parts walking, talking destiny." He knows a lot about

Dinky, but the biggest secret he knows is that Dinky was somehow involved in the death of Skipper Brannigan, his old nemesis from the Kart Korral at the grocery store and a friend of a friend of Eddie Dean's brother, Henry.

Dinky has a rare power involving an intuitive understanding of special, lethal designs and shapes. As a child, he could kill flies by making circles and triangles with his fingers. When the neighbor's dog terrorized him, he killed it by drawing his special symbols on the sidewalk in chalk, reminiscent of the way low men communicate with each other. The dog didn't die immediately—the effect was similar to what happened when Atropos, the agent of Random from *Insomnia,* snipped a victim's balloon cord.

Sharpton, who works for Trans Corporation, a subsidiary of North Central Positronics, employs a group of people—low men—who look for people like Dinky with extrasensory talents: precogs, postcogs, people with telepathy, pyrokinesis or telempathy. "They can actually see fellows and gals like you, Dink, the way certain satellites in space can see nuclear piles and power-plants. . . . They crisscross the country . . . looking for that bright yellow glow. Looking for matchheads in the darkness." Sharpton estimates that there are no more than a few thousand "trannies" in the entire world. He tells Dinky he wants to help him sharpen and focus his talent and use it for the betterment of mankind. Like Richard Sayre, Sharpton is a convincing liar.

Sharpton sends Dinky to Peoria, where he is tested and programmed for his new task, but no one tells him what his work is. He's set up in a nice house with its fringe benefits and $70-a-week allowance. "There's not a whole lot of cash in it, at least to begin with, but there's a lot of satisfaction," Sharpton tells him. When Ted and Dinky compare notes in Devar-Toi, they decide the Crimson King is trying to bring about the end of creation on the budget plan.

He's left to his own devices, cut off from friends and family who might ask awkward questions. One night, his mission comes to him in a dream. His computer contains all the tools he needs: a folder with every mystical, magical symbol he's ever imagined and thousands more. A modem connects him to a database of potential targets. He devises and sends special e-mail messages—sometimes he has to resort to regular mail—only mildly curious about what happens to the intended recipients.

One day, he accidentally sees a story about one of his victims, a man who committed suicide. Dinky starts feeling a little paranoid about his job.[29] After doing research on a library computer, he realizes he's a serial murderer, but he doesn't stop. Like Ted Brautigan, he's had an itch all his life that he's finally able to scratch. He rationalizes that his watchers would be suspicious if his work habits changed.

Someone intervenes to help him, but the story doesn't reveal who. Perhaps it is ka, or Stephen King, assisting his creation. Dinky composes one of his "eventual" e-mail message for Sharpton. The special word he adds to make it work is "Excalibur," another subtle link to the *Dark Tower*. It's the name of Arthur Eld's sword, from which Roland's guns are made. After he kills Sharpton he tries to run away, but the low men catch him and take him to Devar-Toi.

The Talisman *and* Black House

The Talisman's ties to the *Dark Tower* series are tenuous. The Territories, where Jack Sawyer travels when he's not in America, are a borderland near Mid-World, a place akin to the region where the Callas are located. The primary conceptual relationship between *The Talisman* and the *Dark Tower* is the notion of twins, as mentioned previously.

Peter Straub calls *The Talisman* "all but" a *Dark Tower* book.[30] The Agincourt, the Black Hotel in California that contains the Talisman, is an axis of all universes and could be the Dark Tower's representation in that reality. Jack is one of a few people who can enter it because he is single natured. His equivalent (Twinner) in every other reality except his own has died.

Twins aren't as important to *Black House* as they are to *The Talisman*. Parkus tells Jack Sawyer, "You've got to get that idea out of your mind." The Crimson King's search for Breakers drives the plot of *Black House*, as in "Low Men in Yellow Coats." It was Straub's idea to incorporate the *Dark Tower* mythos into *Black House*. "One of the reasons [I suggested it] is that I wanted to know what that stuff was. I had no idea what a 'Breaker' was, what the Tower was, what the Crimson King was."[31]

When it comes to reaping Breakers, the Crimson King is indiscriminate. He casts a wide net for children, knowing that a small percentage of those he catches have the talent he needs. Those who don't qualify are en-slaved to run the Big Combination, an enormous skyscraper reaching into the clouds and spanning miles in each direction that has consumed bil-lions of children over thousands of years, his terrible power source in End-World. It appears to fuel evil—despots, pedophiles, tyrants and tor-turers—in the great numberless string of universes.

The Crimson King uses minions like the low men or Ed Deepneau when he wants to operate in America. In *Black House,* his End-World henchman, Mr. Munshun, possesses an aged serial killer named Charles Burnside. Burnside thinks of the Big Combination as an engine that turns wheels that turn bigger wheels that power engines of destruction. Roland knows it as An-tak, the King's Forge, and it is responsible for the red glow Susannah sees in the distance from the ramparts of Castle Discordia. Burnside worries that it may be hell itself. "It runs on blood and terror and never takes a day off."

Jack Sawyer, now a grown man, has forgotten everything that hap-pened to him twenty years ago during his quest to find the Talisman that saved his mother's life. His mother starred in old B movies that often fea-tured gunslingerlike characters. One of her films was a comic Western, another blend of genres of the kind King set out to create with the *Dark Tower* series.

Ka needs Jack, a successful LAPD homicide detective, to resolve a crisis in French Landing, a small town in Wisconsin familiar to him through one of his cases. Unsettling reminders of his past cause him to take early retirement and he moves to French Landing, as yet unaware of the evil Black House that is a portal to End-World—the doorway to Ab-balah, the entrance to hell. Abbalah is another name for the Crimson King, but its use is limited to *Black House* and *The Plant.*

Though there's a serial killer at large in the area, the real crisis is the disappearance of Tyler Marshall, who has the potential to be as powerful a Breaker as Ted Brautigan. While wandering around her missing son's room, Judy Marshall mutters, "Saw the eye again. It's a red eye. *His* eye. Eye of the King." Her words seem nonsensical. "Abbalah-doon, the Crimson King! Rats in their ratholes! Abbalah Munshun! The King is in the Tower, eating bread and honey! The Breakers in the basement, mak-ing all the money!" She dreams of a Dark Tower standing in a field of roses. Her husband has her committed because of her erratic behavior.

Jack is haunted by the word "opopanax," the same word applied to the feather used to call meetings in Calla Bryn Sturgis,[32] after he reads about it in the local paper. He resists pleas to help with the serial killer investigation until he has a dream encounter with his old friend Speedy, who tries to explain why Ty Marshall is important. Speedy's ominous message is that if Jack can't bring the boy back, he has to kill him. One more Breaker might be all the Crimson King needs to bring down the Tower.

None of this means much to Jack, but it inspires him to action. Judy thinks Jack can save Ty, who she believes is still alive. When they finally meet in the psychiatric hospital, Jack falls in love with her, or rather with her Twinner, Sophie, the Queen of the Territories. Jack leaps to the Territories, where he is reunited with Speedy's Twinner, Parkus, who explains what's really going on in French County.

He meets Sophie in a pavilion that reminds him of the place where his mother's Twinner, the former queen, lay dying. This tent—a hospital to some and a twin to the room Judy occupied on the other side—is less elegant. It belongs to the Little Sisters of Eluria, perhaps the last one of the dozen or more that once existed in "the Territories, On-World, and Mid-World." Sophie tells Jack about the vampire nurses whose patients never get well. "Don't fear, Jack—they also serve the Beam. All things serve the Beam." He has no idea what the Beam is.

Parkus leads them to an abandoned speaking circle like the many encountered by Roland and his ka-tet. "The Demon may be long gone, but the legends say such things leave a residue that may lighten the tongue." He educates Jack on the nature of existence. "You asked how many worlds. The answer, in the High Speech, is da fan: worlds beyond telling. . . . There is a Tower that binds them in place. Think of it as an axle upon which many wheels spin, if you like. And there is an entity that would bring this Tower down. Ram Abbalah."

Parkus says the Crimson King is a physical being trapped in the Tower,[33] but he has another manifestation that lives in Can-tah Abbalah, the Court of the Crimson King. If the King successfully destroys the Tower, he believes he will be free to wander in the chaos that remains, known as din-tah, the furnace. Some parts of Mid-World have fallen into that furnace already, according to Parkus.

If readers were confused about why the Crimson King wants Breakers, Parkus sets the record straight. For the last two centuries[34] he has been gathering mind readers (the most common), precognates, teleports, world jumpers like Jack and telekinetics (the rarest and most valuable), mostly from Earth and the Territories. "This collection of slaves—this gulag—is his crowning achievement. We call them Breakers." The Crimson King is using them to speed up the destruction of the Beams. Of the six, one collapsed on its own thousands of years ago, part of the ordinary course of decay. Since starting their work, the Breakers have destroyed two Beams and weakened two others. Only one (Gan's Beam) still has its original strength.

Parkus tells Jack that the job of protecting the Beams belonged to the gunslingers, "an ancient war guild of Gilead." They possess a "powerful psychic force . . . one fully capable of countering the Crimson King's Breakers." Though the gunslingers are mostly gone, Parkus has heard that the one surviving member of the line of Eld has made at least three new gunslingers, though he doesn't know how. "If Roland were still alone, the Breakers would have toppled the Tower long since." This new band of gunslingers is the last hope for those who want the Tower to stand, or fall in its own time.

If the Crimson King can break the Beams before Roland and his katet reach the Tower, he will never have to confront them. This is why he has stepped up his search for Breakers. The low men, his knights-errant, perform many duties, but their chief job is to find psychically talented children. He also enlists the help of people like Burnside, the serial killer in French Landing. The Crimson King lets him kill and eat all the children he wants, as long as he turns over any potential Breakers to the demon who possesses him, Mr. Munshun, a quasi-immortal creature similar to Walter—though less artful—who delivers them to the Crimson King.[35]

Parkus tells Jack he must either rescue or kill Tyler because he is one of the two most powerful Breakers in all the history of all the worlds, analogous to a nuclear weapon. The other is Ted Brautigan, of whom Munshun says to Ty, "All the boys like the Chief Breaker . . . Perhaps he'll tell you tales of his many escapes."

Jack has some residual power from touching the Talisman, but it's not enough for him to defeat the Crimson King. "But it may be enough for you to take on Mr. Munshun—to go into the furnace-lands and bring Tyler out."

Knowing that he *must* win does not mean that he *will* win. "Proud empires and noble epochs have gone down in defeat, and the Crimson King may burst out of the Tower and rage through world after world, spreading chaos."

Burny delivers Ty to Mr. Munshun, the Eye of the King, who plans to take him to End-World on a monorail. "Once there were two others . . . Patricia and Blaine. They're gone. Went crazy. Committed suicide." This helps put *Black House* in the context of the *Dark Tower* books. In Mid-World, these events occur after *Wizard and Glass,* and most likely after *Song of Susannah,* because the Forge was still visible to Susannah from Castle Discordia's ramparts.

With the assistance of a ragtag band of erudite motorcycle gang members, Jack frees Ty from Mr. Munshun and gets the boy to use his Breaking powers to destroy the Big Combination. "Up, up in his high, faraway confinement, the Crimson King feels a deep pain in his gut and drops into a chair, grimacing. Something, he knows, something fundamental, has changed in his dreary fiefdom."

In the end, Jack Sawyer is seriously wounded by an old enemy and survives the shooting only by leaping to the Territories, where he must remain. Parkus teases readers by saying, "This business of the Tower is moving toward its climax. I believe Jack Sawyer may have a part to play in that, although I can't say for sure." Readers speculated that Jack would show up in the final books of the series, but perhaps King and Straub have other plans for him. Peter Straub has said on numerous occasions that he anticipates that there will be a third *Talisman* book sometime in the future, this one set mostly in the Territories.

Whatever his destiny, Jack Sawyer appears no more on the road to the Dark Tower.

ENDNOTES

[1] Stanley Wiater, Christopher Golden and Hank Wagner, *The Stephen King Universe,* Renaissance Books, 2001.

[2] For example, the authors postulate that the young boy Jim Gardiner meets on the beach in *The Tommyknockers,* whose mother was killed by a drunk driver, is Jack Sawyer from *The Talisman.* Events seen later in *Black House* do not support this theory. Jack says that his mother died more than five years after he rescued her with the Talisman and implies that it was from a relapse of her cancer.

[3] "The Hardcase Speaks," published in *Contraband* number 2, December 1971. "The Dark Man" and "The Hardcase Speaks" are collected in *The Devil's Wine,* edited by Tom Piccirilli, CD Publications, 2004.

[4] Quotes in each section come from the book under discussion unless otherwise specified.

[5] A reference to an H. P. Lovecraft many-formed character who often takes the guise of a human being while serving the purposes of the elder gods. He is known to use deceit, manipulation and propaganda to achieve his goals, and claims to have a thousand masks. He is also known as the Crawling Chaos and the Black Man.

[6] A reference to the *Necronomicon* invented by H. P. Lovecroft.

[7] The Crimson King and Flagg/Walter suffer numerous eye injuries in their long lives.

[8] Ralph Roberts calls his adventure "Short-Time Life on Harris Avenue, A Tragic-Comedy in Three Acts."

[9] The Crimson King knows who his future enemies will be. He tried to scare King away from writing at the age of seven and periodically made attempts on King's life.

[10] They call themselves the "physicians of last resort." Ralph names them after the Greek Fates. Clotho spun the thread of each life, Lachesis measured it and Atropos snipped it. Fate is nearly synonymous with ka.

[11] The four constants are Life, Death, the Purpose and the Random.

[12] They may be agents of Higher Purpose and Higher Random, though it's also possible that above a certain level there is no Random.

[13] Ralph thinks of Joe Wyzer, Lois and himself as the "Three Insomniacs of the Apocalypse." The elderly leaders of Tet Corporation dubbed themselves the "Old Farts of the Apocalypse."

[14] From *Pet Sematary,* the book that made the existence of *The Gunslinger* widely known.

[15] Benjamin Hanscomb of *It* designed the new Civic Center after the original was destroyed in the flood of 1985.

[16] "Once there was a king. . . . But kings are done, lad. In the world of light, anyway," Roland thinks in *The Gunslinger* (revised edition).

[17] When Ralph defeats the Crimson King, there is a titanic green flash so bright that "for one moment it was as if the Emerald City of Oz had exploded around him." The Emerald Palace shows up in *Wizard and Glass,* written two years after *Insomnia* was published.

[18] At one point, Ralph covers Lois's eyes. "His fingers flashed a momentary white so bright it was almost blinding. Must be the white they're always talking about in the detergent commercials, he thought."

[19] Dorcas is the name of a biblical character, a disciple from Joppa whose name translates to Tabitha, which is Stephen King's wife's name. According to Acts, Dorcas was a woman full of good works and charitable deeds.

[20] *The Regulators* was published under King's pseudonym, Richard Bachman, who some might call King's dark twin. Bachman's wife, Claudia Inez Bachman, becomes the author of *Charlie the Choo-Choo* in later books in the *Dark Tower* series, although a *y* is added to her name to give it nineteen characters.

[21] In *Black House,* Sophie says, "The Little Sisters don't come out when the sun shines," but this proves untrue.

[22] Norma Deepneau surprises him from behind in the lobby of the Black Tower housing the Tet Corporation in 1999. At the time, Roland thinks it hasn't happened since he was a teenager.

[23] When "Low Men in Yellow Coats" was adapted as the movie *Hearts in Atlantis,* all references to low men and Breakers were removed from the script because of the complexities that would have been required to explain the *Dark Tower* mythos to a mainstream audience.

[24] In *It,* both Eddie and Ben think they see the figure of a turtle drawn in chalk on the sidewalk, but it turns out to be just a hopscotch grid.

[25] The car in *From a Buick 8* fits this description, and its driver resembles a low man, but King, in keeping with the book's theme of unexplained mysteries, doesn't explicitly connect the Buick to low men. However, its trunk is a portal to another world. *From a Buick 8* is identified at the front of *Wolves of the Calla* as having ties to the *Dark Tower* series.

[26] The Big Coffin Hunters in *Wizard and Glass,* though human, are also regulators. *The Regulators* is a fictional movie, but its stars, John Payne and Karen Steele, are real and did costar in one film.

[27] Peter Straub, personal communication, July 12, 2000.

[28] *Coogan's Bluff.* King has often said that Roland was inspired by Clint Eastwood.

[29] Dinky remembers a TV show he watched one summer. "*Golden Years,* it was called. You probably don't remember it. Anyway, there was a guy on that show who used to say, 'Perfect paranoia is perfect awareness.'" *The Golden Years* was written by King.

[30] Interview with Jeff Zaleski, *Publishers Weekly,* August 20, 2001.

[31] Ibid.

[32] In *The Plant,* Carlos Detweiller, who prayed to the god Abbalah and utters words from the language of the unformed, also mentions opoponax [sic], which is ironic because the newspaper article in *Black House* mentions "opopanax" as a word that was missed in a spelling bee.

[33] Parkus says the Crimson King is "Tower-pent," echoing the term "prison-pent" from *Look Homeward, Angel,* the Thomas Wolfe book that also contains the phrase "a stone, a leaf, an unfound door."

[34] Parkus says, "On the upper levels of the Tower, there are those who call the last two hundred or so years in your world the Age of Poisoned Thought." This is roughly the length of time the Wolves have been raiding the Callas.

[35] Munshun is "as bald as Yul Brynner," star of *The Magnificent Seven,* part of King's inspiration for *Wolves of the Calla.*

CHAPTER 10

DRAMATIS PERSONAE

Roland Deschain of Gilead

You started as a version of Sergio Leone's Man With No Name. You were okay. A lot of fun to partner up with. But then you changed. Right under my hand. It got so I didn't know if you were the hero, the antihero, or no hero at all.

[DT6]

Roland Deschain, son of Stephen and grandson of Alaric and Henry the Tall, is a descendant of Arthur Eld, the ancestor of all gunslingers, and his wife, Queen Rowena. Alaric went to the now-legendary southern realm of Garlan to slay a dragon, but another king, one who was later murdered, had already killed the last one in that part of the world. This was probably King Roland the Good of Delain.

Arthur Eld was the first king to rise after the Prim receded, and Guardian of the Dark Tower, King of All-World. Steven Deschain, Roland's father, was of the twenty-ninth generation, on the sideline of descent. Roland is the only remaining gunslinger, the last of the line of Eld, the only hope that the world's rueful shuffle toward ruin might still be reversed. Though he graciously extends his lineage to include the members of his new ka-tet, the others know that, at best, they are only a distant shoot, far from the trunk.

He could pass for Stephen King's father when King is thirty, so he must look at least fifty. However, he's ageless. His homeland of Gilead, barony seat of New Canaan, one small mote of land located in the western regions of Mid-World, and center of the Affiliation, has been in ruins for a millennium since a civil war. Roland tells the ka-tet, "I've quested after the Dark Tower for over a thousand years, sometimes skipping over whole generations." Joe Collins says Roland must be older than God. "Some would say so," he responds.

Though King believes all his characters are partly him and partly what he sees in other people, Roland is the one that is most unlike him.[1] King said he doesn't have a clear picture of what any of his characters look like because he is behind their eyes looking out. He commented, though, that Michael Whelan's version of Roland from *The Gunslinger* illustrations is what he sees in his mind's eye when he writes.[2]

Roland's tarot card is the Hanged Man, which by itself symbolizes strength.

He has cold and steady blue eyes, the color of fading Levi's. His black hair is streaked with white by the time he reaches Calla Bryn Sturgis. His face is tanned, lined and weathered. A grizzled but vital star like Paul Newman or Clint Eastwood would play him in a movie, with the dark, mysterious demeanor of Yul Brynner. Jake sees the similarity with Eastwood, but mostly in his eyes. Susannah thinks of him as an existential version of Marshal Dillon from *Gunsmoke*. Not as broad shouldered or as tall as Dillon—though he is considered tall for someone from Gilead—and his face seems to her more that of a tired poet than a Wild West lawman.

His entire youth was spent training to be a gunslinger. He excels at drawing a gun but isn't the smartest in his class. Because he's so close-mouthed, Abel Vannay, his classroom teacher, calls Roland "Gabby," a nickname that brings his mother, Gabriel, to mind. "[W]hen he decided to play his cards close to the vest, he played them very close indeed."

His fighting tutor and mentor, Cort, teased him for lacking imagination, something he's told so often he believes it. "I could always haul a gun faster than any of my mates, and shoot straighter, but I've never been much good at thinking around corners." He's not flashingly intelligent like Cuthbert, or even quick like Jamie. The man in black tells him, "Your slow, plodding, tenacious mind. There has never been one quite like it, in all the history of the world. Perhaps in the history of creation." [DT1] His friend Cuthbert says the wheels in Roland's head grind slow but exceedingly fine.

He is one of only thirteen who completed the rigorous process from a beginning class—the last class—of fifty-six, and the youngest ever to succeed at the trial of manhood. Marten the wizard and traitor, who spied against Roland's father and seduced his mother, underestimates Roland's talents. He goads the boy into challenging Cort at the age of fourteen, intending him to fail and be sent west, where he wouldn't be a threat.

Instead, Roland rises to the challenge. His choice of weapon is ingenious and an early indication of the lengths to which he will go to succeed. He sacrifices his aging friend, David the hawk, in the name of victory. Officially a gunslinger, he is still no match for Marten, and his father sends him out of harm's way with Cuthbert and Alain.

On the morning Roland is sent away, his father looks somberly "at his only son. The one who had lived." [DT4] This enigmatic reference has led to speculation that Roland has a sibling, perhaps one who died in childbirth. In fact, he has two siblings, a brother and a sister.[3] Since both Roland and the Crimson King are descendants of Arthur Eld, according to Walter, some people have wondered if Roland's nemesis is an evil twin. They share a lifelong obsession with the Dark Tower. The Crimson King, though, according to various reports, has been busy trying to destroy the Tower for thousands of years, apparently longer than even Roland has been alive.

In Mejis, Roland falls in love with Susan Delgado, a beautiful woman two years his senior who is promised to Mayor Thorin. He also displays his independence and disregard for his friends and companions when he refuses to share his plans with them. He will always keep secrets from those who would help him, and convince himself it is the right thing to do. Even when he has companions, he operates like he's alone and only his objectives matter.

At the end of that long summer, Roland surrenders Susan in the name of his newfound quest for the Tower, revealed to him by the pink Wizard's Glass, but is traumatized when the townspeople kill her. She was pregnant with the next in the line of Eld. Shortly after he returns to Gilead, he accidentally kills his deceitful mother, tricked by Rhea of Cöos.

Roland joins the futile fight to save Gilead, but only out of duty. The Dark Tower has become his ambition. Farson's forces corner the last surviving gunslingers—including Cuthbert, Jamie and Alain—at Jericho Hill, five hundred miles north of Mejis. According to Flagg's recollection of the battle, Roland escaped by hiding in a cart filled with dead men. At Jericho Hill, Roland leaves behind a horn that once belonged to Arthur Eld, something he will need when he reaches the Tower. He's so focused on the long-term goal that he overlooks this one small detail.

He casts about alone for many years, centuries perhaps, trying to find the man in black, who is the key to reaching the Dark Tower. In Eluria, Roland isn't yet cold-blooded enough to shoot the club-wielding Slow Mutants who threaten him. By the time he reaches Tull, he is destroying everyone in the town. As a seasoned gunslinger, he always feels sick after the big battles. What he doesn't say, though, is that he is never so happy to be alive as when he's preparing to deal death.

His most prized possessions are the items that define his nature—the heavy revolvers with sandalwood stocks and barrels made from Arthur Eld's great sword Excalibur, handed down from father to son for generations along with another inheritance: fantastic pride. He owns little else of value, "other than the ruins of my younger face." His gunna consists of ammunition, tobacco and a leather grow-bag, a continually replenishing source of money or gems.

Roland survives because his dark, dryly romantic nature is overset by his practicality and simplicity. He's the sort of man who would straighten pictures in strange hotel rooms; he guards the secret of his romanticism jealously. He understands that only three things matter: mortality, ka and the Tower. He doesn't care to understand himself deeply; he doesn't discuss philosophy or study history. Things in the past are beyond his power to change, and ka will take care of what's ahead.

Susannah believes Roland underestimates his thinking abilities and imagination. His intuitive understanding of Odetta's disorder and his solution to her split personality is only one example of how creative he really is. He has little use for artful cleverness, but when he fully takes on the mantle of gunslinger he is brilliant. She once thought he was unsubtle, but revises that estimation when he acts as emissary in the Calla. "The fact that he's probably going to get me killed—get all of us killed—doesn't change the fact: He is my hero. The last hero."

He's a Dark Tower junkie addicted to rules and tradition, with little regard for anyone who gets in his way. "Morals may always be beyond you," Roland's father tells him at the age of eleven. "It will make you formidable." He lies when it suits his purpose. "I am like one of the old people's death-machines. One that will either accomplish the task for which it has been made or beat itself to death trying."

Eddie, a heroin addict, understands Roland to the core. "You'd use me and then toss me away like a paper bag if that's what it came down to. God fucked you, my friend. You're just smart enough so it would hurt you to do that, and just hard enough so you'd go ahead and do it anyway." The word "retreat" isn't in his vocabulary. Eddie tells him bluntly, "You're as contrary as a hog on ice-skates." Father Callahan is only a little more tactful when he implies that Roland is on occasion prone to mistaking his own will for ka.

Roland knows that by letting Jake fall so he could catch up with Walter, he has committed a conscious act of damnation. Mia tells Susannah, "The guilt of worlds hangs around his neck like a rotting corpse. Yet he's gone far enough with his dry and lusty determination." Roland's way is the way of the gun—death for those who ride with him or walk beside him.

After losing fingers and toes to the lobstrosities on the beach at the Western Sea, he is no longer in a position to achieve his goals alone, even if he hadn't been poisoned. Jamie once said that Roland could shoot blindfolded because he had eyes in his fingers. That he loses two fingers could be viewed as analogous to being partially blinded.

The group he assembles starts out as a means to an end, necessary to the completion of his journey. Before long, though, Roland finds his focus shifting. He's aware of the trail of enemies and friends whose bodies he left scattered behind him, and believes that he may have found something more important than the Tower for the first time since he left Mejis. He's not sure he can risk losing more friends. "There was a part of me that hadn't moved or spoken in a good many years. I thought it was dead. It isn't. I have learned to love again, and I'm aware that this is probably my last chance to love. I'm slow . . . but I'm not stupid."

"Willpower and dedication are good words," Roland says. "There's a bad one, though, that means the same thing. That one is obsession." He is Captain Ahab, and the Tower is his white whale. While his primary objective is to save the Tower from destruction, even when he achieves that by freeing the Breakers and saving Stephen King's life, he is not content. He has one quest assigned by ka and another of his own choosing. When he continues past the Crimson King's castle, he ventures beyond Gan and the prophecies of Arthur Eld, beyond ka itself. As Mia knew, he had to save the Beams because, if they had broken, the Tower would have fallen and he would never have been able to mount its staircase and find out what's at the top.

When he tells Feemalo and Fimalo that he must press on to fulfill a promise he made to himself, they say he is as crazy as the Crimson King, who thinks he can survive the Tower's destruction. His obsession is contagious. He knows that any of his ka-tet would carry on in his place if he fell. "I may have been a failure at my life's greatest work, but when it comes to making martyrs, I have always done well." [DT5] He wonders what he's done to deserve such enthusiastic protectors. "What, besides tear them out of their known and ordinary lives as ruthlessly as a man might tear weeds out of his garden?"

As he emerges from his self-absorbed state, like Walter o'Dim he fears being called to account.[4] "My score grows ever longer, and the day when it will all have to be totted up, like a long-time drunkard's bill in an alehouse, draws ever nearer. How will I ever pay?" He denies being a good man. "All my life I've had the fastest hands, but at being good I was always a little too slow."

He thinks followers of the traditional God learn that love and murder are inextricably bound and that in the end God always drinks blood. At times he is compelled to confess his actions, but he never seeks absolution. His one great fear is not that God is dead, but that He has become feebleminded and malicious. He still prays, but "it's when folks get the idea that the gods are answering that the trouble starts." He shuns the title Childe, a formal, ancient term that describes a gunslinger on a quest. "We never used it among ourselves, for it means holy, chosen by ka. We never liked to think of ourselves in such terms."

As a gunslinger, he serves as a peace officer, messenger, accountant, diplomat, envoy, mediator, teacher, spy and executioner.[5] He is a soldier of the White, a divine combination of training, observation and hair-trigger intuition, which is his version of the touch. His talents include reloading his weapons without pausing, hypnosis, counting a true minute, speaking five languages and running in the darkness. He can see much farther than any of his companions.

Eddie once mused that he had never seen the bottom of Roland's purse, which was an endless source of needed items. Susannah thinks that after all their time together, she hasn't come close to seeing the bottom of

Roland. She's seen him laughing and crying, sleeping, going to the bath-room, killing and dancing the Rice Song with skill and flair. She never slept with him, but thinks she's seen him in every other circumstance, and he still has depths she's never seen.

Things he cannot do: blend in to New York City culture, read English or pronounce words like "tuna" or "aspirin" and see television. His way of listening to stories his ka-tet tell of Keystone Earth bugs them. He lis-tens like an anthropologist trying to figure out some strange culture by their myths and legends.

Both Cuthbert and Vannay warned Roland that failing to change and failing to learn from the past would be his damnation. He once believed that nothing in the universe could cause him to renounce the Tower. At the beginning of his career he was friendless, childless and heartless. Though he had once loved, he learns to love again. He loves his surrogate son, Jake, more than all the others, including Susan Delgado. When Jake dies, Roland is afraid that he has lost the ability to weep, but the tears finally come. He prays over Jake's body, not because he thinks Jake needs a prayer to send him on his way, but to keep his mind occupied, to keep it from breaking.

Susannah, the only member of his ka-tet to leave without dying, be-lieves that Roland even feels pity for Mordred. Whether he does or not, he kills his demon child after it kills Oy, putting an end to the line of Eld, mutated though it might have been. Roland has had three progeny—two real and one surrogate, and all are now gone, one before it was born.

When the time comes for Susannah to leave, he is suddenly afraid to be alone again and falls to his knees to beg her to stay. However, he must let her go—he owes her that much. His selfish desire to keep her with him is unworthy of his training and unworthy of how much he loves and re-spects her.

Roland suffers his final injury within sight of the Tower when he sev-ers one of the remaining fingers on his right hand while plucking a rose. The hand goes numb to the wrist, and Roland suspects he will never feel it again.

Before he takes the last few steps toward the Tower, he sends Patrick back the way they came. Patrick is the surrogate for all those who have died during his millennium-long quest; the gunslinger won't abandon him here at the end of End-World. He tells the boy they may meet again at the clearing at the end of the path, but he knows there will be no clearing for him. His path ends at the Dark Tower.

Though standing so close to the Tower makes him feel like he's in a dream, he realizes that nothing significant has changed. He's still human, but he feels oddly relieved not to have his heavy guns hanging at his hips any longer. The killing has come to an end, but he is forced to remember all those he left behind as he climbs to the top of the Tower. Eventually, it becomes too painful to take in, and he sets his sights on the room at the top, but there's nothing for him there except the punishment for having failed to change enough.

His existence is near perpetual reincarnation. Each time he is returned to the point in his journey where he is closing in on the man in black. Too late, he thinks, to make the important changes. Ka gives him credit, though, for the progress he has made, and Eld's horn is his reward. If he can hold on to it through another iteration, maybe everything will be different next time and he will learn what the top of the Tower really holds for him.

Will he drop Jake again when torn between rescue and catching the man in black?

"I bear watching, as you well know." [DT4]

John "Jake" Chambers

"Go then. There are other worlds than these." [DT1]

Jake Chambers holds the record for the number of times someone dies in the *Dark Tower* series: three. Roland first encounters him at a way station for the coach line while crossing the desert in pursuit of Walter. Jack Mort, probably under Walter's influence, pushed the boy in front of Enrico Balazar's car, and he ended up in Mid-World after he was killed.

His tarot card is the Sailor, drowning, with no one to cast him a line.

Though Roland estimates his age to be about nine,[6] he is actually eleven. He's small for his age, with sun-bleached blond hair and blue eyes. People don't only underestimate his age; until he cut his hair, he was often mistaken for a girl. Calvin Tower tells him he looks like an only child, which he is. He is clean and well mannered, comely, sensitive. He has a hard time making friends his own age. He doesn't shy away from the girls who notice him; he talks to them with unknowing professionalism and puzzles them away. People bewilder him.

Jake's upbringing—like Roland's—was left to a court of cooks, nannies, tutors and teachers. His parents don't hate him, but they seem to have overlooked him. His father, Elmer R. Chambers,[7] is a ruthless and successful TV network executive, the master of "The Kill," the fine art of putting strong programming against a rival's weaker schedule. He's a gunslinger of sorts, a Big Coffin Hunter in TV land.

The private school Jake attends in New York City is, according to his father, the best in the country for a boy his age. Jake won admission based on his academic record and intelligence, not because of his father's money and influence.

His mother, who is scrawny in a sexy way, drinks prodigiously and cheats on her husband, as did Gabrielle Deschain. She leaves taxi fare for Jake to go to school each day, but he pockets the money and walks if it isn't raining.

The family cook, Greta Shaw, is the strongest parental figure he has in New York. She makes his lunch and nicknames him 'Bama, from a Crimson Tide chant. While his parents go off on their respective adventures, she stays with him. By the age of four, Jake has already fantasized that Greta would become his mother if his parents died in a plane crash.

His bedroom is decorated like that of any young boy living in 1977. He has posters of Stevie Wonder and the Jackson Five on his walls, and a microscope. He likes geography, and bowls in the afternoon. He subconsciously resents professional people, and avoids bowling alleys that use equipment manufactured by companies in which his father owns stock. His career aspirations include bowling on the pro tour.

He's prone to claustrophobia. Eddie jokes that if he had stayed in New York, he would probably have had his own child psychiatrist, working on his unresolved conflicts and his parent issues and perhaps being prescribed a drug like Ritalin.

His sensitivity in New York translates into a special awareness in Mid-World that Roland calls the touch. His talent is stronger than that of Roland's old friend and fellow gunslinger Alain Johns. After he sees the rose in the vacant lot, his talent increases. He can lift thoughts from the top of Roland's mind without trying hard, and could defeat the gunslinger in a battle of the minds, even with Roland trying his hardest to defend himself. The strength of his touch might have made him a fine Breaker. Jake is scrupulous about his talent, though. He believes that reading people's minds is as wrong as watching them undress through binoculars.

Jake's second death comes at the hands of the man who will become his surrogate father. The boy is sensitive enough even at that early stage of their relationship to know in advance that Roland will betray him for his quest. Several times he calls on Roland to turn aside or leave him behind, but he's only a boy and has no one to watch out for him in Mid-World.

Ka wants him so badly that it found a way around death to put him back at Roland's side. Roland kills Jack Mort, thereby preventing Jake's first death. This sets up a mental conflict in both the gunslinger and the boy. They each remember both previous timelines, the one in which Jake dies and the one in which he doesn't.

Once he returns to Mid-World, the mental echo vanishes and he grows to trust Roland and love him as a father. In Lud, when Gasher threatens the ka-tet with a hand grenade, Jake willingly goes with him to defuse the situation, trusting that Roland won't let him down again. By the time they are reunited after searching for Susannah in 1999, Jake fully accepts Roland as his surrogate father, certainly more of a father than Elmer Chambers ever was.

From the moment he meets Oy, the billy-bumbler is his constant companion, and Jake's touch connection with Oy increases during his time in Mid-World. At times he believes he can read the creature's mind, and at one point the two actually switch minds temporarily.

In Mid-World, Jake shoulders adult responsibility when he's younger than Roland was when the gunslinger took his test of manhood. Officially an apprentice, he's as deadly a shot as the others. When he isn't called on to be a gunslinger, though, he's still only a child. He makes grown-up excuses to spend time with Benny Slightman in the Calla, seemingly ashamed to want to do boyish things. "This was the part that had been despoiled by the door-keeper in Dutch Hill, by Gasher, by the Tick-Tock Man and by Roland himself."

At times, he is vaguely jealous of Mordred for being Roland's blood offspring. He's not beyond getting angry with Roland when he discovers that the gunslinger has been keeping secrets from the group. He understands, though, that to defy Roland would be more serious than adolescent rebellion. Roland is his dinh, and a serious act of defiance would mean he'd have to face Roland in a test of manhood that he would surely fail.

He's resourceful enough to keep his own secrets when he trails Ben Slightman and Andy to the Dogan near the Calla. Realizing that he has to betray his friendship with Benny by telling what he's seen, he understands a little better what Roland had to do in the mountains. "Jake had thought there could be no worse betrayal than that. Now he wasn't so sure."

Jake is enraged when the Wolves kill Benny, and he becomes a killing machine at the sight of his dead friend. "It should have been his fucking father," Jake cries. He shoots Wolves in much the same way Roland shot down the population of Tull.

Jake's touch is integral to helping the Manni reopen the UNFOUND doorway, giving the ka-tet access to Earth after Susannah and Mia vanish. He, Oy and Father Callahan arrive in the middle of a busy New York street, and he is nearly struck by a taxi. Angry at the near miss, Jake pulls his Ruger on the impressively tall taxi driver, displaying a temper that he certainly would have had to manage as an adult, given the chance. More counseling, on top of his parent issues.

He's fully prepared to die trying to save Susannah. He takes Roland's place as the leader of the team when he and Callahan prepare to invade the Dixie Pig, laying out the general plan of attack while leaving room for improvisation, should unforeseen circumstances arise.

He sometimes chides himself for having stolen his father's gun and doesn't always like the person he becomes when he wears it. Though he has "guts a yard," Jake never loses the humanity gunslingers so often abandon. He is tempted to kill Jochabim, the washer boy in the Dixie Pig's kitchen, but he pauses. He knows that Roland would not have hesitated and suspects Eddie and Susannah wouldn't have, either. "I love them, but I hope I die before it gets me so bad it stops making any difference if the ones against me deserve [to die] or not."

Jake is devastated when Eddie is shot during the liberation of Blue Heaven. The members of the ka-tet had sensed something was going to happen and the sensation—ka-shume—reminded Jake of how he felt before Roland let him fall beneath the mountains. During the hours that follow, Jake doesn't know how to react since he's never had to face the death of a loved one before.

He knows his limitations. When Roland needs someone to drive the truck in Maine, he doesn't bluff his way into doing something beyond his capabilities.

Roland doesn't plan for Jake to die a third time when they rescue Stephen King from the wayward minivan. If ka demands a sacrifice, the gunslinger intends it be him who dies. His body fails him, though, and Jake takes his place, a gunslinger to the end, acting on instinct. He seizes King and shields him with his own body. He urges Roland to attend to King rather than him, since it is King they came to save. "This is dying— I know what it is because I've done it before," he tells Roland, who is trying to convince himself Jake's injuries are slight.

Jake dies while Roland is attending to King, but not before he passes important instructions to Oy and to Irene Tassenbaum. Roland once told him, "You needn't die happy but you must die satisfied, for you have lived your life from beginning to end and ka is always served." With Oy at his side, Roland buries Jake in a shallow grave at the side of the road and asks Irene to plant wild roses nearby. "This is Jake, you gods, who lived well and died as ka would have it. Each man owes a death.[8] This is Jake. Give him peace."

Death is not the end for Jake, though. Susannah encounters him in another New York, where he is Jake Toren, younger brother to Eddie. Both of them have been dreaming of a woman named Susannah who will join them in Central Park, where they begin their new lives together.

Eddie Dean (Edward Cantor[9] Dean)

The first is young, dark-haired. He stands on the brink of robbery and murder. A demon has infested him. The name of the demon is HEROIN. [DT1]

When Roland first encounters Eddie Dean aboard a flight from the Bahamas to New York, a pound of cocaine strapped under each arm, the young man is nearing bottom. He's smuggling the drugs to finance his heroin habit and that of his older brother, Henry.

He has black hair, hazel, almost green eyes and long fingers. In a movie, some "hot young star" like Tom Cruise, Emilio Estevez or Rob Lowe[10] would play him. He grew up in the projects, and his street accent becomes more pronounced when he's angry, as if he were speaking through his nose instead of his mouth.

Eddie is the first member to join Roland's ka-tet, and the first to leave it. He was born in February 1964, which would make him twenty-three in 1987.[11] He lives in a two-bedroom apartment with his brother in Co-Op City, which, in Eddie's reality, is in Brooklyn instead of the Bronx. Both of his parents are dead, but when his mother was still alive she frequently reminded Eddie that he was responsible for his older brother's lack of opportunity in life. Henry believes this, too, but perhaps only because his mother said it so often.

A drunk driver killed Henry and Eddie's sister[12] while she was watching a game of hopscotch on the sidewalk when Eddie was two and she was six. Since their mother worked during the day, Henry—eight years older than Eddie—was given the responsibility of making sure nothing similar happened to his brother.

His tarot card is the Prisoner, a name Roland often calls him during their early days. The card depicts a young man with a whip-wielding baboon on his back whose disturbingly human fingers are buried so deeply in the man's neck that their tips disappear in flesh. The face of the ridden man seems to writhe in wordless terror.

The baboon represents his addiction, but it also represents his brother, Henry, who pulled Eddie down into the muck of drugs and laziness with him. Eddie became a convenient excuse for his brother's failures in life. Henry couldn't play school sports, not because he was scrawny and uncoordinated but because he had to look after Eddie. His grades were too low to earn scholarships, not because he wasn't smart but because he spent so much time keeping Eddie safe. Without a scholarship, Henry couldn't go to college and was sent to Vietnam, coming back minus a knee and hooked on morphine, none of which was his fault.

Believing his mother and brother sacrificed everything so he could be happy robbed Eddie of what little self-esteem he'd been able to develop. "As for me, I don't matter much," thirteen-year-old Eddie tells Jake in a dream when instructing the boy on how to find the doorway to Mid-World. "I'm supposed to guide you, that's all." [DT3]

Henry is responsible for Eddie's descent into a life of crime. Stealing comic books escalates into grand theft auto when Henry steals a car and drives into Manhattan. Scared and crying, Eddie lies about seeing a cop and convinces Henry to abandon the car. Henry runs off at first, but comes back for Eddie. He explains their late return home by telling their mother he'd been teaching Eddie to play basketball. Didn't Eddie have the best big brother in the world?

When Henry does teach Eddie basketball, Eddie quickly becomes better than his brother, as he is with most things, in spite of being much younger. He hides his superiority because if he shows Henry up, Henry would punch him hard on the arm, supposedly as a joke but actually as a warning. Eddie also hides his skill because he adores his big brother. His decision to not excel past his brother is a severe limitation, because Henry isn't much good at anything.[13]

During a conversation about who they'd like to have at their side if they got into a brawl, Henry surprises everyone by saying that he'd want Eddie, "Because when Eddie's in that fuckin zone, he could talk the devil into setting himself on fire."

Eddie catches his brother snorting heroin after he returns from Vietnam, shortly after their mother died. Following a huge fight, Henry threatens to leave, then guilts Eddie into begging him to stay. After all, Henry was injured in the war and got hooked on pain meds because he'd had to look after Eddie after school.

Before long, Eddie is snorting heroin, too. Eddie manages his habit better than his brother, of course. Their positions reverse and Eddie must look after his brother. Henry's addiction worsens, leading to shooting up, another confrontation, another guilt trip resulting in Eddie's needle habit and ultimately his trip to the Bahamas. Once Henry started shooting, Eddie knew his brother wouldn't survive six months without him—he'd end up in jail or a psych ward.

Eddie lingers under his brother's shadow even after Henry dies. "All you have to do to hurt him is to say his brother's name. It's like poking an open sore with a stick." [DT2] He protects his brother's memory to Roland, telling the gunslinger that though Henry was always scared, he always came back. Roland believes it would have been better for Eddie if Henry hadn't come back. "People like Henry always came back because they knew how to use trust. It was the only thing Henry did know how to use. First they changed trust into need, then they changed need into a drug and once that was done they pushed it."

Roland sees deep steel in Eddie from the very first. He proved his mettle in the Bahamas when he stood up to the man who wanted to stiff him in the drugs-for-cash transaction. He impresses the gunslinger by entering the gun battle with Balazar's men naked. A compliment from Roland makes him feel like king of the world. He learns quickly, naturally and easily. His facility with the gun reminds him of stories of reincarnation, an intuition possibly due to the cyclical nature of Roland's existence. He's lived through these experiences countless times with Roland and may have some recollection of skills he learned on previous iterations.

What stops Eddie from killing himself while going cold turkey after Roland draws him to Mid-World is the fact that Roland is deathly ill and needs him. When Odetta is brought through, confused and afraid, Roland thinks, "His brother is dead but he has someone else to take care of so Eddie will be all right now." Eddie falls in love with her and the integrated person who becomes Susannah Dean. He hasn't had a girlfriend since he started using heroin.

"I think I started loving you because you were everything Roland took me away from—in New York, I mean—but it's a lot more than that now, because I don't want to go back anymore." No matter how much Susannah might love him, he's sure he would always love her more. He sees it as his job to make it as good as possible as long as he can. He doesn't believe ka is a friend to him and Susannah and that it will end badly between them. He tells her, "It's good to make someone glad. I didn't use to know that."

Roland recognizes him as Cuthbert's twin, saying he's sure Eddie will die talking, as Bert did.[14] Eddie surpasses Cuthbert in many ways. Roland reflects, "If I underestimate him . . . I'm apt to come away with a bloody paw. And if I let him down, or do something that looks to him like a double-cross, he'll probably try to kill me." [DT3]

For all his strength and skill as a gunslinger, Eddie's dominant characteristic is the speed at which he runs his mouth. Roland, who thinks of Eddie as ka's fool, sometimes feels like shaking him until his nose bleeds and his teeth fall out. He possesses Cuthbert's annoying sense of the ridiculous, which enables him to defeat Blaine the Mono with his unique weapon of illogic. Arguing comes as naturally to him as breathing. He is sometimes weak and self-centered, but possessed of reservoirs of courage and heart and occasionally has deep flashes of intuition.

Never really maturing past the man-boy stage, he is analogous to Horst Buchholz's character in *The Magnificent Seven*. Roland thinks that no one can laugh as fully as Eddie Dean when amused. The Eddie Dean Special is something funny and stinging at the same time. Roland often uses his loquaciousness to advantage by having Eddie act as his mouthpiece.

Eddie respects Roland's skills and talents but understands the addiction that drives the gunslinger as only another addict could. Eventually, he comes to think of Roland as his father but he hates it when Roland relies on ka, calling it "ka-ka." Even so, Roland's quest becomes his own. If Roland were to die on their journey, Eddie would continue with the others, for having dreamt of the Tower and the field of roses, the compulsion to reach the Tower claims him, too.

Eddie shoulders more responsibility as time goes by. He deals with Andolini in Tower's storage room like a hardcase, and he negotiates with Tower, although with less finesse than Roland. He is patient with the Calla-folken but not with anyone who seems likely to cross him.

Pimli Prentiss, the headmaster of Algul Siento, shoots Eddie in the head in the aftermath of the assault on Blue Heaven. He lingers for fourteen hours, mortally injured but unwilling to let go. At the end, he tells Susannah to wait for him, tells Jake and Oy to protect Roland and tells Roland that this new life was better. His final words to Roland are "Thank you, father."

In 1987, in another world, Eddie Cantor Dean becomes Eddie Toren from White Plains. For months he's been dreaming of Susannah, whom he loves already, although he doesn't understand how or why this can possibly be. Voices told him and his younger brother, Jake, to meet her in Central Park when she comes through from End-World. He extends his hand to her, a familiar, well-loved hand, in the hopes that now ka will be on their side.

Susannah Dean, Odetta Susannah Holmes, Detta Susannah Walker, Mia

I am three women . . . I who was; I who had no right to be but was; I am the woman who you saved. [DT2]

When Odetta Holmes was five years old, she was struck in the head by a brick while her family was up north for her aunt's wedding. They were walking to the train station after a taxi driver refused to pick them up because they were black. Odetta was on the inside of the sidewalk, to keep her from getting too close to the traffic. The police never found out if the brick was dropped deliberately or if it fell by accident. She was in a coma for three weeks, and after she recovered she suffered periodic blackout spells that were the earliest manifestations of a mental schism. The brick may have caused this mental illness, though Odetta may have already been predisposed to it and ka just helped out.

Her tarot card is the Lady of Shadows, she of two faces, symbolized by Janus.

An only child—more or less—Odetta is the daughter of a small-town dentist who became wealthy after patenting several dental processes. After her mother died, Odetta took care of her father until he died of a heart attack in 1962, leaving her heir to a fortune worth $8 to $10 million. She grows up to be a pleasant, socially gracious, refined and cultured young woman. She may not have been educated at Morehouse—a reference to Ralph Ellison's *Invisible Man*—but she has a college degree from Columbia.

In the late 1950s, she is inspired to become a civil rights activist by Rosa Parks, but also by her memory of the prejudiced taxi driver. In Oxford, Mississippi, where she allows her friends to call her "Det," the police aim fire hoses at her group and she's put in jail. Occasionally resentful of her treatment at the hands of white people, she knows that hate will only hinder her work. "Man of Constant Sorrow" is the avatar of songs that inspires her to the movement.

Though she tells Eddie on the beach by the Western Sea that she has never been with a white man before, she in fact had a white lover named Daryl while at Oxford. All her life she works to gain self-respect, despite the barely suspected saboteur lurking in her mind. She thinks of herself as Negro and is offended by Eddie's use of the word "black." Her parents never spoke of their difficult past in the South, even when she became interested in her own background. Her father told her, "I don't talk about that part of my life, Odetta, or think about it. It would be pointless. The world had moved on since then."

At the age of twenty-five, she inherits the Holmes Dental fortune. Her home is a luxury penthouse apartment at the corner of Fifth and Central Park West. Perhaps the only black person in the exclusive building, she is literally "above" the others who live there. She's almost as well known as Martin Luther King. Her face has been on the cover of *Time* magazine.

The biggest change in her life prior to being sucked into Mid-World in 1964 occurs on August 19, 1959. Though she's wealthy enough to be chauffeured everywhere, she doesn't want to become a "limousine liberal," so she rides the subway. While waiting at Christopher Street station for the fabled A train Duke Ellington held in such high regard,[15] someone pushes her. She knows only that it was a white man, not realizing that it was the same man who dropped the brick on her head when she was five—any more than Jack Mort realizes he's victimizing her a second time. She misses the third rail, but the train cuts off her legs at the knees.

During the ambulance ride, both of her personalities fully manifest as she freely drifts between calm, polite Odetta and foul, vindictive, dangerous Detta Walker, who appeared only infrequently during the years since her head injury.

After she loses her legs, she disappears occasionally, sometimes for hours, days, even weeks, and often returns bearing bruises. A different car brings her back each time. Odetta isn't aware of these episodes. Her mind fabricates alternate memories that fill in the blanks. She rubs her temples lightly with the tips of her fingers each time Detta threatens to take control.

Detta is Odetta's mirror opposite. Odetta is a civil rights advocate; Detta Walker hates white people passionately. Detta doesn't know about the penthouse; Odetta doesn't know about the dingy loft apartment in Greenwich Village where Detta stays.

Detta is at least partially aware of the vast blanks in her life and suspects something is wrong but doesn't know what. Compared to Odetta, she has much more missing time to account for. She doesn't think about it much, though, because when she's in charge "her needs were too sudden and pressing for any extended contemplation, and she simply fulfilled what needed to be fulfilled, did what needed to be done. Roland would have understood."

Detta talks like a cartoon black woman, "Butterfly McQueen[16] gone Looney Tunes," like a cliché. She curses in a gutter patois so darkly Southern that even Eddie can't understand it. She's an equal opportunity hater, but she has two primary targets: white people and her aunt Sophia. She blames her aunt because Odetta was hurt while they attended Sophia's wedding, but she doesn't consider that the accident is responsible for her existence. Detta objectifies her anger, focusing it on the blue plate her mother gave Sophia as a gift. She steals the "forspecial" plate and crushes it beneath her foot while she masturbates. Susannah Dean will use similar plates as weapons in the Calla. Subtle irony . . . or ka.

To vent her racial anger, she picks up white boys at roadhouses and teases them into a sexual frenzy before cutting them off. It's a dangerous game, and she's been beaten a few times, but she prides herself that she has never been raped. Every one has gone home with blue balls, making her the undefeated queen prick tease.

Detta likes to steal trinkets from fancy New York stores. She doesn't care what she takes—she throws the items away afterward. Taking is what matters. She sees herself as cheap, like the objects she pilfers.

Roland entered Eddie's mind undetected. Detta recognizes his presence as soon as crosses through the doorway. Her split mind is used to compensating for alien personalities. Roland experiences a sensation "like lying naked in the dark while venomous snakes crawled all over you." Detta is intelligent but ruthless, hateful and as deadly as a lobstrosity.

She is heart-stoppingly beautiful, but when Detta is in control her beauty only enhances her interior ugliness. Her grin "seemed the most evil expression he had ever seen on a human face." Roland recognizes that she does things purely out of meanness and that her only real goal in life is probably to be killed by a white man—which means that Odetta will die, too.

Though Roland has no understanding of psychology, he unites Odetta and Detta by forcing them to acknowledge each other. When Odetta sees Detta through the doorway—and vice versa—she can no longer deny the other's existence. While Jack Mort is being cut in half by a subway train, Odetta and Detta divide physically, struggle and reunite as a new entity, who takes the name Susannah, the middle name of both facets of her personality. The name has greater significance: the Hebrew version, Shoshana, means "rose."[17]

Odetta was a combination of her parents' attributes—her mother's shyness and her father's unblinking toughness. Susannah has features from both of her previous personalities: Detta's "fight until you drop" stamina tempered by Odetta's calm humanity. She is hard and soft, passionate and acerbic, stronger and better than either of her components.

When she shoots she channels Detta, and when stirred to anger it is often Detta's voice that emerges. During those times, Detta "dances the commala in her eyes." Often she doesn't realize it until she replays in her mind what she has just said. She is scared of Detta, but knows that this part of her is shrewd. Detta is the one who solves the riddle of the prime numbers in Lud. Odetta never got better than a C in math in her whole life, and Detta claims she wouldn't have done that well without her help. "Poitry-readin bitch like her too good for a little *ars mathematica*, you see?" [DT3]

There are indications that she has more aspects than just these two. When she travels as Mia, Roland hears her speaking in numerous other voices, and when Eddie is shot in Algul Siento, she flits through an array of personalities. Walter said she has at least two faces.

She has a casual way of speaking and calls her friends "sugar" or simply "sug." She remembers enjoying some of the things she did as Detta. "I know I'd do it all again, if the circumstances were right." She loves Eddie, who had loved Odetta, and ritualizes their marriage by taking Dean as her last name. "If she did not call herself Susannah Dean with pride as well as happiness, it was only because her mother had taught her that pride goeth before a fall."

She is often the voice of calm reason to counter her husband's brashness. Susannah loves Eddie because he makes her feel whole and freed her from "a foul-mouthed, cock-teasing thief" and "a self-righteous, pompous prig." She proudly wears on a leather thong around her neck the wooden ring he carved for her. It was a surprise gift, too large for her hand, but she won't let him make her a new one. Eddie fills the hole in her heart that she believes all people are born with and exist with until they find their true love. She wants so much to bear his child that she dismisses the early signs of her pregnancy, fearing that it is hysterical.

Her feelings for Roland are more ambivalent. Her love for him is a mixture of fear, admiration and pity. The Detta part of her hates him for forcing her into this strange land. She admires his strength and indefatigable single-mindedness. Though she understands him at least as well as he understands himself, he still has the capacity to surprise her.

Susannah is arguably the only member of the ka-tet from New York who doesn't have to grow up. She's the oldest, but also the only one who had a well-adjusted childhood. Her parents were an active, loving presence in her life—unlike Jake's absentee parents—and she doesn't have the shadow of guilt that Eddie's mother and brother gifted him with. By the time Roland draws her and unifies her, she is reasonably balanced and mature and rarely descends to the levels of immaturity Eddie is still prone to.

Perhaps ka countered her emotional maturity by breaking her physically. Though she is strong, her missing legs make her vulnerable and she sometimes has to acquiesce to being carried around on a sling. She tolerates this, but in the same way Oy tolerates being carried by someone other than Jake, and there's always a chance she might bite because though Odetta seems to be permanently gone from her personality, Detta still lurks in the wings.

Roland's world is Susannah's birthplace, and is a world where no one calls her names for being black (except Eben Took in the Calla, and she quickly puts him in his place), where she has found love and friendship. She excels as a gunslinger, never lacks for courage, and takes quickly to new weapons, like the Oriza plates she uses against the Wolves and again in Algul Siento. They give her an elemental satisfaction. After she kills everyone in the Fedic Dogan, she's eager for more, believing that becoming a killing machine is what she was made for.

She likes to play parts—as she does when she pretends to be Roland's gilly during their first meeting with the Calla-folken—and is aware that an understanding of her psychosis might have illuminated her childhood joy at pretending to be someone else. Exposure to Mid-World enhances her playacting to the level where she can imagine things and make them tangible, like the mental Dogan she creates to control her pregnancy.

Though her unified personality is strong, she meets her match when Mia possesses her to supervise the progress of her pregnancy. Mia cares nothing about Susannah, Odetta or Detta except when she needs them to help with her "new chap." She implies that one of Susannah's aspects invited her in, like a vampire is invited into a house. Though Susannah denies Mia's presence at first, she excuses herself from strategy sessions where Mia might learn things that would compromise the ka-tet's preparations for the battle against the Wolves.

Susannah knows that Mia lies and doesn't care for her, but she agrees to help the demon because the baby is hers, too. Little is made of Susannah's part as Mordred's mother. She often refers to Mordred as "the other one" without acknowledging her maternity. She feels sympathy for Mordred's plight while he struggles through the cold after them, but her feelings aren't maternal. Her genetic influence seems minor, and she is rarely shown contemplating the nature of her child. When she and Mia separate to palaver, the pregnancy follows Mia. Perhaps Mia's presence prevented her from integrating her motherhood into her personality.

She sympathizes with Mia's single-minded drive to have a baby, someone to love and raise. Under different circumstances, they might have been friends. "She meant no harm to the universe," Susannah says of the woman she calls the "body mother." When she has trouble communicating with Mia—or when Mia has trouble speaking for herself—it is Detta who comes to the rescue. She seems to have a better understanding of the maternal imperative than Susannah does. "Ain't hardly nothin in the world as pow'ful as a pissed-off Mommy," she tells Susannah.

After Eddie dies in the battle to free the Breakers, Susannah agrees to continue with Roland and Jake. "Not because I want to—all the spit and git is out of me, Roland—but because [Eddie] wanted me to." Part of her wants to see the Tower as much as Eddie did. Her destiny, though, doesn't include reaching the Tower. She accompanies Roland through the hardest part of his journey, but after their encounter with Dandelo, she becomes depressed and has puzzling dreams of meeting Eddie and Jake in New York.

Other than Roland, she's the only member of the ka-tet to escape death. In her final moments with Roland, she reverts to Detta, whom she often relies on when she wants to distance herself emotionally from a situation.

Though she became a true gunslinger over the course of her time in Mid-World, it causes her only a moment's anguish to throw away Roland's gun. She knows that if there is a life ahead for her in the version of New York where fate takes her, she must face it without a weapon. Once it's gone, she doesn't pause or look back. She knows ka is working in her favor this time, and the force of ka is enormous.

Susannah takes Eddie Toren's hand and thinks she will die of joy.

Oy

Take one much-loved family pet, a Corgi with short legs, big ears and expressive eyes, give him a voice and a limited vocabulary and hey-presto! You end up with one billy-bumbler named Oy. [DT6]

Oy is a billy-bumbler, also known as a throcken. He has black-and-gray-striped, silky fur thick enough at his neck to make Jake's fingers disappear entirely. His gold-ringed black eyes make him look like a raccoon crossed with a badger or woodchuck, with a dash of dachshund thrown in for good measure. He has a sharp, whiskery snout and a toothy grin. His muzzle is dark and his teeth are needle sharp.

Shortly after Jake returns to Mid-World, Oy joins the travelers and adopts Jake. He doesn't like being carried by anyone except Jake, but he puts up with it when necessary. When Roland carries him while they search for Jake in Lud, the gunslinger feels "his claws splayed against the flesh of his chest and belly like small sharp knives. Then they withdrew." [DT3]

He is normally shy of strangers, but occasionally surprises Jake by flattening his ears and elongating his neck to improve the petting surface for someone, like Benny Slightman or Reverend Harrigan. He even allows the Roderick Haylis of Cheyvin to pet him outside Algul Siento.

When he joins the group he bears the wound from a bite that looks like it came from another bumbler. Roland believes Oy was driven away by his own pack. He suspects that Oy is one of the few bumblers who remember men and that the others might have decided he was "too bright—or too uppity—for their taste." His extraordinary chattiness may have provoked the others in his tet to expel him.

His voice is low and deep, almost a bark—"the voice of an English footballer with a bad cold in his throat." Usually, he echoes words he overhears, but occasionally says something that seems like original thought. He startles Irene Tassenbaum by swearing, a skill he learned from Eddie, and charms the Calla-folken when he introduces himself by standing on his hind legs, making the ritual foot-forward bow, holding his front paws palms up and saying, "Oy! Eld! Thankee!"

Good bumblers are supposed to be good luck. They were once very tame but not useful for much other than amusing children and hunting rats. They are faithful, but not as loyal as dogs. In the wild, they are scavengers. "Not dangerous, but a pain in the ass."

Oy displays emotion and can follow complex commands, such as waking Jake when the moon rises. He emulates some human gestures, like shrugging, but cannot master winking. Jake thinks that Oy can sometimes read his mind. Oy cries when he thinks he's going to be left behind in the Doorway Cave when the others go through the UNFOUND door.

Some bumblers can add, and Oy can count, as he demonstrates outside Tick-Tock Man's lair. He's also capable of independent thought. For example, he knows Jake will be interested to see Ben Slightman and Andy skulking around late at night and brings it to his friend's attention.

He's a true member of the tet and proves his courage on several occasions. In the Dixie Pig, he tackles the scuttling black bugs under the table. Callahan believes Oy was bred for this, like a terrier. Susannah, who calls him an idiot savant, says he would have been worthy of the title gunslinger had he but a gun to sling and a hand to sling it with. He switches minds with Jake to get past the mind trap, though he has to struggle to maintain Jake's body's balance.

After Roland buries Jake, he leaves it up to Oy to either stay at Jake's graveside and die of starvation or continue the quest. His work with Roland and Susannah isn't finished; he returns to Roland's side after a brief period of mourning. Jake gave him instructions just before he died, and Oy abides by his friend's deathbed wish. He tries to repeat the message to Roland but words fail him. Roland can hear Jake's voice, though, when he performs a ritual reminiscent of a Vulcan mind meld.

After they pass through the tunnels leading out of Fedic, Oy remains mute until they meet up with Dandelo. He shakes hands with Collins, says his name and eats gumdrops. Given the choice to go through the doorway with Susannah, he decides to stay with Roland. Part of the task Eddie gave him still lies ahead.

After Susannah leaves Mid-World, Oy stops eating. Roland sees an emptiness in his eyes and a kind of loss that hurts him deep inside, not unlike ka-shume. Roland chides Oy for not having gone with Susannah, hurting the bumbler's feelings. Later Roland apologizes, but Oy doesn't appear to forgive him. After Oy dies, Roland wonders if the bumbler had been sad because he knew it was to be his last day, and that his dying would be hard.

Oy saves Roland's life when Mordred attacks, leaping into the spider's grip. He could probably have gotten free if he wanted to, but instead of escaping, he extends his long neck and bites Mordred on the side. Before Oy, Roland had never seen a bumbler that would choose fight over flight, but this wasn't the first time Oy had done so. Oy's spine cracks in Mordred's grip but he keeps on biting the spider's body.

Mordred throws Oy into the air, where he is impaled on the branch of a cottonwood tree. He cries out in pain and collapses. After killing Mordred, Roland goes to the tree, where he finds that the last of his ka-tet is still alive. Though he risks being bitten—perhaps even wants to be bitten—Roland stretches out his hand. "Oy, we all say thank you. I say thank you, Oy." Oy doesn't bite or speak. He licks Roland's hand a single time, then hangs his head down and dies.

Oy is Roland's last sacrifice, but like Eddie and Jake, Oy chose to die for the quest. Patrick helps bury Oy, but it doesn't take long; "the body was far smaller than the heart it had held."

Father Donald Frank Callahan

Donald Callahan graduated from Boston seminary in 1957. He became a problem drinker during his years at his first parish in Lowell, Massachusetts. His drinking unsettled him spiritually, so he moved to Spofford, Ohio, and was later transferred to Jerusalem's Lot, Maine, where he became parish priest of St. Andrew's. At that time he was fifty-three, with silvery hair, a ruddy complexion and direct, piercing blue eyes threaded with tiny snaps of red surrounded by Irish laugh wrinkles; his mouth was firm, his slightly cleft chin firmer still. He thinks he will soon look like Spencer Tracy.

He knows the golden age poets, and his calling to the priesthood enhanced his childhood interest in the occult. Priests must plumb the depths of human nature as well as aspire to its heights, he would say, but the truth is that he liked to shudder as much as anyone else. He's been working for seven years—ever since the onset of his drinking problem—on notes for a history of the Catholic Church in New England, which he occasionally suspects he will never write.

Callahan resists the enlightened popery and believes that his church

only acknowledges true evil ritualistically, concentrating instead on social evils that arise from everyone's collective subconscious—stupendous,
but impersonal and impossible to banish. "I think it's an abomination. It's
the Catholic Church's way of saying that God isn't dead, only a little se-
nile." This echoes Roland's fear that he would climb to the top of the
Tower only to discover that God was feebleminded or malicious.

As a priest, he seeks a challenge beyond social problems. He wants to
lead an army against EVIL.[18] When the ka-tet of 'Salem's Lot approaches
him with stories of vampires and ancient evils, Callahan sees this as the
opportunity he's been waiting for. "I still believe enough in the awesome,
mystical, and apotheotic power of the church which stands behind me to
tremble a bit at the thought of accepting your request lightly.... The
church is a Force . . . and one does not set a Force in motion lightly." [SL]

He's exhilarated and, for the first time in years, loses his craving for alcohol. He doesn't know if he's up to the challenge, which jeopardizes his
immortal soul. The vampire Barlow understands Callahan better than he
understands himself. "Your faith in the White is weak and soft. . . . Only
when you speak of the bottle are you informed." [SL]

Finally face-to-face with EVIL, Callahan tries to hide behind his plas-
ter crucifix, a gift from his mother. When the vampire challenges him to
throw his cross aside, he hesitates. He has condemned younger priests for
relying on the trappings of the Church as mere icons, but now he is guilty
of the same thing. His faith is tested, and found wanting. If he'd found the
power to put the cross aside and stand strong in his beliefs, he would have
won the battle that night.

Instead of killing Callahan, Barlow forces him to take Communion
from the font of blood gushing from the vampire's neck. Barlow's blood
marks him. He's safe from the other vampires in 'Salem's Lot, but his
church rejects him, burning his hand in a flash of blue light when he tries
to enter. He's unclean. He casts off his priest's vestments and takes the
next bus out of town, which happens to be going to New York.[19] He wanders the streets, feeling Barlow's blood work into him. The world smells,
looks and tastes different. Eddie speculates that Father Callahan had already crossed over to another reality by this time without ever realizing it.

He has no hope of salvation, but he wants to atone. For the next nine
months, he works at the Home, a wet shelter only two blocks from the vacant lot containing the rose. He falls in love with his male coworker, Lupe

Delgado, but their relationship never advances beyond a kiss on the cheek that Callahan remembers like a lovesick teenager.

His newfound stability collapses when Callahan discovers that he can see vampires. Though he does nothing at first, he is spurred to action when Lupe gets AIDS from a vampire bite. Starting in 1976, killing vampires becomes his new mission in life. Elton John's "Someone Saved My Life Tonight" plays in the background, a song that will be the sound track for his adventures.

Unlike Barlow, these Type Threes can be killed as easily as swatting bugs on a wall. He starts drinking heavily again. His activities bring him to the attention of the low men, and he becomes the hunted.

Fleeing New York, he "[s]tumbles upon a great, possibly endless, confluence of worlds. They are all America, but they are all different." He travels the road for the next five years, sometimes killing vampires, but mostly leaving them alone. When the low men catch scent of him, he hears todash chimes. His subconscious has a way of pulling him across realities to evade his pursuers.

He ends up in California, but is lured back to New York when he reads about a friend who was assaulted by a couple of local thugs called the Hitler Brothers.[20] Callahan was their real target, and shortly after he gets back to the city they assault him and muscle him into the Turtle Bay Washateria. His attackers are arguing over who gets to finish carving their trademark swastika into his forehead when they are interrupted by two unlikely saviors, Calvin Tower and Aaron Deepneau. Callahan is left with a broken jaw and a cross-shaped scar that the Calla-folken believe was self-inflicted.

He sets out on the road again, drinking constantly and ignoring vampires. Jailed in Topeka for assaulting a police officer, he hits bottom when he suffers seizures and refractures his jaw. He reflects that the two men saved his life in New York and he has been squandering their gift. Callahan vows to kill himself if he hasn't given up drinking in a year. Of all the venal sins, the one that Callahan seems least constrained by is suicide, promising to kill himself once and actually doing it twice.

In Detroit he finds work at a shelter.[21] He no longer sees vampires or low men, which he takes as a good sign without realizing it is because they have gotten cleverer. In 1983, he's lured to a meeting at the offices of Sombra Corporation, the business arm of North Central Positronics in

Keystone Earth, by an offer of a $1 million grant to support the shelter, another trap. He ends up in a room full of vampires and low men led by Richard P. Sayre. They don't intend to kill him, just put him out of action by giving him AIDS.

Callahan won't let vampires taint him again. He calls on God for the first time since his encounter with Barlow, and decides to kill himself by jumping through the window. He's afraid the glass won't break, but it shatters all around him.[22] His last thought is "This is the last thought I'll ever have. This is goodbye."

He ends up in the way station shortly after Roland and Jake left it. Walter is waiting for him; Callahan is to be another of Walter's traps. He transports the former priest through a doorway to the Calla, sending Black Thirteen with him.

He arrives in the Calla, where the Manni tend him back to full strength and he starts making a living working in the fields. Eventually, he begins to preach again and the people of the Calla build him a church, which he calls Our Lady of Serenity. He hides Black Thirteen beneath the church's floor, trusting the building's sanctity to contain the ball's awesome power.

He converts more than half of the residents of Calla Bryn Sturgis to his way of spiritual thinking, but when Black Thirteen wakes Callahan thinks it is driving God out of his church. It speaks to him, tempting him to use it. The ball sent him todash twice; once to Mexico in the mid-1990s for Ben Mears's[23] funeral and once to the castle of the Crimson King.

When Tian Jaffords's anger-fueled enthusiasm to fight the Wolves threatens to be shouted down by the rich farmers of the Calla, Callahan steps in to help. He has read a book that explains the moral code of gunslingers and believes the group traveling nearby can help. His motives aren't entirely pure—he's looking for someone to take Black Thirteen off his hands.

The people of the Calla call him the Old Fella. They know he is from some other world, but he never speaks of it. Calla Bryn Sturgis is his home. He no longer considers himself a priest, but rather a man of God. "Perhaps one day again, with the blessing, but not now." He still wears a cross around his neck and he can once again dip his fingers in holy water. "God has taken me back . . . although I think only on what might be called 'a trial basis,'" he tells Roland.

He retains his fundamental Catholic beliefs, threatening to raise everyone in the Calla against Roland if the gunslinger allows Susannah to abort her demon child or even suggests it to her. Eddie comments, "For a guy who doesn't want to be called Father, you have taken some very Fatherly stands just lately."

Callahan feels like a full member of Roland's ka-tet when he sees the rose in New York. The foundations of his reality are rocked when Roland discovers a copy of *'Salem's Lot* among Calvin Tower's books. He has been downgraded from a human being to a character in a novel. He is in a universe where the town of 'Salem's Lot no longer exists on any map.

The failed priest is given another chance to confront EVIL when he and Jake follow Susannah's trail to the Dixie Pig in New York. He accepts the challenge, knowing he probably won't survive. He makes a stand similar to the one in the Petrie house in now-fictional 'Salem's Lot. When a vampire dares him to throw away his cross, Callahan says he needn't stake his faith on the challenge of such a creature, and he'd never throw away such an old friend, but he will *put* it away—and returns it to its resting place inside his shirt.

His faith is greater than any talisman—the power of God and the White radiates through him. Callahan's attackers include more than vampires, though, and the low men and taheen are beyond God's power. They fall upon him and bite into his neck, and the smell of blood draws the vampires to him.

God answers his call for strength, and he kills two of the low creatures. Rather than allow himself to be despoiled by the vampires, Callahan uses Jake's Ruger to kill himself again. The last thing he hears is a salute from Roland: "Hile, gunslinger!"

Father Callahan was one of King's tragic figures, last seen riding out of town in shame like a failed gunslinger sent into exile, on a self-destructive path. King occasionally discussed returning to the priest's story to explore what became of him after the night he failed his faith. However, King later said that the time for a sequel to *'Salem's Lot* had passed, leaving Callahan in limbo.

Nearly thirty years on, King allowed Father Callahan to find his redemption at the end of his journey along the road to the Dark Tower.

Patrick Danville

When Patrick Danville was a four-year-old boy in Derry, Maine, the Crimson King sent Ed Deepneau to kill him. Ralph Roberts first sees him playing in a park with his mother, Sonia. Ralph notes that Patrick's face had an extraordinary translucence, a beauty that was enhanced by the rose-colored aura revolving about his head. He has a hook-shaped scar across the bridge of his nose[24] caused by a fall when he was eight months old. His rosy aura is scarlet around the scar.

Named after his grandfather, Patrick is a burgeoning artist, making families out of Play-Doh and creating intricate crayon drawings. Sonia knows her son is special and that the world tried to root out people like him.

His father drinks too much and abuses his mother. Ralph and Lois Chasse save Patrick and Sonia twice, once at a halfway house, where young Patrick perceives them as angels. The second time is during Ed Deepneau's assault on the Derry Civic Center. Patrick wouldn't have been there that day except his babysitter was injured, probably not by accident. The Crimson King wanted Patrick where Ed could get at him.

He sometimes has ideas for pictures that he is compelled to draw. While he and his mother wait in the Civic Center for Susan Day, the main speaker, to take the stage, he falls under one of these compulsions. The drawing he creates features a soot-colored tower in a field of vivid red roses. A hatefully jealous man in a red robe looks down at a gunslinger from the top of the tower. He identifies the two people as "the Red King" and Roland, who is also a king. Patrick dreams about Roland sometimes. The drawing sends a chill through Sonia.

Ralph and Lois know only that Patrick is one of the Great Ones, someone whose life always serves Purpose. His life affects those on many levels above and below the Short-Time world, and his life will have more impact on reality than Caesar, Hitler or Winston Churchill, according to Clotho and Lachesis. If he were to be killed before his time, the Tower would fall and even the bald docs can't comprehend the full implications of that happening.

After Ralph stops Ed, Clotho and Lachesis tell him that Patrick is safe and that eighteen years in the future he will save the lives of two men, one of them crucial to maintaining the balance between Random and Purpose.

Roland learns about Patrick from the Calvins at Tet Corporation, who know about him from studying *Insomnia*. They say that Roland should look for him when he returns to End-World. He could be the key to the Dark Tower.

Roland sees Patrick's name on two paintings in Sayre's office in Fedic. One depicts Mordred with Arthur Eld's horse, which is dead. The other shows the Dark Tower. "It is as if I could touch the texture of every brick. The person who painted it must have been there. Must have set up his easel in the very roses." [DT7] Roland later realizes that Patrick hasn't done these paintings yet and that Sayre collected them from some future world through a doorway, which means that Patrick survived after Roland sent him back toward Outpost 19.

Susannah and Roland find Patrick imprisoned in the basement of Dandelo's hut in Empathica. He's so scrawny he reminds Susannah of a concentration camp prisoner. No one knows how long he's been there. His hair hangs all the way to his shoulders, but he has only the faintest haze of a beard on his cheeks. He looks seventeen; Roland thinks he might be as old as thirty. According to Clotho and Lachesis's story, he should be around twenty-two.

He communicates only through grunts and sign language; Dandelo pulled out his tongue and has been regularly feeding on his emotions. Patrick received the bare minimum of food necessary to keep him alive, and his mind has been terribly damaged.

Roland and Susannah discover his artistic skill. He seems to have no need for erasers, for either he doesn't make mistakes or he incorporates them into his drawings in a way that makes them little acts of genius. His pictures give him all the voice he needs. He produces them with harrowing clarity, rapidly and with clear pleasure. Drawing had always made him happy, but Susannah and Roland show him that his pictures could make others happy, too. Susannah uncovers Patrick's real talent when she gets him to erase the cancerous blemish from her portrait. He can uncreate by erasing; he can also create by drawing, something both she and Roland should have noticed when he drew a picture of some buffalo and the herd seemed closer after he completed the drawing, because he drew them that way.

He provides Susannah with the mechanism for escaping End-World by drawing a doorway for her. Given the choice of going with her or staying with Roland, he chooses to stay. "Scared to go sumplace new," he writes. His tongueless mouth will brand him in another place. Even here, he smiles with his teeth closed to hide the dark hole in his mouth. Drawing is all he has; everything else has been taken from him—his home world as well as his mother and his tongue and whatever brains he might once have had.

His time in Mid-World has not been completely detrimental to him; he has acquired some of the touch and can project thoughts and ideas to Roland.

He is eager to please, slow-witted and naïve, but his hands are as talented as Roland's. Patrick appreciates his own skill with a young man's arrogance that is disturbingly familiar to the gunslinger. Roland believes Patrick has a third eye that looks out from his imagination, seeing everything. His portrait of the Crimson King is genius. Challenged, the boy soars above himself.

Patrick makes a pigment from a paste of saliva, rose petals and Roland's blood and puts in two daubs for the Crimson King's eyes. When he's finished he seems fascinated, as if he can see Gan's face in his work. Erasing the Crimson King removes Roland's final barrier to attaining the Dark Tower.

Patrick is immune to the fate that accompanies most of Roland's fellow travelers because he has never been ka-tet. Even so, he represents all those who died along the way on Roland's quest, and the gunslinger won't see one more innocent perish for his cause. He sends Patrick back to find Stutterin' Bill and possibly to a doorway to America-side. "Here the darkness hides him from my storyteller's eye and he must go on alone."

The Man in Black, Walter o'Dim, Marten Broadcloak, Randall Flagg . . .

"You may not have been [Roland's] greatest enemy, Walter Padick . . . but you were his oldest." He heard for the first time in a thousand years the name a boy from a farm in Delain had once answered to: Walter Padick. Walter, son of Sam the Miller in the Eastar'd Barony. He who had run away from home at thirteen, been raped in the ass by another wanderer a year later and yet had somehow withstood the temptation to go crawling back. [DT7]

For centuries before the Crimson King enlisted him, Flagg stirred up trouble in Delain, causing wars and revolutions during the reigns of numerous kings. These may have been acts of revenge for his treatment as a child.

As the court wizard in Delain, he murdered King Roland so he could put the king's easily influenced son on the throne. He possessed a ball that enabled him to see the past and future—like one of the Wizard's Rainbow—and the ability to make himself dim so he could sneak about the castle undetected.

In one version of Earth—another level of the Tower—Randall Flagg represented the forces of evil against those aligned with Mother Abigail in a cataclysmic confrontation.

Stephen King and Randall Flagg have a lifelong relationship. In 1969, King wrote a poem called "The Dark Man" on the back of a place mat in a diner. Later published in *Ubris,* a University of Maine literary magazine, the poem tells of a man who wanders the country like a vagabond, riding the rails, observing everything. The poem turns dark when the narrator confesses to rape and murder.

> a savage sacrifice
> and a sign to those who creep in
> fixed ways:
> i am a dark man.[25]

"[T]hat idea of the guy never left my mind. The thing about him that really attracted me was the idea of the villain as somebody who was always on the outside looking in and hated people who had good fellowship and good conversation and friends."[26] He didn't belong to any of the "cliques and cults and faiths and factions that had arisen in the confused years since the Tower began to totter," though he pretended to when it suited him.

This fifteen-hundred-year-old, nearly immortal man in black goes by many names and weaves a fabric of truth mixed with lies. He creates a multiplicity of aliases that makes it seem like the gunslinger has more enemies than he really does: Marten the enchanter, Walter o'Dim, John Farson, Randall Flagg and numerous others. He often travels in disguise, but always he is a grinning, laughing man. "I'm a man of many handles," Flagg tells the Tick-Tock Man. "I have been called the Ageless Stranger. . . . I've also been called Merlin or Maerlyn—and who cares, because I was never that one, although I never denied it, either. I am sometimes called the Magician . . . or the Wizard."[27] Much of what he says about himself cannot be trusted. As Browning wrote, "My first thought was, he lied in every word."

In certain provinces to the south even of Garlan[28] he had been known as Walter Hodji, the latter word meaning both "dim" and "hood." He often adopts aliases with the initials R. F., as in Richard Fanin and Raymond Fiegler, the name he used when he showed Carol Gerber the trick of becoming dim.

In the synopses at the beginning of each of the last three stories that make up *The Gunslinger* as they originally appeared in F&SF, King's idea of the relationship between Walter and Marten evolves. Before "The Oracle and the Mountains," he writes, "Marten, the sorcerer physician who may have been the half brother of the man in black." Before "The Slow Mutants" he adds, "Or is he the man in black himself?" And before the final story, he says, "The court sorcerer who may have somehow been transformed into the man in black he now pursues, and who, as the charismatic Good Man [i.e., Farson], pulled down the last kingdom of light." See Appendix V.

A description of his appearance would be meaningless, as he can take whatever form suits him. When Roland sees him as Walter, he sports a handsome, regular face, bearing "none of the marks and twists which indicate a person who has been through awesome times and who has been privy to great and unknown secrets." He has a pallid complexion, ragged, matted black hair, a high forehead, dark and brilliant eyes, a nondescript nose and full and sensual lips. To others, when he drops his hood, he has the snarling face of a human weasel.

Flagg's face is fair and broad browed but not, for all its pleasant looks, in any way human. His cheeks are rosy.

[H]is blue-green eyes sparkled with a gusty joy far too wild to be sane; his blue-black hair stood up in zany clumps like the feathers of a raven; his lips, lushly red, parted to reveal the teeth of a cannibal. . . . His voice is whispery, penetrating. His laughter chilled the skin; it was like the howl of a wolf. . . . His smiles do not broaden his face but instead contract his features into a narrow and spiteful grimace. [DT3]

Walter is the farthest minion of the Dark Tower . . . or rather of he who dwells there: the Crimson King. He calls his master Legion,[29] a name he takes for himself as Flagg in *The Stand* and also used by Linoge in *Storm of the Century* and Munshun in *Black House*. This shouldn't imply that Linoge and Munshun are different aspects of Walter/Flagg, but rather that they are parts of the larger EVIL that serves the Crimson King. Mia tells Susannah that Walter can best be described as the Crimson King's Prime Minister. Sayre of Sombra Corporation reports to him, as do the Big Coffin Hunters in Mejis.

He claims never to have seen his master, who came to him in a dream thousands of years ago and imbued him with his duty. He's terrified of his master. "To speak of [him] is to speak of the ruination of one's own soul." He has done many errands for the Crimson King, including enlisting Mia as a vessel to bear Mordred, but his primary task has been to confound Roland, from his earliest days in Gilead and every step along the way. "You see, someone has taken you seriously," he tells Roland when they meet the first time.

The note the man in black leaves Allie in Tull is signed Walter o'Dim, which is how he normally thinks of himself. Roland doesn't make the connection among all these creatures until near the end of his quest, but it doesn't matter. He addresses each one in turn as necessity requires.

Roland first knew of him as Marten, a man who served as Gilead's court magician and counselor. Marten seduced his mother, Gabrielle, and tried to manipulate Roland into condemning himself to exile, but instead authored Roland's early advance to manhood. He's a man of many neat tricks, but isn't as clever as he thinks. He regularly underestimates Roland, who remembers him as a glutton behind a grave ascetic's exterior.

Roland knew Walter as a member of Marten's entourage. As John Farson, he is responsible for the downfall of Gilead, the last bastion of civilization. He barely misses Roland in Mejis and, under the name Randolph Filaro, he fought against the last gunslingers in Jericho Hill and killed Roland's childhood friend Cuthbert with an arrow through the eye.

Roland encounters him near the end of Gilead's reign when Dennis and Thomas from Delain are pursuing him to bring him to justice for his crimes in their kingdom, but he doesn't make the connection.

After Gilead's fall, Roland casts about for the man in black, understanding that he is the way to the Dark Tower. How he comes by this knowledge or where he first picked up Walter's trail is never revealed. Walter's fires leave peculiar ideograms that Roland tracks across the desert.[30] They please Roland because they confirm his essential humanity.

Walter sets traps for Roland along the way, including Sylvia Pittston in Tull, Jake in the desert and Father Callahan with Black Thirteen in Calla Bryn Sturgis. Callahan tells Walter he is cruel and is surprised to see genuine hurt in his eyes. "I am what ka and the King and the Tower have made me. We all are. We're caught." When Callahan suggests that Roland is above ka, Walter recoils, as if struck. Callahan realizes he's blasphemed, and with Walter that's no mean feat. "No one's above ka, false priest. The room at the top of the Tower is empty. I know it."

Walter isn't above ka. When Roland catches him after years of pursuit, he, like a leprechaun, must perform certain duties, which include showing Roland his future and explaining the nature of the universe and the Tower. He could have killed Roland during their long night of palaver, but he feared what would have happened to the Tower if he had. Besides, he needs Roland to complete the transaction that would give rise to Mordred.

Roland and Walter/Marten/Flagg are opposite sides of the same coin. Flagg believes that Roland completes him, making him greater than his own destiny. Before Roland, Walter had been little more than a wanderer left over from the old days, a mercenary who had done his share of murder with a vague ambition to penetrate the Tower before it was brought down.

Now his goal is to become Walter of End-World, Walter of All-World. Like Roland, he wants to climb the Tower and see what—if anything— lives at the top. He wants to use Mordred, whom he helped create and whom he fears, to attain the Tower and dethrone the Crimson King so he can rule the chaos that will follow its downfall. His plan is to allow Mordred to kill Roland and then kill Mordred himself and take his valuable red heel, the key to the Tower. In his last moments, he realizes that he's been mistaken all along, for it is the red mark, the hourglass on the spider form's belly, that would have granted him access.

He despises Roland, who has stood against him at every turn. In frustration, he loses sight of his goal.

> "'Tisn't the Dark Tower at all, if you want the truth; it's Roland,"
> he tells Mordred. "I want him dead. . . . For the long and dusty
> leagues he's chased me; for all the trouble he's caused me . . . for
> his presumption in refusing to give over his quest no matter what
> obstacles were placed in his path; most of all for the death of his
> mother, whom I once loved . . . or at least coveted . . . All I know
> is that Roland of Gilead has lived too long and *I want that son of a*
> *bitch in the ground.*" [DT7]

Walter meets his match in the baby Mordred Deschain. The wizard believes he's taken preventive measures against Mordred, but they are ineffective. Mordred thinks Walter is a "fool who was too full of his own past exploits to sense his present danger . . . Walter had also grown old, although he was too vain to realize it. Old and lethally sure of himself. Old and lethally stupid."

In his final moments, Walter understands that he has vastly underestimated Mordred's powers. As punishment for allowing his hatred to blind him, Mordred symbolically forces Walter to pluck out his eyes and give them to Mordred. Walter o'Dim becomes Walter the Blind. His centuries of knowledge pass into Mordred as he is consumed. In his final moments, he learns what "almost mortal" means.

Mordred Deschain

> *[T]hough we must keep our fingers away from his mouth (he snaps, this one;*
> *snaps like a crocodile), we are allowed to pity him a little. If ka is a train then*
> *this nasty little lycanthrope is its most vulnerable hostage. Not tied to the tracks*
> *like little Nell but strapped to the train's very nose.* [DT7]

Mordred Deschain has four parents—Roland, Susannah, Mia (daughter of none) and the Crimson King. Both of his fathers are killers. Walter o'Dim arranged his conception to foil Roland's quest and as an heir to the Crimson King's throne. From birth, Mordred has few imperatives other than to survive, to eat and to kill his White father.

Walter o'Dim plans to let Mordred deal with Roland, but then he intends to use the red birthmark on Mordred's left heel to gain access to the
Dark Tower, where he will confront the Crimson King and perhaps defeat
him. Mordred's Red father used to bear the same mark on his heel, but he
scorched it off, thereby imprisoning himself on one of the Tower's balconies.

Mordred's conception began when Roland exchanged sex for information with the oracle in the mountains. Roland's seed was preserved by
the old people's science while the demon elemental turned itself inside
out into its female aspect. The egg is Susannah's, from when she was
raped in the ring of stones during Jake's return to Mid-World.

Mia, who possesses Susannah, nourishes Mordred—it is her pregnancy and not Susannah's. The Crimson King somehow reimpregnated
her, either by his physical presence or via preserved sperm.

Mia drew Mordred's name from Susannah's mind. In legend, King
Arthur's father, Uther Pendragon, used Merlin's wizardry to sleep with
the wife of one of his enemies. Mordred, the son of Uther's illegitimate
daughter, grows up to lead a rebellion against Arthur, and the two kill
each other on the battlefield.

"King of Kings he might be, or destroyer of worlds, but he embarked
upon life as had so many before him, squalling with outrage." [DT7]
Mordred Deschain is born with a mouth full of teeth, a head full of black
hair and a fully erect penis. He grows much more quickly than a normal
child, reminiscent of the children in *The Village of the Damned,* a movie
Bobby Garfield sees with Ted Brautigan in *Hearts in Atlantis.* "[T]hey
grew up faster than normal kids, they were super-smart, they could make
people do what they wanted . . . and they were ruthless." [HA]

He has two physical forms: human and black widow spider. The transformation between these forms requires large amounts of energy. As a
spider, his birthmark becomes a red hourglass on his belly; this symbol is
the real key to the Dark Tower. A white node rises from the spider's back,
containing his human face with blue sparks of eyes identical to Roland's.
As a spider, which is closer to his true form, his metabolism runs hot and
fast. His thoughts become dark, primitive urges uncolored by emotion.

Shortly after he's born he transforms into spider form and sucks the
life from his surrogate mother. Susannah shoots off one of his legs. In human form, this injury translates to an open wound on his arm that seeps

blood and will never heal. Mordred mentally screams at Susannah, "I'll pay you back. My father and I, we'll pay you back!"

Mia expects her "chap" to become the avatar of every gunslinger that ever was. He's an A-bomb of a Breaker and can possibly destroy the remaining Beams by himself. Mordred has no maternal thoughts toward Susannah, referring to her as "the brown bitch." He has Mia's thoughts and memories and many stolen from Susannah, as well. Still, he knows more than he has any right to, and doesn't know why he has this knowledge or how he came by it. Understanding how to use machinery—the creations of man, not gods—is one of his talents. He is a child that knows both too much and too little.

He's both vulnerable and mortal. "[E]ven gods could die once their divinity had been diluted with human blood." As a twenty-pound child, he is more than a match for Walter o'Dim, but he still needs a diaper.

He is the last miracle to ever be spawned by the still-standing Dark Tower, the wedding of the rational and the irrational, the natural and the supernatural, and yet he is alone and he is always hungry. Destiny might have intended him to rule a chain of universes, or destroy them all, but so far he has succeeded in establishing dominion over nothing but one old domestic robot who has now gone to the clearing at the end of the path. [DT7]

He hates Roland for no other reason than he was bred to do so and to rule in his Red father's place, but his hate is tinctured by sadness and loneliness and love. He will remain outside of Roland's circle—it is his ka—and he resents the ka-tet's connection, something he will never have. From his vantage point spying on the gunslingers, though, he considers himself part of the ka-tet. He shares their khef and feels what they do.

Part of him—he attributes it to "the gullible voice of his mother"— longs to go to Roland and call him father and call the others his siblings. He knows the gunslingers would probably kill him the moment they saw him, but if they welcomed him into their circle he would have to accept Roland as dinh in both of its meanings—leader and father—something he will never do.

He feels no more loyalty to the Crimson King than to Roland. He hears the music of the Tower, but what Roland hears in a major key, he hears in a minor. Where Roland hears many voices, Mordred hears only one, the Crimson King, telling him to kill the others and join him. The voice says they will destroy the Dark Tower and rule todash together for eternity.

He follows the ka-tet and plots his revenge. He could have turned them in to the keepers of Devar-Toi, but he wants the privilege of killing Roland for himself. He needs meat to grow, and soon he'll need to switch his diet to human flesh if he is to develop. He calls rooks to him when he's hungry, and they have no choice but to come. To keep from choking on this rough food, he must convert to his spider form. By the time he reaches the size of a nine-year-old boy, starvation has made him haggard and thin. His skin is discolored and covered with sores.

Plodding through the deadly cold, he conserves energy by staying in his human form, even though he would have been less vulnerable to the elements in his spider form. His complicated genetic inheritance allows him to survive where a human would not. The only thing stopping him from giving up and returning to his Red father's castle is hatred. He cries in the darkness at the thought that Roland and Susannah have each other when he has no one.

When he leaves Dandelo's cabin, he looks about twenty years old, tall, straight and fair. In spider form, he unwisely consumes Dandelo's dead, poisonous horse, sickening himself. He relies on his single-minded determination and obsession to force himself to eat enough to keep up his strength so he can maintain control over his shape-shifting. The poison that is slowly killing him in human form would be fanned by his spider's faster metabolism and would kill him rapidly.

> Not since the Prim receded had there been such a creature as Mordred Deschain, who was part human and part of that rich and potent soup. The being whose coming had been prophesied for thousands of years (mostly by the Manni folk, and usually in frightened whispers), the being who would grow to be half-human and half-god, the being who would oversee the end of humanity and the return of the Prim . . . that being had finally arrived as a naïve and bad-hearted child who had grown to a young man and was now dying from a bellyful of poisoned horsemeat. [DT7]

He knows he's dying and his opportunity for revenge is running out. He still thinks he can defeat Roland, though, and wants him to realize that his son killed him mere hours before he reached his precious Tower. He's willing to take a couple of bullets if necessary, but the Crimson King helps him, sending out a pulse from the Tower that lulls Patrick, Roland's ill-chosen night watch, to sleep.

So focused is he on Roland that Mordred forgets the third member of Roland's party. Oy intercepts Mordred, giving Roland time to regain his wits and draw his weapons. Roland offers to let him go free in exchange for Oy's life, but it is a moot point—Mordred will die soon, regardless of what he does. He thrusts Oy aside and attacks, but in spite of Mia's wishes for him, he's no match for a real gunslinger. He dies in a hail of his father's bullets, falls into Roland's campfire and burns.

> Ka could have had no part in this, and Stephen King surely did not conceive it; what writer worth his salt would ever concoct such an end for the villain of the piece? [DT7]

The Crimson King (Ram Abbalah)

The King is in the Tower, eating bread and honey! The Breakers in the basement, making all the money! [BH]

The Crimson King is Roland's greatest enemy and has been his ancestors' foil for generations. When Walter o'Dim, one of his chief knights, greets Mordred in Fedic, he claims that the Crimson King, like Roland, is a descendent of Arthur Eld, which makes them distant cousins, or perhaps twins. "Hile, Mordred Deschain, son of Roland and of the Crimson King whose name was once hiled from End-World to Out-World; hile you son of two fathers, both of them descended from Arthur Eld." [DT7]

Also known as Ram Abbalah,[31] the Crimson King believes that he will survive the Dark Tower's collapse to rule the ensuing todash chaos. Unwilling to wait for the Beams supporting the Tower to decay naturally, the Crimson King has been trying to bring about its downfall "for time out of mind, maybe forever." [BH] In two hundred years, his Breakers have destroyed two of the five remaining Beams and severely weakened two others.

According to Parkus, even though the Crimson King is a physical being trapped in the Tower, he has another manifestation that lives in Can-tah Abbalah—the Court of the Crimson King. In effect, the Crimson King is his own twin. Though he seems to bear some similarities to Pennywise from *It,* the Crimson King is a more powerful creature with greater aspi-rations.

Parkus tells Jack Sawyer that the Crimson King is too strong for Sawyer to take on, even with the lingering power given him by the Talis-man. "The abbalah would blow you out like a candle." Jack senses that there may be some counterbalancing force, possibly female, working against the king, perhaps personified in the immense swarm of bees that accom-panies his gang into End-World.

The Crimson King's low men have performed many tasks over the generations, but their chief job has been to find Breakers, telepathic slaves mostly from Earth and the Territories—a borderland in Roland's reality where part of *The Talisman* is set—who generate a force that will disrupt the Beams. Children who don't qualify as Breakers are sent to the Big Combination, a Dickensian power plant that fuels evil in all uni-verses. The Crimson King hopes to hold Roland back and finish destroy-ing the Tower while he and his band are still at a distance.

Apparently capable of foreseeing the future, the Crimson King goes after anyone with the potential to challenge him long before it happens. Stephen King, known to the Lord of Discordia from an early age, is one of these future threats. He tries repeatedly to divert King from writing about the Dark Tower. If he can successfully discourage the author, Roland's quest cannot succeed. When King hears the song of the Turtle and writes, he is more vulnerable.

The Crimson King sends Atropos to manipulate Ed Deepneau into or-chestrating Patrick Danville's death when the boy is only four. Like any good villain, the Crimson King deceives his followers. Deepneau thinks he is fighting against the Crimson King, who he believes is another incar-nation of King Herod, out to slaughter more babies.

Ralph, the aging insomniac chosen by the Purpose to battle the Crimson King, gets closer to him than any one of his other enemies. Even Roland only comes within shouting distance in the field of roses outside the Dark Tower. While Ralph is trying to prevent Deepneau's kamikaze attack on the Derry Civic Center, the Crimson King appears before him in the guise of Ralph's long-dead mother. Like Pennywise, the Crimson King uses people's childhood fears against them. He transforms into a catfish, reminding Ralph of a traumatic occurrence from his youth. Ralph pierces one of the bulging fish eyes with the point of Lois's earring.

When the Crimson King shows himself in human form, Ralph sees an old man with a long sandy beard and hair and wearing a white robe. The eye that Ralph damaged "was filled with the fierce, splintered glow of diamonds." [INS] This injury does not seem to affect the version of the Crimson King who is trapped at the Tower—his eyes are intact. Maybe Ralph injured the Crimson King's other manifestation, Ram Abbalah. Black Thirteen is rumored to be the Crimson King's eye—perhaps this orb is somehow connected to the eye Ralph injured above Derry.

The aura Ralph perceives around the Crimson King is a fearful red, almost choleric, the color of sickness and pain. He transforms again into a tall and coldly handsome man with blond hair. Finally, he grows ancient and twisted, "less human than the strangest creature to ever flop or hop its way along the Short-Time level of existence." [INS]

Using a booby trap planted by Clotho and Lachesis, Ralph sends the Crimson King back through the doorway that had allowed him direct access to his world, one of a series of defeats—including Ty Marshall's destruction of the Great Combination, the ka-tet's victory in Calla Bryn Sturgis and their attack on Blue Heaven—that drives him crazy, though he always was Gan's crazy side. He once covered the region around Thunderclap with poison and killed almost everyone, probably as a lark. The darkness at Algul Siento is the lingering result.

Roland first hears about the Crimson King from Sylvia Pittston in Tull, and again shortly afterward from Walter. The ka-tet sees graffiti containing his name outside Topeka. Roland knows only that he lives in the West, either in Thunderclap or beyond. "I believe he may be a guardian of the Dark Tower. He may even think he owns it."

Two conflicting compulsions bring the Crimson King to the brink of madness: to destroy the Tower, and to get there ahead of Roland and slay whatever lives behind that final door. In this he is not so different from Roland, but he has no desire to understand the Tower. He only wants to beat Roland to something he wanted and then snatch it away. "He's like the old dog in some fable or other, wanting to make sure that if he can't get any good from the hay, no one else will, either." [DT7]

At some point and through unknown means, the Crimson King adds his own genetic material to Roland and Susannah's fetus. Mordred is to be both Roland's downfall and the ultimate Breaker, accelerating the Tower's downfall.

The Crimson King owned six of the surviving Wizard's glasses, which he smashed before fleeing his castle for the Tower. Using these orbs may also have contributed to his fragile mental state. Flagg told Mordred that his father's madness came from having lived so close to the Tower for so long, and having thought upon it so deeply.

Before abandoning his castle, he made most of his staff take poison as they stood in front of him. Rando Thoughtful, his Minister of State, says, "He could have killed them in their sleep if he'd wanted to by no more than wishing it on them but instead he made them take rat poison. His throne is made of skulls. He sat there with his elbow on his knee and his fist on his chin, like a man thinking long thoughts, all the while watching them writhe and vomit and convulse on the floor of the Audience Chamber." [DT7]

The Crimson King, known to Thoughtful as Los' the Red, killed himself by swallowing a sharpened spoon, fulfilling an age-old prophecy and putting him beyond the reach of Roland's guns; Roland can't kill a man who's already dead. Before leaving, he set a dead-line around the castle to keep any survivors from escaping and to trap anyone foolish enough to wander in. Undead, he mounted the greatest of the gray horses[32] and rode into the white lands of Empathica. He travels in his own portable storm. Joe Collins sensed him passing and hid in his cellar.

The Crimson King comes to fear Roland, insofar as he can fear. The ka-tet's success at Devar-Toi means that his only chance for victory lay in conquering the Tower or killing the gunslinger. After becoming trapped on a balcony outside the Tower, he scorches off his birthmark in a fit of rage. If Mordred, who also bears the mark of the line of Eld, gets through to the Tower, the Crimson King can reenter and climb to the top.

At Federal Outpost 19, the monitor that once showed the Dark Tower no longer works. "I don't think the Red King liked being on television," Stutterin' Bill says.

Once he's trapped, he can't climb to the top of the Tower, but he has enough ammunition with him to keep Roland out. Roland's guns are useless against him, but he could take them and use them to free himself and gain the Tower. If he were so inclined, the mad, dead king could rule from the top of the Tower, but given his insanity, he'd rather bring it down, which he may be able to do even though the Beams are safe and regenerating.

He monitors Mordred's progress as he pursues Roland across the wastelands. When Mordred plans to launch a desperate attack against Roland while Patrick keeps watch, he sends out a pulse from the Tower to lull Patrick to sleep. After Roland kills Mordred, he hears a howl of outraged fury in his head. "My son! My only son! You've murdered him!" Roland responds that Mordred was his own son, too. "Who sent him to me? Who sent him to his death, ye red boggart?"[33]

At the Tower, the Crimson King attacks Roland with his stockpile of sneetches. He's an old man with a snowy white beard growing down to his chest and a flushed face. His red robe is covered with cabalistic symbols like the ones on the cases the Manni use to store their holy instruments. His eyes burn with hell's own fire.

To the New Yorkers he would have looked like Father Christmas. To Roland he looked like what he was: Hell incarnate. A greedy and questioning long face. Cheeks and forehead marked by creases so deep they might have been bottomless. The lips within the beard full and cruel. It was the mouth of a man who would turn a kiss into a bite if the spirit took him, and the spirit often would. The eyes were wide and terrible, the eyes of a were-dragon in human form.

The reek of meat would accompany each outflow of breath. A tuft of hair curls from one of his nostrils. A tiny thread of scar wove in and out of his right eyebrow like a bit of string. [DT7]

He looks down at the gunslinger with an expression of mingled hate and fear. His hands also appear to be red, as in Patrick Danville's crayon sketch. Roland and the Crimson King taunt each other, but Roland takes the goading better than his enemy, who leaps up and down, screaming and shaking his hands beside his face in a way that is almost comical. Roland thinks the Red King will split his own head wide with such cries.

The Crimson King knows his adversary well, saying, "Murderer! Murderer of your mother, murderer of your friends—aye, every one—and now murderer of your own son!" Realizing that Roland is capable of defending himself against the sneetches and resisting his taunts, the Crimson King has enough sanity left to fall silent and let the call of the Tower lure Roland into the open, where he would be easy prey.

As soon as Patrick starts drawing him, the Crimson King knows something bad is happening. When Patrick begins to erase his drawing, he understands what's happening and screams in pain and horror. He throws more sneetches in desperation, but once Patrick removes his hands, he can throw no more. He shrieks and whines until Patrick erases his mouth.

In the end, Patrick removes everything but the red eyes, which his eraser won't touch. When Roland approaches the Tower, the eyes continue to stare down at him, burning with hatred. Roland supposes that they would remain up there forever, watching the field of roses while their owner wanders the world to which Patrick's eraser and enchanted artist's eyes had sent him—or, more likely, to the space between the worlds.

Stephen King[34]

When the real Stephen King announced[35] that he would be a character in the *Dark Tower* series, he told his audience that he wasn't surprised to find himself part of the story, but he was taken aback to discover that he wasn't one of the good guys, but rather a secondary character.

Though the version of the author who first appears in *Song of Susannah* is not a leading character, he is pivotal to the series. How could God not be crucial? For the King within the tale is the tale's creator and, therefore, Roland's maker, as well as the Crimson King's, even though the latter seems to predate him and tried to thwart him when he was a young boy.

King's name is first mentioned on the deli board at Calvin Tower's bookstore when Jake revisits the day he died in 1977. Later, when Tower insists that Eddie hide his most valuable books in the Doorway Cave, Roland finds among them *'Salem's Lot*. The separation of reality and fiction grows hazy. Father Callahan discovers that his life is someone else's invented story.

King shows up in person in 1977, a writer not particularly well known outside of his home state, but not a starving artist, either. He's thirty years old, has three young children, and could pass for Roland's son. His dark beard has a few threads of gray. He's tall and pale, heading toward being fat, and shows the potential for alcoholism. One bow of the frames on his thick glasses is mended with tape. His way of talking reminds Eddie of everyone he's ever known. In the author's note at the end of *The Dark Tower,* King says that this version of him is "very close to the Stephen King I remember living with at that time."

Since King is Eddie and Roland's creator—Roland thinks of him as his biographer—his mistakes and continuity errors are real to them, which is why Eddie's hometown of Co-Op City is in Brooklyn instead of the Bronx. He's as much in awe of his creations as they are of him. Eddie thinks he's likable enough, but reminds himself that King is responsible for the deaths of everyone in his family.

Though he's their god, he's not immortal. If the Crimson King can interfere with his work and discourage him from transcribing the *Dark Tower* series, Roland's quest will fail. The Crimson King has tried to kill him many times during his life. Sometimes he's rescued; sometimes he steps aside and saves himself. The first attempt on his life happened when he was six or seven. He and his brother were sentenced to saw wood in the barn as punishment for trying to run away. There they find some dead chickens, killed by avian flu. The diseased fowls' bodies are covered with red spots, and red spiders crawl on them.

King is afraid that if the spiders get on him he'll catch the flu and die and come back as a vampire, a pet writer, slave to the Lord of the Spiders. Eddie, in one of his forms, saved King from the spiders and won him over to Roland's side. King made up a magic gunslinger to keep him safe in the future from whatever scared him in that barn. In *It,* King writes about George's paper boat floating into the sewer neck and neck with a dead chicken, and later Mike Hanlon tells about someone killing all the chickens in their barn. Richie Tozier quotes Jerry Lee Lewis singing about chickens in the barn. Clearly this episode stayed with King.

One of the real King's frequently asked interview questions is: What happened to you as a child to makes you write the things you do? King expresses frustration with the premise behind this question. He finds modern society tiresomely Freudian and claims to be more Jungian in his philosophy, subscribing to the notions of race and cultural archetypes rather than overbearing importance of childhood trauma. His regular references to spiders throughout the series may be his way of poking fun at pop psychology.

> So there you go, an easy lesson in the psychology of fiction: take an imaginative boy, add a few dead chickens, pop in one common spider, stir well, and bake for roughly forty years. Result? Low men with red spots between their eyes (bloody circles that never heal), and one spider princeling. [DT6]

Very few of the things King has written since starting the *Dark Tower* series in 1970 were just stories. The Calvins, who research his books for Tet Corporation, believe he is leaving messages in his books in the hope they'll reach Roland and help him gain his goal. Roland planted this suggestion in King's mind when he hypnotized him during the summer of 1977.

King thinks he is either the creative force known as Gan, or possessed by Gan. "Maybe there's no difference," he tells Roland and Eddie. [DT6] Greedy old ka demands more from him beyond just turning aside from Discordia. Ka comes to him and he translates it. He hates ka for making him do some of the things he writes.

He is being carried by the tidal wave that runs along the Path of the Beam, a wave he may be creating himself. Jake thinks of him as a tele-caster. He's not thinking things up, like the key and the scrimshaw turtle. He's just broadcasting them. He didn't make the ka-tet; he facilitated it.

His life is a constant battle with ka and the story it wants him to write. When he opens his eyes to Roland's world, the Crimson King sees him more clearly and turns his attention to him. He stopped writing the series at the end of *The Gunslinger* because he didn't want to be the creative force, but also because he was afraid.

The *Dark Tower* series was going to be his epic, but the story and its hero got away from him and its scope exhausted him. By the end of *The Gunslinger* he was no longer sure of Roland's nature—was he hero or anti-hero? He abandoned his plans for the series, but Roland hypnotizes him to return to it when he hears the song of the Turtle. Over the next twenty years, he works on it in bursts, but he finds it harder and harder to return after each book.

Arachnophobia

What should a reader make of all the spiders, some with more than eight legs, that appear throughout the series? Are they an unconscious manifestation of King's childhood experience in the barn? The ones Roland encounters in the basement of the way station are disturbingly large, have eyes on stalks and have as many as sixteen legs. The lobstrosities are described as looking like a crossbreeding of prawn, lobster and spider. Instead of the Queen of Spades, the playing card Roland knows is the "Bloody Black Bitch Queen of Spiders."

Eddie speaks of the halls of the dead "where the spiders spin and the great circuits fall quiet one by one." He mistakenly associates the Dr. Doom masks with Spider-Man, when he was actually primarily in the *Fantastic Four* comics.

Bloated spiders bite Jake on the hand and the neck in the house where he passes back through to Mid-World. The bridge over the River Send has steel cables "like the web of some great spider."

Roland's horse in Mejis is afraid of spiders, and Rimer is described as a "disgusting spider of a chancellor." Susan Delgado is afraid of biting spiders among the oil fields outside Hambry and pretends that one had frightened her to explain her delay while spying on Rhea of Cöos. "I hate the look of them," she tells Rhea, who bears a mark beside her mouth that looks like a spider bite and whose cat looks like it has been crossed with a spider.

Viewed from the Little Needle, the train station at Thunderclap contains a spiderweb of tracks. Todash highways radiate from New York "like some crazy spider's web," and the members of Roland's ka-tet think Susannah's baby might look like a spiderling, which it does in one of its forms, for it is a "were-spider." In the Dogan near the Calla, Jake wonders how many generations of spiders had been born in a skeleton's empty cavity. In the banquet hall where Mia feeds, she sees a dead black widow spider in a goblet. Roland tells the people of Calla about the plague that befell the blossy trees in Gilead when he was ten; the trees were covered in a canopy of spiderwebs.

Spiders extend beyond the *Dark Tower* series. The creature in *It* is best visualized as a spider, and Rose Madder's face turns into "a spider's face, twisted with hunger and crazy intelligence." The Fisherman in *Black House* stashed Ty Marshall in another dimension "like a spider stashing a fly." The original version of the *Creepshow* screenplay specified spiderlike bugs instead of cockroaches for the final story, "They're Creeping Up on You," and the beast in "The Crate" was also described as spiderlike.

Finally, while Roland is plucking a rose outside the Dark Tower to make pigment for Patrick, thorns slash through his glove like it was nothing more than cobwebs, severing one of the remaining fingers on that hand. The spider's last bite.

In the late 1980s, he finally hears the song his wife has been singing and gets sober. After that, the only thing they argue about is the dangerous route he takes on his long walks.

By 1997, he knows the rest of the story and realizes he's going to have to tackle the three remaining books all at once. It means swimming across deep water to the other side, and there's a chance he may drown. He decides against returning to the Tower, but he can't separate it from his writing. His undermind is always thinking of it.

Walter tells Mordred that King was a "damnably quick writer, one with genuine talent" who "turned himself into a shoddy (but rich) quick-sketch artist, a rhymeless Algernon Swinburne."[36] After reading four or five of his books, Irene Tassenbaum decided King wasn't a very good writer. However, when Roland asks, "If he's not very good, why didn't you stop at one?" she concedes the point. "He is readable, I'll give him that—tells a good story, but has very little ear for language." Roland tells her that he hears the right voices and sings the right songs.

Roland dislikes and distrusts King, though, believing the author has turned lazy and relies on ka to protect him against trouble. When King decides to avoid the song of the Turtle in 1999, the ka of the rational world has had enough of his frittering and conspires to kill him. Roland and Jake must counter ka's will and save his life. If they don't, King will die in a fatal auto-pedestrian accident at the age of fifty-two in the most important version of reality.

At some point, the song of the Turtle became Jake's death song. King can't ignore the song, for that would be to abandon "the trail of bread-crumbs he must follow if he is ever to emerge from this bewildering forest of plot he has planted"—if, indeed, he is the one who planted it. He regrets that Jake died—is sorrier about him than about Eddie, although Eddie was always his favorite character.

Jake sacrifices his life so King, though badly injured, will live to finish the tale. Afterward, he tells Roland he wished he could write, "And they lived happily ever after until the end of their days," but he's not God and he must write the story no matter how the tale falls.

King tells Roland to save his hate for someone who deserves it. "I didn't make your ka any more than I made Gan or the world and we both know it. Put your foolishness behind you—and your grief—and do as you'd have me do. Finish the job."

He's prepared for reader reaction to Jake's death when the books are published. When the little boy in *Cujo* died, one reader sent him a dog turd via first-class mail.

The Tower's earliest readers have known Jake Chambers for twenty years. Yes, some of them will be wild, and when he writes back and says he's as sorry as they are, as surprised as they are, will they believe him? Not on your tintype, as his grandfather used to say. He thinks of Annie Wilkes shouting at Paul Sheldon, calling him the God to his characters. He doesn't have to kill any of them if he doesn't want to. [DT7]

Three years later, the accident is a distant memory, but not the pain. He's suffering a mild version of post-traumatic stress disorder, and part of his memory of the accident has been blinded white, hidden by Roland's hypnotic suggestion. He considers hypnotherapy to recover the lost memories, but never follows through.

As he nears the end, King grows weary of the journey. The trip has been long and the cost high. No great thing was ever attained easily, he reflects. A long tale, like a tall Tower, must be built a stone at a time.

"It is the tale, not he who tells it," Stevens the butler once said in "The Breathing Method,"[37] [DS] but he who tells it plays a crucial role in the process, too. "I can stop now, put my pen down, and rest my weary hand, although probably not forever; the hand that tells the tales has a mind of its own, and a way of growing restless." [DT7]

ENDNOTES

[1] AOL chat, September 22, 1998.

[2] www.stephenking.com, June 2002.

[3] Stephen King, personal communication, October 2003. He didn't elaborate on this surprising revelation.

[4] Charles Burnside, the serial killer who delivers Breakers to the Crimson King in *Black House,* has a similar worry. "What if there's more to pay for the things he has done over the course of his long career? . . . What if such a place [as the Big Combination] waits for him?" [BH]

[5] Jake remarks that "with Roland, you were always in school. Even when you were in the shadow of death there were lessons to be learned."

[6] In the revised edition of *The Gunslinger,* Roland is better at estimating Jake's age.

[7] The *R* doesn't stand for "Roland" or anything else. His middle name is just an initial.

[8] This is a Manni prayer, but the sentiment is reminiscent of *The Green Mile.*

[9] Eddie Cantor was a silent movie star and comic singer famous in the early years of the twentieth century. He died in 1964, which would be around when Eddie was born (he was about thirteen in 1977).

[10] Estevez and Lowe have starred in adaptations of King stories, Lowe most recently in a remake of *'Salem's Lot.*

[11] Though some text references put him at twenty-one, he seems to be twenty-three in the early part of the series and is described as twenty-five in *Wolves of the Calla.*

[12] Her name is either Selina [DT2] or Gloria [DT3].

[13] When Jake sees Eddie deliberately losing to Henry at basketball, he muses, "I think your little brother has been playing you like a violin for a long time now, and you don't have the slightest idea, do you?"

[14] He's a year older than Cuthbert was when he died on Jericho Hill.

[15] In *Song of Susannah,* Odetta says that the A train never stopped at Christopher Street. "It was just another little continuity mistake, like putting Co-Op City in Brooklyn."

[16] An actress in *Gone with the Wind.*

[17] "Susan" and "Susannah" both mean lily—it is interesting to note that calla is a kind of lily.

[18] King told Janet Beaulieu of the *Bangor Daily News* that he's interested in whether or not there are powers of evil that exist outside ourselves.

[19] This is where Callahan's story ends in *'Salem's Lot.*

[20] Callahan dubs his two assailants Lenny and George after characters from Steinbeck's *Of Mice and Men.* King often mentions this novel and it's one of the books Ted Brautigan leaves for Bobby Garfield in *Hearts in Atlantis.*

[21] In an interview in *Prevue* magazine in May 1982, King discussed the plot of his then-planned sequel to *'Salem's Lot.* He said Father Callahan, who no longer considered himself a priest, was working in a soup kitchen in Detroit when he got word things weren't over in 'Salem's Lot. Twenty years later, part of that vision came true.

[22] Reminiscent of how Dayna Jurgens escaped from Randall Flagg in *The Stand.*

[23] The head of the 'Salem's Lot ka-tet.

[24] Reminiscent of Ralphie Anderson's fairy-saddle birthmark in *Storm of the Century.*

[25] *Ubris,* 1969, and *Moth,* 1970; *The Devil's Wine,* Cemetery Dance Publications, Tom Piccirilli, ed., 2004.

[26] *Walden Book Report,* July 2003. This description of Flagg the outsider also applies to Mordred Deschain.

[27] In Calla, when talk turns to Walter, Roland still wonders if Marten was Maerlyn, "the old rogue wizard of legend."

[28] In Roland's youth, Garlan is as mythical as Gilead will become in his adult years. It is a land "where carpets sometimes fly, and where holy men sometimes pipe ropes up from wicker baskets, climb them, and disappear at the tops, never to be seen again." [ED] People who went there seeking knowledge usually disappeared, but those who returned were not always changed for the better. On maps, the regions south of Garlan are mostly white spaces.

[29] The Beast in the original version of *The Gunslinger.*

[30] Reminiscent of a scene early in *The Good, the Bad and the Ugly,* which inspired King to write *The Gunslinger.*

[31] Carlos Detweiler's deity in *The Plant* is also called Abbalah.

[32] The horse's name is Nis, after the land of sleep and dreams.

[33] Boggarts are mischievous spirits that inhabit homes but can also be transported in household items.

[34] Unless otherwise specified, this section deals with the fictionalized character who appears in *Song of Susannah* and *The Dark Tower,* not the real person.

[35] Master's Tea, Yale University, April 21, 2003.

[36] Swinburne was a contemporary of Browning, and was both a poet and a critic. He wrote "A Sequence of Sonnets on the Death of Robert Browning" in 1890.

[37] The library in 249B East Thirty-fifth contains a book called *Breakers* by an author who doesn't exist outside the building. Unknown manufacturer names adorn the jukebox and billiards table. The house has rooms that go on forever, with entrances and exits throughout.

CHAPTER 11

EPICS, INFLUENCES AND KA

What in the midst lay but the Tower itself?
The round squat turret, blind as the fool's heart,
Built of brown stone, without a counterpart
In the whole world.[1]

The wheel which turns our lives is remorseless; always it comes
around to the same place again.

[DT3]

When Stephen King started working on the first story of the first book that would become the *Dark Tower* series, his intentions were nothing grander than to write the longest popular novel in history. Now a grandfather in his late fifties, King looks back with sympathy and understanding at the youthful hubris that gave rise to such an aspiration. "At nineteen, it seems to me, one has a right to be arrogant. . . . Nineteen is the age where you say *Look out world, I'm smokin' TNT and I'm drinkin' dynamite, so if you know what's good for ya, get out of my way—here comes Stevie.*"[2]

The Lord of the Rings inspired King, though he had no intention of replicating Tolkien's creations, for his inspirations went beyond that epic quest fantasy to embrace romantic poetry and the spaghetti westerns of the 1960s and 1970s. After graduating from college, he decided it was time to stop playing around and tackle something serious. He began a novel "that contained Tolkien's sense of quest and magic but set against [director Sergio] Leone's almost absurdly majestic Western backdrop."[3]

In the afterword to *Wizard and Glass,* King calls the *Dark Tower* books cowboy romances. Through Roland, he comments on mixing genres when Eddie explains the differences between mysteries, suspense stories, science fiction, Westerns and fairy tales. "Do people in your world always want only one story-flavor at a time? Only one taste in their mouths? . . .

Does no one eat stew?" Roland asks. Eddie admits that it sounds boring expressed that way. "When it comes to entertainment, we *do* tend to stick with one flavor at a time." The scene brings to mind a line from *Adventures of Huckleberry Finn*: "In a barrel of odds and ends it is different; things get mixed up, and the juice kind of swaps around, and the things go better."

In his review of *The Waste Lands*, Edward Bryant says, "One of the astonishments of these books is King's seemingly cavalier but still utterly coherent method of merging science fictional constructs with irrational fantasy. He shoves the superficially disparate concepts together with such force, the generated heat melds the elements."[4]

While most modern fantasy derives from Tolkien in one way or another, the epic quest dates back to the beginning of written language. The earliest surviving fiction is the *Epic of Gilgamesh,* composed more than four thousand years ago. This ancient story about unknown people in an unknown time displays characteristics of epic adventures that persist in modern fiction. Though Gilgamesh—and his companion Enkidu— accomplishes legendary feats, the story emphasizes what he learned along the way. Quests are as much about the trip as the goal.

In his inimitable pithy manner, King reflects on this in the closing pages of *The Dark Tower*. He addresses imaginary readers who won't be satisfied until they learn what awaits Roland within the Tower.

> You are the grim, goal-oriented ones who will not believe that the joy is in the journey rather than the destination no matter how many times it has been proven to you. You are the unfortunate ones who still get the lovemaking all confused with the paltry squirt that comes to end the lovemaking. . . . You are the cruel ones who deny the Grey Havens,[5] where tired characters go to rest. . . . I hope most of you know better. Want better. I hope you came to hear the tale, and not the ending. For an ending, you only have to turn to the last page and see what is there writ upon. But endings are heartless. An ending is a closed door no man . . . can open. [DT7]

The Odyssey is mostly about what befalls Odysseus during his travels. He has a specific goal—to return to Utica after the Trojan War and regain his kingdom—but he learns more about himself during his twenty years of travel than he would have in twenty years of peaceful existence with his wife and son. He is forced to make decisions that affect not only his own fate but also the lives of those who accompany him. He's not perfect; he makes his share of mistakes. What makes him heroic is the way he gains moral clarity by understanding his errors.

Though he is a strong leader, his quest is sometimes jeopardized by the independent actions of his companions, for each of them has a life to live, too, and their goals are not always compatible. Curiosity blended with distrust provokes some of his men into opening the sack holding unfavorable winds when his ships are within sight of home, blowing them far off track and ultimately condemning all but Odysseus to death in foreign lands.

Poems of epic quests are part of the oral tradition of literature. In French, these poems are called *Chansons de Geste,* songs of heroic deeds, the oldest surviving of which is the "Chanson de Roland" (see below). Though these poems were often based on historical events—many of them inspired by Charlemagne's life and deeds—traveling musicians turned them into legends when they embroidered them as songs performed from village to village.

Quests have goals, indeed. Bilbo's goal is to get back home alive after he's dragged out of his comfortable hole to help steal a dragon's treasure. Frodo needs to get the One Ring to Mordor and destroy it. King Arthur and his knights hope that by finding the Holy Grail they can strengthen their faltering fellowship. The travelers in the *Canterbury Tales* are on a religious pilgrimage. Captain Ahab seeks vengeance against the beast that crippled him. Don Quixote seeks adventure itself. Dante traverses purgatory and hell to find a way back home, a common element in many quests, including *The Wizard of Oz,* on which King draws in *Wizard and Glass.*

One thing that sets the *Dark Tower* apart from these earlier works—aside from its greater length—is the way in which the story was meted out to readers over such a long period of time. The words "What happened next?" have always been treasured by storytellers, but with the *Dark Tower,* the author has not always been prepared to reveal more of the story right away.

"It's the one project I've ever had that seems to wait for me," King said in 1988.[6] "Epileptics, I have heard, either see or sense aura of some sort before a seizure. In much the same way I would, from time to time, find myself thinking of Roland and his queer, sad world . . . and then there would be a brief writing seizure."[7] Within the story, King attributes these long lapses to the phenomenon of waiting to hear the song that carries the tale.

Roland's quest to reach the Dark Tower is an Aristotelian epic, in which a hero who was already larger than life, possessed of unique strengths, sets out on a journey, encounters great challenges and learns from both his travels and his encounters with others.

Unlike Odysseus, Roland doesn't have a large company of men. He starts out alone and fully intends to complete his journey alone until events conspire against him. When it seems like his goal is within his grasp, though it is still thousands of miles away, he is disabled. He loses some of his unique strength and is forced to rely on others who are conscripted to assist him but who ultimately adopt his quest as their own. Roland's obsession with the Tower infects them. If he were to fall, the others would carry on without him.

Roland's primary calling is to save all of existence, a task that has been prophesied and the one that fate and destiny—called ka—conspire to facilitate. The Dark Tower, the axis around which an infinity of universes and realities rotate, is failing. It will collapse if Roland cannot stop its decline, and if it does, existence will come to an end, to be replaced by a vast chaos known as Discordia.

However, saving the Tower is a means to an end for Roland. If the Tower were to fall, he wouldn't be able to climb the staircase to the room at the top. The Tower is made of the flesh of creation, and those who know of it and believe in it think that something dwells—or once dwelled—there. God? No one knows for sure, but Roland, Walter and the Crimson King all believe that by reaching the Tower they will be able to discover what is at the root of existence. The latter two aspire to control, destroy or replace it. Walter is worried that he might be called to account for all he has done in his life. Roland's fear is that he will mount the stairs and find nothing.

Nothing drives Roland to go beyond saving the Tower other than his own curiosity, the age-old drive to discover the nature of existence. Is there a God? Does He control creation from atop the Tower, or has He abdicated or passed on to the clearing at the end of the path? In biblical times, the people of Babel attempted to build a similar tower that would reach to heaven to find their maker.

After completing *The Drawing of the Three,* King told an interviewer, "I think everybody keeps a Dark Tower in their heart that they want to find and they know it's destructive and it will probably mean the end of them, but there's that urge to make it your own or to destroy it, one or the other. So I thought: Maybe it's different things to different people. . . . And as I write along I'll find out what it is to Roland."[8]

Roland's choice to continue past the Crimson King's castle and confront the Tower carries enormous risks. The Crimson King, unable to conquer the Tower on his own, waits for someone to bring him a sigul that will readmit him from the balcony where he is trapped. If Roland turns back, the dead king will be trapped forever where he is. However, if he carries on, confronts the Crimson King and loses, he will undo everything he and his ka-tet have fought and died for. He will live up to Walter's expectations and become an instrument of creation's destruction. Nothing sends him farther—not Gan, not the prophecies of Arthur Eld and certainly not the Tet Corporation, which will defeat Sombra and North Central Positronics in the years to come and scatter their remains to every point of the compass.

Towers are often used to symbolize an individual's self-constructed existence, perception, philosophy or consciousness. Unlike a mountain, a tower is man-made, though both stand alone. A quest to conquer a tower may be seen as a voyage of self-discovery.

Walter tells Roland's future during the long night in the Golgotha using a special—and probably stacked—deck of tarot cards. The first card represents Roland, and the next four symbolize people he will need to accomplish his quest. Walter spreads them around Roland's Hanged Man like satellites surrounding a star. The sixth card is the Tower, which he places directly on top of the Hanged Man, refusing to tell the gunslinger what it represents.

The Tower is one of the major tarot arcana, known as a villain card because very little good is ever implied by it, regardless of its orientation. On the card, a lightning bolt strikes a tower, setting it on fire or separating the top from the base. Two figures—thought to represent madness and despair or the conscious and subconscious minds—tumble from it as if they've been cast out of their high place.

At its worst, it represents the complete destruction of an existing way of life, the overturning of beliefs. It can also foretell the loss of love or long-term friendships. Old systems will be broken down or replaced through a cosmic intervention that is usually external and impersonal. In Roland's world, the old ways are already breaking down. Technology is failing. He has lost his one love and his childhood friends are all dead.

Even at its best, the card stands for necessary change, sometimes a blessing in disguise. For Roland, this may be the transition from an insular lifestyle to opening himself to others. By the time he finds Walter's trail, Roland has become a hard man and his isolation makes him harder still. His eye is fixed on his goal, and he wants to remain invulnerable until he accomplishes it. As soon as he becomes the leader of a group, he loses autonomy and becomes susceptible to the whims and needs of others. A threat to one of his ka-tet is a threat to him. What he wants cannot always be paramount, as much as he might wish otherwise.

His ka-given objective is worthy—what purer goal could there be than to save all of creation or die trying? Roland can easily justify sacrificing the lives of countless others en route to his destiny. Without sacrificing his hawk, David, when he is only fourteen, he can't become a gunslinger and try to restore family unity when Marten the enchanter comes between his parents. Without sacrificing Jake, an innocent plucked from one harsh world and dropped into another like a pawn in a game of multidimensional chess, Roland cannot catch the man in black, who he believes holds the key to the opening phases of his quest.

It's the same theme debated in the *Star Trek* movie *The Wrath of Khan*. Should one person be sacrificed to save others? Which is paramount, the good of the one or the good of the many? Roland nearly always chooses the abstract good of everyone in creation, though the harsh question he never answers is whether he is acting selflessly or merely trying to achieve his own selfish objective. Father Callahan understands that Roland is prone to confusing his own desires with the will of ka.

STEPHEN KING ISN'T THE FIRST PERSON to write about a man named Roland whose goal was to find and perhaps conquer a mysterious Dark Tower. He was inspired by the feel of Robert Browning's somewhat obtuse "Childe Roland to the Dark Tower Came," written in Paris on January 2, 1852, during the denouement of Napoleon's coup d'état. The poem, which King had been assigned in a class covering the earlier romantics poets, combines romance and existentialism, atypical of Browning's other work and ahead of its time in its Weltschmerz. "Childe" refers to a young or unproven knight. Roland tells Susannah that to him the word is a formal, ancient and almost holy term that describes a gunslinger who has been chosen by ka for a quest.

Browning, in turn, borrowed his title from a line in Shakespeare's *King Lear* uttered by Edgar during his mad ravings while disguised as Poor Tom: "Childe Rowland to the Dark Tower came, His word was so still—Fie, foh and fom / I smell the blood of a British man."[9] King clearly knew of this reference; he named the creatures Roland and Susannah encounter at the Crimson King's castle Feemalo, Fimalo and Fumalo.

Tom was likely referring to an old Scottish ballad titled "Child Rowland and Burd Ellen" wherein Rowland, a son of King Arthur, rescues his sister, Lady Ellen, from the King of Elfland's Dark Tower after his older brothers try and fail to return. Merlin the magician tells Rowland that, to avoid being caught by the king, he must lop off the heads of everyone who speaks to him in the land of Fairy until he finds his sister. He is also to refuse any food offered to him. In *The Dark Tower*, Roland and Susannah also must resist the temptation of food at the Crimson King's castle. The King of Elfland utters the legendary words, "Fee, fi, fo, fum," which also connects to the scene at the Crimson King's castle.

In the Scottish ballad, Rowland uses his father's sword Excalibur—the source of metal for Roland Deschain's guns—to strike the King of Elfland to the ground. The king begs for his life and agrees to set not only Roland's sister, but also his two brothers, free.[10]

In the early books of the series, King does not rely heavily on Browning's poem. He extracts some details from the text (Roland's boyhood friend Cuthbert is mentioned in stanza XVI) and ignores others (a character named Giles in stanza XVII, for example, has no counterpart in the *Dark Tower* series). However, in the final book, *The Dark Tower*, King makes more extensive and literal use of the poem. He physically delivers it into Roland's hands with important stanzas highlighted. Roland and Susannah's encounter with the vampire Dandelo is strongly influenced by Browning, a fact King acknowledges by naming Dandelo's horse Lippy, as in "Fra Lippo Lippi." Stanzas XIII and XIV describe the beast: "One stiff blind horse, his every bone a-stare."[11]

Browning's poem is far from a beaming light of clarity. King told Matt

Lauer on the *Today Show* that he didn't understand what it was about. The poet wrote in 1887, "I was conscious of no allegorical intention in writing it. . . . Childe Roland came upon me as a kind of dream. I had to write it then and there, and I finished it the same day, I believe. But it was simply that I had to do it. I did not know then what I meant beyond that, and I'm sure I don't know now. But I'm very fond of it." Since Browning writes of Roland's adventures, perhaps he was one of Stephen King's predecessors as the channel of Gan.

The mood of Browning's poem is even bleaker than that of *The Gunslinger*. The poem's persona—and everyone else—feels that his quest is doomed to fail: "Heard failure prophesied so oft, been writ / So many times." He is depressed by the loss of his companions and continues his journey because "naught else remained to do." The reason for his nightmarish quest is clear neither to the protagonist nor to the reader.

The terrain Browning's speaker crosses is as desolate as the wastelands in Mid-World, places so ruined that "Last Judgement's fire must cure" them. The poem pauses in the middle for "one taste of the old time," a period of reflection analogous to Roland's long story in *Wizard and Glass*.

Most of the poem is taken up with the protagonist's journey through hateful lands. Everything he encounters is terrible; his adversary seems to be nature itself. In the final stanzas he emerges from the last of this horrible terrain to encounter what he has spent a life training to reach. Browning's Tower is a squat brown turret, apparently inspired by a tower the author saw in Italy.[12] It is built of an unusual stone not known anywhere else in the world. King's Tower is not made of stone at all, but the living essence of creation: Gan.

Browning's Roland, like King's, hears the names of all his lost friends as he approaches the Tower and reflects on their individual strengths ("How such a one was strong, and such was bold / And such was fortunate . . . one moment knelled the woe of years"). In the end, he puts his "slug-horn"[13] to his lips and blows. What he hopes to challenge is left unsaid—a situation King addresses when his own Roland reaches the Tower.

Victor Kelleher turned the poem into a children's book called *To the Dark Tower*. When the hero, Tom Roland, reaches the goal of his long quest, he finds that it has been a delusion and there is no paradise to be won. Critic Harold Bloom—not King's number one fan—suggests that Browning's poem may begin again to form a closed cycle, an infinite loop.[14]

Roland lost his horn, handed down through the generations from Arthur Eld, and thus cannot blow it in challenge or celebration. He left it beside the body of his friend Cuthbert, who had borrowed it because he claimed he could blow it sweeter than Roland could. "Neglect not to pick it up, Roland, for it's your property," Cuthbert said, anticipating his death and Roland's survival. Roland was so focused on his quest that he ignored Cuthbert's advice. "In his grief and bloodlust he will forget all about Eld's Horn." [DT5]

Though he may have been inspired by the Scottish ballad, Browning's use of the horn calls to mind the original Roland, who was immortalized in the "Chanson de Roland," an epic poem probably written by the Norman poet Turold around A.D. 1100.[15] The historical Roland—Hruodlandus, governor of a borderland of Brittany—was killed by the Basques in the Pyrenees Mountains in 788 while leading the rear guard of future emperor Charlemagne's forces returning from their invasion of Spain. In some legends, Charlemagne is both Roland's uncle and father, having sired him via an incestuous relationship with his sister, bringing to mind the Arthurian legend of Mordred, which King exploits in the *Dark Tower* series. The poet transformed the Basque enemies into the Saracens,[16] and moved the battle to Roncesvalles.

Roland's stepfather, Ganelon, is sent to negotiate peace with the Saracens at Roland's suggestion. Already resentful of his stepson's arrogance and prowess—Ganelon isn't pleased at being nominated for such hazardous duty—he plots with the Saracens, who were ready to accept peace, to bring about Roland's defeat. They attack his forces in the mountain pass.

Roland carried with him the legendary sword Durendal, which contained the tooth of St. Peter and the blood of St. Basil secreted in its hilt. Brave, but also reckless and proud, he refused to call for help until their situation was desperate.[17] In the face of defeat, he blew his ivory horn, named Oliphant or Olivant, cracking his own temples with the strain. Roland is the last of his men to die. On his deathbed, he tries to destroy Durendal, reminiscent of King Arthur's attempts to return Excalibur to the Lady of the Lake before he died.

Charlemagne heard Roland's call for help, but arrived in time only to avenge Roland and his lost army. He discovers Ganelon's treason and has him tried and executed.[18]

• • •

THE SYMBOL OF THE TOWER appears often in epic fiction. It con-
jures an image of isolation, strength and impenetrability. Where else
would Sauron have dwelt and schemed if not in a Black Tower in the land
of Mordor? Even Dr. Who tries to breach the Dark Tower of Rassilon,
which President Borusa hopes to enter and claim immortality in *The Five
Doctors*.

C. S. Lewis[19] was inspired, at least in part, by Browning in Lewis's unfinished novella *The Dark Tower,* written in 1938 and published in 1974.[20]
Five men gather in a room at Cambridge University to use their newly invented chronoscope, a kind of projecting telescope that allows them to
look in on other times.[21] They have no control over what the projector will
reveal—akin to Rhea's experience with the pink Wizard's Glass—but the
locations they see are always close to a Dark Tower, which they associate
with Browning. Slaves supervised by automatons called Jerkies are con-
structing the Tower. The Jerkies report to the Stingingman, who has a
stinger protruding from his forehead.

The men realize that the Tower is identical to the one at the Cambridge
library, and some of the faces they see are familiar, including a facsimile
of one of the men watching the scene. The duplicate grows a forehead
stinger and replaces the Stingingman. Enraged, the original viewer dashes
at the projection screen and switches places with his evil double (his
Twinner), ending up in another time frame, a parallel reality.

Also inspired by Browning's poem, Louis MacNeice wrote a radio
play called *The Dark Tower* at the end of the Second World War. In his introduction to a collection of scripts, MacNeice comments that the poem
eludes analysis and its moral and meaning are unclear.[22]

The self-described parable play is cast as a dream. Roland is the seventh son of a family in which every male for generations has learned to
play a trumpet challenge call before setting out by ship in search of the
Dark Tower, never to return, as in the old Scottish ballad. As Aunt Talitha
of River Crossing tells Roland and his ka-tet in *The Waste Lands,* "No one
who ever went in search of that black dog ever came back."

MacNeice's Dark Tower, sometimes called a Dragon, is the source of
evil throughout the world. Though it is immortal, men are compelled to
try to defeat it. When Roland asks his tutor what would happen if people

decided to just leave the Tower alone, he is told that some people would live longer (that is, those who die trying to defeat it) but everyone's lives would be degraded and the Dragon (evil) would reign supreme. "Honor" and "duty" are obsolete terms—Roland and his family quest after the Tower because of tradition. The play ends, like Browning's poem, with Roland uttering a challenge on his trumpet, a phrase that he has perfected under intense tutelage. What happens thereafter is not revealed.

IN THE *DARK TOWER* SERIES, King constructed a new world and, over the course of the seven main books and ancillary novels, composed its history back to the beginning of time. He posited parallel realities, some that are mostly the same as our own and others that are starkly different. King acknowledges drawing inspiration from Clifford D. Simak's novel *Ring Around the Sun,* which "postulates the idea that there are a number of worlds like ours. Not other planets but other Earths, *parallel* Earths, in a kind of ring around the sun." [HA]

As Jack Sawyer comes to realize, "Worlds spin around him, worlds within worlds and other worlds along side them, separated by a thin membrane composed of a thousand thousand doors, if you only know how to find them." [BH] Death is one of these doorways, as Jake and Callahan discover.

It's not unreasonable to speculate that the parallel universes in King's creation all began from the same spark and were propagated independently, which would explain why so many of them are similar. Michael Moorcock coined the term "multiverse" to describe these infinite alternate realities that sometimes intersect, and addressed the possibility that one could meet a different version of oneself when traveling between realities. While King's characters never meet themselves when they reality hop, different versions of themselves come into play. For example, a young Eddie points Jake in the right direction to get back to Mid-World while his older self works to create a doorway on the other side.

Is Roland's land a postapocalyptic version of Earth? That's one possible explanation. There seems to have been some sort of radiation incident in Mid-World's history causing mutations in people and livestock. The bloodlines are beginning to clarify in some regions (the so-called "threaded stock") and there are fewer mutants, but in other places the lingering effects of whatever cataclysm took place are still in evidence. Slow Mutants, horribly deformed humans, lurk beneath the mountains Jake and Roland traverse. The region beyond Lud is a wasteland that the ka-tet could never have survived without riding Blaine the Mono. In the Territories, another of Mid-World's borderlands, nuclear testing in one reality created the Blasted Lands in the other.

Even if all realities, which number beyond telling, began at a common point—and nothing in the *Dark Tower* series requires this—time is free to travel at different speeds from one reality to another, a phenomenon that the ka-tet has to contend with as their quest proceeds. Time passes more slowly in Jake's world than in Mid-World, but faster in Keystone Earth. Roland's land may represent a reality that evolved similarly to Earth but at a faster rate, proceeding beyond the currently known state of things to some undefined cataclysm that destroyed everything. How else to explain the preponderance of things in Mid-World that are known on Earth—machinery, oil plants, the Bible, "Hey Jude"?

Another explanation is that people in Mid-World borrowed these things from Earth by traveling through the doorways that connect realities. Blaine the Mono knows about Earth culture because of doorways. In his supersonic travels he may even have crossed the boundaries between worlds in thin places, which would explain how he derails in an Earth-like version of Topeka. The Manni have often passed between worlds, and the travel posters and brochures near some doorways in New York and Fedic indicate that Earth was a popular tourist destination for Mid-Worlders in times gone by. The only place on Earth where this interdimensional travel is noticeable is in western Maine, where walk-ins started appearing in the late 1970s.

Of the infinite worlds, only two are important to the continuation of existence: Mid-World, also known as the Tower Keystone, and Keystone Earth. The Tower exists as itself only in Mid-World. In many others it is a rose or an immortal tiger. In at least one it is the ur-dog Rover. In one version of Earth it may be a black hotel in California.

Keystone Earth is different from all others in that time flows in only one direction. Roland and his followers can travel across todash space into Keystone Earth, but each time they will arrive later than the time before.[23] If they make mistakes, they can't double back and fix things. Roland says that in Keystone Earth most species still breed true, many lives are sweet and there is still energy and hope. Each world has its own ka—the ka of 19 in one and the ka of 99 in the other.

Since shortly after the beginning of creation, when the Prim receded, an order of men arose whose purpose is protecting the Tower and the Beams of power that support it. These gunslingers of the line of Arthur Eld, the first great champion of ka, produce a type of energy that feeds the six Beams crisscrossing Roland's reality, intersecting at the Tower. Once there were Great Old Ones who ruled and knew magic, but the magic of creation eventually retreated everywhere except at the Tower. The Old Ones panicked, not realizing that the magic was sufficient to keep the Tower forever, and replaced it with technology. Magic relied on faith; technology did not. However, things created by technology are doomed to fail, though they may last for millennia. This includes the Beams, which run on technology.

The world has moved on, people say. It's running down like the clock spring in an ancient watch. Time is soft, slipping in and out of gear. Some days seem forty hours long. The night Roland told the story of Mejis felt even longer. On some afternoons, night seems to rush over the horizon. The points of the compass can no longer be trusted. What was dead west today might be southwest tomorrow.

The gunslingers in Gilead, in the barony of New Canaan in In-World, are benign rulers, but their primary destiny makes them aloof. The Affiliation of Baronies that comprises their universe frays at the edges because the people who live in the distant lands—Mejis, for example—don't feel their influence. These people pay tribute—and taxes, presumably—to Gilead, but it's like the Roman Empire, collapsing under its own weight. Roland's father, Stephen, is unwilling to exert much energy fighting the rebels and insurrectionists who challenge his authority because he believes the rebellion is unimportant in the grander scheme.

To succeed Roland must overcome the flawed notion that everything is unimportant except for the Tower's well-being because everything, in some small way, contributes to the Tower's well-being. Stephen Deschain doesn't understand that the rebellion is an indirect threat to the Tower. As the uprising expands and finds sympathy even among people within the ivory tower of Gilead, the gunslingers are outnumbered and ultimately destroyed.

The master Trickster behind it all is Walter o'Dim, who works on behalf of the Crimson King, a fallen dark angel who has turned away from the line of Eld. The Crimson King's goal is to bring about the downfall of the Tower and rule the resulting discord. No one knows why the Crimson King believes he can survive the Tower's fall. Someone promised it to him or he promised it to himself, deluding himself into thinking he is beyond ka.

The Crimson King rarely acts directly, but rather enlists minions in his own world and others. He knows what destiny holds for him and tries to intervene, though not always successfully, to guarantee triumph. He sent Ed Deepneau to kill Patrick Danville, knowing that the boy would grow up to become the talented artist who would pose a threat to him. He tried to terrorize Stephen King as a young boy to prevent him from writing the *Dark Tower*. If King doesn't create Roland and his fellow gunslingers and guide them along the path toward the Tower, the Crimson King would be unopposed.

Walter o'Dim is the adversary Roland fences with over his millennium-long existence. As Marten the enchanter, he is counselor to the gunslingers of Gilead, causing discord from within. He corrupts Roland's mother so thoroughly that she is prepared to murder her husband. Marten goads Roland into taking his test of manhood early by flagrantly displaying his mother's infidelity, the first of many times when he underestimates Roland. As John Farson, he leads the insurrection against Gilead. In this he is successful—the gunslingers win some battles but lose the war. In the end, only Roland survives of all the people in Gilead and In-World. The gunslingers of his father's generation and of his own are all killed. The castles of Gilead are abandoned to nests of Slow Mutants and other corrupt beings.

Roland is called to save the Dark Tower via his vision in the "grapefruit" he and his friends acquire in Mejis. While some heroes must be convinced to take on the burden of a quest[24]—Stephen R. Donaldson's Thomas Covenant is probably the most extreme case—Roland doesn't hesitate. He likely doesn't realize how his goal will ultimately split into two facets—personal and universal—but his answer to the call to adventure is a resounding yes, even though it means abandoning the love of his life. His goal, as in all quests, is to return the ordinary world to its former balance.

How Roland ends up on Walter's trail and why he thinks the man in black can help him is never revealed. Their duel continues for years beyond telling. They seem incapable of killing each other; Roland's Mid-World bullets are useless against Walter.

Walter allows Roland to catch up with him after their passage through the mountains, after circling around to meet Father Callahan and returning to the trail, but he is genuinely afraid Roland might kill him during their encounter. Roland is a wild card, an agent of Purpose who sometimes acts like he is governed by Random. Though most people think he is unimaginative, he often comes up with surprisingly original solutions to problems.

Walter fulfills many of the archetypes associated with quests. He's the threshold guardian whose challenges Roland must pass to begin his real journey. He's the herald, laying out important details of the upcoming mission, and the shadow, representing Roland's darkest desires. He's the trickster, using laughter and ridicule to make Roland inspect his own motives and disrupting the quest whenever possible. He's also the shapeshifter, hiding behind several masks while attempting to thwart Roland. He's even something of a mentor, though much of what he says cannot be trusted.

Walter can't kill Roland in the Golgotha because the Crimson King needs him to beget Mordred, the son who the Crimson King would corrupt and who, like his Arthurian namesake, would hate his White father his entire life. As a descendant of the line of Eld, he could free his Red father from the prison the Tower has become for him.

For all the parts he plays, Walter is little more than the Crimson King's flunky. Higher powers are involved in Roland's quest. Walter tells him in the Golgotha, "Someone has taken an interest in you." The force that is manipulating destiny wants Roland and his followers to succeed. Roland never learns who this external power is. Perhaps it is the sheer will of the universes to survive, a Gaia that denies chaos. Maybe the Great Old Ones survive, looking down like Olympian gods, toying with the lives of mortals, aiding them when it suits their will, thwarting them otherwise.

All things serve the Beam, even the man in black. "I am compelled to tell you, partly because of the sacrifice of the boy, and partly because it is the law; the natural law of things. Water must run downhill, and you must be told." [DT1] Everything conspires to aid Roland. Even the Little Sisters of Eluria serve the Beam, Jack Sawyer is told.

Ka is King's great invention, a powerful and nearly irresistible force that guides Roland's quest from the beginning. He is gifted with an intuition of what is to come and the right thing to do when it happens. He grows to rely on ka. When he *needs* something, he *knows* it will be provided . . . because he needs it. If his group tries to go against ka, ka will shepherd them back on course. If ka wants them to go through Lud and they start to go around it, circumstances will force them back. Ka's only rule is "Stand aside and let me work." [DT6] It has no heart or mind. According to Parkus, "ka is a friend to evil as well as to good. It embraces both." [BH] Ka is like a Path of the Beam—it's the way to the Tower. It isn't omnipotent, though. Ka can be fought and changed, but only at a great cost.

"In matters of the Tower, fate became a thing as merciful as the lighter that had saved his life and as painful as the fire the miracle had ignited. Like the wheels of the oncoming train, it followed a course both logical and crushingly brutal, a course against which only steel and sweetness could stand." [DT2]

Some purpose—or perhaps Purpose, as defined in *Insomnia*—is on Roland's side. In *Black House,* the narrators comment that an event was "too meaningless to be called a coincidence. Coincidence brings together two previously unrelated elements of a larger story. Here nothing connected and there was no larger story." [BH]

Coincidence becomes an active participant in the *Dark Tower* series, a character unto itself. Each fluke is another click in some great turning cog. Everything is happening for a reason. Eddie starts carving a key without knowing what it is for so it will be ready when he needs it. Twice Roland encounters useful people in the mercantile store in Maine.

Jack Mort, little more than a bit player, is responsible for life-shaping events in the lives of both Jake and Susannah. He dropped the brick on Susannah that gave rise to her split personality, and pushed her in front of the train twenty years later without realizing she was the same person. He also pushed Jake in front of a car driven by Enrico Balazar, the crime lord who sent Eddie to the Bahamas to buy drugs.

When Roland hears that Jake and Susannah both know the poem about the turtle he learned when he was a child, he says, "It's another connection, one that really tells us something, although I'm not sure it's anything we need to know. . . . Still, one never knows when a little understanding may come in handy." Roland is aware of ka's goal, though he may not always understand the minutiae of its day-to-day operations.

Some force that knew whom Roland would need to complete his quest provided the doorways through which he draws his ka-tet. They are very specific doorways, targeted on precise people, and only Roland can open them. On the beach, he intuitively heads north toward them without knowing they exist. Without them and the people they bring into his life, not only would Roland have failed in his quest but he would have died from infection.

There are Towers everywhere. When Balazar's lieutenant, Jack Andolini, takes Eddie to their headquarters, they pull up in front of a restaurant called The Leaning Tower. Balazar, known for building houses of cards, was once observed building a tower nine levels high before it collapsed. The man who witnessed this felt that the tower of cards "explained the stars." Jake passes Tower Records after he leaves the Manhattan bookshop owned by Calvin Tower, the guardian of the rose, which is the Tower's representation in New York.

Susannah had a college teacher who hated the sort of easy coincidences often found in Dickens novels. Roland responds that her teacher was a man who either didn't know about ka or didn't believe in it.

Is Stephen King the force of ka? When he enters the *Dark Tower* as a character, this notion becomes a distinct possibility. No one wants Roland to succeed more than the author. He spent the entire span of his publishing career pushing the ka-tet along the Path of the Beam toward the Tower. But King denies that he is ka; instead he is just another of its instruments. "And still ka comes to me, comes *from* me, I translate it, am *made* to translate it, ka flows out of my navel like a ribbon. I am not ka, I am not the ribbon, it's just what comes through me." [DT6]

Ka isn't always a kind mistress. It is an enormous wheel with more momentum than most people can oppose. It's the answer to every hateful question. "Why must life always demand so much and give so little? Ka." [BH] When its translator grows lazy and decides to abandon Roland's story, ka loses patience with him and orchestrates his death.

In 438 B.C., Alcestis wrote, "I have found power in the mysteries of thought / exaltation in the changing of the Muses; / I have been versed in the reasonings of men; / But Fate is stronger than anything I have known."

Ka is Roland's usual answer to why things are the way they are, and his reliance upon it as a panacea often frustrates his friends.

There was one thing about ka they didn't tell us, [Ralph] thought. It's slippery. Slippery as some nasty old fish that won't come off the hook but just keeps flopping around in your hand. And it was like climbing a sand dune, too—you slid one step back for every two you managed to lunge ahead. . . . Because ka was like a fish, ka was like a sand dune, ka was like a wheel that didn't want to stop but only roll on and on, crushing whatever might happen to be in its path. A wheel of many spokes. But most of all perhaps, ka was like a ring. Like a wedding ring. Life is a wheel. Sooner or later everything you thought you'd left behind comes around again. For good or ill, it comes around again. [INS]

Eddie is the character most frustrated by greedy old ka. He comes to refer to it as "ka-ka." It's the net from which none ever escaped, and he is struck by the way things from his world are bleeding over into Roland's. Things in Mid-World are tangible, but on one level they don't seem real to him.

Why do people over here sing "Hey Jude?" I don't know. That cyborg bear, Shardik . . . all that shit about the Wizard of Oz, Roland—all that happened to us. I have no doubt of it, but at the same time it doesn't seem real to me. . . . And what happens after the Green Palace? Why, we walk into the woods, just like Hansel and Gretel. There's a road for us to walk on. Muffin-balls for us to pick. Civilization has ended. Everything is coming unraveled. You told us so. We saw it in Lud. Except guess what? It's not. . . . The joke is that, out here a billion miles from nowhere, we come upon a storybook town. Civilized. Decent. The kind of folks you feel you know . . . The storybook town has a fairy-tale problem. And so the storybook people call on a band of movie-show heroes to save them from the fairy-tale villains. I know it's real—people are going to die, very likely, and the blood will be real, the screams will be real—but at the same time there's something about it that

feels no more real than stage scenery. [New York feels] the same. . . .
Out of all the hoods in New York, Balazar shows up. [DT5]

Another take on ka and the sense of omniscience it lends to the characters is the cyclical nature of Roland's existence. Eddie comes close to
realizing this at one point, commenting that the way he intuitively knows
how to ride a horse and how quickly he learned to shoot is like stories of
reincarnation. If Roland has been repeating his life over and over again,
then Eddie, Jake, Susannah and Oy have likely done so, too. Have they
learned from their past experiences and gotten better each time? It's like
a computer adventure game. Sometimes a mistake made early on doesn't
manifest itself until far later, and the player has to go back to the beginning and try again.[25]

King draws from Hindu mythology throughout the series. The god
Vishnu took the form of a turtle called Kurma to carry the world on his
back after a huge flood. In *The Dark Tower,* the turtle "sees the truth but
mayn't aid." In other books King uses the turtle to symbolize a guardian
of the universe, though in *It* the turtle was old and mostly impotent. Pennywise even suggested the turtle was dead. King compares the red dot on
the low men's foreheads to Hindu caste marks, and identifies Gan—perhaps incorrectly—as a Hindu creation.

Within the pages of the final two *Dark Tower* books, King reveals
some trivia about his inspirations for other elements in the series. The
town of Calla Bryn Sturgis was named for *The Magnificent Seven* director, John Sturges, and the film's star Yul *Bryn*ner. However, King realized
that he had misspelled the director's last name after the prologue had been
posted—published, in a sense—on his official Web site.

He also wonders if he misspelled the name of the vampiric man
Roland and Susannah encounter at the beginning of Tower Road. Dandelo
is a reference to the family cat who was the subject of the researcher's
first, failed attempt at teleportation in the Vincent Price version of the
movie *The Fly,* based on a story by George Langlahan. King probably had
teleportation on his mind after assigning that power to Sheemie Ruiz.

King borrowed from many other sources in creating his magnum
opus—Tolkien, spaghetti westerns, *The Wizard of Oz,* T. S. Eliot, *The
Lord of the Rings,* the Harry Potter books, *Don Quixote,* Edgar Allan Poe,

Thomas Wolfe, *Romeo and Juliet,* and Greek mythology. From these diverse influences he has created something unique. Edward Bryant says, "[I]t's strangely unfamiliar, dissimilar to anything else the author is doing. And if the imagination itself can be considered a bone that supports the musculature, flesh, and hide of a writer's private associative creative processes, then I suspect this work of King's cuts close to it."[26]

In the end, it is not clear whether to call Roland a tragic or a dramatic hero. He successfully completes the task to which he was destined, though he left many companions strewn behind him, but so did Odysseus. Although he undergoes a kind of resurrection, he fails his personal quest. King provides readers with a glimmer of hope that the last gunslinger is evolving and one day may understand ka's message, complete his transformation and climb to the top of the Tower, mounting each level in groups of nineteen steps, and find . . . what? The destiny that Robert Browning left to the imagination of his readers?

Or maybe he will come to understand that his personal quest is too costly in terms of the sacrifices it requires of him. Perhaps he will decide that saving the world is enough purpose for one man and that the real way for him to discover the truth of creation is to live out the rest of his natural days without ever completing the road to the Dark Tower.

ENDNOTES

[1] Robert Browning, "Childe Roland to the Dark Tower Came," stanza XXXI.

[2] "On Being Nineteen (and a Few Other Things)," Viking, 2003.

[3] Ibid.

[4] Edward Bryant, *Locus* magazine, vol. 27, no. 6, December 1991.

[5] A reference to *The Lord of the Rings,* analogous to Avalon in Arthurian legends.

[6] Interview with Janet C. Beaulieu of the *Bangor Daily News,* November 17, 1988.

[7] "The Politics of Limited Editions," part 1, *Castle Rock Newsletter,* vol. 1, no. 6, June 1995.

[8] Interview with Janet C. Beaulieu, op cit.

[9] *King Lear,* Act III, Scene IV, 178–80.

[10] Robert Browning, *Selected Poetry,* The Penguin Poetry Library, edited by Daniel Karlin, Penguin Books, 1989. Synopsis derived from *The Book of Knowledge, The Children's Encyclopedia,* Grolier, 1923.

[11] Browning reportedly had in his drawing room a tapestry featuring an emaciated horse. Jim Rockhill, "The Weird Review: Childe Roland," www.violetbooks.com/REVIEWS/rockhill-browning.html.

[12] Ibid.

[13] Browning perpetuates a mistake in using this term that dates to "The Battle of Hastings" by poet Thomas Chatteton (1752–1770). Though intended to refer to a trumpet, the word is actually the etymological root of "slogan," or battle cry. Robert Browning, *Selected Poetry,* The Penguin Poetry Library, op cit.

[14] *Robert Browning: A Collection of Critical Essays,* Harold Bloom and Adrienne Munich, eds. Prentice Hall, Inc. 1977.

[15] *The Norton Anthology of World Literature,* Second Edition, Volume B, W. W. Norton & Company, 2002.

[16] This was often done to convert the gestes into triumphs of Christianity, of which Charlemagne was a champion.

[17] Though this is often seen as pride on Roland's part, it may also have been an act of loyalty. The rear guard's duty was to protect the main army from attack from behind, and to call the army back into battle might have led to their destruction. Roland had sworn an oath to Charlemagne to fight to the death to protect the army.

[18] *Merriam-Webster's Encyclopedia of Literature,* Merriam-Webster, Incorporated, 1995, and *The Columbia Encyclopedia,* Sixth Edition, Columbia University Press, 2001.

[19] Beezer, one of the Thunder Five in *Black House,* was a fan of C. S. Lewis.

[20] The author of a book called *The C. S. Lewis Hoax* claimed that *The Dark Tower* wasn't by Lewis, but a forensic documents expert confirmed that the work was indeed his.

[21] The story features Dr. Elwin Ransom and the skeptical MacPhee, from Lewis's *Out of the Silent Planet. The Dark Tower* may have been intended as part of his science fiction series.

[22] Louis MacNeice, *The Dark Tower,* Faber and Faber Limited, London, 1947.

[23] A possible logical problem crops up here. If Mid-World people vacationed in New York in 2001, shouldn't that have prevented the ka-tet from going to a previous time? Though they never get to test this theory, the ka-tet believes that if any one of them travels to a certain time, none of them can revisit that time. Perhaps the Mid-World Tourism Bureau only accesses worlds other than Keystone Earth.

[24] Jack Sawyer is reluctant to come out of retirement to assist in the serial murder case in *Black House,* for example.

[25] For example, in the old text adventure game based on Douglas Adams's *Hitchhiker's Guide to the Galaxy,* if a player fails to give a dog a sandwich very early in the game, the mission is doomed to failure regardless of whatever else the player does. It's a small detail, like Roland failing to reclaim Arthur Eld's horn at Jericho Hill, but a crucial one. The hungry dog always wins, and there's only one chance to feed it.

[26] Edward Bryant, *Locus* magazine, vol. 27, no. 6, December 1991.

CHAPTER 12

ART AND THE ACT OF CREATION

Two patterns, art and craft, were welded together.

[DT1]

All he needs to do is write the right story.
Because some stories do live forever.

[DT7]

In the window of The Manhattan Restaurant of the Mind, bookstore owner Calvin Tower maintains a deli board announcing the day's specials. FRESH-BROILED JOHN D. MACDONALD, it says. PAN-FRIED WILLIAM FAULKNER and CHILLED STEPHEN KING.

For Stephen King to show up in his own novels isn't unprecedented. His books have become so much a part of the cultural consciousness that characters who live in a simulacrum of our world need to be aware of them and mention them to be realistic. When there's a fire at a graduation dance in *The Dead Zone,* the characters automatically think of *Carrie,* a book Dinky mentions during the aftermath of the battle at Algul Siento. Flaherty, the human who pursues Jake down the corridors behind the Dixie Pig, read *The Eyes of the Dragon* when he was a kid. Part of the "feeling of reality" that F&SF editor Ed Ferman identified in the series is the characters' awareness of all the fantasy that has gone before them. Though they are living in a fantasy world, they are conversant with *The Lord of the Rings, The Wizard of Oz, The Chronicles of Narnia* and *Watership Down.*

Eddie has seen Stanley Kubrick's adaptation of *The Shining,* but he has also read a book by Ben Mears, a character in *'Salem's Lot.* He doesn't seem to know King's name and later says that he thinks King exists only in Keystone Earth. *The Shining* may be one of those stories, like *Charlie the Choo-Choo,* that is so important that it is written by different authors in different realities. Eddie also dreams of the first line of *The Gunslinger,* though in his dream it is attributed to Thomas Wolfe. Father Callahan believes that the man who thought him up may exist in only one world.

King occasionally inserts references to himself as a writer within his books, sometimes obliquely,[1] sometimes explicitly.[2] However, he takes self-reference a step farther when, in *Song of Susannah,* Eddie and Roland visit a younger version of himself living in western Maine in 1977. King transcends the characters' common consciousness to take part in the action, going beyond simple author intrusion.[3]

In "Slade," a precursor to the *Dark Tower* series (see the introduction), the imperiled heroine cries, "You came just in time!" to which Slade replies, "I always do. Steve King sees to that."[4] Slade is aware he's fictional, but King isn't a character in the story.

In "The Blue Air Compressor," the author halts the action to speak to readers, but still doesn't participate in the action.

> My own name, of course, is Steve King, and you'll pardon my intrusion on your mind—or I hope you will. I could argue that the drawing-aside of the curtain of presumption between reader and author is permissible because I am the writer; i.e., since it's my story I'll do any goddam thing I please with it—but since that leaves the reader out of it completely, that is not valid. Rule One for all writers is that the teller is not worth a tin tinker's fart when compared to the listener. Let us drop the matter, if we may. I am intruding for the same reason that the Pope defecates: we both have to.[5]

Characters in the story are unaware that they are cast in a work of fiction, but King reminds readers that what they are reading is made up. "I invented [Gerald Nately] first during a moment of eight o'clock boredom in a class taught by Carroll F. Terrell of the University of Maine English faculty. . . . In truth, he was guided by an invisible hand—mine." It's a risky approach because readers are pulled out of the story in a fashion similar to what happens when a movie character breaks the fourth wall and speaks directly to the audience.

King and Peter Straub insert themselves into *Black House* in a different way, relating much of the action as omniscient narrators who offer readers a literal bird's-eye view of events. Late in the book, the authors step briefly from behind the curtain to explain who they are, calling themselves "the scribbling fellows." They occasionally comment on their own writing structure, in one place noting that to change scene during certain events would be "bad narrative business."

The literary term for self-aware or self-referential fiction is "metafiction," probably coined by William H. Gass in 1970. In his afterword to *The Dark Tower,* King says he hates this "smarmy academic term." Metafiction—or the less frequently used metafantasy—is not really what King is up to in the *Dark Tower* series. Books to which this label is applied examine the story-telling process, exploring the relationship between the apparent reality portrayed in the fiction and genuine reality. "The Blue Air Compressor" is metafiction, a commentary on narrative reality, or the lack thereof. In the *Dark Tower* series, King explores the creative process, but does not often criticize the process or fiction in general.

> I'm in here because I've known for some time now (consciously since writing *Insomnia* in 1995) that many of my fictions refer back to Roland's world and Roland's story. Since I was the one who wrote them, it seemed logical that I was part of the gunslinger's ka. My idea was to use the Dark Tower stories as a kind of summation, a way of unifying as many of my previous stories as possible beneath the arch of some über-tale. I never meant that to be pretentious (and I hope it isn't), but only as a way of clearing my desk once and for all. . . . It was all about reaching the Tower, mine as well as Roland's, and that has finally been accomplished.[6] [DT7]

One of the earliest instances of fiction transcending itself is Cervantes's *Don Quixote*. Cervantes, who is quoted by Feemalo at the Crimson King's castle,[7] is both the author and the book's narrator and, as such, a literal presence in the fiction. He's retelling Quixote's story to set the record straight from the original Arabic "history," which contained inaccuracies compounded by mistakes made by the translator. This means that Quixote has three fictional people and the real author telling his story in nested layers, all of whom are, to varying degrees, unreliable.

After the success of the original book, Alonzo Fernández de Aval-laneda wrote an unauthorized sequel. Furious not only about the sequel but also about a personal attack in the preface, Cervantes wrote his own sequel in which Don Quixote and Sancho Panza are aware of the first book and the false sequel. They—and people they meet—know of Cervantes and their fictional representations in the original book, but they believe themselves to be real.

In the *Dark Tower* series, Father Callahan is the first character to discover that his reality is someone else's fiction. The story of his life recounted in *'Salem's Lot* contains details known only to him. Roland and Eddie are less concerned that somewhere a writer is making up their lives as they go along, creating their reality a step ahead of them—or, as it happens, a step behind them. Their only concern is that he not stop, or their quest will fail.

Patricia Waugh, who has written extensively about metafiction, says that its purpose is to pose questions about the relationship between fiction and reality.[8] The metafictional novel often parodies novel conventions, thereby making the reader conscious of these conventions, and uses that awareness to evaluate them. In "The Blue Air Compressor," King indulges in a running commentary on the story and on the genre. "In a horror story, it is imperative that the grotesque be elevated to the status of the abnormal." In *The Dark Tower,* when Susannah asks Nigel the robot the way to the doorway, she realizes it is a crucial question. Nigel, being a robot, though, makes no effort to keep her in suspense as a character in a book might. He has no sense of dramatic tension, well read though he may be.

If King parodies anything in the *Dark Tower* series, it is the notion of deus ex machina—God in the work. In ancient Greek drama, starting with Euripides,[9] gods often came onstage to intercede on behalf of characters or hand them convenient solutions to their problems.

Fiction has to be truer than reality or else it seems like contrivance. An author who relies on convenient solutions to too great a degree is seen as artless and unsophisticated. If characters only show up to deliver important bits of information or if heroes happen upon the very item they need to complete the next stage of their quest, critics—and readers—scream, "Cheat!"

When Eddie and Roland encounter John Cullum in the general store in western Maine and the man proves extremely useful, Eddie claims that someone like him would never "come off the bench to save the day" in fiction. It wouldn't be considered realistic. Roland says, "In life, I'm sure it happens all the time."

The Fates, who control the span of an individual's life, appear in *Insomnia,* telling Ralph and Lois only as much as they need to know to accomplish their task. Without them, Ralph would never have understood what was going on in Derry and stood no chance of succeeding.

Over the course of the series—and in related books—King intercedes on behalf of his characters to help them. In *Insomnia,* Dorrance Marstellar acts on his behalf, delivering important warning messages to Ralph. Speedy does the same thing in *Black House,* phoning Jack to tell him how to handle crises and leaving some powerful flowers for him in the bathroom. In *The Waste Lands,* King leaves a key in the vacant lot that Jake will need to cross into Mid-World, and he provides a bowling bag that will block some of Black Thirteen's terrible power. Hidden within the bag is a talisman that helps Susannah survive in New York with Mia and allows Jake and Callahan to battle insurmountable odds at the Dixie Pig.

King sends a message directly to Jake at the hotel in New York, providing him with the key card they need to access Mia's room. He packs the group a lunch after they leave the Emerald Palace, and pokes fun at the chain of coincidences in *The Dark Tower* when Susannah finds a message in the bathroom at Dandelo's house explaining to her what's going on. The note points her toward a copy of "Childe Roland to the Dark Tower Came" left by King, who is the deus in this machina.

Eddie calls these little author-provided gifts "get out of jail free" cards. Although deus ex machina is no longer fashionable, Eddie thinks that a popular novelist like King still relies on it, perhaps in a way disguised a little better than classic playwrights did. Jake argues that King isn't thinking up these clues; he's just broadcasting them on behalf of ka.

Though King interjects himself into the story, he rarely narrates. Readers observe him as an active participant in the tale. When he does push back the "curtain of presumption" to comment on proceedings, it is usually to absolve himself of responsibility for what has happened or to claim reluctance to tell certain parts of the story. As he foreshadows Eddie's death in Algul Siento, King identifies an incident that "moves us a step closer to that you will not want to hear and I will not want to tell." [DT7]

In *The Eyes of the Dragon,* when Dennis is sneaking through the sewer into the castle, he narrowly misses the passage containing poisonous fumes left over from the Dragon Sand that Flagg washed down the drain. "Perhaps it was luck that saved him, or fate, or those gods he prayed to; I'll not take a stand on the matter. I tell tales, not tea leaves, and on the subject of Dennis's survival, I leave you to your own conclusions." [ED]

Roland has two gods manipulating his actions, though he prays to neither. Stephen King is his creator, albeit one who proves himself to be lazy and weak. The other is a mystery and as much King's creator as King is Roland's: Gan, the universal creative force, the ultimate representation of the White, the power of good.

The Crimson King and Walter think they can challenge whoever lives at the top of the Tower and take over. Roland simply wants to meet the creature living there to convince himself that someone is still actively interested in creation. Though he claims he's neither philosophical nor introspective, Roland is searching for the meaning of existence and looking for the source of good. Ted Brautigan tells Bobby Garfield that literature's "only excuses" were exploring the questions of innocence and experience, good and evil.

While Roland searches for his maker, King attempts to elucidate where stories come from. He refuses to take credit for creating his tales, but instead likens writing to archeology. In *On Writing: A Memoir of the Craft,* he addresses the subject directly:

> [M]y basic belief about the making of stories is that they pretty much make themselves. The job of the writer is to give them a place to grow (and to transcribe them, of course). . . . When, during the course of an interview for *The New Yorker,* I told the interviewer (Mark Singer) that I believed stories are found things, like fossils in the ground, he said that he didn't believe me. I replied that that was fine, as long as he believed that *I* believe it. . . . Stories are relics, part of an undiscovered pre-existing world. The writer's job is to use the tools in his or her toolbox to get as much of each one out of the ground intact as possible. [OW]

As King tells Roland and Eddie, "To peek in Gan's navel does not make one Gan, though many creative people seem to think so." Because he sees something in his mind's eye and writes it down does not make him responsible for having created it. He says he once thought he was Gan, but that was pride. Artists are prophets or singers of that which they discover—a little more genteel than "the teller is not worth a tin tinker's fart," but the idea is the same.

Pennywise believed in an Outsider, a force beyond the universe, the Turtle's creator and "the author of all there was." That description might apply to Stephen King. He claims he killed Jake in *The Gunslinger* because he didn't know what else to do with him. "That's why you usually got rid of characters." He attempts to allay Roland's discomfort when the subject comes up. "It was me, after all. I was the one who made you do it." He recants a few minutes later, admitting that he had lied and that Roland let Jake fall on his own.

When the time arrives for King to write of Jake's final death, he again distances himself from responsibility, stating that the song of the Turtle, the voice that carries messages from Gan, became Jake's death song, something he could not ignore. He knows it's going to anger many readers, but it's the truth of the story. "He died on his own. I didn't tell him to," he often said in defense of Tad's death in *Cujo*. "I just looked back at him and he was gone."[10]

He tells Roland he would have been much better off if the gunslinger had died on the Western Sea beach after his encounter with the lobstrosities. "I love to write stories, but I don't want to write your story." Often he's an unwilling instrument, hating ka for making him kill beloved characters. He has no choice. That's how the artifact revealed itself when King exposed it.

When *The Waste Lands* ended in a cliff-hanger, King wrote in the afterword, "Books which write themselves (as this one did for the most part) must be allowed to end themselves." Around the same time, he told *Writer's Digest* that working on the *Dark Tower* was like excavating a huge buried city. In a pessimistic mood, he said he'd never live to uncover it all.

In a letter to fans prior to the release of *Wizard and Glass,* he wrote, "The creative part of what passed for my mind does not run on a timetable." In the book's afterword, he echoes words uttered by Susannah

Dean to describe returning to the series after each prolonged break between books: "It's hard to begin." But in the coda to *Song of Susannah,* his fictional counterpart says, "Writing this story is the one that always feels like coming home."

King's history with the *Dark Tower* can be summed up with this quote: "The wind blows and the story comes. Then it stops blowing, and all I can do is wait, the same as you." With no clear idea where the story was going, each time he sat down to work on the next installment after a break of four or five years, he had to open himself up to whatever the Muses had in store for him. "This [story] is so out of control it's ridiculous. It really is more like watching something happen—or listening to a song—than writing a damned made up story." [DT6]

Though he once created a complex outline of the series, he lost it. In *On Writing* he talks about writers "enslaved to . . . the tiresome tyranny of the outline." People asked him how the story was going to turn out, afraid they wouldn't live to see the next installment or that King wouldn't live to complete the story. He sympathized, but couldn't answer. "To know I have to write . . . I have no more idea what's inside that damned Tower than . . . well, than Oy does!" [DT6] The parts of the story that he hadn't written yet were trapped, sleeping inarticulate in his subconscious, "creatures without breath locked behind an unfound door," as Walter o'Dim said. [DT7]

When Roland and Eddie meet King, they have already lived beyond the part of the story he's written. King hasn't uncovered Eddie yet, and knows nothing of Breakers or the Crimson King. His own creations force him to continue the story, but they never tell him what to write. They leave hints of things that have already happened to them, but nothing more.

At the same time, though, the members of the ka-tet seem to acquire knowledge that King has discovered about the series while writing non-series books. For example, most of Roland's information about the Crimson King and his intentions comes from no outside source, yet he goes from barely recognizing the name in *The Gunslinger* to knowing ancient prophecies about him in *The Dark Tower*. King, apparently, imparts his discoveries to his creations.

Roland understands how Gan is working through King and trusts ka to do what it will. King isn't meant to force the story or try to map it out. Roland tells him, "When you can't tell any more, when the Turtle's song and the Bear's cry grow faint in your ears, then will you rest. And when you can begin again, you will begin again." [DT6]

As creator, King's mistakes and continuity errors become reality for his characters. He mistakenly placed Eddie's home of Co-Op City in Brooklyn instead of the Bronx. As far as Eddie is concerned, Co-Op City *is* in Brooklyn. He grew up and played basketball with his brother there. "I refuse to believe that I was raised in Brooklyn simply because of some writer's mistake, something that will eventually be fixed in the second draft," Eddie says.

Odetta Holmes lost her legs under the A train at the Christopher Street station. The only problem with that is that the A train doesn't go to Christopher Street in Keystone Earth, the 1/9 does. That little detail is small comfort to Odetta, legless in spite of King's error.

King's characters also express some of his views about being a public person. After a lengthy meet-and-greet session on the steps at Took's General Store in Calla Bryn Sturgis, Eddie notes how draining it was and observes how he and his friends sometimes resorted to giving "weaselly politicians' answers" to the villagers. In an interview with Janet Beaulieu, King talked about how there is a tendency to pull "little cassettes" off the shelf and play them in response to questions he's been asked before, conveniently brief answers that aren't necessarily true but satisfy the interviewer.

When the Calla-folken pester Jake with questions while he is tending to Oy's water bowl, the scene is reminiscent of a story King has often told about how tourists photographed him while he walked his dog Marlowe (on whom Oy is based).

King's real-life accident in 1999 motivated him to finish the last three books in the series. He worried that he might not live long enough to complete the story and, having built the *Dark Tower* in the collective imagination of a million readers, felt responsible for keeping it safe for as long as people wanted to read the books. Roland's way of making the Tower safe is by removing the threat to the Beams. King had to do it by finishing the story.

SOMETIMES IN THE NIGHT, when King wakes up from dreams he can't quite remember, he hears voices. As a writer, it comes with the territory, he says. It's like he has a Cave of Voices inside his head. When he interviewed himself on his Web site during the late stages of writing *The Dark Tower,* he said, "All writers talk to themselves. This [self-interview] is just another version of that."[11]

Many of his characters share this trait, not only in the *Dark Tower* series but also in other novels and stories. In *Gerald's Game,* trapped alone in a cabin, handcuffed to the bed, Jessie Burlingame holds extended conversations with voices whom she identifies either as other forms of herself or as friends from her past. Ms. Practical-Sensible offers Rosie advice in *Rose Madder*.

Roland has a head full of voices offering unsolicited advice. Often it is Cort, his old tutor, nagging him or berating him when something goes wrong. He also hears from Abel Vannay and from Walter and Cuthbert. Eddie sometimes thinks in the voices of other people. "He guessed lots of people did that—it was a way of changing perspective a little, seeing stuff from another angle." [DT5] Most often he hears his late brother's voice.

Members of the ka-tet routinely hear each other's voices advising them, setting them straight. Some of this can be attributed to the extrasensory contact they have with each other, but mostly it comes from their psychological makeup. When Susannah attempts to communicate with Eddie in her Dogan, she gets no answer and thinks that this "wasn't a situation where talking to herself in Eddie's voice would do any good." [DT6]

Secondary characters aren't immune to this phenomenon. Tian Jaffords hears the voice of his dead father when he has the jitters before the Town Hall meeting in Calla Bryn Sturgis. The voices aren't always from the subconscious, though it may seem that way. Roland knows that "often the voices that sound the most like our own when they speak in our heads are those of the most terrible outsiders, dangerous intruders." [DT4]

King's narrative appearances within *The Dark Tower* are like his subconscious voice speaking to the reader. With only fifty manuscript pages left, he speaks again, this time referring to himself a little more obliquely.

The road and the tale have both been long, would you not say so? And as Stephen King nears the point where the pages of his manuscript must be told in four figures instead of three, we are all weary of journeying (none more than King himself, who was hurt badly that day on the highway and is still not entirely better of it). The trip has been long and the cost has been high . . . but what of that? No great thing was ever attained easily. A long tale, like a tall Tower, must be built a stone at a time. [DT7]

When Roland is about to see the Tower for the first time, King positions himself with the reader at the top of the hill as the gunslinger and Patrick approach.

Don't worry, he can't see us (although he may in truth sense the weight of our eyes). He crests the hill, so close to us that we can smell the sour tang of his sweat. . . . And it's here we must join him—sink into him—although how we will ever con the territory of Roland's heart at such a moment as this, when the single-minded goal of his lifetime at last comes in sight, is more than I can tell. Some moments are beyond imagination. [DT7]

Like Johnny Smith from *The Dead Zone,* the author and his audience are in the vision but unable to interact with anything, only watch. They've been swept up on a Beam hurricane. This omniscient viewpoint is reminiscent of the one used in *Black House.* King wraps his arm around the reader's shoulder and personally shows him events of incredible import. Reaching this part of the story has been King's lifelong quest, as well as Roland's and some of King's readers'.

One of the most difficult transitions in the series takes place during the night after Roland becomes a gunslinger. In 1970, King wrote the scene in which Roland bests Cort. He returned to Gilead twenty-six years later in *Wizard and Glass,* continuing with events the following morning. "I found myself confronting myself across a whore's bed—the unemployed schoolboy with the long black hair and beard on one side, the successful popular novelist . . . on the other." [DT4] King asked himself if he was capable of tackling a story of youthful romance.

"*I will help you with that part,* came the reply. I didn't know who the voice belonged to on that day . . . but I do now, because I have looked into his eyes across a whore's bed in a land that exists very clearly in my imagination. Roland's love for Susan Delgado (and hers for him) is what was told to me by the boy who began this story." [DT4] By twenty-two-year-old Stephen King, in other words.

King calls himself a popular novelist, the kind who asks what a story would mean to others, as opposed to the literary novelist who asks what writing a certain story would mean to himself. The "serious" novelist is looking for answers; the "popular" novelist is looking for an audience. Both are equally selfish, he says. "I believe now that the best stories are stories that are generous and welcome the reader in."[12]

Ted Brautigan warns against being a snob, citing the Clifford D. Simak novel that was King's inspiration for parallel universes. Brautigan says Simak's story is great, but the writing is not so great. "Not bad, I don't mean to say that, but take it from me, there is better." There are also books full of great writing without good stories. Brautigan counsels Bobby to read sometimes for the story and sometimes for the language. "When you find a book that has both a good story and good words, treasure that book." [HA] Good books, he says, don't give up all their secrets at once. "A book is like a pump. It gives nothing unless first you give to it. You prime a pump with your own water, you work the handle with your own strength. You do this because you expect to get back more than you give . . . eventually." [HA][13]

In his dedication to the final book, King writes, "He who speaks without an attentive ear is mute. Therefore, Constant Reader, this final book in the Dark Tower cycle is dedicated to you," acknowledging his readership as a necessary part in the process. Though he welcomes readers into the story, in the afterword he is careful to keep this invitation from seeming more than it is. "My books are my way of knowing you. Let them be your way of knowing me, as well. It's enough." [DT7]

Roland reaches the Dark Tower a thousand years after he set out from Gilead and more than three decades after King wrote, "The man in black fled across the desert, and the gunslinger followed." For the author, the story could have ended there. After all, "Fair is whatever God wants to do," as he writes in an epigraph at the beginning of Song of Susannah.

From his long experience with fans, though, King knows that merely standing Roland in front of the door of the Tower, bringing together the man and the object of his quest, as Robert Browning did, will not be enough. For King, the journey and what was learned along the way is

what's important, not the goal itself. Addressing those hypothetical readers who would shriek in outrage if the series ended there, those who
would insist they paid their money to follow Roland into the Tower, King
says, "You are the cruel ones who deny the Grey Havens, where tired
characters go to rest."

"I hope you came to hear the tale, and not the ending," he writes. Endings are nothing more than the final page in a book, which readers could
turn to without experiencing the journey. He writes endings only because
it is the "custom of the country," like putting on his pants in the morning.
There has never been an ending as happy as a beginning like "Once upon
a time." Endings are heartless, just another word for good-bye. Closed
doors that can never be opened.

Elsewhere, he says:

> Did they all live happily ever after?[14] They did not. No one ever
> does, in spite of what the stories may say. They had their good
> days, as you do, and they had their bad days, and you know about
> those. They had their victories, as you do, and they had their de-
> feats, and you know about those, too. There were times when they
> felt ashamed of themselves, knowing that they had not done their
> best, and there were times when they knew they had stood where
> their God had meant them to stand. All I'm trying to say is that
> they lived as well as they could, each and every one of them; some
> lived longer than others, but all lived well, and bravely, and I love
> them all, and am not ashamed of my love. [ED]

Roland once said, "No one ever does live happily ever after, but we
leave the children to find that out for themselves, don't we?" [DT5] King
has provided one ending already, as close to "happily ever after" as he
could get. Eddie, Susannah and Jake are together with a promise that
some version of Oy might join their happy little family. He warns readers
that they may not find what comes next as satisfying.

He takes that last key from his belt and opens the UNFOUND door—
which now reads FOUND—and follows Roland through the portal to a staircase that winds upward through his life, until he at last reaches the top.

Did the series end as he planned? "It's like shooting a nuclear missile
over 3,000 miles. You're happy if it lands in the same neighborhood where

you wanted it to finish up. And that's pretty much what I did. I would say that once I got a little way down the path, I was pretty well locked in on where it was going to come out."[15]

In the final afterword, though, he writes,

I wasn't that crazy about the ending, either, if you want to know the truth, but it's the right ending. The only ending, in fact. You have to remember that I don't make these things up, exactly; I only write down what I see.

I never worked harder on a project in my life, and I know—none better, alas—that it has not been entirely successful. What work of make-believe ever is? And yet for all that, I would not give back a single minute of the time that I lived in Roland's world. Those days in Mid-World and End-World were quite extraordinary.

Thank you for going there with me. [DT7]

ENDNOTES

[1] "Also, she wrote good old Western stories that you could really sink your teeth into, not all full of make-believe monsters and a bunch of dirty words, like the books that fellow who lived up Bangor way wrote." [TK]

[2] "You were starting to sound a little like a Stephen King novel for a while there" (*Thinner,* by Richard Bachman).

[3] For a slightly different take on the relationship between art and creation, see King's novelette "Stationary Bike" in *Borderlands 5,* Borderlands Press, 2003.

[4] "Slade," *The Maine Campus,* June–August 1970.

[5] "The Blue Air Compressor," first published in *Onan* magazine (The University of Maine, Orono), January 1971. Later revised for *Heavy Metal* magazine, July 1981.

[6] The irony here is that, having reached the top of his Tower, the end of his own personal quest for closure to a series that has occupied his life, King returns to the beginning, to a line he wrote in 1970, and Roland returns to the point in his quest where he sensed there was a chance he might succeed.

NOTE: Some quotes in this chapter are from the real Stephen King and others are from King the fictional character. While King is probably echoing his own sentiments through his fictional representation, what the character says does not necessarily reflect King's real beliefs. Fiction is not reality after all. Or is it?

[7] "Honesty's the best policy."

[8] "What Is Metafiction and Why Are They Saying Such Awful Things About It" in *Metafiction,* Mark Currie, ed., Harlow, 1995.

⁹ According to Ted Brautigan.

¹⁰ For example, in an interview with the *Bangor Daily News,* November 1988.

¹¹ www.stephenking.com, June 2002.

¹² Interview on *NewsNight with Aaron Brown,* June 24, 2003.

¹³ He also says that one nice thing about science fiction and mystery writers is that they rarely "dither" five years between books. "That is the prerogative of serious writers who drink whiskey and have affairs."

¹⁴ King repeats this line in *The Dark Tower* after Susannah reunites with Jake and Eddie Toren.

¹⁵ Interview on Amazon.com, May 2003.

MAGNUM OPUS?

On the way to the Dark Tower, anything is possible.

[DT2]

Magnum Opus: From the Latin for "Great Work," usually the masterpiece or greatest work of an artist's life.

Who decides what is the greatest work of a person's career? Is it determined during the artist's lifetime or not until the dispassionate eye of the future casts its gaze over the entire body of work that person produced? Can a writer have more than one magnum opus?

Will future critics even care? The first indication that they might came when the National Book Foundation named King as the 2003 recipient of a medal for Distinguished Contribution to American Letters. While some self-appointed gatekeepers of the literary canon criticized giving the award to a popular writer, the response to this decision was overwhelmingly positive.

Individuals will have different opinions about what work qualifies as Stephen King's magnum opus. For some fans, it will be *The Stand,* that enormous, tapestried exploration of good versus evil. "[A]s far as the most passionate of the '*Stand*-fans' are concerned, I could have died in 1980 without making the world a noticeably poorer place," King said, referring to the strongly held belief of many readers that *The Stand* was his best book. [DT1, foreword]

Others will choose *It,* which rivals *The Stand* both in size and scope. These two books usually battle for the number one and two positions on fans' favorites lists. Critics may well consider the complex and insightful *The Shining* as one of King's most powerful and sophisticated works.

Or the poignant *The Green Mile*. The literary style of *Bag of Bones* made many critics sit up and pay attention to King as more than a genre writer.

Many of King's creations have become part of the lexicon of modern society. Think of a mad dog? *Cujo*. Scary car? *Christine*. Prom night? *Carrie*. Worst vacation resort? The Overlook. Vampires? *'Salem's Lot*, a book that inspired many others to exhume horror from traditionally Gothic settings and bring it into the bright light of contemporary society. Even people who haven't read King's books are familiar with many of these icons.

Apart from these stands the *Dark Tower* series, seven books totaling nearly 4,000 pages that span the entirety of King's writing career to date. Janet Maslin, book and film critic with the *New York Times*, called it his magnum opus even before the complete series was published.[1]

As the preceding chapters have shown, these seven books have exerted their influence on many of his nonseries novels. Still, a substantial percentage of King's core readership has yet to visit Mid-World. Perhaps with the publication of the final volumes, that will change.

King has known for more than fifteen years where he wanted to go with the series. "In that sense, the long pauses between the books have worked for me, because the books that I wrote instead of the Dark Tower from probably 1988 on . . . all of them refer to the Dark Tower books in some way or another."[2]

Peter Straub, King's collaborator on two books with Dark Tower connections, says that the way King has interwoven the fictional reality of his novels is both playful and serious.

[I]t has given him the liberty to create a grand, gestural suggestiveness as to moral and theological depths ordinarily beyond the scope of individual works of fiction. Great, explanatory meanings hover in the air, musically, as resolution seems to draw near. We know the author has something magnificently significant in mind, and that he is working, maybe even groping, his way toward it. It's very gutsy. This goes well beyond the normal wish to have all of one's work eventually be seen as a single entity. . . . What is surprising is that even a writer as true to himself as Stephen King could find so much ongoing possibility, so much space so full of unexpected promise, in an idea which first came to him in his late teens. . . . That King can and wishes to do so indicates two things about him: that his imagination has been internally consistent since his youth, and that even very early on he had an instinct for what would evoke emotional power from him.[3]

King explores the significance of the *Dark Tower* series as a part of his body of work in the afterword to *Wizard and Glass:*

Roland's story is my Jupiter—a planet that dwarfs all the others (at least from my own perspective), a place of strange atmosphere, crazy landscape, and savage gravitational pull. Dwarfs the others, did I say? I think there's more to it than that, actually. I am coming to understand that Roland's world (or worlds) actually *contains* all the others of my making; there is a place in Mid-World for Randall Flagg, Ralph Roberts, the wandering boys from *The Eyes of the Dragon,* even Father Callahan, the damned priest from *'Salem's Lot,* who rode out of New England on a Greyhound bus and wound up dwelling on the border of a terrible Mid-World land called Thunderclap. This seems to be where they all finish up, and why not? Mid-World was here first, before all of them, dreaming under the blue gaze of Roland's bombardier eyes. [DT4]

When asked if he believed the *Dark Tower* series was his magnum opus, King responded:

Yep, I do. Each time I would stop, I would come back and say, "This time it's going to be really hard and this time I'm really going to have to dig and force myself to do the job." And every time it was like the story was just waiting to take me back in. I would say to myself, "Why did I ever stop for as long as I did?" There's no real answer to that except that when I finished each book there seemed to have to be a pause for the well to refill. . . . Having finished the Dark Tower, it puts a real bow on the whole package. It does kind of summarize everything else. And I think, after that, that everything would be almost kind of like an epilogue to what I've done with my life's work.[4]

"The Dark Tower finishes everything that I really wanted to say."[5] What else, then, is a magnum opus if not something that both ties together and summarizes a person's life's work? On the *Today Show,* King said that he started working on a novel after finishing the last volume of the *Dark Tower* series, but it "just went belly-up." He said he told his wife, "Maybe I really did break it [his creative ability] working on these last three gunslinger books."[6]

"I think that probably I'll find some other things to write. And if I like them, I'll publish them," he told Rene Rodriguez of the *Miami Herald,* but he told the *Walden Book Report,* "I really don't know what comes next."[7] As recently as October 2003, King said that he'd tried a couple of times to write a novel but claimed to be struggling. "I'm real flat when it comes to that. I need a little creative Viagra, I guess."[8]

King also says that, eventually, all the *Dark Tower* books will be rewritten. "The same way that if you finished a novel in first or second draft, you'd want to redo it and polish it and make it shine. But I really wanted people to read the new volumes, five, six and seven, because I worked hard on all of them and because the whole thing is finally done."[9]

Many readers have traveled with Roland for more than twenty years. Now, the entire story is told, the secrets of Roland's universe are revealed and the Dark Tower stands firm again as the Beams that support it mend themselves and the field of roses sing.

Roland is back in the desert on the trail of the man in black, but this time there is hope that he will grasp the significance of his quest. That he will come to understand the universe and his place in it. That, in fully understanding himself, he will prevail.

That's pretty close to "happily ever after."

A road lined with roses still leads to this slate gray Dark Tower that contains everything, both universal and personal. The magnum opus around which all of King's realities revolve.

Will people travel down the road to the Dark Tower in years—in generations—to come?

As they say in Mid-World, there will be water if God wills it. In the end, there is only ka.

ENDNOTES

[1] Interview with Janet Maslin at the Jacob Burns Film Center, October 30, 2003.

[2] *Walden Book Report,* July 2003.

[3] Peter Straub, in "The Dark Tower's Architecture," posted to the Penguin Web site in 1997.

[4] Interview with Ben Reese on Amazon.com, March 2003.

[5] Interview with Rene Rodriguez, *Miami Herald,* May 19, 2003.

[6] Interview with Matt Lauer, the *Today Show,* June 23, 2003.

[7] Interview with *Walden Book Report,* July 2003.

[8] Interview with Janet Maslin at the Jacob Burns Film Center, October 30, 2003.

[9] Interview with *Walden Book Report,* July 2003.

APPENDIX I:

TIMELINE (FACT)

- Fall 1969: Poem "The Dark Man" published in *Ubris.*
- June–August 1970: "Slade" is published in the *Maine Campus* newspaper.
- June 19, 1970: King starts writing "The Gunslinger."
- December 1971: Poem "The Hardcase Speaks" published in *Contraband #2.*
- October 1978: "The Gunslinger" is published in *The Magazine of Fantasy and Science Fiction* (F&SF).
- October 1979: "The Way Station" is accepted for publication in F&SF.
- April 1980: "The Way Station" is published in F&SF.
- June 1980: King tells his agent, Kirby McCauley, to complete the deal for *The Gunslinger* with Donald M. Grant.
- February 1981: " The Oracle and the Mountains" appears in F&SF.
- July 1981: "The Slow Mutants" appears in F&SF.
- November 1981: "The Gunslinger and the Dark Man" appears in F&SF.
- August 1982: Donald M. Grant publishes *The Gunslinger.*
- September 1983: *Pet Sematary* is published, and the existence of *The Gunslinger* becomes known to the world at large.
- January 1984: *The Gunslinger,* second edition, published by Donald M. Grant.
- August 1984: NAL pitches the idea of a trade paperback release of *The Gunslinger,* but King passes.
- January 1985: Second printing of *The Gunslinger* sold out from the publisher. *Castle Rock Newsletter* (CRN) reports seeing *The Gunslinger* offered for $50–$100.
- February 1985: CRN reports on a Norfolk, Virginia, article that speculated the reason why *The Gunslinger* was so hard to find was that it was a "dark flop." The article gave King's mailing address, which inspired a lot of mail from Virginia.
- July 1985: CRN reports $165 for a first printing of *The Gunslinger;* $65–$85 for second.
- October 1985: A 1986 publication date for *The Drawing of the Three* is postulated.
- January 1986: *The Gunslinger* second printings $75; first printings $200.
- June 15, 1986: King begins to write *The Drawing of the Three.* A tentative release date of "sometime in early 1987" is given in CRN.
- September 1986: King finishes writing *The Drawing of the Three.*
- February 1987: Donald M. Grant starts taking orders for *The Drawing of the Three:* 800 signed ($100) and 30,000 trade ($35 postpaid) copies. Paperback sale of *The Gunslinger* and *The Drawing of the Three* for a proposed 1988 release.

- April/May 1987: Excerpt of *The Drawing of the Three* released in CRN.
- June 1987: *The Drawing of the Three* is published. NAL trade paperback of *The Gunslinger* and *The Drawing of the Three* announced for late 1988 release with a mass-market paperback to follow.
- September 1987: Last call from Donald M. Grant on the limited trade of *The Drawing of the Three.* Signed edition is out of print and appears in ads for $500.
- May 1988: NAL audio of *The Gunslinger* released.
- September 1988: Plume trade paperback of *The Gunslinger* released.
- January 1989: NAL audio of *The Drawing of the Three* released. Grant trade hardcover selling for $75–$100.
- March 1989: Plume trade paperback of *The Drawing of the Three* released. King says in CRN that volume three is two or three years away from publication.
- June 1989: Paperback of *The Drawing of the Three* is fifth on the best-seller list.
- October 1989: King begins *The Waste Lands.*
- January 1990: King completes *The Waste Lands.*
- December 1990: "The Bear," an excerpt of *The Waste Lands,* appears in F&SF.
- 1991: NAL audio of *The Waste Lands* issued.
- August 1991: Donald M. Grant edition of *The Waste Lands* published.
- January 1992: Plume trade paperback of *The Waste Lands* published.
- April 1994: *Insomnia* published.
- August 29, 1994: King says on *Larry King Live* that he will finish the *Dark Tower* series in back-to-back books.
- July 1995: *Rose Madder* published.
- May 1996: A summer 1997 release of *Wizard and Glass* is announced in *The Green Mile,* part 3, "Coffey's Hands."
- July 4, 1996: King begins *Wizard and Glass.*
- September 1996: *Desperation* and *The Regulators* published.
- October 1996: King writes introduction to *Wizard and Glass* preview booklet.
- November 1996: Preview booklet of *Wizard and Glass* released in time for Christmas, bundled with *Desperation* and *The Regulators.* King issues his infamous "pissing and moaning" commentary to newsgroup alt.books.stephenking.
- March 1997: First draft of *Wizard and Glass* complete. Plume release date announced.
- April 3, 1997: Donald M. Grant gets the final draft of *Wizard and Glass.*
- August 9, 1997: First copies of *Wizard and Glass* ship.
- August 15, 1997: *Wizard and Glass* appears.
- September 20, 1997: *Wizard and Glass* appears on the *New York Times* hardcover list, the first time a book from a specialty publisher has ever done so.
- October/November 1997: "Everything's Eventual" appears in F&SF.
- November 15, 1997: Plume trade paperback of *Wizard and Glass* appears.
- Fall 1997: Donald M. Grant *Wizard and Glass* out of print.

- September 1998: Donald M. Grant issues *The Gunslinger* (third printing), *The Drawing of the Three* (second edition) and *The Waste Lands* (first edition) as a slipcased gift set.
- October 1998: "The Little Sisters of Eluria" published in *Legends.*
- June 19, 1999: King is struck and nearly killed by a minivan while walking along the roadside near his summer home.
- September 1999: *Hearts in Atlantis* published.
- July 2001: King starts writing *Wolves of the Calla.*
- August 21, 2001: Prologue from *Wolves of the Calla* posted at www.stephen-king.com. King announces plans to finish the series back-to-back. Estimated time to publication: two years.
- September 11, 2001: King writes the chapter from *Wolves of the Calla* dealing with Father Callahan as he travels across America, fighting vampires and keeping ahead of the low men.
- September 15, 2001: *Black House* published.
- October 3, 2001: Stephen King day at UMO. King reads the section written September 11, 2001.
- December 8, 2001: King finishes *Wolves of the Calla* and announces the title and illustrator (Bernie Wrightson). Immediately begins Book VI, as yet untitled.
- February 24, 2002: King visits Frank Muller. Writes the chapter where Roland and Eddie meet King en route.
- March 2002: Grant begins production of *Wolves of the Calla.*
- March 24, 2002: King finishes writing *Song of Susannah.*
- April 2002: King announces title of *Song of Susannah.* Begins *The Dark Tower.* Illustrator for *Song of Susannah* and *The Dark Tower* announced.
- June 2002: King interviews himself about the *Dark Tower* books on Web site. He's a third of the way through *The Dark Tower* and will take a month off to recharge after producing 1,900 manuscript pages in the past year.
- July 2002: King returns to *The Dark Tower.*
- September 2002: Tentative publication dates for *Wolves of the Calla, Song of Susannah* and *The Dark Tower* issued by King's official Web site.
- September 30, 2002: King tells Mitch Albom he has two or three pages left to *The Dark Tower.*
- October 3, 2002: King finishes the first draft of *The Dark Tower.*
- January 26, 2003: King writes introduction to Robin Furth's *Dark Tower* Concordance.
- February 2003: "The Tale of Gray Dick," an excerpt from *Wolves of the Calla,* published in *McSweeney's Mammoth Treasury of Thrilling Tales,* edited by Michael Chabon.
- February 13, 2003: Joint press release from Viking, Grant and Scribner outlining their publication schedules.
- February 25, 2003: King explains his decision to rewrite *The Gunslinger* for the new hardcover issue.
- March 11, 2003: King finishes revisions and proofing of *Wolves of the Calla.*
- May 28, 2003: King finishes revising *Song of Susannah.*

- June 23, 2003: First four *Dark Tower* books reissued in trade hardcover by Viking with new introductions. *The Gunslinger* is revised and expanded.
- June 24, 2003: First four *Dark Tower* books reissued in trade paperback by Plume.
- July 2003: Volume I of Robin Furth's *Concordance* is published.
- July 3, 2003: Grant starts taking orders for *Wolves of the Calla*.
- November 4, 2003: Grant and Scribner publish *Wolves of the Calla*.
- June 8, 2004: Grant and Scribner publish *Song of Susannah*.
- September 2004: Volume II of *Concordance* is published.
- September 21, 2004: Grant and Scribner publish *The Dark Tower*.
- January 2005: *Wolves of the Calla* appears in trade paperback.
- April 2005: *Song of Susannah* appears in trade paperback.
- July 2005: *The Dark Tower* appears in trade paperback.

APPENDIX II:
TIMELINE (FICTION)

Part 1: Mid-World

- (DT1). Roland, 11, hears Hax conspiring to aid the Good Man.
- (DT1). Roland, 14, sees Marten with his mother, takes his test to become a gunslinger, and sleeps with a woman for the first time.
- (DT4)+1 day. Roland is sent east by his father to avoid Marten's treachery.
- (DT4)+1 month. Roland meets Susan Delgado in Mejis.
- (DT4)+1 day. Roland, Alain and Cuthbert present themselves to Sheriff Avery.
- (DT4)+1 day. Dinner at the home of Thorin, the Mayor of Hambry. Showdown with the Big Coffin Hunters at the Travellers' Rest.
- (DT4)+1 week. Roland sends an apology to Susan via Sheemie.
- (DT4)+1 day. Susan rejects Roland's invitation to meet.
- (DT4)+2 weeks. Susan and Cordelia fight. Susan meets up with "Will Dearborn." Roy Depape learns about Stephen Deschain in Ritzy.
- (DT4)+3 days. Roland, Alain and Cuthbert explore the thinny.
- (DT4)+4 days. Thorin sends a second horse to Susan; Alain passes a message from Will to Susan.
- (DT4)+1 day. Susan passes a note to Cuthbert refusing to meet Will.
- (DT4)+1 day. Susan sends Will a packet of seeds and a note to meet her at moonrise.
- (DT4)+2 weeks. Susan and Roland declare and consummate their love.
- (DT4)+5 weeks. Roland and Susan succumb to the drug of true love.
- (DT4)+3 days. The Affiliation brats announce their intention to count horses.
- (DT4)+7 days. A week of bad weather. Cordelia tells Eldred Jonas of her suspicions about Susan. Eldred finds Cuthbert's rook skull at Citgo.
- (DT4)+1 day. Eldred Jonas visits the Bar K Ranch with a can of paint. Cuthbert hits Roland.
- (DT4)+1 day. Roland and his ka-tet visit Rhea as gunslingers.
- (DT4)+3 days. Susan meets with the ka-tet.
- (DT4)+2 days. Susan and Sheemie send fireworks to the Bar K. Alain and Cuthbert bury gunpowder.
- (DT4)+2 days. Susan discovers someone has cut pages from her father's ledger, fights with Cordelia and leaves the house permanently.
- (DT4)+1 day. Roland tells Susan what to do if he dies. They make love for the last time.
- (DT4)+1 day. The Big Coffin Hunters murder Mayor Thorin and Rimer, the Chancellor of Mejis. Roland and his ka-tet are arrested. Susan and Sheemie free them.

- (DT4)+1 day. Reaping Fair Day. Explosions at Citgo; Roland and Susan part. Jonas captures Susan. Sheemie and Olive Thorin free her. Roland and his ka-tet destroy the Big Coffin Hunters and their local help. Roland travels inside the Wizard's Glass. Massacre at Eyebolt Canyon. Susan burns.
- (DT4)+1 day. The gunslingers ride to Il Bosque, west of Mejis.
- (DT4)+1 month (est.). Roland, Alain and Cuthbert return to Gilead.
- (DT4)+3 days. Banquet to celebrate their return. Roland goes into the Wizard's Glass again.
- (DT4)+3 days. Roland shoots his mother to death.

- (DT4)+2 years. The fall of Gilead. Cuthbert, Alain and Jamie die. Roland's father dies.

- (LS). Roland encounters the Little Sisters of Eluria.

- (DT1). The man in black raises Nort from the dead.
- (DT1). Roland buys a mule in Pricetown.
- (DT1). Roland arrives in Tull.
- (DT1)+7 days. Roland kills everyone in Tull.
- (DT1)+1 day. Roland leaves Tull.
- (DT1)+20 days. Roland meets Brown and Zoltan.
- (DT1)+1 day. Roland leaves Brown.
- (DT1)+15 days. **The man in black fled across the desert, and the gunslinger followed.**
- (DT1)+1 day. Roland discovers Jake at the way station.
- (DT1)+1 day. Roland and Jake leave the way station. Father Callahan enters Mid-World (DT5).
- (DT1)+3 days. Roland thinks he sees the light of another fire.
- (DT1)+1 day. Roland recalls the story of Hax.
- (DT1)+2 days. Roland and Jake see the man in black for the first time.
- (DT1)+1 day. They continue into the foothills.
- (DT1)+1 day. Jake and Roland rest.
- (DT1)+1 day. They encounter the oracle. Roland learns of the three.
- (DT1)+1 day. Another day of travel for Jake and Roland.
- (DT1)+1 day. Roland tells Jake of New Canaan and Gilead.
- (DT1)+1 day. They climb the foothills.
- (DT1)+1 day. Roland finds a footprint.
- (DT1)+7 days. Roland and Jake speak with the man in black.
- (DT1)+1 day. They go beneath the mountain.
- (DT1)+3 days. They find the railway tracks.
- (DT1)+4 days. Jake runs into a handcar in the darkness.
- (DT1)+? Roland tells of his coming of age.
- (DT1)+1 day. Roland and Jake encounter the Slow Mutants.
- (DT1)+1 day. They travel without incident.
- (DT1)+1 day. They enter the switching station.
- (DT1)+3 days. Roland lets Jake fall from the trestle.

- (DT1)+1 day. The long night palaver with the man in black.
- (DT1)+10 years? Roland arrives at the Western Sea.

- (DT2) Seven hours later; Roland versus the lobstrosities.
- (DT2)+1 day. Roland cleans his guns.
- (DT2)+1 day. The first door—the Prisoner. Welcome Eddie Dean.
- (DT2)+1 week. Roland battles the fever with Keflex.
- (DT2)+1 day. Eddie drags Roland north on a travois.
- (DT2)+3 days. More travel north along the beach. Eddie talks about Henry.
- (DT2)+1 day. The second door—the Lady of Shadows. Odetta Holmes comes through the doorway.
- (DT2)+1 day. Detta Walker on the other side.
- (DT2)+1 day. The threesome travels north.
- (DT2)+1 day. Detta wakes them with screams. They cover three miles.
- (DT2)+1 day. The threesome manages only two miles.
- (DT2)+1 day. Odetta reappears. Eddie and Odetta look for the third door, make love.
- (DT2)+1 day. The third door—the Pusher.
- (DT2)+1 day. Eddie returns for Roland.
- (DT2)+1 day. Eddie pushes Roland up the beach. Roland meets Jack Mort. Susannah Dean is born.
- (DT2)+6 days. Everyone recovers.

- (DT3)+2 months or more. Roland and Susannah destroy Shardik/Mir.
- (DT3)+1 day. Eddie's dream. The gunslingers follow Shardik's back trail.
- (DT3)+1 day. Shardik's lair. The Path of the Beam.
- (DT3)+1 day. Eddie dreams again. Roland has a nightmare and gives up his guns.
- (DT3)+8 days. Jake telegraphs a message to Eddie about the key.
- (DT3)+1 day. Jake crosses back to Mid-World. Susannah and the demon.
- (DT3)+4 days. Oy joins the ka-tet.
- (DT3)+1 day. The ka-tet visits Aunt Talitha at River Crossing.
- (DT3)+3 days. The downed airplane.
- (DT3)+3 days. Mutant honeybees and poisoned honey.
- (DT3)+1 day. The ka-tet hears fighting from Lud.
- (DT3)+1 day. Crossing the Send River, Gasher, Tick-Tock Man, Blaine the Mono.

- (DT4) Later that same day. Blaine the Mono and Topeka.
- (DT4)+1 day. The ka-tet takes the Interstate.
- (DT4)+1 day. Eddie's dream. They see the crystal palace in the distance.
- (DT4)+1 day. Roland tells his story.
- (DT4)+1 day? Inside the Emerald Palace.
- (DT4)+? After the journey inside the pink Wizard's ball. Time has slipped again, but no one knows how much.

- (DT5)+7 weeks. The end of Full or Wide Earth (summer) in Calla Bryn Sturgis. Andy brings news of the Wolves. Jake finds muffin balls and notices they are being watched. The ka-tet goes todash to Jake's New York. Mia forages for food.
- (DT5)+1 day. Palaver about the trip todash. Father Callahan and the other representatives of the Calla approach.
- (DT5)+1 day. Another trip todash trip to New York.
- (DT5)+1 day. Riding to Calla Bryn Sturgis. Singing and dancing at the pavilion.
- (DT5)+1 day. Father Callahan tells the first part of his story. Shows Roland Black Thirteen. The Tale of Gray Dick. The Orizas. Gran-Pere Jaffords tells of killing a Wolf.
- (DT5)+1 day. Mia hunts again, followed by Jake. Father Callahan tells the end of his story. Susannah tells the others she might be pregnant.
- (DT5)+1 day. The end of ritual and preparation. The beginning of the business. Roland says his confession to Callahan.
- (DT5)+5 days. Roland and the others schmooze the Calla-folken.
- (DT5)+2 days. Susannah displays her skills with the Orizas.
- (DT5)+2 days. The Sisters of Oriza have a contest.
- (DT5)+1 day. Eddie goes to New York and convinces Tower to leave town. Jake crosses the Whye and sees Andy and Ben Slightman the elder at the Dogan.
- (DT5)+1 day. Jake tells about Slightman and Andy. Father Callahan goes to New York to get the zip code and date.
- (DT5)+4 days. The town hall meeting.
- (DT5)+1 day. Father Callahan goes to Maine. Eddie almost jumps to his death.
- (DT5)+1 day. Susannah has contractions and a three-hour fugue.
- (DT5)+1 day. Eddie and Tian Jaffords mislead Andy with news of heavy artillery.
- (DT5)+2 days. Wolf's Eve. Andy is decommissioned. The people of the Calla bring their children to town. The Big Feast.
- (DT5)+1 day. The Day of the East Road Battle. Mia/Susannah escapes through the UNFOUND door. The ka-tet discovers 'Salem's Lot.

- (DT6) The same day. Roland consults Henchick about reopening the door. The Calla experiences a Beamquake.
- (DT6)+1 day. Henchick and his Manni open the doorway. Callahan, Jake and Oy follow Susannah; Roland and Eddie go to Maine to deal with Tower and meet Stephen King.

- (DT7) The same day. The Dixie Pig. Bridgton. Mordred's birth and Mia's death. Eddie and Roland send Cullum to New York, then cross over to 1999 and into Fedic. Reunion.
- (DT7)+1 day. Onward to Thunderclap. Walter o'Dim dies. The ka-tet meets Ted, Dinky and Sheemie. Plans for battle. Ka-shume. Ted's tapes.
- (DT7)+1 day. The attack on Algul Siento. Eddie is killed. Say sorry.

- (DT7)+2 days. Roland returns to Fedic and rejoins Susannah. They spend the night in Fedic.
- (DT7)+1 day. Beneath Fedic. Past Castle Discordia into the badlands.
- (DT7)+weeks. Walking across the badlands. Roland, Susannah and Oy reach the outpost of the Crimson King's castle.
- (DT7)+3 days. They walk at night again.
- (DT7)+1 day. They reach the village near the Crimson King's castle.
- (DT7)+1 day. The castle. Feemalo, Fimalo and Fumalo.
- (DT7)+1 day. The first trees since Calla Bryn Sturgis.
- (DT7)+3 days. The deer hunt. Preparing hides.
- (DT7)+1 day. Dehairing the hides.
- (DT7)+1 day. Tanning the hides.
- (DT7)+1 day. Roland and Susannah make garments.
- (DT7)+3 weeks. Roland, Susannah and Oy emerge from the forest. Joe Collins.
- (DT7)+3 days. Roland, Susannah, Oy and Patrick Danville camp in the barn outside Dandelo's cabin.
- (DT7)+2 days. Stutterin' Bill drops them off at Federal Outpost 19.
- (DT7)+1 day. A herd of buffalo.
- (DT7)+1 day. Susannah looks for an UNFOUND door.
- (DT7)+1 day. Patrick draws the UNFOUND door. Susannah passes through. The first rose.
- (DT7)+1 day. Mordred's attack. Oy's death. Mordred's death. The Dark Tower.
- (DT7)+1 day. Patrick walks back toward the Federal Outpost.

Part 2: Keystone Earth

- March 19, 1846: Calvin Tower's great-great-great-grandfather writes his will.
- September 21, 1859: Tak first released in the China Pit mine.
- 1898: Ted Brautigan is born in Milford, Connecticut.
- 1916: Ted Brautigan tries to enlist as a telepath but goes to Harvard instead.
- 1935: Ted Brautigan is mugged in Akron and kills his attacker.
- 1936: Claudia y Inez Bachman writes *Charlie the Choo-Choo*. (A year of 19.)
- 1938: Beryl Evans writes *Charlie the Choo-Choo*.
- 1938: Odetta Walker is born.
- 1943: Benjamin Slightman Jr. publishes *The Dogan/The Hogan*.
- 1943: A brick hits Odetta Walker.
- October 1946: Susannah shows Mia her mother.
- 1947: Stephen King is born. Ed Deepneau dies.
- August 1948: Ice cream snow flurries in western Maine.
- September 1955: Ted Brautigan applies for a job.
- October 31, 1955: Ted Brautigan becomes a Breaker.
- 1956: Henry Dean is born.
- 1957: Odetta becomes involved in the Movement.

- 1957: Father Callahan graduates from seminary in Boston, goes to Lowell, Massachusetts.
- July 1959: Snowfall in western Maine.
- August 19, 1959: Odetta loses her legs from the knees down—and half her mind.
- October 1959: Dan Holmes has the first of many heart attacks.
- April 26, 1960: Ted Brautigan escapes from Devar-Toi to Connecticut.
- 1962: Odetta's father dies, leaving her millions in trust until she turns twenty-five.
- Summer 1963: Odetta vanishes for three weeks. Returns with a bruise on her cheek.
- November 22, 1963: JFK is assassinated.
- 1964: Father Callahan requests a transfer from Lowell, Massachusetts, to Spofford, Ohio.
- February 1964: Eddie Dean is born.
- February 21, 1964: Odetta goes to Oxford, Mississippi.
- June 19, 1964: Three voter-registration workers go missing in Mississippi.
- July 19, 1964: Susannah stays at the Blue Moon Hotel in Oxford. Sings "Maid of Constant Sorrow."
- July 20, 1964: Odetta goes to jail in Oxford.
- August 5, 1964: Missing voter-registration workers' bodies are found in Mississippi.
- 1965: Bobby Garfield gets a letter from Ted Brautigan full of rose petals.
- 1966: Jake Chambers is born. A drunk driver kills Eddie's sister.
- 1969: Callahan transfers from Dayton to 'Salem's Lot, Maine.
- 1970: Paul Prentiss is laid off from Attica and becomes warden of Blue Heaven.
- January 1971: A tornado in western Maine.
- Summer 1972: Joe Collins enters Mid-World.
- 1974: Callahan fights vampires in 'Salem's Lot.
- March 1975: A Type Three vampire bites Lupe Delgado.
- April 1975: Callahan kills his first vampire.
- October 1975: Callahan flees 'Salem's Lot for New York. Works at the Home shelter.
- December 1975: Callahan sees his first vampire in New York.
- May 1976: Lupe falls ill with AIDS and dies. Callahan falls off the wagon.
- Summer 1976: Callahan wanders, does day jobs, drinks, and kills vampires.
- July 15, 1976: Calvin Tower signs a letter agreeing not to sell the lot at the corner of Forty-sixth and Second, in return for which he receives $100,000 from Enrico Balazar.
- August 1976: Callahan's vampire toll hits six. Low men are following him. Decides to leave New York. Crosses into a different America.
- May 9, 1977: Jake dies at the hands of Jack Mort, run over by a car.
- May 9, 1977: Jake doesn't die at the hands of Jack Mort.
- May 31, 1977: Jake goes truant. He meets Calvin Tower, buys a book of jokes and *Charlie the Choo-Choo*. He enters the empty lot, finds a key and sees the rose. Jake, Eddie and Oy return to this date when they go todash near the Calla.

- May 31, 1977: Jake, Eddie and Oy go todash to New York.
- June 1, 1977: Jake takes his father's gun, meets young Eddie Dean in Co-Op City (Brooklyn), and opens the door to Mid-World.
- June 2, 1977: The ka-tet goes todash to New York, where time is moving fast.
- June 23, 1977: Eddie goes to New York to make a deal with Calvin Tower.
- June 24, 1977: Callahan goes to New York to get the zip code.
- June 26, 1977: Callahan steals a book of maps from the New York Public Library.
- June 27, 1977: Callahan goes to Stoneham, Maine.
- July 9, 1977: Eddie and Roland go to Stoneham, Maine. The ambush.
- July 12, 1977: Stephen King decides Roland needs some friends.
- July 15, 1977: Calvin Tower's agreement with Balazar expires.
- July 19, 1977: Stephen King sees *Star Wars*. Decides to publish the five parts of *The Gunslinger* in F&SF.
- August 9, 1978: Kirby McCauley sells the first part of *The Gunslinger* to F&SF.
- September 9, 1978: F&SF magazine with "The Gunslinger" comes out.
- 1979: Stephen King buys Cara Laughs on Turtleback Lane.
- October 29, 1979: "The Way Station" accepted by F&SF. King lives in Orrington, the inspiration for *Pet Sematary*.
- June 19, 1980: Don Grant suggests doing *The Gunslinger* as a limited edition.
- Spring 1981: Callahan arrives in California after five years of wandering Americas.
- May 19, 1981: Callahan is attacked by the Hitler Brothers. Cross carved in his forehead. Rescued by Tower and Aaron Deepneau.
- May 25, 1981: Callahan released from the hospital.
- May 31, 1981: The Hitler Brothers found shot to death.
- February 1982: Callahan hits bottom in a jail cell in Topeka. Gives himself a year to quit drinking.
- Fall 1982: Callahan no longer wants to drink. Sees traces of the low men, so moves to Detroit and works at the Lighthouse Shelter.
- July 27, 1983: King decides to add *The Dark Tower* to the front of *Pet Sematary*.
- December 1983: Sombra Corporation invites Father Callahan to accept grant.
- December 19, 1983: Father Callahan dies and goes to the way station in the desert.
- February 21, 1984: Publication of *Pet Sematary* generates an onslaught of demand for *The Gunslinger*. Owen King's seventh birthday.
- August 14, 1984: NAL and King's agent pitch him the idea of doing *The Gunslinger* as a trade paperback, but King passes. Wants to work on *It* instead.
- November 18, 1984: King comes up with the notion of the world resting on a turtle's back to solve a plotting problem in *It*.
- 1986: Eddie and Henry Dean solemnly pledge to never become needle freaks.
- June 10, 1986: King starts to think about returning to the *Dark Tower* story.
- June 13, 1986: King has a dream of Roland telling him to start with the lobstrosities.

- June 15, 1986: King starts *The Drawing of the Three.*
- June 24, 1986: Captain Trips ravages the world the ka-tet enters in Topeka.
- July 16, 1986: King has written three hundred pages of *The Drawing of the Three.*
- September 19, 1986: King finishes *The Drawing of the Three,* two days before his birthday.
- Fall 1986: Eddie crosses from the land of Recreational Drugs into the Kingdom of Really Bad Habits.
- 1987: Eddie smuggles drugs. Roland and Eddie kill Enrico Balazar and Jack Andolini.
- June 19, 1987: King receives his copy of *The Drawing of the Three* from Grant. Decides to let NAL do the first two books as trade paperbacks.
- August 5, 1987: Helen and Ed Deepneau are married.
- October 19, 1987: King starts to confront his drinking problems.
- December 1987: Susannah joins Eddie and Jake Toren in Central Park.
- 1988: The Tet Corporation firebombs Sombra Enterprises in New Delhi.
- April 12, 1988: Walk-ins article pasted into King's journal.
- June 19, 1989: King has been sober for a year.
- July 12, 1989: King reads *Shardik* by Richard Adams.
- 1989: John Cullum is shot and killed by low men.
- September 21, 1989: King receives roses for his birthday. Hypnotizes himself. Ready to return to the *Dark Tower.*
- October 7, 1989: King starts writing *The Wastelands.*
- October 9, 1989: King decides to call it *The Waste Lands* instead.
- January 9, 1990: King finishes *The Waste Lands.*
- 1990: Calvin Tower dies of a heart attack.
- November 27, 1991: King starts getting mail about the cliff-hanger ending to *The Waste Lands.*
- 1992: Aaron Deepneau dies of cancer.
- March 23, 1992: King receives a letter from a cancer patient asking for the ending of the *Dark Tower* series.
- July 1992: Ed Deepneau flips out; Ralph Roberts hears about the Crimson King.
- September 22, 1992: Grant edition of *The Waste Lands* sells out.
- April 1993: Ralph Roberts gets insomnia.
- 1993: Tyler Marshall is born.
- October 8, 1993: Ralph meets the Crimson King, saves Patrick Danville's life.
- January 2, 1994: Ralph marries Lois Chasse.
- July 9, 1994: A driver kills Chip McCausland on Route 7 in western Maine.
- 1994: The Tassenbaums buy John Cullum's house in western Maine.
- 1994: Chew Chew Mama's becomes Dennis's Waffles and Pancakes.
- July 1995: Tak unleashed and possibly destroyed in Desperation, Nevada.
- June 19, 1995: King feels the wind blowing again.
- July 19, 1995: King is two hundred pages into *Wizard and Glass.*
- September 2, 1995: King watches *The Seven Samurai* and sees in it inspiration for the next book.

- October 19, 1995: King finishes *Wizard and Glass.*
- Mid-1990s: Callahan travels todash to Mexico for Ben Mears's funeral.
- 1997: Moses Carver retires as head of Tet Corporation.
- August 19, 1997: King gets first copies of *Wizard and Glass.*
- Summer 1997: King knows story of *Wolves of the Calla*, but it seems like too much work. Starts on *Hearts in Atlantis* instead.
- July 6, 1998: King works on *Hearts in Atlantis* and sees the *Dark Tower* as his überstory. He contemplates easing back or retiring when it's finished.
- August 1998: Ralph Roberts dies in Derry, Maine.
- August 7, 1998: King hears about walk-ins.
- January 2, 1999: King dreams about June 19, 1999. O Discordia.
- June 1, 1999: Mia crosses from the Calla into New York.
- June 12, 1999: The Kings move back to the summerhouse by the lake. Mordred kills Randall Flagg/Walter o'Dim.
- June 17, 1999: King talks about doing *Rose Red* as a miniseries.
- June 18, 1999: Eddie is killed in Blue Heaven.
- June 19, 1999: King is killed in an auto-pedestrian accident in Maine.
- June 19, 1999: Jake sacrifices his life to save King. Roland and Irene drive toward New York.
- June 20, 1999: Irene and Roland stay in Harwich, Connecticut.
- June 21, 1999: Roland goes to New York one last time.
- Summer 1999: Bobby Garfield receives a message from Ted Brautigan.
- September 11, 2001: Black Thirteen is crushed beneath the World Trade Center.
- August 2002: Stephen King writes about Roland rejoining Susannah in Fedic.

APPENDIX III:
MID-WORLD GLOSSARY

In *The Dark Tower*, King says that his editor usually forces him to change words he makes up if they are too strange. However, over the course of the past few decades, King managed to slip a few unusual words past him. The following list contains expressions mostly from High Speech that refer to concepts in the *Dark Tower* mythos. Some are common phrases from Mid-World speech.

Alleyo: Running away.

An-tak: The Big Combination. The Crimson King's child-powered engine that Roland knows as the King's Forge. Its energy output fuels evils in the myriad universes of existence.

An-tet: The position of a person who follows a dinh.

Aven kal: A tidal wave of disastrous proportions that runs along the Path of the Beam. Sometimes it becomes a hurricane or tsunami, sweeping people along with it. This indicates the very Beam means to speak with these people, who would do well to listen. King's creative force made real.

Can Calah: Angels.

Can Calyx: The Dark Tower, aka the Hall of Resumption.

Can'-Ka No Rey: The red road leading up to the Dark Tower.

Can Steek-Tete: The Little Needle. A sharp upthrust of rock in Thunderclap.

Can-tah: The little gods. The turtle scrimshaw is one.

Can tam: Little doctors; the black bugs associated with Type One vampires.

Can toi: The low men, taheen-human hybrids; sometimes called the third people. They wear human masks, take human names and hope to replace humans after the fall of the Tower. Roland calls these soldiers of the Crimson King the fayen-folken.

Commala: Refers to rice and the festivals associated with it. Also a dance and a festival of fertility. The word is used in numerous ways, many of them expletive. See *Wolves of the Calla* for a summary of its meanings.

Dan-dinh: An implicit agreement between someone who is an-tet and his dinh. When presenting a personal problem dan-dinh, the follower opens his heart to his leader and agrees to do what the leader says. This tradition predates Arthur Eld.

Dan-tete: Little savior. John Cullum is a little savior for Roland and Eddie.

Dash-dinh: A religious leader.

Devar-tete: Little torture chamber.

Devar-Toi: Prison where the Breakers are held. Known as Algul Siento—Blue Heaven.

Dinh: The leader of a ka-tet. It also means "king" and "father." This latter ties Mordred to the legends of Arthur and Charlemagne, where children were born of incestuous relationships. Roland is Susannah's dinh, in some ways a father. Walter o'Dim thinks of Mordred as his new dinh.

Din-tah: The furnace of destruction. Chaos.

Discordia: The great chaos. All that will remain if the Tower falls.

Fan-gon: Exiled one.

Gan: Supposedly the creative force in Hindu mythology according to fictional Stephen King.[1] It is everything that is not Discordia, a force too great to be called God. Gan rose from the void (the Prim) and gave birth to the universe through his navel. Then he tipped it with his finger and set it rolling, and that was time. Gan is responsible for the creative force in King. The Tower is Gan itself.

Gilly: A woman usually taken to bear children outside wedlock. Concubine or mistress.

Graf: Apple beer.

Gunna: A person's worldly possessions.

Howken: Roland's hypnosis trick in which he uses a bullet that dances along his fingers.

Ka: A force of fate and destiny. When someone doesn't know what to do in a certain situation, they throw themselves into ka's hands.

Kai-mai: A friend of ka, someone who carries out ka's will, like Father Callahan bringing Black Thirteen to the Calla from the way station.

Ka-mai: Ka's fool, a term Roland applies to Eddie. Mia says it is one who has been given hope but no choices.

Ka-me: Someone who acts wisely.

Kammen: The bells that accompany a todash journey.

Ka-shume: A melancholy awareness of an approaching break in a ka-tet.

Kas-ka Gan: Prophets of Gan or singers of Gan, for example, authors, like Stephen King and, perhaps, Robert Browning.

Ka-tel: Roland's gunslinger class.

Ka-tet: A group of people bound together by fate, broken only by death or treachery. Cort believed that since death and treachery are also spokes on the wheel of ka, a ka-tet could never be broken. Roland says, "Each member of a ka-tet is like a piece in a puzzle. Taken by itself, each piece is a mystery, but when they are put together, they make a picture." Roland believes he's not a full member of the ka-tet because he's not from New York. However, Oy is a member of the ka-tet, and even Mordred falls within its scope.

Kaven: The persistence of magic.

Khef: Life force. The sharing of water by those whom ka has welded together for good or for ill—by those who were ka-tet. "Water" and "birth" are other meanings. In Greek, the word "kefi" means "spirit."

Ki'-dam: Shit-for-brains. Dinky's nickname for the warden of Devar-Toi, Prentiss.

Kra Kammen: House of Ghosts. What the Manni call the Doorway Cave.

Ma-sun: War chest, like the cave filled with munitions at Little Needle above Devar-Toi.

Moit: A group of five or six people.

Over, the: The God of the Manni. The primordial soup (Prim) of creation, the greater Discordia. Henchick sometimes refers to it as the Force, as in *Star Wars*.

Pol kam: A dance from the Great Hall days of Gilead.

Saita: A great, magical snake slain by Arthur Eld on a quest.

Seppe-sai: Death seller (i.e., gunslinger).

Taheen: Creatures neither of the Prim nor of the natural world, but misbegotten things from somewhere between the two.

Te-ka: Destiny's friend. Used by a low man to describe Ted's relationship with Bobby Garfield.

Telamei: To gossip about someone you shouldn't gossip about.

Ter-tah: An unflattering term used by Munshun to refer to our world.

Tet-ka can Gan: The navel, derived from the belief that Gan created the universe through his navel.

Todana: Deathbag. The black aura Roland and Eddie observe surrounding King.

Todash: The passing between worlds and the empty voids between worlds. The Manni consider going todash to be the holiest of rites and the most exalted of states. Some pieces of the Wizard's Rainbow can send people todash against their will. Terrible creatures live in the todash spaces.

Todash Tahken: Holes in reality (thinnies).

Trum: Someone who can convince people to do things they wouldn't ordinarily do, like stick their head in a rock cat's mouth. Roland is trum.

Urs-A-Ka-Gan: The cry or the scream of the bear.[2]

Ves'-Ka Gan: The song of the Turtle. Sometimes the Song of Susannah. Perhaps an analog of the Voice of the Turtle in *It* that tells characters when it's time to act.

ENDNOTES

[1] Hindu scriptures credit Kaal Purush or Aadi Purush for being the creative force from whose body the universe was born via his navel. The sky came from his head, the earth from his feet and all directions from his ears. "Gan Eden" refers to paradise in Judaism.

[2] When translating this phrase, Roland comments that it was hardly the time for semantics in deciding whether the words mean "cry" or "scream." King may be using this odd aside to subtly chide readers who complained that he got the title of Edvard Munch's painting wrong in *Bag of Bones*. Commonly known as *The Scream*, King calls it *The Cry* throughout that novel. Many legitimate sources translate the painting's title as *The Cry*.

APPENDIX IV:
THE DARK TOWER ON THE WEB*

- Official Stephen King Web presence
  www.stephenking.com/DarkTower/

- Scribner Dark Tower site
  www.simonsays.com/subs/index.cfm?areaid=21

- Penguin Dark Tower site
  www.penguin.com/darktower

- Donald M. Grant
  www.grantbooks.com/

- Hodder & Stoughton (U.K. publisher)
  www.madaboutbooks.com/darktower

- The Dark Tower dot Net
  www.thedarktower.net

- Yahoo group discussion of the Dark Tower
  groups.yahoo.com/group/The_Dark_Tower/

- The Dark Tower FAQ by Jordan Lund
  www.geocities.com/jordanlund/dtfaq1.htm

- The Dark Tower Compendium by Anthony Schwethelm
  www.darktowercompendium.com/

- The Nitpicker's Guide
  www.geocities.com/darktowercompendium/nitpicker-menu.html

- The Road to the Dark Tower
  www.BevVincent.com/

Stephen King fan pages

- Lilja's Library
  www.liljas-library.com/

- Needful Things
  free.hostdepartment.com/n/needfulthings

- Charnel House
  www.charnelhouse.net

* Note: These URLs were valid as of March 2004.

- The Collector
  www.stephenkingcollector.com/

- Stephen King News
  www.stephenkingnews.com/

- SKEMERs (e-mail newsletter)
  www.skemers.com/

- Stephen King resources on the Web
  scarletking.20m.com/

APPENDIX V:
SYNOPSES AND NOTES FROM
The Magazine of Fantasy and Science Fiction

"The Gunslinger"

Thus ends what is written in the first Book of Roland, and his Quest for the Tower which stands at the root of Time. [This is the first time Roland is named.]

"The Way Station"

SYNOPSIS: The dark days have come; the last of the lights are guttering, flickering out—in the minds of men as well as in their dwellings. The world has moved on. Something has, perhaps, happened to the continuum itself. Dark things haunt the dark; communities stand alone and isolated. Some houses, shunned, have become the dens of demons.

Against this dying, twilit landscape, the gunslinger—last of his kind, and wearing the sandalwood-inlaid pistols of his father—pursues the man in black into the desert, leaving the last, tattered vestiges of life and civilization behind. In the town of Tull, now miles and days at his back, the man in black set him a snare; reanimated a corpse and set the town against him. The gunslinger has left them all dead, victims of the man in black's mordant prank and the deadly, mindless speed of his own hands.

Following the ashes of days-old fires, the gunslinger pursues the man in black.

He may be gaining, and it may be that the man in black knows the secret of the Dark Tower, which stands at the root of time. For it is not ultimately the man in black which the gunslinger seeks; it is the Tower.

The dark days have come.

The world has moved on.

"The Oracle and the Mountain"

SYNOPSIS: This is the third tale of Roland, the last gunslinger, and his quest for the Dark Tower which stands at the root of time.

Time is the problem; the dark days have come and the world has moved on. Demons haunt the dark and monsters walk in empty places. The time of light and knowledge has passed, and only remnants—and revenants—remain.

Against this twilit landscape, the gunslinger pursues the man in black into the desert, leaving behind the town of Tull, where the man he pursues—if he is a man—set him a snare . . .

Three-quarters of the way across the desert he comes upon the husk of a way station that served the stagelines years (or centuries, or millennia) ago.

Yet there is life here; not the man in black but a puzzling young boy named Jake, who has no understanding of how he came to be there. The gunslinger hypnotizes the boy and hears a puzzling, disquieting tale: Jake remembers a great city whose harbor is guarded by "a lady with a torch"; he remembers going to a private school and wearing a tie; he remembers yellow vehicles that pedestrians could hire.

And he remembers being killed.

Pushed from behind in front of an oncoming vehicle (called a "Cadillac"), Jake was run over. Who pushed him?

It was the man in black, he says.

There is water enough at the way station for two pilgrims to continue onward, across the rest of the desert to the foothills . . . and the mountains beyond. And in the cellar of the way station, Roland discovers a Speaking Demon in the wall which tells him: "Go slow, gunslinger. Go slow past the Drawers. While you travel with the boy, the man in black travels with your soul in his pocket."

According to the old ways, a Speaking Demon may only speak through the mouth of a corpse; reaching into the wall, Roland discovers a jawbone which he takes with him.

As Jake and the gunslinger continue toward the mountains, the campfire remnants of the man in black grow fresher. And as Jake sleeps, the gunslinger works laboriously over the figures in his own past: Gabrielle, his mother . . . Marten, the sorcerer-physician who may have been the half-brother of the man in black . . . Roland, his father[1] . . . Cort, his teacher . . . Cuthbert, his friend . . . and David, the falcon, "God's gunslinger."

He remembers the death of a traitor, the cook Hax, by hanging . . . and how he and Cuthbert broke bread beneath the hanged man's feet as an offering to the rooks. He remembers "the good man," in whose service Hax died, "the good man" who has ushered in this dark age. The good man. Marten. His mother's lover . . . and the man in black?

As Jake and the gunslinger reach the first hilly upswells marking the far edge of the desert, the boy points upward and, far above and miles beyond, the gunslinger sees the man in black, climbing up and up toward what the gunslinger feels may be another killing ground.

The man in black has set him snares before on this terrible progress toward the Tower.

Roland fears the boy Jake may be another—and Roland has come to love him.

"The Slow Mutants"

SYNOPSIS: This is the fourth tale of Roland, the last gunslinger, and his quest for the Dark Tower which stands at the root of time. Time is the problem: the dark days have come and the world has moved on. Demons haunt the dark and monsters walk in empty places. The time of light and knowledge has passed.

Against this twilit landscape, the gunslinger pursues the man in black into the desert. . . .

The campfire remnants of the man in black grow fresher. And as Jake sleeps, the gunslinger works laboriously over the figures in his own past: Gabrielle, his mother . . . Marten, the sorcerer-physician who may have been the half-brother of the man in black . . . Roland, his father . . . Cort, his teacher . . . Cuthbert, his friend . . . and David, the falcon, "God's gunslinger."

He remembers the execution of a traitor, the cook Hax, by hanging and "the good man" who has ushered in this new dark age. The good man. Marten. His mother's lover. The half-brother of the man in black . . . or is he the man in black himself?

Roland and Jake follow the man in black into the mountains toward what the gunslinger feels may be another killing ground. The man in black has set him snares before on this terrible progress toward the Tower. Roland fears Jake may be another—and Roland has come to love him.

His fears for Jake are nearly justified on their first night in the foothills when Jake is nearly caught in the toils of a sexual vampire that has been caught for eons in a cage of Druid stones. This unformed sexual creature is also an oracle, and after taking mescaline, the gunslinger approaches it. In exchange for a sexual encounter that nearly kills him, the oracle provides disquieting information.

"Three is the number of your fate," the oracle tells Roland. "The first is young, dark-haired. He stands on the brink of robbery and murder. A demon has infested him. The name of the demon is HEROIN. The second comes on wheels; her mind is iron, but her heart and eyes are soft. The third comes in chains."

The oracle will tell Roland no more of these three, but speaks grimly of the boy Jake's future: "The boy is your gateway to the man in black. The man in black is your gate to the three. The three are your way to the Tower . . . some, gunslinger, live on blood. Even, I understand, the blood of young boys."

The gunslinger asks if there is no way Jake can be saved from the mysterious and terrible fate of being killed a second time. The oracle responds that there is one: if Roland gives up his quest of the Tower, the boy may be saved— and this the gunslinger cannot do.

They climb into the mountains together, and the gunslinger finally confronts the man in black standing on a ledge where a mountain river gushes out of a dark fault in the stone. The man in black, almost within reach, mockingly promises Roland the answers he has sought for twelve years.

Answers, he says, on the other side. Just the two of us.

He disappears into the blackness under the mountains, leaving the gunslinger his final decision: give over, and save the boy he has come to love and his own soul, or push on in search of the Tower . . . and be damned forever.

The gunslinger begins to climb toward the dark opening from which the river spills, the opening which leads under the mountains . . . and Jake, the boy, his sacrifice, follows.

They go into the darkness together.

"The Gunslinger and the Dark Man"

SYNOPSIS: This is the fifth tale of Roland, the last gunslinger, and his quest for the Dark Tower which stands at the root of time. . . .

As they pursue the man in black, Roland the gunslinger recalls his strange, marked past: his mother, Gabrielle, Marten, the court sorcerer who may have somehow been transformed into the man in black he now pursues (and who, as the charismatic Good Man, pulled down the last kingdom of light), Cort, his teacher, Cuthbert, his friend, and David, the falcon, "God's gunslinger."

In spite of his own fears and Jake's growing premonition of doom, the two of them plunge into the passageway after the dark man. In that darkness the gunslinger recalls the great lighted balls and fetes of his childhood . . . and his mother's growing enchantment with Marten, the sorcerer. They follow a river in the dark, and this leads them to an old rail-line . . . and a handcar.

Flying through the dark, the gunslinger tells Jake of his coming of age, a combat-rite of manhood which he attempted early, horrifyingly early, due more than anything else to his growing realization that Marten and his mother have become lovers. He wished to challenge Marten, he tells Jake obliquely, but he could only do that as a man . . . even if the combat-rite ended in his premature exile from the kingdom he had always known.

In the horrifying combat which followed, Roland bested Cort, his teacher, by using David, his falcon, as his weapon. Jake is unimpressed by the story. *It was a game, wasn't it?* he says. *Do grown men always have to play games?*

On their sixth day/night under the mountains, they encounter the Slow Mutants, horrible, starving subhuman creatures who subsist on whatever they may find . . . including human flesh. They fight their way through them, thanks to Jake's courage and Roland's sandalwood-inlaid guns.

Perhaps a week's travel further on (in the darkness, both Jake and the gunslinger find time nearly incalculable), they come to a trestle which bridges a wide chasm through which the river has cut its path. The trestle is old and rotted but they can see daylight on the far side. They begin to walk across, leaving the handcar behind.

They have nearly negotiated all of the harrowing passage when the man in black appears at the exit-point. Almost simultaneously, the rotted metal ties Jake has been standing on give way. He falls . . . and dangles by one hand. And, from a mere thirty yards ahead, the man in black issues his challenge to Roland, the last gunslinger. "Come now . . . or catch me never."

After a moment of agonizing choice, the gunslinger leaves Jake to fall into the abyss, electing to follow the man in black; even at the price of his soul, he is unable to give up his quest for the Tower.

"Go then," Jake calls to him as he falls. "There are other worlds than these."

The gunslinger emerges. The man in black is there. And the gunslinger follows him in broken boots to the place of counseling.

ENDNOTE

[1] At this time, King called Roland's father Roland as well.

APPENDIX VI:

"CHILDE ROWLAND TO THE DARK TOWER CAME"

by Robert Browning

(See Edgar's song in *"Lear"*)

I.

My first thought was, he lied in every word,
   That hoary cripple, with malicious eye
   Askance to watch the working of his lie
On mine, and mouth scarce able to afford
Suppression of the glee that pursed and scored
   Its edge, at one more victim gained thereby.

II.

What else should he be set for, with his staff?
   What, save to waylay with his lies, ensnare
   All travellers who might find him posted there,
And ask the road? I guessed what skull-like laugh
Would break, what crutch 'gin write my epitaph
   For pastime in the dusty thoroughfare,

III.

If at his counsel I should turn aside
   Into that ominous tract which, all agree,
   Hides the Dark Tower. Yet acquiescingly
I did turn as he pointed: neither pride
Nor hope rekindling at the end descried,
   So much as gladness that some end might be.

IV.

For, what with my whole world-wide wandering,
   What with my search drawn out thro' years, my hope
   Dwindled into a ghost not fit to cope
With that obstreperous joy success would bring,
I hardly tried now to rebuke the spring
   My heart made, finding failure in its scope.

V.

As when a sick man very near to death
   Seems dead indeed, and feels begin and end
   The tears and takes the farewell of each friend,
And hears one bid the other go, draw breath

Freelier outside ("since all is o'er," he saith,
  "And the blow fallen no grieving can amend;")

VI.

  While some discuss if near the other graves
    Be room enough for this, and when a day
    Suits best for carrying the corpse away,
  With care about the banners, scarves and staves:
  And still the man hears all, and only craves
    He may not shame such tender love and stay.

VII.

  Thus, I had so long suffered in this quest,
    Heard failure prophesied so oft, been writ
    So many times among "The Band"—to wit,
  The knights who to the Dark Tower's search addressed
  Their steps—that just to fail as they, seemed best,
    And all the doubt was now—should I be fit?

VIII.

  So, quiet as despair, I turned from him,
    That hateful cripple, out of his highway
    Into the path he pointed. All the day
  Had been a dreary one at best, and dim
  Was settling to its close, yet shot one grim
    Red leer to see the plain catch its estray.

IX.

  For mark! no sooner was I fairly found
    Pledged to the plain, after a pace or two,
    Than, pausing to throw backward a last view
  O'er the safe road, 'twas gone; grey plain all round:
  Nothing but plain to the horizon's bound.
    I might go on; nought else remained to do.

X.

  So, on I went. I think I never saw
    Such starved ignoble nature; nothing throve:
    For flowers—as well expect a cedar grove!
  But cockle, spurge, according to their law
  Might propagate their kind, with none to awe,
    You'd think; a burr had been a treasure trove.

XI.

  No! penury, inertness and grimace,
    In some strange sort, were the land's portion. "See

Or shut your eyes," said Nature peevishly,
"It nothing skills: I cannot help my case:
'Tis the Last Judgment's fire must cure this place,
    Calcine its clods and set my prisoners free."

XII.

If there pushed any ragged thistle-stalk
    Above its mates, the head was chopped; the bents
    Were jealous else. What made those holes and rents
In the dock's harsh swarth leaves, bruised as to baulk
All hope of greenness? 'tis a brute must walk
    Pashing their life out, with a brute's intents.

XIII.

As for the grass, it grew as scant as hair
    In leprosy; thin dry blades pricked the mud
    Which underneath looked kneaded up with blood.
One stiff blind horse, his every bone a-stare,
Stood stupefied, however he came there:
    Thrust out past service from the devil's stud!

XIV.

Alive? he might be dead for aught I know,
    With that red gaunt and colloped neck a-strain,
    And shut eyes underneath the rusty mane;
Seldom went such grotesqueness with such woe;
I never saw a brute I hated so;
    He must be wicked to deserve such pain.

XV.

I shut my eyes and turned them on my heart.
    As a man calls for wine before he fights,
    I asked one draught of earlier, happier sights,
Ere fitly I could hope to play my part.
Think first, fight afterwards—the soldier's art:
    One taste of the old time sets all to rights.

XVI.

Not it! I fancied Cuthbert's reddening face
    Beneath its garniture of curly gold,
    Dear fellow, till I almost felt him fold
An arm in mine to fix me to the place
That way he used. Alas, one night's disgrace!
    Out went my heart's new fire and left it cold.

XVII.

    Giles then, the soul of honour—there he stands
        Frank as ten years ago when knighted first.
        What honest men should dare (he said) he durst.
    Good—but the scene shifts—faugh! what hangman hands
    Pin to his breast a parchment? His own bands
        Read it. Poor traitor, spit upon and curst!

XVIII.

    Better this present than a past like that;
        Back therefore to my darkening path again!
        No sound, no sight as far as eye could strain.
    Will the night send a howlet or a bat?
    I asked: when something on the dismal flat
        Came to arrest my thoughts and change their train.

XIX.

    A sudden little river crossed my path
        As unexpected as a serpent comes.
        No sluggish tide congenial to the glooms;
    This, as it frothed by, might have been a bath
    For the fiend's glowing hoof—to see the wrath
        Of its black eddy bespate with flakes and spumes.

XX.

    So petty yet so spiteful! All along
        Low scrubby alders kneeled down over it;
        Drenched willows flung them headlong in a fit
    Of mute despair, a suicidal throng:
    The river which had done them all the wrong,
        Whate'er that was, rolled by, deterred no whit.

XXI.

    Which, while I forded,—good saints, how I feared
        To set my foot upon a dead man's cheek,
        Each step, or feel the spear I thrust to seek
    For hollows, tangled in his hair or beard!
    —It may have been a water-rat I speared,
        But, ugh! it sounded like a baby's shriek.

XXII.

    Glad was I when I reached the other bank.
        Now for a better country. Vain presage!
        Who were the strugglers, what war did they wage,
    Whose savage trample thus could pad the dank

Soil to a plash? Toads in a poisoned tank,
  Or wild cats in a red-hot iron cage—

XXIII.

  The fight must so have seemed in that fell cirque.
    What penned them there, with all the plain to choose?
    No foot-print leading to that horrid mews,
  None out of it. Mad brewage set to work
  Their brains, no doubt, like galley-slaves the Turk
    Pits for his pastime, Christians against Jews.

XXIV.

  And more than that—a furlong on—why, there!
    What bad use was that engine for, that wheel,
    Or brake, not wheel—that harrow fit to reel
  Men's bodies out like silk? with all the air
  Of Tophet's tool, on earth left unaware,
    Or brought to sharpen its rusty teeth of steel.

XXV.

  Then came a bit of stubbed ground, once a wood,
    Next a marsh, it would seem, and now mere earth
    Desperate and done with; (so a fool finds mirth,
  Makes a thing and then mars it, till his mood
  Changes and off he goes!) within a rood—
    Bog, clay and rubble, sand and stark black dearth.

XXVI.

  Now blotches rankling, coloured gay and grim,
    Now patches where some leanness of the soil's
    Broke into moss or substances like boils;
  Then came some palsied oak, a cleft in him
  Like a distorted mouth that splits its rim
    Gaping at death, and dies while it recoils.

XXVII.

  And just as far as ever from the end!
    Nought in the distance but the evening, nought
    To point my footstep further! At the thought,
  A great black bird, Apollyon's bosom-friend,
  Sailed past, nor beat his wide wing dragon-penned
    That brushed my cap—perchance the guide I sought.

XXVIII.

  For, looking up, aware I somehow grew,
    'Spite of the dusk, the plain had given place

All round to mountains—with such name to grace
Mere ugly heights and heaps now stolen in view.
How thus they had surprised me,—solve it, you!
    How to get from them was no clearer case.

XXIX.

    Yet half I seemed to recognise some trick
        Of mischief happened to me, God knows when—
        In a bad dream perhaps. Here ended, then,
Progress this way. When, in the very nick
Of giving up, one time more, came a click
    As when a trap shuts—you're inside the den!

XXX.

    Burningly it came on me all at once,
        This was the place! those two hills on the right,
        Crouched like two bulls locked horn in horn in fight;
While to the left, a tall scalped mountain . . . Dunce,
Dotard, a-dozing at the very nonce,
    After a life spent training for the sight!

XXXI.

    What in the midst lay but the Tower itself?
        The round squat turret, blind as the fool's heart
        Built of brown stone, without a counterpart
In the whole world. The tempest's mocking elf
Points to the shipman thus the unseen shelf
    He strikes on, only when the timbers start.

XXXII.

    Not see? because of night perhaps?—why, day
        Came back again for that! before it left,
        The dying sunset kindled through a cleft:
The hills, like giants at a hunting, lay
Chin upon hand, to see the game at bay,—
    "Now stab and end the creature—to the heft!"

XXXIII.

    Not hear? when noise was everywhere! it tolled
        Increasing like a bell. Names in my ears
        Of all the lost adventurers my peers,—
How such a one was strong, and such was bold,
And such was fortunate, yet each of old
    Lost, lost! one moment knelled the woe of years.

XXXIV.

There they stood, ranged along the hillsides, met
   To view the last of me, a living frame
   For one more picture! in a sheet of flame
I saw them and I knew them all. And yet
Dauntless the slug-horn to my lips I set,
   And blew. *"Childe Roland to the Dark Tower came."*

REFERENCES AND ACKNOWLEDGMENTS

One person alone rarely produces a book. Each of the following people's fingerprints appears on these pages, and I would like to acknowledge their assistance and support.

Stephen King's generosity in allowing me access to the final three *Dark Tower* books before they were published turned my vague notion of a book that I might write one day into something imminent and vital. It seems trite to say that without him this project wouldn't have happened, for that is self-evident, but his contribution goes far beyond the thirty years of creative energy that went into creating the *Dark Tower* mythos.

Marsha DeFilippo always graciously and patiently answered what must have seemed to her like a steady stream of questions.

Ron Martirano took the stack of chapters I first sent him and showed me how to turn it into a book. He's the first editor I've ever worked with who understood the big picture of the project, who had his own vision of what the book should look like while respecting mine. He's also the only person I could discuss *Dark Tower* philosophy with for nearly a year, and our correspondence concerning some of the more profound implications of the final books helped me to solidify my own thinking on the subject. Ron also braved a cold, snowy winter day to take the photographs that grace this volume.

Michael Psaltis not only saw the promise in this project, but has become steadfastly interested in my future as a writer, which is music to any author's ears.

Rich Chizmar was the first person to tell me he thought the idea for this book was sound, and encouraged me to take it on. Rich has been a great friend for several years, and I'm one of only a few people who can claim to have seen him wearing a tuxedo. He cleans up *good*.

Thanks to Peter Straub and Edward Bryant for allowing me to quote from their essays, interviews and reviews in this work.

Susan Moldow at Scribner encouraged me to pursue this project, which helped boost my confidence in the early stages of the process.

There's a group of people whom I've taken to calling the triumvirate of Stephen King webmasters. It's composed of Hans-Ake Lilja (Lilja's Library), Rosandra Montequin (Needful Things) and Kev Quigley (Charnel House). If you're looking for all the news that's fit to e-print, check out one of these sites. See appendix IV for links.

Robin Furth's *Concordance* was an invaluable reference tool while I worked on this book, as were our e-mail exchanges as we delved into esoteric details of Roland's world. Thanks also to Chuck Verrill, who answered my questions when I tried to spread them around so as to not be too much of a pest to any one person.

Rocky Wood, David Rawsthorne and Norma Blackburn are the authors of the CD-ROM encyclopedia *The Complete Guide to the Works of Stephen King.* There will never be a more exhaustive and thorough tool for anyone working on a project related to Stephen King's fiction. When I needed to track down some detail for my research, this is where I turned first.

For the better part of a year, I watched discussions of the series at The Dark Tower dot Net and on SKEMERs, as well as on my own message board. Comments made in these forums inspired me to think about some *Dark Tower* concepts that I might not have considered otherwise. I've especially enjoyed watching fans of the series guess what might happen in the as-yet-unpublished books, and it's been hard to keep from confirming or denying their speculations.

Finally, my wife and daughter have had to deal with the crazy schedule of a writer who also has a day job during this whole process since I started *The Road to the Dark Tower* in late 2002. They've both been incredibly supportive and put up with me when I was less than available, especially during deadline periods. To Mary Anne, thank you for encouraging me to reach higher when I might otherwise have let opportunity pass me by. I love you and I promise to always love you! To Ginny, I love you, and I'm very proud of the young woman you've become. The world, your quest, still lies before you.

I would like to thank Stephen King for giving permission to quote from his published works in this book. The following abbreviations are used in the text to identify the source of quoted material, all of which are copyright Stephen King. Quotes from *Song of Susannah* and *The Dark Tower* come from prerelease manuscripts and may be different from what appears in the final versions.

DT1: *The Gunslinger*, Donald M. Grant, 1982. Revised and expanded version, Viking, 2003. Individual stories originally published in *The Magazine of Fantasy and Science Fiction* between 1978 and 1981.

DT2: *The Drawing of the Three*, Donald M. Grant, 1987.

DT3: *The Waste Lands*, Donald M. Grant, 1991.

DT4: *Wizard and Glass*, Donald M. Grant, 1997.

DT5: *Wolves of the Calla*, Donald M. Grant and Scribner, 2003.

DT6: *Song of Susannah*, Donald M. Grant and Scribner, 2004.

DT7: *The Dark Tower*, Donald M. Grant and Scribner, 2004.

SL: *'Salem's Lot*, Doubleday, 1975.

TS: *The Stand*, Doubleday, 1978. Revised and expanded edition, Doubleday, 1990.

DS: *Different Seasons*, Viking, 1982.

TT: *The Talisman*, with Peter Straub, Viking, 1984.

ED: *The Eyes of the Dragon*, Philtrum Press, 1984. Revised edition, Viking, 1987.

TK: *The Tommyknockers*, G. P. Putnam & Sons, 1987.

INS: *Insomnia*, Viking, 1994.

RM: *Rose Madder*, Viking, 1995.

LS: "The Little Sisters of Eluria," in *Legends: Short Novels by the Masters of Modern Fantasy*, edited by Robert Silverberg, Tor, 1998. Collected in *Everything's Eventual*, Scribner, 2002.

HA: *Hearts in Atlantis*, Scribner, 1999.

OW: *On Writing*, Scribner, 2000.

BH: *Black House*, with Peter Straub, Random House, 2001.

EE: *Everything's Eventual*, Scribner, 2002. The novella of the same name first appeared in *The Magazine of Fantasy and Science Fiction*, 1997.

FB8: *From a Buick 8*, Scribner, 2002.

Bev Vincent is the author of more than two dozen short sto-
ries and the Stephen King column "News from the Dead
Zone," featured in *Cemetery Dance* magazine. He lives in
Texas with his wife and teenage daughter.

Printed in the United States
by Baker & Taylor Publisher Services